Blackstone's
INTERNATIONAL HUMAN RIGHTS
DOCUMENTS

Blackstone's

INTERNATIONAL HUMAN RIGHTS DOCUMENTS

Edited by

P. R. Ghandhi

M.A. (Oxon), LLM (Lond), Solicitor of the Supreme Court,
Senior Lecturer in Law, University of Reading

BLACKSTONE
PRESS LIMITED

First published in Great Britain 1995 by Blackstone Press Limited,
9-15 Aldine Street, London W12 8AW. Telephone 0181-740 1173

© P. R. Ghandhi, 1995

ISBN: 1 85431 409 2

British Library Cataloguing in Publication Data
A CIP catalogue record for this book is available from the British Library

Typeset by Style Photosetting Limited, Mayfield, East Sussex
Printed by Livesey Limited, Shrewsbury, Shropshire

CONTENTS

EDITOR'S PREFACE

Human rights have been described as the 'great idea of our time'. The international law of human rights increasingly appears as a separate subject in its own right in undergraduate degree programmes, and no longer as simply a part of the syllabus in a general course on public international law. This development, together with the sheer quantity of documentation in the human rights field, now demands a documents book dealing exclusively with human rights.

The purpose of this compilation is to provide students of international human rights with a collection of texts, which gather within the confines of one cover, a multitude of UN human rights conventions, covenants and declarations together with the texts of various regional human rights protection mechanisms, including those under the C.S.C.E. arrangements. As any student of the subject will know, some documents, such as the relevant provisions of the UN Charter, the Universal Declaration and the two UN Covenants are self-selecting. I have included a selection of other instruments which, in my judgment, are likely to appear in any human rights course. Naturally, it has been impossible to include, in particular, *all* the UN human rights instruments. It has been difficult to decide what to omit. If I have been guilty of too savage a pruning, I hope to put that right in the next edition. Owing to the printing schedule it has not been possible to include the Final Document of the Belgrade Review Conference which was concluded in December 1994.

In arranging the material for this book I have chosen to adopt generally a chronological approach within each subject heading; occasionally, this has required modification as, for example, in the case of subsequent additional protocols to particular treaties and the 1953 Protocol Amending the Slavery Convention of 1926. Generally, the full texts of the instruments in question have been provided so that a particular provision may be seen in the round; however, there are exceptions to this practice, as for example, in the case of the UN Charter when only the so-called 'human rights clauses' have been reproduced.

Finally, I have to express my gratitude to the Publications Board of the UN and the Centre for Human Rights for permission to reproduce the UN texts, the Organization of American States for permission to publish the Inter-American documents, the Prague Office of the Secretariat of the Conference on Security and Co-operation in Europe for authority to re-print the C.S.C.E. texts, The African Commission on Human and Peoples' Rights for granting me permission to include the African Charter and last, but not least, the Publishing and Documentation Service of the Council of Europe with whose permission the text of the European Convention on Human Rights and its first 10 additional Protocols (ISBN 92–871–1961–9), Protocol No. 11 (ISBN 92–871–2513–9), the European Convention for the Prevention of Torture and Inhuman or Degrading Treatment or Punishment (ISBN 92–871–1526–5), Protocol No. 1, (92–871–2454–X) and Protocol No. 2 (92–871–2455–8) are inserted.

P. R. Ghandhi

INTERNATIONAL INSTRUMENTS

THE COVENANT OF THE LEAGUE OF NATIONS (1919)

The High Contracting Parties,
In order to promote international co-operation and to achieve international peace and security
    by the acceptance of obligations not to resort to war,
    by the prescription of open, just and honourable relations between nations,
    by the firm establishment of the understandings of international law as the actual rule of conduct among Governments, and
    by the maintenance of justice and a scrupulous respect for all treaty obligations in the dealings of organised peoples with one another,
Agree to this Covenant of the League of Nations.

Article 22

1. To those colonies and territories which as a consequence of the late war have ceased to be under the sovereignty of the States which formerly governed them and which are inhabited by peoples not yet able to stand by themselves under the strenuous conditions of the modern world, there should be applied the principle that the well-being and development of such peoples form a sacred trust of civilisation and that securities for the performance of this trust should be embodied in this Covenant.

2. The best method of giving practical effect to this principle is that the tutelage of such peoples should be entrusted to advanced nations who by reason of their resources, their experience or their geographical position can best undertake this responsibility, and who are willing to accept it, and that this tutelage should be exercised by them as Mandatories on behalf of the League.

3. The character of the mandate must differ according to the stage of the development of the people, the geographical situation of the territory, its economic conditions and other similar circumstances.

4. Certain communities formerly belonging to the Turkish Empire have reached a stage of development where their existence as independent nations can be pro-visionally recognised subject to the rendering of administrative advice and assistance by a Mandatory until such time as they are able to stand alone. The wishes of these communities must be a principal consideration in the selection of the Mandatory.

5. Other peoples, especially those of Central Africa, are at such a stage that the Mandatory must be responsible for the administration of the territory under con-ditions which will guarantee freedom of conscience and religion, subject only to the maintenance of public order and morals, the prohibition of abuses such as the slave trade, the arms traffic and the liquor traffic, and the prevention of the establishment of fortifications or military and naval bases and of military training of the natives for other than police purposes and the defence of territory, and will also secure equal opportunities for the trade and commerce of other Members of the League.

6. There are territories, such as South-West Africa and certain of the South Pacific Islands, which, owing to the sparseness of their population, or their small size, or their remoteness from the centres of civilisation, or their geographical contiguity to the territory of the Mandatory, and other circumstances, can be best administered under the laws of the Mandatory as integral portions of its territory, subject to the safeguards above mentioned in the interests of the indigenous population.

7. In every case of mandate, the Mandatory shall render to the Council an annual report in reference to the territory committed to its charge.

8. The degree of authority, control, or administration to be exercised by the Mandatory shall, if not previously agreed upon by the Members of the League, be explicitly defined in each case by the Council.

9. A permanent Commission shall be constituted to receive and examine the annual reports of the Mandatories and to advise the Council on all matters relating to the observance of the mandates.

Article 23
Subject to and in accordance with the provisions of international conventions existing or hereafter to be agreed upon, the Members of the League:

(a) will endeavour to secure and maintain fair and humane conditions of labour for men, women, and children, both in their own countries and in all countries to which their commercial and industrial relations extend, and for that purpose will establish and maintain the necessary international organisations;

(b) undertake to secure just treatment of the native inhabitants of territories under their control;

(c) will entrust the League with the general supervision over the execution of agreements with regard to the traffic in women and children, and the traffic in opium and other dangerous drugs;

(d) will entrust the League with the general supervision of the trade in arms and ammunition with the countries in which the control of this traffic is necessary in the common interest;

(e) will make provision to secure and maintain freedom of communications and of transit and equitable treatment for the commerce of all Members of the League. In this connection the special necessities of the regions devastated during the war of 1914-1918 shall be borne in mind;

(f) will endeavour to take steps in matters of international concern for the prevention and control of disease.

SLAVERY CONVENTION (1926)

Whereas the signatories of the General Act of the Brussels Conference of 1889–90 declared that they were equally animated by the firm intention of putting an end to the traffic in African slaves,

Whereas the signatories of the Convention of Saint-Germain-en-Laye of 1919, to revise the General Act of Berlin of 1885 and the General Act and Declaration of Brussels of 1890, affirmed their intention of securing the complete suppression of slavery in all its forms and of the slave trade by land and sea,

Taking into consideration the report of the Temporary Slavery Commission appointed by the Council of the League of Nations on June 12th, 1924,

Desiring to complete and extend the work accomplished under the Brussels Act and to find a means of giving practical effect throughout the world to such intentions as were expressed in regard to slave trade and slavery by the signatories of the Convention of Saint-Germain-en-Laye, and recognising that it is necessary to conclude to that end more detailed arrangements than are contained in that Convention,

Considering, moreover, that it is necessary to prevent forced labour from developing into conditions analogous to slavery,

Have decided to conclude a Convention and have accordingly appointed as their Plenipotentiaries [*names omitted*]

. . . *have agreed* as follows:

Article 1
For the purpose of the present Convention, the following definitions are agreed upon:

(1) Slavery is the status or condition of a person over whom any or all of the powers attaching to the right of ownership are exercised.

(2)   The slave trade includes all acts involved in the capture, acquisition or disposal of a person with intent to reduce him to slavery; all acts involved in the acquisition of a slave with a view to selling or exchanging him; all acts of disposal by sale or exchange of a slave acquired with a view to being sold or exchanged, and, in general, every act of trade or transport in slaves.

Article 2
The High Contracting Parties undertake, each in respect of the territories placed under its sovereignty, jurisdiction, protection, suzerainty or tutelage, so far as they have not already taken the necessary steps:
(a)   To prevent and suppress the slave trade;
(b)   To bring about, progressively and as soon as possible, the complete abolition of slavery in all its forms.

Article 3
The High Contracting Parties undertake to adopt all appropriate measures with a view to preventing and suppressing the embarkation, dis-embarkation and transport of slaves in their territorial waters and upon all vessels flying their respective flags.

The High Contracting Parties undertake to negotiate as soon as possible a general Convention with regard to the slave trade which will give them rights and impose upon them duties of the same nature as those provided for in the Convention of June 17th, 1925, relative to the International Trade in Arms (Articles 12, 20, 21, 22, 23, 24 and paragraphs 3, 4 and 5 of Section II of Annex II), with the necessary adaptations, it being understood that this general Convention will not place the ships (even of small tonnage) of any High Contracting Parties in a position different from that of the other High Contracting Parties.

It is also understood that, before or after the coming into force of this general Convention, the High Contracting Parties are entirely free to conclude between themselves, without, however, derogating from the principles laid down in the preceding paragraph, such special agreements as, by reason of their peculiar situation, might appear to be suitable in order to bring about as soon as possible the complete disappearance of the slave trade.

Article 4
The High Contracting Parties shall give to one another every assistance with the object of securing the abolition of slavery and the slave trade.

Article 5
The High Contracting Parties recognise that recourse to compulsory or forced labour may have grave consequences and undertake, each in respect of the territories placed under its sovereignty, jurisdiction, protection, suzerainty or tutelage, to take all necessary measures to prevent compulsory or forced labour from developing into conditions analogous to slavery.

It is agreed that:
(1)   Subject to the transitional provisions laid down in paragraph (2) below, compulsory or forced labour may only be exacted for public purposes.
(2)   In territories in which compulsory or forced labour for other than public purposes still survives, the High Contracting Parties shall endeavour progressively and as soon as possible to put an end to the practice. So long as such forced or compulsory labour exists, this labour shall invariably be of an exceptional character, shall always receive adequate remuneration, and shall not involve the removal of the labourers from their usual place of residence.
(3)   In all cases, the responsibility for any recourse to compulsory or forced labour shall rest with the competent central authorities of the territory concerned.

Article 6
Those of the High Contracting Parties whose laws do not at present make adequate provision for the punishment of infractions of laws and regulations enacted with a view to giving effect to the purposes of the present Convention undertake to adopt the necessary measures in order that severe penalties may be imposed in respect of such infractions.

Article 7
The High Contracting Parties undertake to communicate to each other and to the Secretary-General of the League of Nations any laws and regulations which they may enact with a view to the application of the provisions of the present Convention.

Article 8
The High Contracting Parties agree that disputes arising between them relating to the interpretation or application of this Convention shall, if they cannot be settled by direct negotiation, be referred for decision to the Permanent Court of International Justice. In case either or both of the States Parties to such a dispute should not be Parties to the Protocol of December 16th, 1920, relating to the Permanent Court of International Justice, the dispute shall be referred, at the choice of the Parties and in accordance with the constitutional procedure of each State, either to the Permanent Court of International Justice or to a court of arbitration constituted in accordance with the Convention of October 18th, 1907, for the Pacific Settlement of International Disputes, or to some other court of arbitration.

Article 9
At the time of signature or of ratification or of accession, any High Contracting Party may declare that its acceptance of the present Convention does not bind some or all of the territories placed under its sovereignty, jurisdiction, protection, suzerainty or tutelage in respect of all or any provisions of the Convention; it may subsequently accede separately on behalf of any one of them or in respect of any provision to which any one of them is not a Party.

Article 10
In the event of a High Contracting Party wishing to denounce the present Convention, the denunciation shall be notified in writing to the Secretary-General of the League of Nations, who will at once communicate a certified true copy of the notification to all the other High Contracting Parties, informing them of the date on which it was received.

The denunciation shall only have effect in regard to the notifying State, and one year after the notification has reached the Secretary-General of the League of Nations.

Denunciation may also be made separately in respect of any territory placed under its sovereignty, jurisdiction, protection, suzerainty or tutelage.

Article 11
The present Convention, which will bear this day's date and of which the French and English texts are both authentic, will remain open for signature by the States Members of the League of Nations until April 1st, 1927.

The Secretary-General of the League of Nations will subsequently bring the present Convention to the notice of States which have not signed it, including States which are not Members of the League of Nations, and invite them to accede thereto.

A State desiring to accede to the Convention shall notify its intention in writing to the Secretary-General of the League of Nations and transmit to him the instrument of accession, which shall be deposited in the archives of the League.

The Secretary-General shall immediately transmit to all the other High Contracting Parties a certified true copy of the notification and of the instrument of accession, informing them of the date on which he received them.

Article 12
The present Convention will be ratified and the instruments of ratification shall be deposited in the office of the Secretary-General of the League of Nations. The Secretary-General will inform all the High Contracting Parties of such deposit.

The Convention will come into operation for each State on the date of the deposit of its ratification or of its accession.

IN FAITH WHEREOF the Plenipotentiaries signed the present Convention.

DONE at Geneva the twenty-fifth day of September, one thousand nine hundred and twenty-six, in one copy, which will be deposited in the archives of the League of Nations. A certified copy shall be forwarded to each signatory State.

PROTOCOL AMENDING THE SLAVERY CONVENTION (1953)

The States Parties to the present Protocol,
Considering that under the Slavery Convention signed at Geneva on 25 September 1926 (hereinafter called 'the Convention') the League of Nations was invested with certain duties and functions, and

Considering that it is expedient that these duties and functions should be continued by the United Nations,

Have agreed as follows:

Article I
The States Parties to the present Protocol undertake that as between themselves they will, in accordance with the provisions of the Protocol, attribute full legal force and effect to and duly apply the amendments to the Convention set forth in the annex to the Protocol.

Article II
1. The present Protocol shall be open for signature or acceptance by any of the States Parties to the Convention to which the Secretary-General has communicated for this purpose a copy of the Protocol.
2. States may become Parties to the present Protocol by:
   (a) Signature without reservation as to acceptance;
   (b) Signature with reservation as to acceptance, followed by acceptance;
   (c) Acceptance.
3. Acceptance shall be effected by the deposit of a formal instrument with the Secretary-General of the United Nations.

Article III
1. The present Protocol shall come into force on the date on which two States shall have become Parties thereto, and shall thereafter come into force in respect of each State upon the date on which it becomes a Party to the Protocol.
2. The amendments set forth in the annex to the present Protocol shall come into force when twenty-three States shall have become Parties to the Protocol, and consequently any State becoming a Party to the Convention, after the amendments thereto have come into force, shall become a Party to the Convention as so amended.

Article IV
In accordance with paragraph 1 of Article 102 of the Charter of the United Nations and the regulations pursuant thereto adopted by the General Assembly, the Secretary-General of the United Nations is authorized to effect registration of the present Protocol and of the amendments made in the Convention by the Protocol on the respective dates of their entry into force and to publish the Protocol and the amended text of the Convention as soon as possible after registration.

Article V
The present Protocol, of which the Chinese, English, French, Russian and Spanish texts are equally authentic, shall be deposited in the archives of the United Nations Secretariat. The texts of the Convention to be amended in accordance with the annex being authentic in the English and French languages only, the English and French texts of the annex shall be equally authentic, and the Chinese, Russian and Spanish texts shall be translations. The Secretary-General shall prepare certified copies of the Protocol, including the annex, for communication to States Parties to the Convention, as well as to all other States Members of the United Nations. He shall likewise prepare for communication to States including States not Members of the United Nations, upon the entry into force of the amendments as provided in article III, certified copies of the Convention as so amended.

IN WITNESS WHEREOF the undersigned, being duly authorized thereto by their respective Governments, signed the present Protocol on the date appearing opposite their respective signatures.

DONE at the Headquarters of the United Nations, New York, this seventh day of December one thousand nine hundred and fifty-three.

ANNEX TO THE PROTOCOL AMENDING THE SLAVERY CONVENTION SIGNED AT GENEVA ON 25 SEPTEMBER 1926

In article 7 'the Secretary-General of the United Nations,' shall be substituted for 'the Secretary-General of the League of Nations'.

In article 8 'the International Court of Justice' shall be substituted for the 'Permanent Court of International Justice', and 'the Statute of the International Court of Justice' shall be substituted for 'the Protocol of December 16th, 1920, relating to the Permanent Court of International Justice'.

In the first and second paragraphs of article 10, 'the United Nations' shall be substituted for 'the League of Nations'.

The last three paragraphs of article 11 shall be deleted and the following substituted:

'The present Convention shall be open to accession by all States, including States which are not Members of the United Nations, to which the Secretary-General of the United Nations shall have communicated a certified copy of the Convention.

'Accession shall be effected by the deposit of a formal instrument with the Secretary-General of the United Nations, who shall give notice thereof to all States Parties to the Convention and to all other States contemplated in the present article, informing them of the date on which each such instrument of accession was received in deposit.'

In article 12 'the United Nations' shall be substituted for 'the League of Nations'.

CONVENTION CONCERNING FORCED LABOUR (1930)

The General Conference of the International Labour Organisation

Having been convened at Geneva by the Governing Body of the International Labour Office, and having met in its fourteenth session on 10 June 1930, and

Having decided upon the adoption of certain proposals with regard to forced or compulsory labour, which is included in the first item on the agenda of the session, and

Having determined that these proposals shall take the form of an international Convention,

Adopts this twenty-eighth day of June of the year one thousand nine hundred and thirty the following Convention, which may be cited as the Forced Labour Convention, 1930, for ratification by the Members of the International Labour Organisation in accordance with the provisions of the Constitution of the International Labour Organisation:

Article 1

1. Each Member of the International Labour Organisation which ratifies this Convention undertakes to suppress the use of forced or compulsory labour in all its forms within the shortest possible period.

2. With a view to this complete suppression, recourse to forced or compulsory labour may be had, during the transitional period, for public purposes only and as an exceptional measure, subject to the conditions and guarantees hereinafter provided.

3. At the expiration of a period of five years after the coming into force of this Convention, and when the Governing Body of the International Labour Office prepares the report provided for in article 31 below, the said Governing Body shall consider the possibility of the suppression of forced or compulsory labour in all its forms without a further transitional period and the desirability of placing this question on the agenda of the Conference.

Article 2

1. For the purposes of this Convention the term 'forced or compulsory labour' shall mean all work or service which is exacted from any person under the menace of any penalty and for which the said person has not offered himself voluntarily.

2. Nevertheless, for the purposes of this Convention the term 'forced or compulsory labour' shall not include:

(a) Any work or service exacted in virtue of compulsory military service laws for work of a purely military character;

(b) Any work or service which forms part of the normal civic obligations of the citizens of a fully self-governing country;

(c) Any work or service exacted from any person as a consequence of a conviction in a court of law, provided that the said work or service is carried out under the supervision and control of a public authority and that the said person is not hired to or placed at the disposal of private individuals, companies or associations;

(d) Any work or service exacted in cases of emergency, that is to say, in the event of war or of a calamity or threatened calamity, such as fire, flood, famine, earthquake, violent epidemic or epizootic diseases, invasion by animal, insect or vegetable pests, and in general any circumstance that would endanger the existence or the well-being of the whole or part of the population;

(e) Minor communal services of a kind which, being performed by the members of the community in the direct interest of the said community, can therefore be considered as normal civic obligations incumbent upon the members of the community, provided that the members of the community or their direct representatives shall have the right to be consulted in regard to the need for such services.

Article 3

For the purposes of this Convention the term 'competent authority' shall mean either an authority of the metropolitan country or the highest central authority in the territory concerned.

Article 4

1. The competent authority shall not impose or permit the imposition of forced or compulsory labour for the benefit of private individuals, companies or associations.

2. Where such forced or compulsory labour for the benefit of private individuals, companies or associations exists at the date on which a Member's ratification of this Convention is registered by the Director-General of the International Labour Office, the Member shall completely suppress such forced or compulsory labour from the date on which this Convention comes into force for that Member.

Article 5

1. No concession granted to private individuals, companies or associations shall involve any form of forced or compulsory labour for the production or the collection of products which such private individuals, companies or associations utilise or in which they trade.

2. Where concessions exist containing provisions involving such forced or compulsory labour, such provisions shall be rescinded as soon as possible, in order to comply with article 1 of this Convention.

Article 6

Officials of the administration, even when they have the duty of encouraging the populations under their charge to engage in some form of labour, shall not put constraint upon the said populations or upon any individual members thereof to work for private individuals, companies or associations.

Article 7

1. Chiefs who do not exercise administrative functions shall not have recourse to forced or compulsory labour.

2. Chiefs who exercise administrative functions may, with the express permission of the competent authority, have recourse to forced or compulsory labour, subject to the provisions of article 10 of this Convention.

3. Chiefs who are duly recognised and who do not receive adequate remuneration in other forms may have the enjoyment of personal services, subject to due regulation and provided that all necessary measures are taken to prevent abuses.

Article 8

1. The responsibility for every decision to have recourse to forced or compulsory labour shall rest with the highest civil authority in the territory concerned.

2. Nevertheless, that authority may delegate powers to the highest local authorities to exact forced or compulsory labour which does not involve the removal of the workers from their place of habitual residence. That authority may also delegate, for such periods and subject to such conditions as may be laid down in the regulations provided for in article 23 of this Convention, powers to the highest local authorities to exact forced or compulsory labour which involves the removal of the workers from their place of habitual residence for the purpose of facilitating the movement of officials of the administration, when on duty, and for the transport of Government stores.

Article 9

Except as otherwise provided for in article 10 of this Convention, any authority competent to exact forced or compulsory labour shall, before deciding to have recourse to such labour, satisfy itself:

(a)   That the work to be done or the service to be rendered is of important direct interest for the community called upon to do the work or render the service;

(b)   That the work or service is of present or imminent necessity;

(c)   That it has been impossible to obtain voluntary labour for carrying out the work or rendering the service by the offer of rates of wages and conditions of labour not less favourable than those prevailing in the area concerned for similar work or service; and

(d)   That the work or service will not lay too heavy a burden upon the present population, having regard to the labour available and its capacity to undertake the work.

Article 10

1. Forced or compulsory labour exacted as a tax and forced or compulsory labour to which recourse is had for the execution of public works by chiefs who exercise administrative functions shall be progressively abolished.

2.   Meanwhile, where forced or compulsory labour is exacted as a tax, and where recourse is had to forced or compulsory labour for the execution of public works by chiefs who exercise administrative functions, the authority concerned shall first satisfy itself:

(a)   That the work to be done or the service to be rendered is of important direct interest for the community called upon to do the work or render the service.

(b)   That the work or the service is of present or imminent necessity;

(c)   That the work or service will not lay too heavy a burden upon the present population, having regard to the labour available and its capacity to undertake the work.

(d)   That the work or service will not entail the removal of the workers from their place of habitual residence;

(e)   That the execution of the work or the rendering of the service will be directed in accordance with the exigencies of religion, social life and agriculture.

Article 11

1.   Only adult able-bodied males who are of an apparent age of not less than 18 and not more than 45 years may be called upon for forced or compulsory labour. Except in respect of the kinds of labour provided for in article 10 of this Convention, the following limitations and conditions shall apply:

(a)   Whenever possible prior determination by a medical officer appointed by the administration that the persons concerned are not suffering from any infectious or contagious disease and that they are physically fit for the work required and for the conditions under which it is to be carried out;

(b)   Exemption of school teachers and pupils and of officials of the administration in general;

(c)   The maintenance in each community of the number of adult able-bodied men indispensable for family and social life;

(d)   Respect for conjugal and family ties.

2.   For the purposes of subparagraph (c) of the preceding paragraph, the regulations provided for in article 23 of this Convention shall fix the proportion of the resident adult able-bodied males who may be taken at any one time for forced or compulsory labour, provided always that this proportion shall in no case exceed 25 per cent. In fixing this proportion the competent authority shall take account of the density of the population, of its social and physical development, of the seasons, and of the work which must be done by the persons concerned on their own behalf in their locality, and, generally, shall have regard to the economic and social necessities of the normal life of the community concerned.

Article 12

1.   The maximum period for which any person may be taken for forced or compulsory labour of all kinds in any one period of twelve months shall not exceed sixty days, including the time spent in going to and from the place of work.

2.   Every person from whom forced or compulsory labour is exacted shall be furnished with a certificate indicating the periods of such labour which he has completed.

Article 13

1.   The normal working hours of any person from whom forced or compulsory labour is exacted shall be the same as those prevailing in the case of voluntary labour, and the hours worked in excess of the normal working hours shall be remunerated at the rates prevailing in the case of overtime for voluntary labour.

2.   A weekly day of rest shall be granted to all persons from whom forced or compulsory labour of any kind is exacted and this day shall coincide as far as possible with the day fixed by tradition or custom in the territories or regions concerned.

Article 14

1. With the exception of the forced or compulsory labour provided for in article 10 of this Convention, forced or compulsory labour of all kinds shall be remunerated in cash at rates not less than those prevailing for similar kinds of work either in the district in which the labour is employed or in the district from which the labour is recruited, whichever may be the higher.

2. In the case of labour to which recourse is had by chiefs in the exercise of their administrative functions, payment of wages in accordance with the provisions of the preceding paragraph shall be introduced as soon as possible.

3. The wages shall be paid to each worker individually and not to his tribal chief or to any other authority.

4. For the purpose of payment of wages the days spent in travelling to and from the place of work shall be counted as working days.

5. Nothing in this article shall prevent ordinary rations being given as a part of wages, such rations to be at least equivalent in value to the money payment they are taken to represent, but deductions from wages shall not be made either for the payment of taxes or for special food, clothing or accommodation supplied to a worker for the purpose of maintaining him in a fit condition to carry on his work under the special conditions of any employment, or for the supply of tools.

Article 15

1. Any laws or regulations relating to workmen's compensation for accidents or sickness arising out of the employment of the worker and any laws or regulations providing compensation for the dependants of deceased or incapacitated workers which are or shall be in force in the territory concerned shall be equally applicable to persons from whom forced or compulsory labour is exacted and to voluntary workers.

2. In any case it shall be an obligation on any authority employing any worker on forced or compulsory labour to ensure the subsistence of any such worker who, by accident or sickness arising out of his employment, is rendered wholly or partially incapable of providing for himself, and to take measures to ensure the maintenance of any persons actually dependent upon such a worker in the event of his incapacity or decease arising out of his employment.

Article 16

1. Except in cases of special necessity, persons from whom forced or compulsory labour is exacted shall not be transferred to districts where the food and climate differ so considerably from those to which they have been accustomed as to endanger their health.

2. In no case shall the transfer of such workers be permitted unless all measures relating to hygiene and accommodation which are necessary to adapt such workers to the conditions and to safeguard their health can be strictly applied.

3. When such transfer cannot be avoided, measures of gradual habituation to the new conditions of diet and of climate shall be adopted on competent medical advice.

4. In cases where such workers are required to perform regular work to which they are not accustomed, measures shall be taken to ensure their habituation to it, especially as regards progressive training, the hours of work and the provision of rest intervals, and any increase or amelioration of diet which may be necessary.

Article 17

Before permitting recourse to forced or compulsory labour for works of construction or maintenance which entail the workers remaining at the work-places for considerable periods, the competent authority shall satisfy itself:

(1) That all necessary measures are taken to safeguard the health of the workers and to guarantee the necessary medical care, and, in particular, (a) that the workers

are medically examined before commencing the work and at fixed intervals during the period of service, (b) that there is an adequate medical staff, provided with the dispensaries, infirmaries, hospitals and equipment necessary to meet all requirements, and (c) that the sanitary conditions of the workplaces, the supply of drinking water, food, fuel, and cooking utensils, and, where necessary, of housing and clothing are satisfactory;

(2)   That definite arrangements are made to ensure the subsistence of the families of the workers, in particular by facilitating the remittance, by a safe method, of part of the wages to the family, at the request or with the consent of the workers;

(3)   That the journey of the workers to and from the workplaces are made at the expense and under the responsibility of the administration, which shall facilitate such journeys by making the fullest use of all available means of transport;

(4)   That, in case of illness or accident causing incapacity to work of a certain duration, the worker is repatriated at the expense of the administration;

(5)   That any worker who may wish to remain as a voluntary worker at the end of his period of forced or compulsory labour is permitted to do so without, for a period of two years, losing his right to repatriation free of expense to himself.

Article 18

1.   Forced or compulsory labour for the transport of persons or goods, such as the labour of porters or boatmen, shall be abolished within the shortest possible period. Meanwhile the competent authority shall promulgate regulations determining, *inter alia*, (a) that such labour shall only be employed for the purpose of facilitating the movement of officials of the administration, when on duty, or for the transport of Government stores, or, in cases of very urgent necessity, the transport of persons other than officials, (b) that the workers so employed shall be medically certified to be physically fit, where medical examination is possible, and that where such medical examination is not practicable the person employing such workers shall be held responsible for ensuring that they are physically fit and not suffering from any infectious or contagious diseases, (c) the maximum load which these workers may carry, (d) the maximum distance from their homes to which they may be taken, (e) the maximum number of days per month or other period for which they may be taken, including the days spent in returning to their homes, and (f) the persons entitled to demand this form of forced or compulsory labour and the extent to which they are entitled to demand it.

2.   In fixing the maxima referred to under (c), (d) and (e) in the foregoing paragraph, the competent authority shall have regard to all relevant factors, including the physical development of the population from which the workers are recruited, the nature of the country through which they must travel and the climatic conditions.

3.   The competent authority shall further provide that the normal daily journey of such workers shall not exceed a distance corresponding to an average working day of eight hours, it being understood that account shall be taken not only of the weight to be carried and the distance to be covered, but also of the nature of the road, the season and all other relevant factors, and that, where hours of journey in excess of the normal daily journey are exacted, they shall be remunerated at rates higher than the normal rates.

Article 19

1.   The competent authority shall only authorise recourse to compulsory cultivation as a method of precaution against famine or a deficiency of food supplies and always under the condition that the food or produce shall remain the property of the individuals or the community producing it.

2.   Nothing in this article shall be construed as abrogating the obligation on members of a community, where production is organised on a communal basis by

virtue of law or custom and where the procedure or any profit accruing from the sale thereof remain the property of the community, to perform the work demanded by the community by virtue of law or custom.

Article 20
Collective punishment laws under which a community may be punished for crimes committed by any of its members shall not contain provisions for forced or compulsory labour by the community as one of the methods of punishment.

Article 21
Forced or compulsory labour shall not be used for work underground in mines.

Article 22
The annual reports that Members which ratify this Convention agree to make to the International Labour Office, pursuant to the provisions of article 22 of the Constitution of the International Labour Organisation, on the measures they have taken to give effect to the provisions of this Convention, shall contain as full information as possible, in respect of each territory concerned, regarding the extent to which recourse has been had to forced or compulsory labour in that territory, the purposes for which it has been employed, the sickness and death rates, hours of work, methods of payment of wages and rates of wages, and any other relevant information.

Article 23
1.   To give effect to the provisions of this Convention the competent authority shall issue complete and precise regulations governing the use of forced or compulsory labour.

2.   These regulations shall contain, *inter alia*, rules permitting any person from whom forced or compulsory labour is exacted to forward all complaints relative to the conditions of labour to the authorities and ensuring that such complaints will be examined and taken into consideration.

Article 24
Adequate measures shall in all cases be taken to ensure that the regulations governing the employment of forced or compulsory labour are strictly applied, either by extending the duties of any existing labour inspectorate which has been established for the inspection of voluntary labour to cover the inspection of forced or compulsory labour or in some other appropriate manner. Measures shall also be taken to ensure that the regulations are brought to the knowledge of persons from whom such labour is exacted.

Article 25
The illegal exaction of forced or compulsory labour shall be punishable as a penal offence, and it shall be an obligation on any Member ratifying this Convention to ensure that the penalties imposed by law are really adequate and are strictly enforced.

Article 26
1.   Each Member of the International Labour Organisation which ratifies this Convention undertakes to apply it to the territories placed under its sovereignty, jurisdiction, protection, suzerainty, tutelage or authority, so far as it has the right to accept obligations affecting matters of internal jurisdiction; provided that, if such Member may desire to take advantage of the provisions of article 35 of the Constitution of the International Labour Organisation, it shall append to its ratification a declaration stating:

(1)   The territories to which it intends to apply the provisions of this Convention without modification;

(2)   The territories to which it intends to apply the provisions of this Convention with modifications, together with details of the said modifications;

(3)   The territories in respect of which it reserves its decision.

2.   The aforesaid declaration shall be deemed to be an integral part of the ratification and shall have the force of ratification. It shall be open to any Member, by a subsequent declaration, to cancel in whole or in part the reservations made, in pursuance of the provisions of subparagraphs (2) and (3) of this article, in the original declaration.

Article 27
The formal ratifications of this Convention under the conditions set forth in the Constitution of the International Labour Organisation shall be communicated to the Director-General of the International Labour Office for registration.

Article 28
1.   This Convention shall be binding only upon those Members whose ratifications have been registered with the International Labour Office.

2.   It shall come into force twelve months after the date on which the ratifications of two Members of the International Labour Organisation have been registered with the Director-General.

3.   Thereafter, this Convention shall come into force for any Member twelve months after the date on which the ratification has been registered.

Article 29
As soon as the ratifications of two Members of the International Labour Organisation have been registered with the International Labour Office, the Director-General of the International Labour Office shall so notify all the Members of the International Labour Organisation. He shall likewise notify them of the registation of ratifications which may be communicated subsequently by other Members of the Organisation.

Article 30
1.   A Member which has ratified this Convention may denounce it after the expiration of ten years from the date on which the Convention first comes into force, by an act communicated to the Director-General of the International Labour Office for registration. Such denunciation shall not take effect until one year after the date on which it is registered with the International Labour Office.

2.   Each Member which has ratified this Convention and which does not, within the year following the expiration of the period of ten years mentioned in the preceding paragraph, exercise the right of denunciation provided for in this article, will be bound for another period of five years and, thereafter, may denounce this Convention at the expiration of each period of five years under the terms provided for in this article.

Article 31
At the expiration of each period of five years after the coming into force of this Convention, the Governing Body of the International Labour Office shall present to the General Conference a report on the working of this Convention and shall consider the desirability of placing on the agenda of the Conference the question of its revision in whole or in part.

Article 32
1.   Should the Conference adopt a new Convention revising this Convention in whole or in part, the ratification by a Member of the new revising Convention shall *ipso jure* involve denunciation of this Convention without any requirement of delay, notwithstanding the provisions of article 30 above, if and when the new revising Convention shall have come into force.

2.   As from the date of the coming into force of the new revising Convention, the present Convention shall cease to be open to ratification by the Members.

3.   Nevertheless, this Convention shall remain in force in its actual form and content for those Members which have ratified it but have not ratified the revising Convention.

Article 33
The French and English texts of this Convention shall both be authentic.

CHARTER OF THE UNITED NATIONS (1945)[1]

WE THE PEOPLES OF THE UNITED NATIONS DETERMINED
   to save succeeding generations from the scourge of war, which twice in our lifetime has brought untold sorrow to mankind, and
   to reaffirm faith in fundamental human rights, in the dignity and worth of the human person, in the equal rights of men and women and of nations large and small, and
   to establish conditions under which justice and respect for the obligations arising from treaties and other sources of international law can be maintained, and
   to promote social progress and better standards of life in larger freedom, AND FOR THESE ENDS
   to practise tolerance and live together in peace with one another as good neighbours, and
   to unite our strength to maintain international peace and security, and
   to ensure, by the acceptance of principles and the institution of methods, that armed force shall not be used, save in the common interest, and
   to employ international machinery for the promotion of the economic and social advancement of all peoples,
HAVE RESOLVED TO COMBINE OUR EFFORTS TO ACCOMPLISH THESE AIMS
Accordingly, our respective Governments, through representatives assembled in the City of San Francisco, who have exhibited their full powers found to be in good and due form, have agreed to the present Charter of the United Nations and do hereby establish an international organization to be known as the United Nations.

CHAPTER I   PURPOSES AND PRINCIPLES

Article 1
The Purposes of the United Nations are:
   1.   To maintain international peace and security, and to that end: to take effective collective measures for the prevention and removal of threats to the peace, and for the suppression of acts of aggression or other breaches of the peace, and to bring about by peaceful means, and in conformity with the principles of justice and international law, adjustment or settlement of international disputes or situations which might lead to a breach of the peace;
   2.   To develop friendly relations among nations based on respect for the principle of equal rights and self-determination of peoples, and to take other appropriate measures to strengthen universal peace;
   3.   To achieve international co-operation in solving international problems of an economic, social, cultural or humanitarian character, and in promoting and encouraging respect for human rights and for fundamental freedoms for all without distinction as to race, sex, language, or religion; and
   4.   To be a centre for harmonizing the actions of nations in the attainment of these common ends.

---

[1]As amended. Amendments to Articles 23, 27 and 61 in force 31 August 1965. Article 61 further amended, in force 24 September 1973. Amendment to Article 109 in force 12 June 1968.

Article 2

The Organization and its Members, in pursuit of the Purposes stated in Article 1, shall act in accordance with the following Principles:

1.   The Organization is based on the principle of the sovereign equality of all its Members.

2.   All Members, in order to ensure to all of them the rights and benefits resulting from membership, shall fulfil in good faith the obligations assumed by them in accordance with the present Charter.

3.   All Members shall settle their international disputes by peaceful means in such a manner that international peace and security, and justice, are not endangered.

4.   All Members shall refrain in their international relations from the threat or use of force against the territorial integrity or political independence of any State, or in any other manner inconsistent with the Purposes of the United Nations.

5.   All Members shall give the United Nations every assistance in any action it takes in accordance with the present Charter, and shall refrain from giving assistance to any State against which the United Nations is taking preventive or enforcement action.

6.   The Organization shall ensure that States which are not Members of the United Nations act in accordance with these Principles so far as may be necessary for the maintenance of international peace and security.

7.   Nothing contained in the present Charter shall authorize the United Nations to intervene in matters which are essentially within the domestic jurisdiction of any State or shall require the Members to submit such matters to settlement under the present Charter; but this principle shall not prejudice the application of enforcement measures under Chapter VII.

CHAPTER IV   THE GENERAL ASSEMBLY

Functions and Powers

Article 10

The General Assembly may discuss any questions or any matters within the scope of the present Charter or relating to the powers and functions of any organs provided for in the present Charter, and, except as provided in Article 12, may make recommendations to the Members of the United Nations or to the Security Council or to both on any such questions or matters.

Article 12

1.   While the Security Council is exercising in respect of any dispute or situation the functions assigned to it in the present Charter, the General Assembly shall not make any recommendation with regard to that dispute or situation unless the Security Council so requests.

2.   The Secretary-General, with the consent of the Security Council, shall notify the General Assembly at each session of any matters relative to the maintenance of international peace and security which are being dealt with by the Security Council and shall similarly notify the General Assembly, or the Members of the United Nations if the General Assembly is not in session, immediately the Security Council ceases to deal with such matters.

Article 13

1.   The General Assembly shall initiate studies and make recommendations for the purpose of:

(a)   promoting international co-operation in the political field and encouraging the progressive development of international law and its codification;

(b)   promoting international co-operation in the economic, social, cultural, educational, and health fields, and assisting in the realization of human rights and fundamental freedoms for all without distinction as to race, sex, language, or religion.

2.   The further responsibilities, functions, and powers of the General Assembly with respect to matters mentioned in paragraph 1 (b) above are set forth in Chapters IX and X.

Article 14

Subject to the provisions of Article 12, the General Assembly may recommend measures for the peaceful adjustment of any situation, regardless of origin, which it deems likely to impair the general welfare or friendly relations among nations, including situations resulting from a violation of the provisions of the present Charter setting forth the Purposes and Principles of the United Nations.

Article 16

The General Assembly shall perform such functions with respect to the international trusteeship system as are assigned to it under Chapters XII and XIII, including the approval of the trusteeship agreements for areas not designated as strategic.

CHAPTER IX   INTERNATIONAL ECONOMIC AND SOCIAL CO-OPERATION

Article 55

With a view to the creation of conditions of stability and well-being which are necessary for peaceful and friendly relations among nations based on respect for the principle of equal rights and self-determination of peoples, the United Nations shall promote:

(a)   higher standards of living, full employment, and conditions of economic and social progress and development;

(b)   solutions of international economic, social, health, and related problems; and international cultural and educational co-operation; and

(c)   universal respect for, and observance of, human rights and fundamental freedoms for all without distinction as to race, sex, language, or religion.

Article 56

All Members pledge themselves to take joint and separate action in co-operation with the Organization for the achievement of the purposes set forth in Article 55.

Article 60

Responsibility for the discharge of the functions of the Organization set forth in this Chapter shall be vested in the General Assembly and, under the authority of the General Assembly, in the Economic and Social Council, which shall have for this purpose the powers set forth in Chapter X.

CHAPTER X   THE ECONOMIC AND SOCIAL COUNCIL
Composition

Article 61

1.   The Economic and Social Council shall consist of fifty-four[1] Members of the United Nations elected by the General Assembly.

2.   Subject to the provisions of paragraph 3, eighteen members of the Economic and Social Council shall be elected each year for a term of three years. A retiring member shall be eligible for immediate re-election.

3.   At the first election after the increase in the membership of the Economic and Social Council from twenty-seven to fifty-four members, in addition to the members

---

[1]Originally eighteen, increased to twenty-seven (1965).

elected in place of the nine members whose term of office expires at the end of that year, twenty-seven additional members shall be elected. Of these twenty-seven additional members, the term of office of nine members so elected shall expire at the end of one year, and of nine other members at the end of two years, in accordance with arrangements made by the General Assembly.

4. Each member of the Economic and Social Council shall have one representative.

Functions and Powers

Article 62

1. The Economic and Social Council may make or initiate studies and reports with respect to international economic, social, cultural, educational, health, and related matters and may make recommendations with respect to any such matters to the General Assembly, to the Members of the United Nations, and to the specialized agencies concerned.

2. It may make recommendations for the purpose of promoting respect for, and observance of, human rights and fundamental freedoms for all.

3. It may prepare draft conventions for submission to the General Assembly, with respect to matters falling within its competence.

4. It may call, in accordance with the rules prescribed by the United Nations, international conferences on matters failing within its competence.

Article 65

The Economic and Social Council may furnish information to the Security Council and shall assist the Security Council upon its request.

Article 66

1. The Economic and Social Council shall perform such functions as fall within its competence in connexion with the carrying out of the recommendations of the General Assembly.

2. It may, with the approval of the General Assembly, perform services at the request of Members of the United Nations and at the request of specialized agencies.

3. It shall perform such other functions as are specified elsewhere in the present Charter or as may be assigned to it by the General Assembly.

CHAPTER XI   DECLARATION REGARDING NON-SELF-GOVERNING TERRITORIES

Article 73

Members of the United Nations which have or assume responsibilities for the administration of territories whose peoples have not yet attained a full measure of self-government recognize the principle that the interests of the inhabitants of these territories are paramount, and accept as a sacred trust the obligation to promote to the utmost, within the system of international peace and security established by the present Charter, the well-being of the inhabitants of these territories, and to this end:

(a)   to ensure, with due respect for the culture of the peoples concerned, their political, economic, social and educational advancement, their just treatment, and their protection against abuses;

(b)   to develop self-government, to take due account of the political aspirations of the peoples, and to assist them in the progressive development of their free political institutions, according to the particular circumstances of each territory and its peoples and their varying stages of advancement;

(c)   to further international peace and security;

(d)   to promote constructive measures of development, to encourage research, and to co-operate with one another and, when and where appropriate, with specialized international bodies with a view to the practical achievement of the social, economic, and scientific purposes set forth in this Article; and

(e) to transmit regularly to the Secretary-General for information purposes, subject to such limitation as security and constitutional considerations may require, statistical and other information of a technical nature relating to economic, social, and educational conditions in the territories for which they are respectively responsible other than those territories to which Chapters XII and XIII apply.

CHAPTER XII INTERNATIONAL TRUSTEESHIP SYSTEM

Article 75
The United Nations shall establish under its authority an international trusteeship system for the administration and supervision of such territories as may be placed thereunder by subsequent individual agreements. These territories are hereinafter referred to as trust territories.

Article 76
The basic objectives of the trusteeship system, in accordance with the Purposes of the United Nations laid down in Article 1 of the present Charter, shall be:
    (a) to further international peace and security;
    (b) to promote the political, economic, social, and educational advancement of the inhabitants of the trust territories, and their progressive development towards self-government or independence as may be appropriate to the particular circumstances of each territory and its peoples and the freely expressed wishes of the people concerned, and as may be provided by the terms of each trusteeship agreement;
    (c) to encourage respect for human rights and for fundamental freedoms for all without distinction as to race, sex, language, or religion, and to encourage recognition of the interdependence of the peoples of the world; and
    (d) to ensure equal treatment in social, economic and commercial matters for all Members of the United Nations and their nationals, and also equal treatment for the latter in the administration of justice, without prejudice to the attainment of the foregoing objectives and subject to the provisions of Article 80.

Article 77
1. The trusteeship system shall apply to such territories in the following categories as may be placed thereunder by means of trusteeship agreements:
    (a) territories now held under mandate;
    (b) territories which may be detached from enemy States as a result of the Second World War; and
    (c) territories voluntarily placed under the system by States responsible for their administration.
2. It will be a matter for subsequent agreement as to which territories in the foregoing categories will be brought under the trusteeship system and upon what terms.

Article 78
The trusteeship system shall not apply to territories which have become Members of the United Nations, relationship among which shall be based on respect for the principle of sovereign equality.

CONVENTION ON THE PREVENTION AND PUNISHMENT OF THE CRIME OF GENOCIDE (1948)

THE CONTRACTING PARTIES,
    HAVING CONSIDERED the declaration made by the General Assembly of the United Nations in its resolution 96 (I) dated 11 December 1946 that genocide is a crime under international law, contrary to the spirit and aims of the United Nations and condemned by the civilized world;

RECOGNIZING that at all periods of history genocide has inflicted great losses on humanity; and

BEING CONVINCED that, in order to liberate mankind from such an odious scourge, international co-operation is required:

HEREBY AGREE AS HEREINAFTER PROVIDED:

Article I

The Contracting Parties confirm that genocide, whether committed in time of peace or in time of war, is a crime under international law which they undertake to prevent and to punish.

Article II

In the present Convention, genocide means any of the following acts committed with intent to destroy, in whole or in part, a national, ethnical, racial or religious groups, as such:

    (a)   killing members of the group;

    (b)   causing serious bodily or mental harm to members of the group;

    (c)   deliberately inflicting on the group conditions of life calculated to bring about its physical destruction in whole or in part,

    (d)   imposing measures intended to prevent births within the group;

    (e)   forcibly transferring children of the group to another group.

Article III

The following acts shall be punishable:

    (a)   genocide;

    (b)   conspiracy to commit genocide;

    (c)   direct and public incitement to commit genocide;

    (d)   attempt to commit genocide;

    (e)   complicity in genocide.

Article IV

Persons committing genocide or any of the other acts enumerated in Article III shall be punished, whether they are constitutionally responsible rulers, public officials or private individuals.

Article V

The Contracting Parties undertake to enact, in accordance with their respective Constitutions, the necessary legislation to give effect to the provisions of the present Convention and, in particular, to provide effective penalties for persons guilty of genocide or of any of the other acts enumerated in Article III.

Article VI

Persons charged with genocide or any of the other acts enumerated in Article III shall be tried by a competent tribunal of the State in the territory of which the act was committed, or by such international penal tribunal as may have jurisdiction with respect to those Contracting Parties which shall have accepted its jurisdiction.

Article VII

Genocide and the other acts enumerated in Article III shall not be considered as political crimes for the purpose of extradition.

The Contracting Parties pledge themselves in such cases to grant extradition in accordance with their laws and treaties in force.

Article VIII

Any Contracting Party may call upon the competent organs of the United Nations to take such action under the Charter of the United Nations as they consider appropriate for the prevention and suppression of acts of genocide or any of the other acts enumerated in Article III.

Article IX
Disputes between the Contracting Parties relating to the interpretation, application or fulfilment of the present Convention, including those relating to the responsibility of a State for genocide or for any of the other acts enumerated in Article III, shall be submitted to the International Court of Justice at the request of any of the parties to the dispute.

Article X
The present Convention, of which the Chinese, English, French, Russian and Spanish texts are equally authentic, shall bear the date of 9 December 1948.

Article XI
The present Convention shall be open until 31 December 1949 for signature on behalf of any Member of the United Nations and of any non-member State to which an invitation to sign has been addressed by the General Assembly.

The present Convention shall be ratified, and the instruments of ratification shall be deposited with the Secretary-General of the United Nations.

After 1 January 1950 the present Convention may be acceded to on behalf of any Member of the United Nations and of any non-member State which has received an invitation as aforesaid.

Instruments of accession shall be deposited with the Secretary-General of the United Nations.

Article XII
Any Contracting Party may at any time, by notification addressed to the Secretary-General of the United Nations, extend the application of the present Convention to all or any of the territories for the conduct of whose foreign relations that Contracting Party is responsible.

Article XIII
On the day when the first twenty instruments of ratification or accession have been deposited, the Secretary-General shall draw up a *procès-verbal* and transmit a copy thereof to each Member of the United Nations and to each of the non-member States contemplated in Article XI.

The present Convention shall come into force on the ninetieth day following the date of deposit of the twentieth instrument of ratification or accession.

Any ratification or accession effected subsequent to the latter date shall become effective on the ninetieth day following the deposit of the instrument of ratification or accession.

Article XIV
The present Convention shall remain in effect for a period of ten years as from the date of its coming into force.

It shall thereafter remain in force for successive periods of five years for such Contracting Parties as have not denounced it at least six months before the expiration of the current period.

Denunciation shall be effected by a written notification addressed to the Secretary-General of the United Nations.

Article XV
If, as a result of denunciations, the number of Parties to the present Convention should become less than sixteen, the Convention shall cease to be in force as from the date on which the last of these denunciations shall become effective.

Article XVI
A request for the revision of the present Convention may be made at any time by any Contracting Party by means of a notification in writing addressed to the Secretary–General.

The General Assembly shall decide upon the steps, if any, to be taken in respect of such request.

Article XVII

The Secretary-General of the United Nations shall notify all Members of the United Nations and the non-member States contemplated in Article XI of the following:

(a) signatures, ratifications and accessions received in accordance with Article XI;

(b) notifications received in accordance with Article XII;

(c) the date upon which the present Convention comes into force in accordance with Article XIII;

(d) denunciations received in accordance with Article XIV;

(e) the abrogation of the Convention in accordance with Article XV;

(f) notifications received in accordance with Article XVI.

Article XVIII

The original of the present Convention shall be deposited in the archives of the United Nations.

A certified copy of the Convention shall be transmitted to each Member of the United Nations and to each of the non-member States contemplated in Article XI.

Article XIX

The present Convention shall be registered by the Secretary-General of the United Nations on the date of its coming into force.

UNIVERSAL DECLARATION OF HUMAN RIGHTS (1948)

PREAMBLE

Whereas recognition of the inherent dignity and of the equal and inalienable rights of all members of the human family is the foundation of freedom, justice and peace in the world,

Whereas disregard and contempt for human rights have resulted in barbarous acts which have outraged the conscience of mankind, and the advent of a world in which human beings shall enjoy freedom of speech and belief and freedom from fear and want has been proclaimed as the highest aspiration of the common people,

Whereas it is essential, if man is not to be compelled to have recourse, as a last resort, to rebellion against tyranny and oppression, that human rights should be protected by the rule of law,

Whereas it is essential to promote the development of friendly relations between nations,

Whereas the peoples of the United Nations have in the Charter reaffirmed their faith in fundamental human rights, in the dignity and worth of the human person and in the equal rights of men and women and have determined to promote social progress and better standards of life in larger freedom,

Whereas Member States have pledged themselves to achieve, in co-operation with the United Nations, the promotion of universal respect for and observance of human rights and fundamental freedoms,

Whereas a common understanding of these rights and freedoms is of the greatest importance for the full realization of this pledge,

Now, therefore, THE GENERAL ASSEMBLY *proclaims*

This Universal Declaration of Human Rights as a common standard of achievement for all peoples and all nations, to the end that every individual and every organ of society, keeping this Declaration constantly in mind, shall strive by teaching and education to promote respect for these rights and freedoms and by progressive measures, national and international, to secure their universal and effective recognition and observance, both among the peoples of Member States themselves and among the peoples of territories under their jurisdiction.

Article 1
All human beings are born free and equal in dignity and rights. They are endowed with reason and conscience and should act towards one another in a spirit of brotherhood.

Article 2
Everyone is entitled to all the rights and freedoms set forth in this Declaration, without distinction of any kind, such as race, colour, sex, language, religion, political or other opinion, national or social origin, property, birth or other status.

Furthermore, no distinction shall be made on the basis of the political, jurisdictional or international status of the country or territory to which a person belongs, whether it be independent, trust, non-self-governing or under any other limitation of sovereignty.

Article 3
Everyone has the right to life, liberty and the security of person.

Article 4
No one shall be held in slavery or servitude; slavery and the slave trade shall be prohibited in all their forms.

Article 5
No one shall be subjected to torture or to cruel, inhuman or degrading treatment or punishment.

Article 6
Everyone has the right to recognition everywhere as a person before the law.

Article 7
All are equal before the law and are entitled without any discrimination to equal protection of the law. All are entitled to equal protection against any discrimination in violation of this Declaration and against any incitement to such discrimination.

Article 8
Everyone has the right to an effective remedy by the competent national tribunals for acts violating the fundamental rights granted him by the constitution or by law.

Article 9
No one shall be subjected to arbitrary arrest, detention or exile.

Article 10
Everyone is entitled in full equality to a fair and public hearing by an independent and impartial tribunal, in the determination of his rights and obligations and of any criminal charge against him.

Article 11
1. Everyone charged with a penal offence has the right to be presumed innocent until proved guilty according to law in a public trial at which he has had all the guarantees necessary for his defence.

2. No one shall be held guilty of any penal offence on account of any act or omission which did not constitute a penal offence, under national or international law, at the time when it was committed. Nor shall a heavier penalty be imposed than the one that was applicable at the time the penal offence was committed.

Article 12
No one shall be subjected to arbitrary interference with his privacy, family, home or correspondence, nor to attacks upon his honour and reputation. Everyone has the right to the protection of the law against such interference or attacks.

Article 13
1. Everyone has the right to freedom of movement and residence within the borders of each State.
2. Everyone has the right to leave any country, including his own, and to return to his country.

Article 14
1. Everyone has the right to seek and to enjoy in other countries asylum from persecution.
2. This right may not be invoked in the case of prosecutions genuinely arising from non-political crimes or from acts contrary to the purposes and principles of the United Nations.

Article 15
1. Everyone has the right to a nationality.
2. No one shall be arbitrarily deprived of his nationality nor denied the right to change his nationality.

Article 16
1. Men and women of full age, without any limitation due to race, nationality or religion, have the right to marry and to found a family. They are entitled to equal rights as to marriage, during marriage and at its dissolution.
2. Marriage shall be entered into only with the free and full consent of the intending spouses.
3. The family is the natural and fundamental group unit of society and is entitled to protection by society and the State.

Article 17
1. Everyone has the right to own property alone as well as in association with others.
2. No one shall be arbitrarily deprived of his property.

Article 18
Everyone has the right to freedom of thought, conscience and religion; this right includes freedom to change his religion or belief, and freedom, either alone or in community with others and in public or private, to manifest his religion or belief in teaching, practice, worship and observance.

Article 19
Everyone has the right to freedom of opinion and expression; this right includes freedom to hold opinions without interference and to seek, receive and impart information and ideas through any media and regardless of frontiers.

Article 20
1. Everyone has the right to freedom of peaceful assembly and association.
2. No one may be compelled to belong to an association.

Article 21
1. Everyone has the right to take part in the government of his country, directly or through freely chosen representatives.
2. Everyone has the right of equal access to public service in his country.

3.   The will of the people shall be the basis of the authority of government; this will shall be expressed in periodic and genuine elections which shall be by universal and equal suffrage and shall be held by secret vote or by equivalent free voting procedures.

Article 22

Everyone, as a member of society, has the right to social security and is entitled to realization, through national effort and international co-operation and in accordance with the organization and resources of each State, of the economic, social and cultural rights indispensable for his dignity and the free development of his personality.

Article 23

1.   Everyone has the right to work, to free choice of employment, to just and favourable conditions of work and to protection against unemployment.

2.   Everyone, without any discrimination, has the right to equal pay for equal work.

3.   Everyone who works has the right to just and favourable remuneration ensuring for himself and his family an existence worthy of human dignity, and supplemented, if necessary, by other means of social protection.

4.   Everyone has the right to form and to join trade unions for the protection of his interests.

Article 24

Everyone has the right to rest and leisure, including reasonable limitation of working hours and periodic holidays with pay.

Article 25

1.   Everyone has the right to a standard of living adequate for the health and well-being of himself and of his family, including food, clothing, housing and medical care and necessary social services, and the right to security in the event of unemployment, sickness, disability, widowhood, old age or other lack of livelihood in circumstances beyond his control.

2.   Motherhood and childhood are entitled to special care and assistance. All children, whether born in or out of wedlock, shall enjoy the same social protection.

Article 26

1.   Everyone has the right to education. Education shall be free, at least in the elementary and fundamental stages. Elementary education shall be compulsory. Technical and professional education shall be made generally available and higher education shall be equally accessible to all on the basis of merit.

2.   Education shall be directed to the full development of the human personality and to the strengthening of respect for human rights and fundamental freedoms. It shall promote understanding, tolerance and friendship among all nations, racial or religious groups, and shall further the activities of the United Nations for the maintenance of peace.

3.   Parents have a prior right to choose the kind of education that shall be given to their children.

Article 27

1.   Everyone has the right freely to participate in the cultural life of the community, to enjoy the arts and to share in scientific advancement and its benefits.

2.   Everyone has the right to the protection of the moral and material interests resulting from any scientific, literary or artistic production of which he is the author.

Article 28

Everyone is entitled to a social and international order in which the rights and freedoms set forth in this Declaration can be fully realized.

Article 29

1.   Everyone has duties to the community in which alone the free and full development of his personality is possible.

2.   In the exercise of his rights and freedoms, everyone shall be subject only to such limitations as are determined by law solely for the purpose of securing due recognition and respect for the rights and freedoms of others and of meeting the just requirements of morality, public order and the general welfare in a democratic society.

3.   These rights and freedoms may in no case be exercised contrary to the purposes and principles of the United Nations.

Article 30

Nothing in this Declaration may be interpreted as implying for any State, group or person any right to engage in any activity or to perform any act aimed at the destruction of any of the rights and freedoms set forth herein.

CONVENTION FOR THE SUPPRESSION OF THE TRAFFIC IN PERSONS AND OF THE EXPLOITATION OF THE PROSTITUTION OF OTHERS (1949)

PREAMBLE

Whereas prostitution and the accompanying evil of the traffic in persons for the purpose of prostitution are incompatible with the dignity and worth of the human person and endanger the welfare of the individual, the family and the community,

Whereas, with respect to the suppression of the traffic in women and children, the following international instruments are in force:

(1)   International Agreement of 18 May 1904 for the Suppression of the White Slave Traffic, as amended by the Protocol approved by the General Assembly of the United Nations on 3 December 1948,

(2)   International Convention of 4 May 1910 for the Suppression of the White Slave Traffic, as amended by the above-mentioned Protocol,

(3)   International Convention of 30 September 1921 for the Suppression of the Traffic in Women and Children, as amended by the Protocol approved by the General Assembly of the United Nations on 20 October 1947,

(4)   International Convention of 11 October 1933 for the Suppression of the Traffic in Women of Full Age, as amended by the aforesaid Protocol,

Whereas the League of Nations in 1937 prepared a draft Convention extending the scope of the above-mentioned instruments, and

Whereas developments since 1937 make feasible the conclusion of a convention consolidating the above-mentioned instruments and embodying the substance of the 1937 draft Convention as well as desirable alterations therein:

Now therefore
The Contracting parties
Hereby agree as hereinafter provided:

Article 1

The Parties to the present Convention agree to punish any person who, to gratify the passions of another:

(1)   Procures, entices or leads away, for purposes of prostitution, another person, even with the consent of that person;

(2)   Exploits the prostitution of another person, even with the consent of that person.

Article 2

The Parties to the present Convention further agree to punish any person who:

(1)   Keeps or manages, or knowingly finances or takes part in the financing of a brothel;

(2)   Knowingly lets or rents a building or other place or any part thereof for the purpose of the prostitution of others.

Article 3
To the extent permitted by domestic law, attempts to commit any of the offences referred to in articles 1 and 2, and acts preparatory to the commission thereof, shall also be punished.

Article 4
To the extent permitted by domestic law, intentional participation in the acts referred to in articles 1 and 2 above shall also be punishable.

To the extent permitted by domestic law, acts of participation shall be treated as separate offences whenever this is necessary to prevent impunity.

Article 5
In cases where injured persons are entitled under domestic law to be parties to proceedings in respect of any of the offences referred to in the present Convention, aliens shall be so entitled upon the same terms as nationals.

Article 6
Each Party to the present Convention agrees to take all the necessary measures to repeal or abolish any existing law, regulation or administrative provision by virtue of which persons who engage in or are suspected of engaging in prostitution are subject either to special registration or to the possession of a special document or to any exceptional requirements for supervision or notification.

Article 7
Previous convictions pronounced in foreign States for offences referred to in the present Convention shall, to the extent permitted by domestic law, be taken into account for the purpose of:

(1)   Establishing recidivism;

(2)   Disqualifying the offender from the exercise of civil rights.

Article 8
The offences referred to in articles 1 and 2 of the present Convention shall be regarded as extraditable offences in any extradition treaty which has been or may hereafter be concluded between any of the Parties to this Convention.

The Parties to the present Convention which do not make extradition conditional on the existence of a treaty shall henceforward recognize the offences referred to in articles 1 and 2 of the present Convention as cases for extradition between themselves.

Extradition shall be granted in accordance with the law of the State to which the request is made.

Article 9
In States where the extradition of nationals is not permitted by law, nationals who have returned to their own State after the commission abroad of any of the offences referred to in articles 1 and 2 of the present Convention shall be prosecuted in and punished by the courts of their own State.

This provision shall not apply if, in a similar case between the Parties to the present Convention, the extradition of an alien cannot be granted.

Article 10
The provisions of article 9 shall not apply when the person charged with the offence has been tried in a foreign State and, if convicted, has served his sentence or had it remitted or reduced in conformity with the laws of that foreign State.

Article 11

Nothing in the present Convention shall be interpreted as determining the attitude of a Party towards the general question of the limits of criminal jurisdiction under international law.

Article 12

The present Convention does not affect the principle that the offences to which it refers shall in each State be defined, prosecuted and punished in conformity with its domestic law.

Article 13

The Parties to the present Convention shall be bound to execute letters of request relating to offences referred to in the Convention in accordance with their domestic law and practice.

The transmission of letters of request shall be effected:

(1)   By direct communication between the judicial authorities; or

(2)   By direct communication between the Ministers of Justice of the two States, or by direct communication from another competent authority of the State making the request to the Minister of Justice of the State to which the request is made; or

(3)   Through the diplomatic or consular representative of the State making the request in the State to which the request is made; this representative shall send the letters of request direct to the competent judicial authority or to the authority indicated by the Government of the State to which the request is made, and shall receive direct from such authority the papers constituting the execution of the letters of request.

In cases 1 and 3 a copy of the letters of request shall always be sent to the superior authority of the State to which application is made.

Unless otherwise agreed, the letters of request shall be drawn up in the language of the authority making the request, provided always that the State to which the request is made may require a translation in its own language, certified correct by the authority making the request.

Each Party to the present Convention shall notify to each of the other Parties to the Convention the method or methods of transmission mentioned above which it will recognize for the letters of request of the latter State.

Until such notification is made by a State, its existing procedure in regard to letters of request shall remain in force.

Execution of letters of request shall not give rise to a claim for reimbursement of charges or expenses of any nature whatever other than expenses of experts.

Nothing in the present article shall be construed as an undertaking on the part of the Parties to the present Convention to adopt in criminal matters any form or methods of proof contrary to their own domestic laws.

Article 14

Each Party to the present Convention shall establish or maintain a service charged with the co-ordination and centralization of the results of the investigation of offences referred to in the present Convention.

Such services should compile all information calculated to facilitate the prevention and punishment of the offences referred to in the present Convention and should be in close contact with the corresponding services in other States.

Article 15

To the extent permitted by domestic law and to the extent to which the authorities responsible for the services referred to in article 14 may judge desirable, they shall furnish to the authorities responsible for the corresponding services in other States the following information:

(1)   Particulars of any offence referred to in the present Convention or any attempt to commit such offence;

(2)   Particulars of any search for any prosecution, arrest, conviction, refusal of admission or expulsion of persons guilty of any of the offences referred to in the present Convention, the movements of such persons and any other useful information with regard to them.

The information so furnished shall include descriptions of the offenders, their fingerprints, photographs, methods of operation, police records and records of conviction.

Article 16
The Parties to the present Convention agree to take or to encourage, through their public and private educational, health, social, economic and other related services, measures for the prevention of prostitution and for the rehabilitation and social adjustment of the victims of prostitution and of the offences referred to in the present Convention.

Article 17
The Parties to the present Convention undertake, in connection with immigration and emigration, to adopt or maintain such measures as are required, in terms of their obligations under the present Convention, to check the traffic in persons of either sex for the purpose of prostitution.

In particular they undertake:

(1)   To make such regulations as are necessary for the protection of immigrants or emigrants, and in particular, women and children, both at the place of arrival and departure and while *en route*;

(2)   To arrange for appropriate publicity warning the public of the dangers of the aforesaid traffic;

(3)   To take appropriate measures to ensure supervision of railway stations, airports, seaports and *en route*, and of other public places, in order to prevent international traffic in persons for the purpose of prostitution;

(4)   To take appropriate measures in order that the appropriate authorities be informed of the arrival of persons who appear, *prima facie*, to be the principals and accomplices in or victims of such traffic.

Article 18
The Parties to the present Convention undertake, in accordance with the conditions laid down by domestic law, to have declarations taken from aliens who are prostitutes, in order to establish their identity and civil status and to discover who has caused them to leave their State. The information obtained shall be communicated to the authorities of the State of origin of the said persons with a view to their eventual repatriation.

Article 19
The Parties to the present Convention undertake, in accordance with the conditions laid down by domestic law and without prejudice to prosecution or other action for violations therunder and so far as possible:

(1)   Pending the completion of arrangements for the repatriation of destitute victims of international traffic in persons for the purpose of prostitution, to make suitable provisions for their temporary care and maintenance;

(2)   To repatriate persons referred to in article 18 who desire to be repatriated or who may be claimed by persons exercising authority over them or whose expulsion is ordered in conformity with the law. Repatriation shall take place only after agreement is reached with the State of destination as to identity and nationality as well as to the place and date of arrival at frontiers. Each Party to the present Convention shall facilitate the passage of such persons through its territory.

Where the persons referred to in the preceding paragraph cannot themselves repay the cost of repatriation and have neither spouse, relatives nor guardian to pay for them, the cost of repatriation as far as the nearest frontier or port of embarkation or airport in the direction of the State of origin shall be borne by the State where they are in residence, and the cost of the remainder of the journey shall be borne by the State of origin.

Article 20
The Parties to the present Convention shall, if they have not already done so, take the necessary measures for the supervision of employment agencies in order to prevent persons seeking employment, in particular women and children, from being exposed to the danger of prostitution.

Article 21
The Parties to the present Convention shall communicate to the Secretary-General of the United Nations such laws and regulations as have already been promulgated in their States, and thereafter annually such laws and regulations as may be promulgated, relating to the subjects of the present Convention, as well as all measures taken by them concerning the application of the Convention. The information received shall be published periodically by the Secretary-General and sent to all Members of the United Nations and to non-member States to which the present Convention is officially communicated in accordance with article 23.

Article 22
If any dispute shall arise between the Parties to the present Convention relating to its interpretation or application and if such dispute cannot be settled by other means, the dispute shall, at the request of any one of the Parties to the dispute, be referred to the International Court of Justice.

Article 23
The present Convention shall be open for signature on behalf of any Member of the United Nations and also on behalf of any other State to which an invitation has been addressed by the Economic and Social Council.

The present Convention shall be ratified and the instruments of ratification shall be deposited with the Secretary-General of the United Nations.

The States mentioned in the first paragraph which have not signed the Convention may accede to it.

Accession shall be effected by deposit of an instrument of accession with the Secretary-General of the United Nations.

For the purposes of the present Convention the word 'State' shall include all the colonies and Trust Territories of a State signatory or acceding to the Convention and all territories for which such State is internationally responsible.

Article 24
The present Convention shall come into force on the ninetieth day following the date of deposit of the second instrument of ratification or accession.

For each State ratifying or acceding to the Convention after the deposit of the second instrument of ratification or accession, the Convention shall enter into force ninety days after the deposit by such State of its instrument of ratification or accession.

Article 25
After the expiration of five years from the entry into force of the present Convention, any Party to the Convention may denounce it by a written notification addressed to the Secretary-General of the United Nations.

Such denunciation shall take effect for the Party making it one year from the date upon which it is received by the Secretary-General of the United Nations.

Article 26
The Secretary-General of the United Nations shall inform all Members of the United Nations and non-member States referred to in article 23:
(a)   Of signatures, ratifications and accessions received in accordance with article 23;
(b)   Of the date on which the present Convention will come into force in accordance with article 24;
(c)   Of denunciations received in accordance with article 25.

Article 27
Each Party to the present Convention undertakes to adopt, in accordance with its Constitution, the legislative or other measures necessary to ensure the application of the Convention.

Article 28
The provisions of the present Convention shall supersede in the relations between the Parties thereto the provisions of the international instruments referred to in subparagraphs 1, 2, 3 and 4 of the second paragraph of the Preamble, each of which shall be deemed to be terminated when all the Parties thereto shall have become Parties to the present Convention.

FINAL PROTOCOL

Nothing in the present Convention shall be deemed to prejudice any legislation which ensures, for the enforcement of the provisions for securing the suppression of the traffic in persons and of the exploitation of others for purposes of prostitution, stricter conditions than those provided by the present Convention.
The provisions of articles 23 to 26 inclusive of the Convention shall apply to the present Protocol.

CONVENTION ON THE POLITICAL RIGHTS OF WOMEN (1952)

The Contracting Parties,
Desiring to implement the principle of equality of rights for men and women contained in the Charter of the United Nations,
Recognizing that everyone has the right to take part in the government of his country directly or indirectly through freely chosen representatives, and has the right to equal access to public service in his country, and desiring to equalize the status of men and women in the enjoyment and exercise of political rights, in accordance with the provisions of the Charter of the United Nations and of the Universal Declaration of Human Rights,
Having resolved to conclude a Convention for this purpose,
Hereby agree as hereinafter provided:

Article I
Women shall be entitled to vote in all elections on equal terms with men, without any discrimination.

Article II
Women shall be eligible for election to all publicly elected bodies, established by national law, on equal terms with men, without any discrimination.

Article III
Women shall be entitled to hold public office and to exercise all public functions, established by national law, on equal terms with men, without any discrimination.

Article IV

1. This Convention shall be open for signature on behalf of any Member of the United Nations and also on behalf of any other State to which an invitation has been addressed by the General Assembly.

2. This Convention shall be ratified and the instruments of ratification shall be deposited with the Secretary-General of the United Nations.

Article V

1. This Convention shall be open for accession to all States referred to in paragraph 1 of article IV.

2. Accession shall be effected by the deposit of an instrument of accession with the Secretary-General of the United Nations.

Article VI

1. This Convention shall come into force on the ninetieth day following the date of deposit of the sixth instrument of ratification or accession.

2. For each State ratifying or acceding to the Convention after the deposit of the sixth instrument of ratification or accession the Convention shall enter into force on the ninetieth day after deposit by such State of its instrument of ratification or accession.

Article VII

In the event that any State submits a reservation to any of the articles of this Convention at the time of signature, ratification or accession, the Secretary-General shall communicate the text of the reservation to all States which are or may become Parties to this Convention. Any State which objects to the reservation may, within a period of ninety days from the date of the said communication (or upon the date of its becoming a Party to the Convention), notify the Secretary-General that it does not accept it. In such case, the Convention shall not enter into force as between such State and the State making the reservation.

Article VIII

1. Any State may denounce this Convention by written notification to the Secretary-General of the United Nations. Denunciation shall take effect one year after the date of receipt of the notification by the Secretary General.

2. This Convention shall cease to be in force as from the date when the denunciation which reduces the number of Parties to less than six becomes effective.

Article IX

Any dispute which may arise between any two or more Contracting States concerning the interpretation or application of this Convention, which is not settled by negotiation, shall at the request of any one of the parties to the dispute be referred to the International Court of Justice for decision, unless they agree to another mode of settlement.

Article X

The Secretary-General of the United Nations shall notify all Members of the United Nations and the non-member States contemplated in paragraph 1 of article IV of this Convention of the following:

(a) Signatures and instruments of ratification received in accordance with article IV;

(b) Instruments of accession received in accordance with article V;

(c) The date upon which this Convention enters into force in accordance with article VI;

(d) Communications and notifications received in accordance with article VII;

(e) Notifications of denunciation received in accordance with paragraph 1 of article VIII;

(f) Abrogation in accordance with paragraph 2 of article VIII.

Article XI

1. This Convention, of which the Chinese, English, French, Russian and Spanish texts shall be equally authentic, shall be deposited in the archives of the United Nations.

2. The Secretary-General of the United Nations shall transmit a certified copy to all Members of the United Nations and to the non-member States contemplated in paragraph 1 of article IV.

SUPPLEMENTARY CONVENTION ON THE ABOLITION OF SLAVERY, THE SLAVE TRADE, AND INSTITUTIONS AND PRACTICES SIMILAR TO SLAVERY (1956)

PREAMBLE

The States Parties to the present Convention,

Considering that freedom is the birthright of every human being,

Mindful that the peoples of the United Nations reaffirmed in the Charter their faith in the dignity and worth of the human person,

Considering that the Universal Declaration of Human Rights, proclaimed by the General Assembly of the United Nations as a common standard of achievement for all peoples and all nations, states that no one shall be held in slavery or servitude and that slavery and the slave trade shall be prohibited in all their forms,

Recognizing that, since the conclusion of the Slavery Convention signed at Geneva on 25 September 1926, which was designed to secure the abolition of slavery and of the slave trade, further progress has been made towards this end,

Having regard to the Forced Labour Convention of 1930 and to subsequent action by the International Labour Organisation in regard to forced or compulsory labour,

Being aware, however, that slavery, the slave trade and institutions and practices similar to slavery have not yet been eliminated in all parts of the world,

Having decided, therefore, that the Convention of 1926, which remains operative, should now be augmented by the conclusion of a supplementary convention designed to intensify national as well as international efforts towards the abolition of slavery, the slave trade and institutions and practices similar to slavery,

Have agreed as follows:

SECTION 1   INSTITUTIONS AND PRACTICES SIMILAR TO SLAVERY

Article 1

Each of the States Parties to this Convention shall take all practicable and necessary legislative and other measures to bring about progressively and as soon as possible the complete abolition or abandonment of the following institutions and practices, where they still exist and whether or not they are covered by the definition of slavery contained in article 1 of the Slavery Convention signed at Geneva on 25 September 1926:

(a) Debt bondage, that is to say, the status or condition arising from a pledge by a debtor of his personal services or of those of a person under his control as security for a debt, if the value of those services as reasonably assessed is not applied towards the liquidation of the debt or the length and nature of those services are not respectively limited and defined;

(b) Serfdom, that is to say, the condition or status of a tenant who is by law, custom or agreement bound to live and labour on land belonging to another person and to render some determinate service to such other person, whether for reward or not, and is not free to change his status;

(c)   Any institution or practice whereby:

(i)   A woman, without the right to refuse, is promised or given in marriage on payment of a consideration in money or in kind to her parents, guardian, family or any other person or group; or

(ii)   The husband of a woman, his family, or his clan, has the right to transfer her to another person for value received or otherwise; or

(iii)   A woman on the death of her husband is liable to be inherited by another person;

(d)   Any institution or practice whereby a child or young person under the age of 18 years, is delivered by either or both of his natural parents or by his guardian to another person, whether for reward or not, with a view to the exploitation of the child or young person or of his labour.

Article 2
With a view to bringing to an end the institutions and practices mentioned in article 1 (c) of this Convention, the States Parties undertake to prescribe, where appropriate, suitable minimum ages of marriage, to encourage the use of facilities whereby the consent of both parties to a marriage may be freely expressed in the presence of a competent civil or religious authority, and to encourage the registration of marriages.

SECTION II   THE SLAVE TRADE

Article 3
1.   The act of conveying or attempting to convey slaves from one country to another by whatever means of transport, or of being accessory thereto, shall be a criminal offence under the laws of the States Parties to this Convention and persons convicted thereof shall be liable to very severe penalties.

2.   (a)   The States Parties shall take all effective measures to prevent ships and aircraft authorized to fly their flags from conveying slaves and to punish persons guilty of such acts or of using national flags for that purpose.

(b)   The States Parties shall take all effective measures to ensure that their ports, airfields and coasts are not used for the conveyance of slaves.

3.   The States Parties to this Convention shall exchange information in order to ensure the practical co-ordination of the measures taken by them in combating the slave trade and shall inform each other of every case of the slave trade, and of every attempt to commit this criminal offence, which comes to their notice.

Article 4
Any slave who takes refuge on board any vessel of a State Party to this Convention shall *ipso facto* be free.

SECTION III   SLAVERY AND INSTITUTIONS AND PRACTICES SIMILAR TO SLAVERY

Article 5
In a country where the abolition or abandonment of slavery, or of the institutions or practices mentioned in article 1 of this Convention, is not yet complete, the act of mutilating, branding or otherwise marking a slave or a person of servile status in order to indicate his status, or as a punishment, or for any other reason, or of being accessory thereto, shall be a criminal offence under the laws of the States Parties to this Convention and persons convicted thereof shall be liable to punishment.

Article 6
1.   The act of enslaving another person or of inducing another person to give himself or a person dependent upon him into slavery, or of attempting these acts, or

being accessory thereto, or being a party to a conspiracy to accomplish any such acts, shall be a criminal offence under the laws of the States Parties to this Convention and persons convicted thereof shall be liable to punishment.

2. Subject to the provisions of the introductory paragraph of article 1 of this Convention, the provisions of paragraph 1 of the present article shall also apply to the act of inducing another person to place himself or a person dependent upon him into the servile status resulting from any of the institutions or practices mentioned in article 1, to any attempt to perform such acts, to being accessory thereto, and to being a party to a conspiracy to accomplish any such acts.

SECTION IV   DEFINITIONS

Article 7
For the purposes of the present Convention:

(a)   'Slavery' means, as defined in the Slavery Convention of 1926, the status or condition of a person over whom any or all of the powers attaching to the right of ownership are exercised, and 'slave' means a person in such condition or status;

(b)   'A person of servile status' means a person in the condition or status resulting from any of the institutions or practices mentioned in article 1 of this Convention;

(c)   'Slave trade' means and includes all acts involved in the capture, acquisition or disposal of a person with intent to reduce him to slavery; all acts involved in the acquisition of a slave with a view to selling or exchanging him; all acts of disposal by sale or exchange of a person acquired with a view to being sold or exchanged; and, in general, every act of trade or transport in slaves by whatever means of conveyance.

SECTION V   CO-OPERATION BETWEEN STATES PARTIES AND COMMUNICATION OF INFORMATION

Article 8
1. The States Parties to this Convention undertake to co-operate with each other and with the United Nations to give effect to the foregoing provisions.

2. The Parties undertake to communicate to the Secretary-General of the United Nations copies of any laws, regulations and administrative measures enacted or put into effect to implement the provisions of this Convention.

3. The Secretary-General shall communicate the information received under paragraph 2 of this article to the other Parties and to the Economic and Social Council as part of the documentation for any discussion which the Council might undertake with a view to making further recommendations for the abolition of slavery, the slave trade or the institutions and practices which are the subject of this Convention.

SECTION VI   FINAL CLAUSES

Article 9
No reservations may be made to this Convention.

Article 10
Any dispute between States Parties to this Convention relating to its interpretation or application, which is not settled by negotiation, shall be referred to the International Court of Justice at the request of any one of the parties to the dispute, unless the parties concerned agree on another mode of settlement.

Article 11
1. This Convention shall be open until 1 July 1957 for signature by any State Member of the United Nations or of a specialized agency. It shall be subject to ratification by the signatory States, and the instruments of ratification shall be

deposited with the Secretary-General of the United Nations, who shall inform each signatory and acceding State.

2.	After 1 July 1957 this Convention shall be open for accession by any State Member of the United Nations or of a specialized agency, or by any other State to which an invitation to accede has beeen addressed by the General Assembly of the United Nations. Accession shall be effected by the deposit of a formal instrument with the Secretary-General of the United Nations, who shall inform each signatory and acceding State.

Article 12

1.	This Convention shall apply to all non-self-governing trust, colonial and other non-metropolitan territories for the international relations of which any State Party is responsible; the Party concerned shall, subject to the provisions of paragraph 2 of this article, at the time of signature, ratification or accession declare the non-metropolitan territory or territories to which the Convention shall apply *ipso facto* as a result of such signature, ratification or accession.

2.	In any case in which the previous consent of a non-metropolitan territory is required by the constitutional laws or practices of the Party or of the non-metropolitan territory, the Party concerned shall endeavour to secure the needed consent of the non-metropolitan territory within the period of twelve months from the date of signature of the Convention by the metropolitan State, and when such consent has been obtained the Party shall notify the Secretary-General. This Convention shall apply to the territory or territories named in such notification from the date of its receipt by the Secretary-General.

3.	After the expiry of the twelve-month period mentioned in the preceding paragraph, the States Parties concerned shall inform the Secretary-General of the results of the consultations with those non-metropolitan territories for whose international relations they are responsible and whose consent to the application of this Convention may have been withheld.

Article 13

1.	This Convention shall enter into force on the date on which two States have become Parties thereto.

2.	It shall thereafter enter into force with respect to each State and territory on the date of deposit of the instrument of ratification or accession of that State or notification of application to that territory.

Article 14

1.	The application of this Convention shall be divided into successive periods of three years, of which the first shall begin on the date of entry into force of the Convention in accordance with paragraph 1 of article 13.

2.	Any State Party may denounce this Convention by a notice addressed by that State to the Secretary-General not less than six months before the expiration of the current three-year period. The Secretary-General shall notify all other Parties of each such notice and the date of the receipt thereof.

3.	Denunciations shall take effect at the expiration of the current three-year period.

4.	In cases where, in accordance with the provisions of article 12, this Convention has become applicable to a non-metropolitan territory of a Party, that Party may at any time thereafter, with the consent of the territory concerned, give notice to the Secretary-General of the United Nations denouncing this Convention separately in respect of that territory. The denunciation shall take effect one year after the date of the receipt of such notice by the Secretary-General, who shall notify all other Parties of such notice and the date of the receipt thereof.

Article 15
This Convention, of which the Chinese, English, French, Russian and Spanish texts are equally authentic, shall be deposited in the archives of the United Nations Secretariat. The Secretary-General shall prepare a certified copy thereof for communication to States Parties to this Convention, as well as to all other States Members of the United Nations and of the specialized agencies.

IN WITNESS WHEREOF the undersigned, being duly authorized thereto by their respective Governments, have signed this Convention on the date appearing opposite their respective signatures.

DONE at the European Office of the United Nations at Geneva, this seventh day of September one thousand nine hundred and fifty-six.

CONVENTION CONCERNING THE ABOLITION OF FORCED LABOUR (1957)

The General Conference of the International Labour Organisation,

Having been convened at Geneva by the Governing Body of the International Labour Office, and having met in its fortieth session on 5 June 1957, and

Having considered the question of forced labour, which is the fourth item on the agenda of the session, and

Having noted the provisions of the Forced Labour Convention, 1930, and

Having noted that the Slavery Convention, 1926, provides that all necessary measures shall be taken to prevent compulsory or forced labour from developing into conditions analogous to slavery and that the Supplementary Convention on the Abolition of Slavery, the Slave Trade, and Institutions and Practices Similar to Slavery, 1956, provides for the complete abolition of debt bondage and serfdom, and

Having noted that the Protection of Wages Convention, 1949, provides that wages shall be paid regularly and prohibits methods of payment which deprive the worker of a genuine possibility of terminating his employment, and

Having decided upon the adoption of further proposals with regard to the abolition of certain forms of forced or compulsory labour constituting a violation of the rights of man referred to in the Charter of the United Nations and enunciated by the Universal Declaration of Human Rights, and

Having determined that these proposals shall take the form of an international Convention,

Adopts this twenty-fifth day of June of the year one thousand nine hundred and fifty-seven the following Convention, which may be cited as the Abolition of Forced Labour Convention, 1957:

Article 1
Each Member of the International Labour Organisation which ratifies this Convention undertakes to suppress and not to make use of any form of forced or compulsory labour:

    (a) As a means of political coercion or education or as a punishment for holding or expressing political views or views ideologically opposed to the established political, social or economic system;

    (b) As a method of mobilising and using labour for purposes of economic development;

    (c) As a means of labour discipline;

    (d) As a punishment for having participated in strikes;

    (e) As a means of racial, social, national or religious discrimination.

Article 2
Each Member of the International Labour Organisation which ratifies this Convention undertakes to take effective measures to secure the immediate and complete abolition of forced or compulsory labour as specified in article 1 of this Convention.

Article 3
The formal ratifications of this Convention shall be communicated to the Director-General of the International Labour Office for registration.

Article 4
1. This Convention shall be binding only upon those Members of the International Labour Organisation whose ratifications have been registered with the Director-General.

2. It shall come into force twelve months after the date on which the ratifications of two Members have been registered with the Director-General.

3. Thereafter, this Convention shall come into force for any Member twelve months after the date on which its ratification has been registered.

Article 5
1. A Member which has ratified this Convention may denounce it after the expiration of ten years from the date on which the Convention first comes into force, by an act communicated to the Director-General of the International Labour Office for registration. Such denunciation shall not take effect until one year after the date on which it is registered.

2. Each Member which has ratified this Convention and which does not, within the year following the expiration of the period of ten years mentioned in the preceding paragraph, exercise the right of denunciation provided for in this article, will be bound for another period of five years and, thereafter, may denounce this Convention at the expiration of each period of five years under the terms provided for in this article.

Article 6
1. The Director-General of the International Labour Office shall notify all Members of the International Labour Organisation of the registration of all ratifications and denunciations communicated to him by the Members of the Organisation.

2. When notifying the Members of the Organisation of the registration of the second ratification communicated to him the Director-General shall draw the attention of the Members of the Organisation to the date upon which the Convention will come into force.

Article 7
The Director-General of the International Labour Office shall communicate to the Secretary-General of the United Nations for registration in accordance with Article 102 of the Charter of the United Nations full particulars of all ratifications and acts of denunciation registered by him in accordance with the provisions of the preceding articles.

Article 8
At such times as it may consider necessary the Governing Body of the International Labour Office shall present to the General Conference a report on the working of the Convention and shall examine the desirability of placing on the agenda of the Conference the question of its revision in whole or in part.

Article 9
1. Should the Conference adopt a new Convention revising this Convention in whole or in part, then, unless the new Convention otherwise provides:

   (a) The ratification by a Member of the new revising Convention shall *ipso jure* involve the immediate denunciation of this Convention, notwithstanding the provisions of article 5 above, if and when the new revising Convention shall have come into force;

   (b) As from the date when the new revising Convention comes into force this Convention shall cease to be open to ratification by the Members.

2. This Convention shall in any case remain in force in its actual form and content for those Members which have ratified it but have not ratified the revising Convention.

Article 10

The English and French versions of the text of this Convention are equally authoritative.

The foregoing is the authentic text of the Convention duly adopted by the General Conference of the International Labour Organisation during its fortieth session which was held at Geneva and declared closed the twenty-seventh day of June 1957.

IN FAITH WHEREOF we have appended our signatures this fourth day of July 1957.

DECLARATION OF THE RIGHTS OF THE CHILD (1959)

PREAMBLE

Whereas the peoples of the United Nations have, in the Charter, re-affirmed their faith in fundamental human rights and in the dignity and worth of the human person, and have determined to promote social progress and better standards of life in larger freedom,

Whereas the United Nations has, in the Universal Declaration of Human Rights, proclaimed that everyone is entitled to all the rights and freedoms set forth therein, without distinction of any kind, such as race, colour, sex, language, religion, political or other opinion, national or social origin, property, birth or other status,

Whereas the child, by reason of his physical and mental immaturity, needs special safeguards and care, including appropriate legal protection, before as well as after birth,

Whereas the need for such special safeguards has been stated in the Geneva Declaration of the Rights of the Child of 1924, and recognized in the Universal Declaration of Human Rights and in the statutes of specialized agencies and international organizations concerned with the welfare of children,

Whereas mankind owes to the child the best it has to give,

Now therefore,

The General Assembly

Proclaims this Declaration of the Rights of the Child to the end that he may have a happy childhood and enjoy for his own good and for the good of society the rights and freedoms herein set forth, and calls upon parents, upon men and women as individuals, and upon voluntary organizations, local authorities and national Governments to recognize these rights and strive for their observance by legislative and other measures progressively taken in accordance with the following principles:

Principle 1

The child shall enjoy all the rights set forth in this Declaration. Every child, without any exception whatsoever, shall be entitled to these rights, without distinction or discrimination on account of race, colour, sex, language, religion, political or other opinion, national or social origin, property, birth or other status, whether of himself or of his family.

Principle 2

The child shall enjoy special protection, and shall be given opportunities and facilities, by law and by other means, to enable him to develop physically, mentally, morally, spiritually and socially in a healthy and normal manner and in conditions of freedom and dignity. In the enactment of laws for this purpose, the best interests of the child shall be the paramount consideration.

Principle 3

The child shall be entitled from his birth to a name and a nationality.

Principle 4
The child shall enjoy the benefits of social security. He shall be entitled to grow and develop in health; to this end, special care and protection shall be provided both to him and to his mother, including adequate pre-natal and post-natal care. The child shall have the right to adequate nutrition, housing, recreation and medical services.

Principle 5
The child who is physically, mentally or socially handicapped shall be given the special treatment, education and care required by his particular condition.

Principle 6
The child, for the full and harmonious development of his personality, needs love and understanding. He shall, wherever possible, grow up in the care and under the responsibility of his parents, and, in any case, in an atmosphere of affection and of moral and material security; a child of tender years shall not, save in exceptional circumstances, be separated from his mother. Society and the public authorities shall have the duty to extend particular care to children without a family and to those without adequate means of support. Payment of State and other assistance towards the maintenance of children of large families is desirable.

Principle 7
The child is entitled to receive education, which shall be free and compulsory, at least in the elementary stages. He shall be given an education which will promote his general culture and enable him, on a basis of equal opportunity, to develop his abilities, his individual judgement, and his sense of moral and social responsibility, and to become a useful member of society.

The best interests of the child shall be the guiding principle of those responsible for his education and guidance; that responsibility lies in the first place with his parents.

The child shall have full opportunity for play and recreation, which should be directed to the same purposes as education; society and the public authorities shall endeavour to promote the enjoyment of this right.

Principle 8
The child shall in all circumstances be among the first to receive protection and relief.

Principle 9
The child shall be protected against all forms of neglect, cruelty and exploitation. He shall not be the subject of traffic, in any form.

The child shall not be admitted to employment before an appropriate minimum age; he shall in no case be caused or permitted to engage in any occupation or employment which would prejudice his health or education, or interfere with his physical, mental or moral development.

Principle 10
The child shall be protected from practices which may foster racial, religious and any other form of discrimination. He shall be brought up in a spirit of understanding, tolerance, friendship among peoples, peace and universal brotherhood, and in full consciousness that his energy and talents should be devoted to the service of his fellow men.

UNITED NATIONS DECLARATION ON THE ELIMINATION OF ALL FORMS OF RACIAL DISCRIMINATION (1963)

The General Assembly,
Considering that the Charter of the United Nations is based on the principles of the dignity and equality of all human beings and seeks, among other basic objectives, to

achieve international co-operation in promoting and encouraging respect for human rights and fundamental freedoms for all without distinction as to race, sex, language or religion,

Considering that the Universal Declaration of Human Rights proclaims that all human beings are born free and equal in dignity and rights and that everyone is entitled to all the rights and freedoms set out in the Declaration, without distinction of any kind, in particular as to race, colour or national origin,

Considering that the Universal Declaration of Human Rights proclaims further that all are equal before the law and are entitled without any discrimination to equal protection of the law and that all are entitled to equal protection against any discrimination and against any incitement to such discrimination,

Considering that the United Nations has condemned colonialism and all practices of segregation and discrimination associated therewith, and that the Declaration on the Granting of Independence to Colonial Countries and Peoples proclaims in particular the necessity of bringing colonialism to a speedy and unconditional end,

Considering that any doctrine of racial differentiation or superiority is scientifically false, morally condemnable, socially unjust and dangerous, and that there is no justification for racial discrimination either in theory or in practice,

Taking into account the other resolutions adopted by the General Assembly and the international instruments adopted by the specialized agencies, in particular the International Labour Organisation and the United Nations Educational, Scientific and Cultural Organization, in the field of discrimination,

Taking into account the fact that, although international action and efforts in a number of countries have made it possible to achieve progress in that field, discrimination based on race, colour or ethnic origin in certain areas of the world continues none the less to give cause for serious concern,

Alarmed by the manifestations of racial discrimination still in evidence in some areas of the world, some of which are imposed by certain Governments by means of legislative, administrative or other measures, in the form, *inter alia*, of *apartheid*, segregation and separation, as well as by the promotion and dissemination of doctrines of racial superiority and expansionism in certain areas,

Convinced that all forms of racial discrimination and, still more so, governmental policies based on the prejudice of racial superiority or on racial hatred, besides constituting a violation of fundamental human rights, tend to jeopardize friendly relations among peoples, co-operation between nations and international peace and security,

Convinced also that racial discrimination harms not only those who are its objects but also those who practise it.

Convinced further that the building of a world society free from all forms of racial segregation and discrimination, factors which create hatred and division among men, is one of the fundamental objectives of the United Nations,

1. *Solemnly affirms* the necessity of speedily eliminating racial discrimination throughout the world, in all its forms and manifestations, and of securing understanding of and respect for the dignity of the human person;

2. *Solemnly affirms* the necessity of adopting national and international measures to that end, including teaching, education and information, in order to secure the universal and effective recognition and observance of the principles set forth below;

3. *Proclaims* this Declaration:

Article 1
Discrimination between human beings on the ground of race, colour or ethnic origin is an offence to human dignity and shall be condemned as a denial of the principles of the Charter of the United Nations, as a violation of the human rights and

fundamental freedoms proclaimed in the Universal Declaration of Human Rights, as an obstacle to friendly and peaceful relations among nations and as a fact capable of disturbing peace and security among peoples.

Article 2

1. No State, institution, group or individual shall make any discrimination whatsoever in matters of human rights and fundamental freedoms in the treatment of persons, groups of persons or institutions on the ground of race, colour or ethnic origin.

2. No State shall encourage, advocate or lend its support, through police action or otherwise, to any discrimination based on race, colour or ethnic origin by any group, institution or individual.

3. Special concrete measures shall be taken in appropriate circumstances in order to secure adequate development or protection of individuals belonging to certain racial groups with the object of ensuring the full enjoyment by such individuals of human rights and fundamental freedoms. These measures shall in no circumstances have as a consequence the maintenance of unequal or separate rights for different racial groups.

Article 3

1. Particular efforts shall be made to prevent discrimination based on race, colour or ethnic origin, especially in the fields of civil rights, access to citizenship, education, religion, employment, occupation and housing.

2. Everyone shall have equal access to any place or facility intended for use by the general public, without distinction as to race, colour or ethnic origin.

Article 4

All States shall take effective measures to revise governmental and other public policies and to rescind laws and regulations which have the effect of creating and perpetuating racial discrimination wherever it still exists. They should pass legislation for prohibiting such discrimination and should take all appropriate measures to combat those prejudices which lead to racial discrimination.

Article 5

An end shall be put without delay to governmental and other public policies of racial segregation and especially policies of *apartheid*, as well as all forms of racial discrimination and separation resulting from such policies.

Article 6

No discrimination by reason of race, colour or ethnic origin shall be admitted in the enjoyment by any person of political and citizenship rights in his country, in particular the right to participate in elections through universal and equal suffrage and to take part in the government. Everyone has the right of equal access to public service in his country.

Article 7

1. Everyone has the right to equality before the law and to equal justice under the law. Everyone, without distinction as to race, colour or ethnic origin, has the right to security of person and protection by the State against violence or bodily harm, whether inflicted by government officials or by any individual, group or institution.

2. Everyone shall have the right to an effective remedy and protection against any discrimination he may suffer on the ground of race, colour or ethnic origin with respect to his fundamental rights and freedoms through independent national tribunals competent to deal with such matters.

Article 8

All effective steps shall be taken immediately in the fields of teaching, education and information, with a view to eliminating racial discrimination and prejudice and promoting understanding, tolerance and friendship among nations and racial groups, as well as to propagating the purposes and principles of the Charter of the United Nations, of the Universal Declaration of Human Rights, and of the Declaration on the Granting of Independence to Colonial Countries and Peoples.

Article 9

1.   All propaganda and organizations based on ideas or theories of the superiority of one race or group of persons of one colour or ethnic origin with a view to justifying or promoting racial discrimination in any form shall be severely condemned.

2.   All incitement to or acts of violence, whether by individuals or organizations against any race or group of persons of another colour or ethnic origin shall be considered an offence against society and punishable under law.

3.   In order to put into effect the purposes and principles of the present Declaration, all States shall take immediate and positive measures, including legislative and other measures, to prosecute and/or outlaw organizations which promote or incite to racial discrimination, or incite to or use violence for purposes of discrimination based on race, colour or ethnic origin.

Article 10

The United Nations, the specialized agencies, States and non-governmental organizations shall do all in their power to promote energetic action which, by combining legal and other practical measures, will make possible the abolition of all forms of racial discrimination. They shall, in particular, study the causes of such discrimination with a view to recommending appropriate and effective measures to combat and eliminate it.

Article 11

Every State shall promote respect for and observance of human rights and fundamental freedoms in accordance with the Charter of the United Nations and shall fully and faithfully observe the provisions of the present Declaration, the Universal Declaration of Human Rights and the Declaration on the Granting of Independence to Colonial Countries and Peoples.

INTERNATIONAL CONVENTION ON THE ELIMINATION OF ALL FORMS OF RACIAL DISCRIMINATION (1966)

The States Parties to this Convention,

Considering that the Charter of the United Nations is based on the principles of the dignity and equality inherent in all human beings, and that all Member States have pledged themselves to take joint and separate action, in co-operation with the Organization, for the achievement of one of the purposes of the United Nations which is to promote and encourage universal respect for and observance of human rights and fundamental freedoms for all, without distinction as to race, sex, language or religion,

Considering that the Universal Declaration of Human Rights proclaims that all human beings are born free and equal in dignity and rights and that everyone is entitled to all the rights and freedoms set out therein, without distinction of any kind, in particular as to race, colour or national origin,

Considering that all human beings are equal before the law and are entitled to equal protection of the law against any discrimination and against any incitement to discrimination,

Considering that the United Nations has condemned colonialism and all practices of segregation and discrimination associated therewith, in whatever form and wherever they exist, and that the Declaration on the Granting of Independence to Colonial Countries and Peoples of 14 December 1960 (General Assembly resolution 1514 (XV)) has affirmed and solemnly proclaimed the necessity of bringing them to a speedy and unconditional end,

Considering that the United Nations Declaration on the Elimination of All Forms of Racial Discrimination of 20 November 1963 (General Assembly resolution 1904 (XVIII)) solemnly affirms the necessity of speedily eliminating racial discrimination throughout the world in all its forms and manifestations and of securing understanding of and respect for the dignity of the human person,

Convinced that any doctrine of superiority based on racial differentiation is scientifically false, morally condemnable, socially unjust and dangerous, and that there is no justification for racial discrimination, in theory or in practice, anywhere,

Reaffirming that discrimination between human beings on the grounds of race, colour or ethnic origin is an obstacle to friendly and peaceful relations among nations and is capable of disturbing peace and security among peoples and the harmony of persons living side by side even within one and the same State,

Convinced that the existence of racial barriers is repugnant to the ideals of any human society,

Alarmed by manifestations of racial discrimination still in evidence in some areas of the world and by governmental policies based on racial superiority or hatred, such as policies of *apartheid,* segregation or separation,

Resolved to adopt all necessary measures for speedily eliminating racial discrimination in all its forms and manifestations, and to prevent and combat racist doctrines and practices in order to promote understanding between races and to build an international community free from all forms of racial segregation and racial discrimination,

Bearing in mind the Convention concerning Discrimination in respect of Employment and Occupation adopted by the International Labour Organization in 1958, and the Convention against Discrimination in Education adopted by the United Nations Educational, Scientific, and Cultural Organization in 1960,

Desiring to implement the principles embodied in the United Nations Declaration on the Elimination of All Forms of Racial Discrimination and to secure the earliest adoption of practical measures to that end,

Have agreed as follows:

PART I

Article 1

1.   In this Convention, the term 'racial discrimination' shall mean any distinction, exclusion, restriction or preference based on race, colour, descent, or national or ethnic origin which has the purpose or effect of nullifying or impairing the recognition, enjoyment or exercise, on an equal footing, of human rights and fundamental freedoms in the political, economic, social, cultural or any other field of public life.

2.   This Convention shall not apply to distinctions, exclusions, restrictions or preferences made by a State Party to this Convention between citizens and non-citizens.

3.   Nothing in this Convention may be interpreted as affecting in any way the legal provisions of States Parties concerning nationality, citizenship or naturalization, provided that such provisions do not discriminate against any particular nationality.

4.   Special measures taken for the sole purpose of securing adequate advancement of certain racial or ethnic groups or individuals requiring such protection as may be necessary in order to ensure such groups or individuals equal enjoyment or exercise of human rights and fundamental freedoms shall not be deemed racial discrimination, provided, however, that such measures do not, as a consequence, lead to the

maintenance of separate rights for different racial groups and that they shall not be continued after the objectives for which they were taken have been achieved.

Article 2

1.   States Parties condemn racial discrimination and undertake to pursue by all appropriate means and without delay a policy of eliminating racial discrimination in all its forms and promoting understanding among all races, and, to this end:

(a)   each State Party undertakes to engage in no act or practice of racial discrimination against persons, groups of persons or institutions and to ensure that all public authorities and public institutions, national and local, shall act in conformity with this obligation;

(b)   each State Party undertakes not to sponsor, defend or support racial discrimination by any persons or organizations;

(c)   each State Party shall take effective measures to review governmental, national and local policies, and to amend, rescind or nullify any laws and regulations which have the effect of creating or perpetuating racial discrimination wherever it exists;

(d)   each State Party shall prohibit and bring to an end, by all appropriate means, including legislation as required by circumstances, racial discrimination by any persons, group or organization;

(e)   each State Party undertakes to encourage, where appropriate, integrationist multi-racial organizations and movements and other means of eliminating barriers between races, and to discourage anything which tends to strengthen racial division.

2.   States Parties shall, when the circumstances so warrant, take, in the social, economic, cultural and other fields, special and concrete measures to ensure the adequate development and protection of certain racial groups or individuals belonging to them, for the purpose of guaranteeing them the full and equal enjoyment of human rights and fundamental freedoms. These measures shall in no case entail as a consequence the maintenance of unequal or separate rights for different racial groups after the objectives for which they were taken have been achieved.

Article 3

States Parties particularly condemn racial segregation and *apartheid* and undertake to prevent, prohibit and eradicate all practices of this nature in territories under their jurisdiction.

Article 4

States Parties condemn all propaganda and all organizations which are based on ideas or theories of superiority of one race or group of persons of one colour or ethnic origin, or which attempt to justify or promote racial hatred and discrimination in any form, and undertake to adopt immediate and positive measures designed to eradicate all incitement to, or acts of, such discrimination and, to this end, with due regard to the principles embodied in the Universal Declaration of Human Rights and the rights expressly set forth in Article 5 of this Convention, *inter alia:*

(a)   shall declare an offence punishable by law all dissemination of ideas based on racial superiority or hatred, incitement to racial discrimination, as well as all acts of violence or incitement to such acts against any race or group of persons of another colour or ethnic origin, and also the provision of any assistance to racist activities, including the financing thereof;

(b)   shall declare illegal and prohibit organizations, and also organized and all other propaganda activities, which promote and incite racial discrimination, and shall recognize participation in such organizations or activities as an offence punishable by law;

(c)   shall not permit public authorities or public institutions, national or local, to promote or incite racial discrimination.

Article 5

In compliance with the fundamental obligations laid down in Article 2 of this Convention, States Parties undertake to prohibit and to eliminate racial discrimination in all its forms and to guarantee the right of everyone, without distinction as to race, colour, or national or ethnic origin, to equality before the law, notably in the enjoyment of the following rights:

(a) the right to equal treatment before the tribunals and all other organs administering justice;

(b) the right to security of person and protection by the State against violence or bodily harm, whether inflicted by government officials or by any individual, group or institution;

(c) political rights, in particular the rights to participate in elections — to vote and to stand for election — on the basis of universal and equal suffrage, to take part in the Government as well as in the conduct of public affairs at any level and to have equal access to public service;

(d) other civil rights, in particular:

(i) the right to freedom of movement and residence within the border of the State;

(ii) the right to leave any country, including one's own, and to return to one's country;

(iii) the right to nationality;

(iv) the right to marriage and choice of spouse;

(v) the right to own property alone as well as in association with others;

(vi) the right to inherit;

(vii) the right to freedom of thought, conscience and religion;

(viii) the right to freedom of opinion and expression;

(ix) the right to freedom of peaceful assembly and association;

(e) economic, social and cultural rights, in particular:

(i) the rights to work, to free choice of employment, to just and favourable conditions of work, to protection against unemployment, to equal pay for equal work, to just and favourable remuneration;

(ii) the right to form and join trade unions;

(iii) the right to housing;

(iv) the right to public health, medical care, social security and social services;

(v) the right to education and training;

(vi) the right to equal participation in cultural activities;

(f) the right of access to any place or service intended for use by the general public, such as transport, hotels, restaurants, cafés, theatres and parks.

Article 6

States Parties shall assure to everyone within their jurisdiction effective protection and remedies, through the competent national tribunals and other State institutions, against any acts of racial discrimination which violate his human rights and fundamental freedoms contrary to this Convention, as well as the right to seek from such tribunals just and adequate reparation or satisfaction for any damage suffered as a result of such discrimination.

Article 7

States Parties undertake to adopt immediate and effective measures, particularly in the fields of teaching, education, culture and information, with a view to combating prejudices which lead to racial discrimination and to promoting understanding, tolerance and friendship among nations and racial or ethnical groups, as well as to propagating the purposes and principles of the Charter of the United Nations, the Universal Declaration of Human Rights, the United Nations Declaration on the Elimination of All Forms of Racial Discrimination, and this Convention.

PART II

Article 8

1. There shall be established a Committee on the Elimination of Racial Discrimination (hereinafter referred to as the Committee) consisting of eighteen experts of high moral standing and acknowledged impartiality elected by States Parties from among their nationals, who shall serve in their personal capacity, consideration being given to equitable geographical distribution and to the representation of the different forms of civilization as well as of the principal legal systems.

2. The members of the Committee shall be elected by secret ballot from a list of persons nominated by the States Parties. Each State Party may nominate one person from among its own nationals.

3. The initial election shall be held six months after the date of the entry into force of this Convention. At least three months before the date of each election the Secretary-General of the United Nations shall address a letter to the States Parties inviting them to submit their nominations within two months. The Secretary-General shall prepare a list in alphabetical order of all persons thus nominated, indicating the States Parties which have nominated them, and shall submit it to the States Parties.

4. Elections of the members of the Committee shall be held at a meeting of States Parties convened by the Secretary-General at United Nations Headquarters. At that meeting, for which two-thirds of the States Parties shall constitute a quorum, the persons elected to the Committee shall be those nominees who obtain the largest number of votes and an absolute majority of the votes of the representatives of States Parties present and voting.

5.(a) The members of the Committee shall be elected for a term of four years. However, the terms of nine of the members elected at the first election shall expire at the end of two years; immediately after the first election the names of these nine members shall be chosen by lot by the Chairman of the Committee.

(b) For the filling of casual vacancies, the State Party whose expert has ceased to function as a member of the Committee shall appoint another expert from among its nationals, subject to the approval of the Committee.

6. States Parties shall be responsible for the expenses of the members of the Committee while they are in performance of Committee duties.

Article 9

1. States Parties undertake to submit to the Secretary-General of the United Nations, for consideration by the Committee, a report on the legislative, judicial, administrative or other measures which they have adopted and which give effect to the provisions of this Convention: (a) within one year after the entry into force of the Convention for the State concerned; and (b) thereafter every two years and whenever the Committee so requests. The Committee may request further information from the States Parties.

2. The Committee shall report annually, through the Secretary-General, to the General Assembly of the United Nations on its activities and may make suggestions and general recommendations based on the examination of the reports and information received from the States Parties. Such suggestions and general recommendations shall be reported to the General Assembly together with comments, if any, from States Parties.

Article 10

1. The Committee shall adopt its own rules of procedure.

2. The Committee shall elect its officers for a term of two years.

3. The secretariat of the Committee shall be provided by the Secretary-General of the United Nations.

4.   The meetings of the Committee shall normally be held at United Nations Headquarters.

Article 11

1.   If a State Party considers that another State Party is not giving effect to the provisions of this Convention, it may bring the matter to the attention of the Committee. The Committee shall then transmit the communication to the State Party concerned. Within three months, the receiving State shall submit to the Committee written explanations or statements clarifying the matter and the remedy, if any, that may have been taken by that State.

2.   If the matter is not adjusted to the satisfaction of both parties, either by bilateral negotiations or by any other procedure open to them, within six months after the receipt by the receiving State of the initial communication, either State shall have the right to refer the matter again to the Committee by notifying the Committee and also the other State.

3.   The Committee shall deal with a matter referred to it in accordance with paragraph 2 of this Article after it has ascertained that all available domestic remedies have been invoked and exhausted in the case, in conformity with the generally recognized principles of international law. This shall not be the rule where the application of the remedies is unreasonably prolonged.

4.   In any matter referred to it, the Committee may call upon the States Parties concerned to supply any other relevant information.

5.   When any matter arising out of this article is being considered by the Committee, the States Parties concerned shall be entitled to send a representative to take part in the proceedings of the Committee, without voting rights, while the matter is under consideration.

Article 12

1.(a)   After the Committee has obtained and collated all the information it deems necessary, the Chairman shall appoint an *ad hoc* Conciliation Commission (hereinafter referred to as the Commission) comprising five persons who may or may not be members of the Committee. The members of the Commission shall be appointed with the unanimous consent of the parties to the dispute, and its good offices shall be made available to the States concerned with a view to an amicable solution of the matter on the basis of respect for this Convention.

(b)   If the States Parties to the dispute fail to reach agreement within three months on all or part of the composition of the Commission, the members of the Commission not agreed upon by the States Parties to the dispute shall be elected by secret ballot by a two-thirds majority vote of the Committee from among its own members.

2.   The members of the Commission shall serve in their personal capacity. They shall not be nationals of the States Parties to the dispute or of a State not Party to this Convention.

3.   The Commission shall elect its own Chairman and adopt its own rules of procedure.

4.   The meetings of the Commission shall normally be held at United Nations Headquarters or at any other convenient place as determined by the Commission.

5.   The secretariat provided in accordance with Article 10, paragraph 3, of this Convention shall also service the Commission whenever a dispute among States Parties brings the Commission into being.

6.   The States Parties to the dispute shall share equally all the expenses of the members of the Commission in accordance with estimates to be provided by the Secretary-General of the United Nations.

7.   The Secretary-General shall be empowered to pay the expenses of the members of the Commission, if necessary, before reimbursement by the States Parties to the dispute in accordance with paragraph 6 of this Article.

8.   The information obtained and collated by the Committee shall be made available to the Commission, and the Commission may call upon the States concerned to supply any other relevant information.

Article 13

1.   When the Commission has fully considered the matter, it shall prepare and submit to the Chairman of the Committee a report embodying its findings on all questions of fact relevant to the issue between the parties and containing such recommendations as it may think proper for the amicable solution of the dispute.

2.   The Chairman of the Committee shall communicate the report of the Commission to each of the States Parties to the dispute. These States shall, within three months, inform the Chairman of the Committee whether or not they accept the recommendations contained in the report of the Commission.

3.   After the period provided for in paragraph 2 of this Article, the Chairman of the Committee shall communicate the report of the Commission and the declarations of the States Parties concerned to the other States Parties to this Convention.

Article 14

1.   A State Party may at any time declare that it recognizes the competence of the Committee to receive and consider communications from individuals or groups of individuals within its jurisdiction claiming to be victims of a violation by that State Party of any of the rights set forth in this Convention. No communication shall be received by the Committee if it concerns a State Party which has not made such a declaration.

2.   Any State Party which makes a declaration as provided for in paragraph 1 of this Article may establish or indicate a body within its national legal order which shall be competent to receive and consider petitions from individuals and groups of individuals within its jurisdiction who claim to be victims of a violation of any of the rights set forth in this Convention and who have exhausted other available local remedies.

3.   A declaration made in accordance with paragraph 1 of this Article and the name of any body established or indicated in accordance with paragraph 2 of this Article shall be deposited by the State Party concerned with the Secretary-General of the United Nations, who shall transmit copies thereof to the other States Parties. A declaration may be withdrawn at any time by notification to the Secretary-General, but such a withdrawal shall not affect communications pending before the Committee.

4.   A register of petitions shall be kept by the body established or indicated in accordance with paragraph 2 of this Article, and certified copies of the register shall be filed annually through appropriate channels with the Secretary-General on the understanding that the contents shall not be publicly disclosed.

5.   In the event of failure to obtain satisfaction from the body established or indicated in accordance with paragraph 2 of this Article, the petitioner shall have the right to communicate the matter to the Committee within six months.

6.(a)   The Committee shall confidentially bring any communication referred to it to the attention of the State Party alleged to be violating any provision of this Convention, but the identity of the individual or groups of individuals concerned shall not be revealed without his or their express consent. The Committee shall not receive anonymous communications.

(b)   Within three months, the receiving State shall submit to the Committee written explanations or statements clarifying the matter and the remedy, if any, that may have been taken by that State.

7.(a)   The Committee shall consider communications in the light of all information made available to it by the State Party concerned and by the petitioner. The Committee shall not consider any communication from a petitioner unless it has ascertained that the petitioner has exhausted all available domestic remedies. However, this shall not be the rule where the application of the remedies is unreasonably prolonged.

(b)   The Committee shall forward its suggestions and recommendations, if any, to the State Party concerned and to the petitioner.

8.   The Committee shall include in its annual report a summary of such communications and, where appropriate, a summary of the explanations and statements of the States Parties concerned and of its own suggestions and recommendations.

9.   The Committee shall be competent to exercise the functions provided for in this Article only when at least ten States Parties to this Convention are bound by declarations in accordance with paragraph 1 of this Article.

Article 15

1.   Pending the achievement of the objectives of the Declaration on the Granting of Independence to Colonial Countries and Peoples, contained in General Assembly resolution 1514 (XV) of 14 December 1960, the provisions of this Convention shall in no way limit the right of petition granted to these peoples by other international instruments or by the United Nations and its specialized agencies.

2.(a)   The Committee established under Article 8, paragraph 1, of this Convention shall receive copies of the petitions from, and submit expressions of opinion and recommendations on these petitions to, the bodies of the United Nations which deal with matters directly related to the principles and objectives of this Convention in their consideration of petitions from the inhabitants of Trust and Non-Self-Governing Territories and all other territories to which General Assembly resolution 1514 (XV) applies, relating to matters covered by this Convention which are before these bodies.

(b)   The Committee shall receive from the competent bodies of the United Nations copies of the reports concerning the legislative, judicial, administrative or other measures directly related to the principles and objectives of this Convention applied by the administering Powers within the Territories mentioned in sub-paragraph (a) of this paragraph, and shall express opinions and make recommendations to these bodies.

3.   The Committee shall include in its report to the General Assembly a summary of the petitions and reports it has received from United Nations bodies, and the expressions of opinion and recommendations of the Committee relating to the said petitions and reports.

4.   The Committee shall request from the Secretary-General of the United Nations all information relevant to the objectives of this Convention and available to him regarding the Territories mentioned in paragraph 2(a) of this Article.

Article 16

The provisions of this Convention concerning the settlement of disputes or complaints shall be applied without prejudice to other procedures for settling disputes or complaints in the field of discrimination laid down in the constituent instruments of, or in conventions adopted by, the United Nations and its specialized agencies, and shall not prevent the States Parties from having recourse to other procedures for settling a dispute in accordance with general or special international agreements in force between them.

PART III

Article 17

1.   This Convention is open for signature by any State Member of the United Nations or member of any of its specialized agencies, by any State Party to the Statute of the International Court of Justice, and by any other State which has been invited by the General Assembly of the United Nations to become a Party to this Convention.

2. This Convention is subject to ratification. Instruments of ratification shall be deposited with the Secretary-General of the United Nations.

Article 18

1. This Convention shall be open to accession by any State referred to in Article 17, paragraph 1, of the Convention.

2. Accession shall be effected by the deposit of an instrument of accession with the Secretary-General of the United Nations.

Article 19

1. This Convention shall enter into force on the thirtieth day after the date of the deposit with the Secretary-General of the United Nations of the twenty-seventh instrument of ratification or instrument of accession.

2. For each State ratifying this Convention or acceding to it after the deposit of the twenty-seventh instrument of ratification or instrument of accession, the Convention shall enter into force on the thirtieth day after the date of the deposit of its own instrument of ratification or instrument of accession.

Article 20

1. The Secretary-General of the United Nations shall receive and circulate to all States which are or may become Parties to this Convention reservations made by States at the time of ratification or accession. Any State which objects to the reservation shall, within a period of ninety days from the date of the said communication, notify the Secretary-General that it does not accept it.

2. A reservation incompatible with the object and purpose of this Convention shall not be permitted, nor shall a reservation the effect of which would inhibit the operation of any of the bodies established by this Convention be allowed. A reservation shall be considered incompatible or inhibitive if at least two-thirds of the States Parties to this Convention object to it.

3. Reservations may be withdrawn at any time by notification to this effect addressed to the Secretary-General. Such notification shall take effect on the date on which it is received.

Article 21

A State Party may denounce this Convention by written notification to the Secretary-General of the United Nations. Denunciation shall take effect one year after the date of receipt of the notification by the Secretary-General.

Article 22

Any dispute between two or more States Parties with respect to the interpretation or application of this Convention, which is not settled by negotiation or by the procedures expressly provided for in this Convention, shall, at the request of any of the parties to the dispute, be referred to the International Court of Justice for decision, unless the disputants agree to another mode of settlement.

Article 23

1. A request for the revision of this Convention may be made at any time by any State Party by means of a notification in writing addressed to the Secretary-General of the United Nations.

2. The General Assembly of the United Nations shall decide upon the steps, if any, to be taken in respect of such a request.

Article 24

The Secretary-General of the United Nations shall inform all States referred to in Article 17, paragraph 1, of this Convention of the following particulars:

   (a)   signatures, ratifications and accessions under Articles 17 and 18;

(b)   the date of entry into force of this Convention under Article 19;
(c)   communications and declarations received under Articles 14, 20 and 23;
(d)   denunciations under Article 21.

Article 25

1.   This Convention, of which the Chinese, English, French, Russian and Spanish texts are equally authentic, shall be deposited in the archives of the United Nations.
2.   The Secretary-General of the United Nations shall transmit certified copies of this Convention to all States belonging to any of the categories mentioned in Article 17, paragraph 1, of the Convention.

In faith whereof the undersigned, being duly authorized thereto by their respective Governments, have signed the present Convention, opened for signature at New York, on the seventh day of March, one thousand nine hundred and sixty-six.

INTERNATIONAL COVENANT ON CIVIL AND POLITICAL RIGHTS (1966)

PREAMBLE

The States Parties to the Present Covenant,

Considering that, in accordance with the principles proclaimed in the Charter of the United Nations, recognition of the inherent dignity and of the equal and inalienable rights of all members of the human family is the foundation of freedom, justice and peace in the world,

Recognizing that these rights derive from the inherent dignity of the human person,

Recognizing that, in accordance with the Universal Declaration of Human Rights, the ideal of free human beings enjoying civil and political freedom and freedom from fear and want can only be achieved if conditions are created whereby everyone may enjoy his civil and political rights, as well as his economic, social and cultural rights,

Considering the obligation of States under the Charter of the United Nations to promote universal respect for, and observance of, human rights and freedoms,

Realizing that the individual, having duties to other individuals and to the community to which he belongs, is under a responsibility to strive for the promotion and observance of the rights recognized in the present Covenant,

Agree upon the following articles:

PART I

Article 1

1.   All peoples have the right of self-determination. By virtue of that right they freely determine their political status and freely pursue their economic, social and cultural development.
2.   All peoples may, for their own ends, freely dispose of their natural wealth and resources without prejudice to any obligations arising out of international economic co-operation, based upon the principle of mutual benefit, and international law. In no case may a people be deprived of its own means of subsistence.
3.   The States Parties to the present Covenant, including those having responsibility for the administration of Non-Self-Governing and Trust Territories, shall promote the realization of the right of self-determination, and shall respect that right, in conformity with the provisions of the Charter of the United Nations.

PART II

Article 2

1.   Each State Party to the present Covenant undertakes to respect and to ensure to all individuals within its territory and subject to its jurisdiction the rights recognized

in the present Covenant, without distinction of any kind, such as race, colour, sex, language, religion, political or other opinion, national or social origin, property, birth or other status.

2. Where not already provided for by existing legislative or other measures, each State Party to the present Covenant undertakes to take the necessary steps, in accordance with its constitutional processes and with the provisions of the present Covenant, to adopt such legislative or other measures as may be necessary to give effect to the rights recognized in the present Covenant.

3. Each State Party to the present Covenant undertakes:

(a) to ensure that any person whose rights or freedoms as herein recognized are violated shall have an effective remedy, notwithstanding that the violation has been committed by persons acting in an official capacity;

(b) to ensure that any person claiming such a remedy shall have his right thereto determined by competent judicial, administrative or legislative authorities, or by any other competent authority provided for by the legal system of the State, and to develop the possibilities of judicial remedy;

(c) to ensure that the competent authorities shall enforce such remedies when granted.

Article 3
The States Parties to the present Covenant undertake to ensure the equal right of men and women to the enjoyment of all civil and political rights set forth in the present Covenant.

Article 4
1. In time of public emergency which threatens the life of the nation and the existence of which is officially proclaimed, the States Parties to the present Covenant may take measures derogating from their obligations under the present Covenant to the extent strictly required by the exigencies of the situation, provided that such measures are not inconsistent with their other obligations under international law and do not involve discrimination solely on the ground of race, colour, sex, language, religion or social origin.

2. No derogation from articles 6, 7, 8 (paragraphs 1 and 2), 11, 15, 16 and 18 may be made under this provision.

3. Any State Party to the present Covenant availing itself of the right of derogation shall immediately inform the other States Parties to the present Covenant, through the intermediary of the Secretary-General of the United Nations, of the provisions from which it has derogated and of the reasons by which it was actuated. A further communication shall be made, through the same intermediary, on the date on which it terminates such derogation.

Article 5
1. Nothing in the present Covenant may be interpreted as implying for any State, group or person any right to engage in any activity or perform any act aimed at the destruction of any of the rights and freedoms recognized herein or at their limitation to a greater extent than is provided for in the present Covenant.

2. There shall be no restriction upon or derogation from any of the fundamental human rights recognized or existing in any State Party to the present Covenant pursuant to law, conventions, regulations or custom on the pretext that the present Covenant does not recognize such rights or that it recognizes them to a lesser extent.

PART III

Article 6
1. Every human being has the inherent right to life. This right shall be protected by law. No one shall be arbitrarily deprived of his life.

2.   In countries which have not abolished the death penalty, sentence of death may be imposed only for the most serious crimes in accordance with the law in force at the time of the commission of the crime and not contrary to the provisions of the present Covenant and to the Convention on the Prevention and Punishment of the Crime of Genocide. This penalty can only be carried out pursuant to a final judgement rendered by a competent court.

3.   When deprivation of life constitutes the crime of genocide, it is understood that nothing in this article shall authorize any State Party to the present Covenant to derogate in any way from any obligation assumed under the provisions of the Convention on the Prevention and Punishment of the Crime of Genocide.

4.   Anyone sentenced to death shall have the right to seek pardon or commutation of the sentence. Amnesty, pardon or commutation of the sentence of death may be granted in all cases.

5.   Sentence of death shall not be imposed for crimes committed by persons below eighteen years of age and shall not be carried out on pregnant women.

6.   Nothing in this article shall be invoked to delay or to prevent the abolition of capital punishment by any State Party to the present Covenant.

Article 7
No one shall be subjected to torture or to cruel, inhuman or degrading treatment or punishment. In particular, no one shall be subjected without his free consent to medical or scientific experimentation.

Article 8
1.   No one shall be held in slavery; slavery and the slave-trade in all their forms shall be prohibited.

2.   No one shall be held in servitude.

3.(a)   No one shall be required to perform forced or compulsory labour;

(b)   Paragraph 3 (a) shall not be held to preclude, in countries where imprisonment with hard labour may be imposed as a punishment for a crime, the performance of hard labour in pursuance of a sentence to such punishment by a competent court;

(c)   For the purpose of this paragraph the term 'forced or compulsory labour' shall not include:

(i)   any work or service, not referred to in subparagraph (b), normally required of a person who is under detention in consequence of a lawful order of a court, or of a person during conditional release from such detention;

(ii)   any service of a military character and, in countries where conscientious objection is recognized, any national service required by law of conscientious objectors;

(iii)   any service exacted in cases of emergency or calamity threatening the life or well-being of the community;

(iv)   any work or service which forms part of normal civil obligations.

Article 9
1.   Everyone has the right to liberty and security of person. No one shall be subjected to arbitrary arrest or detention. No one shall be deprived of his liberty except on such grounds and in accordance with such procedures as are established by law.

2.   Anyone who is arrested shall be informed, at the time of arrest, of the reasons for his arrest and shall be promptly informed of any charges against him.

3.   Anyone arrested or detained on a criminal charge shall be brought promptly before a judge or other officer authorized by law to exercise judicial power and shall be entitled to trial within a reasonable time or to release. It shall not be the general rule that persons awaiting trial shall be detained in custody, but release may be subject

to guarantees to appear for trial, at any other stage of the judicial proceedings, and, should occasion arise, for execution of the judgement.

4.   Anyone who is deprived of his liberty by arrest or detention shall be entitled to take proceedings before a court, in order that that court may decide without delay on the lawfulness of his detention and order his release if the detention is not lawful.

5.   Anyone who has been the victim of unlawful arrest or detention shall have an enforceable right to compensation.

Article 10

1.   All persons deprived of their liberty shall be treated with humanity and with respect for the inherent dignity of the human person.

2.(a)   Accused persons shall, save in exceptional circumstances, be segregated from convicted persons and shall be subject to separate treatment appropriate to their status as unconvicted persons;

(b)   Accused juvenile persons shall be separated from adults and brought as speedily as possible for adjudication.

3.   The penitentiary system shall comprise treatment of prisoners the essential aim of which shall be their reformation and social rehabilitation. Juvenile offenders shall be segregated from adults and be accorded treatment appropriate to their age and legal status.

Article 11

No one shall be imprisoned merely on the ground of inability to fulfil a contractual obligation.

Article 12

1.   Everyone lawfully within the territory of a State shall, within that territory, have the right to liberty of movement and freedom to choose his residence.

2.   Everyone shall be free to leave any country, including his own.

3.   The above-mentioned rights shall not be subject to any restrictions except those which are provided by law, are necessary to protect national security, public order (ordre public), public health or morals or the rights and freedoms of others, and are consistent with the other rights recognized in the present Covenant.

4.   No one shall be arbitrarily deprived of the right to enter his own country.

Article 13

An alien lawfully in the territory of a State Party to the present Covenant may be expelled therefrom only in pursuance of a decision reached in accordance with law and shall, except where compelling reasons of national security otherwise require, be allowed to submit the reasons against his expulsion and to have his case reviewed by, and be represented for the purpose before, the competent authority or a person or persons especially designated by the competent authority.

Article 14

1.   All persons shall be equal before the courts and tribunals. In the determination of any criminal charge against him, or of his rights and obligations in a suit at law, everyone shall be entitled to a fair and public hearing by a competent, independent and impartial tribunal established by law. The Press and the public may be excluded from all or part of a trial for reasons of morals, public order (ordre public) or national security in a democratic society, or when the interest of the private lives of the parties so requires, or to the extent strictly necessary in the opinion of the court in special circumstances where publicity would prejudice the interests of justice; but any judgement rendered in a criminal case or in a suit at law shall be made public except where the interest of juvenile persons otherwise requires or the proceedings concern matrimonial disputes or the guardianship of children.

2.   Everyone charged with a criminal offence shall have the right to be presumed innocent until proved guilty according to law.

3.   In the determination of any criminal charge against him, everyone shall be entitled to the following minimum guarantees, in full equality:

(a)   to be informed promptly and in detail in a language which he understands of the nature and cause of the charge against him;

(b)   to have adequate time and facilities for the preparation of his defence and to communicate with counsel of his own choosing;

(c)   to be tried without undue delay;

(d)   to be tried in his presence, and to defend himself in person or through legal assistance of his own choosing; to be informed, if he does not have legal assistance, of this right; and to have legal assistance assigned to him, in any case where the interests of justice so require, and without payment by him in any such case if he does not have sufficient means to pay for it;

(e)   to examine, or have examined, the witnesses against him and to obtain the attendance and examination of witnesses on his behalf under the same conditions as witnesses against him;

(f)   to have the free assistance of an interpreter if he cannot understand or speak the language used in court;

(g)   not to be compelled to testify against himself or to confess guilt.

4.   In the case of juvenile persons, the procedure shall be such as will take account of their age and the desirability of promoting their rehabilitation.

5.   Everyone convicted of a crime shall have the right to his conviction and sentence being reviewed by a higher tribunal according to law.

6.   When a person has by a final decision been convicted of a criminal offence and when subsequently his conviction has been reversed or he has been pardoned on the ground that a new or newly discovered fact shows conclusively that there has been a miscarriage of justice, the person who has suffered punishment as a result of such conviction shall be compensated according to law, unless it is proved that the non-disclosure of the unknown fact in time is wholly or partly attributable to him.

7.   No one shall be liable to be tried or punished again for an offence for which he has already been finally convicted or acquitted in accordance with the law and penal procedure of each country.

Article 15

1.   No one shall be held guilty of any criminal offence on account of any act or omission which did not constitute a criminal offence, under national or international law, at the time when it was committed. Nor shall a heavier penalty be imposed than the one that was applicable at the time when the criminal offence was committed. If, subsequent to the commission of the offence, provision is made by law for the imposition of a lighter penalty, the offender shall benefit thereby.

2.   Nothing in this article shall prejudice the trial and punishment of any person for any act or omission which, at the time when it was committed, was criminal according to the general principles of law recognized by the community of nations.

Article 16

Everyone shall have the right to recognition everywhere as a person before the law.

Article 17

1.   No one shall be subjected to arbitrary or unlawful interference with his privacy, family, home or correspondence, nor to unlawful attacks on his honour and reputation.

2.   Everyone has the right to the protection of the law against such interference or attacks.

Article 18

1.   Everyone shall have the right to freedom of thought, conscience and religion. This right shall include freedom to have or to adopt a religion or belief of his choice, and freedom, either individually or in community with others and in public or private, to manifest his religion or belief in worship, observance, practice and teaching.

2.   No one shall be subject to coercion which would impair his freedom to have or to adopt a religion or belief of his choice.

3.   Freedom to manifest one's religion or beliefs may be subject only to such limitations as are prescribed by law and are necessary to protect public safety, order, health, or morals or the fundamental rights and freedoms of others.

4.   The States Parties to the present Covenant undertake to have respect for the liberty of parents and, when applicable, legal guardians to ensure the religious and moral education of their children in conformity with their own convictions.

Article 19

1.   Everyone shall have the right to hold opinions without interference.

2.   Everyone shall have the right to freedom of expression; this right shall include freedom to seek, receive and impart information and ideas of all kinds, regardless of frontiers, either orally, in writing or in print, in the form of art, or through any other media of his choice.

3.   The exercise of the rights provided for in paragraph 2 of this article carries with it special duties and responsibilities. It may therefore be subject to certain restrictions, but these shall only be such as are provided by law and are necessary:

     (a)   for respect of the rights or reputations of others;

     (b)   for the protection of national security or of public order (*ordre public*), or of public health or morals.

Article 20

1.   Any propaganda for war shall be prohibited by law.

2.   Any advocacy of national, racial or religious hatred that constitutes incitement to discrimination, hostility or violence shall be prohibited by law.

Article 21

The right of peaceful assembly shall be recognized. No restrictions may be placed on the exercise of this right other than those imposed in conformity with the law and which are necessary in a democratic society in the interests of national security or public safety, public order (*ordre public*), the protection of public health or morals or the protection of the rights and freedoms of others.

Article 22

1.   Everyone shall have the right to freedom of association with others, including the right to form and join trade unions for the protection of his interests.

2.   No restrictions may be placed on the exercise of this right other than those which are prescribed by law and which are necessary in a democratic society in the interests of national security or public safety, public order (*ordre public*), the protection of public health or morals or the protection of the rights and freedoms of others. This article shall not prevent the imposition of lawful restrictions on members of the armed forces and of the police in their exercise of this right.

3.   Nothing in this article shall authorize States Parties to the International Labour Organisation Convention of 1948 concerning Freedom of Association and Protection of the Right to Organise to take legislative measures which would prejudice, or to apply the law in such a manner as to prejudice, the guarantees provided for in that Convention.

Article 23

1. The family is the natural and fundamental group unit of society and is entitled to protection by society and the State.

2. The right of men and women of marriageable age to marry and to found a family shall be recognized.

3. No marriage shall be entered into without the free and full consent of the intending spouses.

4. States Parties to the present Covenant shall take appropriate steps to ensure equality of rights and responsibilities of spouses as to marriage, during marriage and at its dissolution. In the case of dissolution, provision shall be made for the necessary protection of any children.

Article 24

1. Every child shall have, without any discrimination as to race, colour, sex, language, religion, national or social origin, property or birth, the right to such measures of protection as are required by his status as a minor, on the part of his family, society and the State.

2. Every child shall be registered immediately after birth and shall have a name.

3. Every child has the right to acquire a nationality.

Article 25

Every citizen shall have the right and the opportunity, without any of the distinctions mentioned in article 2 and without unreasonable restrictions:

   (a)   to take part in the conduct of public affairs, directly or through freely chosen representatives;

   (b)   to vote and to be elected at genuine periodic elections which shall be by universal and equal suffrage and shall be held by secret ballot, guaranteeing the free expression of the will of the electors;

   (c)   to have access, on general terms of equality, to public service in his country.

Article 26

All persons are equal before the law and are entitled without any discrimination to the equal protection of the law. In this respect, the law shall prohibit any discrimination and guarantee to all persons equal and effective protection against discrimination on any ground such as race, colour, sex, language, religion, political or other opinion, national or social origin, property, birth or other status.

Article 27

In those States in which ethnic, religious or linguistic minorities exist, persons belonging to such minorities shall not be denied the right, in community with the other members of their group, to enjoy their own culture, to profess and practise their own religion, or to use their own language.

PART IV

Article 28

1. There shall be established a Human Rights Committee (hereafter referred to in the present Covenant as the Committee). It shall consist of eighteen members and shall carry out the functions hereinafter provided.

2. The Committee shall be composed of nationals of the States Parties to the present Covenant who shall be persons of high moral character and recognized competence in the field of human rights, consideration being given to the usefulness of the participation of some persons having legal experience.

3. The members of the Committee shall be elected and shall serve in their personal capacity.

Article 29
1.   The members of the Committee shall be elected by secret ballot from a list of persons possessing the qualifications prescribed in article 28 and nominated for the purpose by the States Parties to the present Covenant.
2.   Each State Party to the present Covenant may nominate not more than two persons. These persons shall be nationals of the nominating State.
3.   A person shall be eligible for renomination.

Article 30
1.   The initial election shall be held no later than six months after the date of the entry into force of the present Covenant.
2.   At least four months before the date of each election to the Committee, other than an election to fill a vacancy declared in accordance with article 34, the Secretary-General of the United Nations shall address a written invitation to the States Parties to the present Covenant to submit their nominations for membership of the Committee within three months.
3.   The Secretary-General of the United Nations shall prepare a list in alphabetical order of all the persons thus nominated, with an indication of the States Parties which have nominated them, and shall submit it to the States Parties to the present Covenant no later than one month before the date of each election.
4.   Elections of the members of the Committee shall be held at a meeting of the States Parties to the present Covenant convened by the Secretary-General of the United Nations at the Headquarters of the United Nations. At that meeting, for which two thirds of the States Parties to the present Covenant shall constitute a quorum, the persons elected to the Committee shall be those nominees who obtain the largest number of votes and an absolute majority of the votes of the representatives of States Parties present and voting.

Article 31
1.   The Committee may not include more than one national of the same State.
2.   In the election of the Committee, consideration shall be given to equitable geographical distribution of membership and to the representation of the different forms of civilization and of the principal legal systems.

Article 32
1.   The members of the Committee shall be elected for a term of four years. They shall be eligible for re-election if renominated. However, the terms of nine of the members elected at the first election shall expire at the end of two years; immediately after the first election, the names of these nine members shall be chosen by lot by the Chairman of the meeting referred to in article 30, paragraph 4.
2.   Elections at the expiry of office shall be held in accordance with the preceding articles of this part of the present Covenant.

Article 33
1.   If, in the unanimous opinion of the other members, a member of the Committee has ceased to carry out his functions for any cause other than absence of a temporary character, the Chairman of the Committee shall notify the Secretary-General of the United Nations, who shall then declare the seat of that member to be vacant.
2.   In the event of the death or the resignation of a member of the Committee, the Chairman shall immediately notify the Secretary-General of the United Nations, who shall declare the seat vacant from the date of death or the date on which the resignation takes effect.

Article 34

1. When a vacancy is declared in accordance with article 33 and if the term of office of the member to be replaced does not expire within six months of the declaration of the vacancy, the Secretary-General of the United Nations shall notify each of the States Parties to the present Covenant, which may within two months submit nominations in accordance with article 29 for the purpose of filling the vacancy.

2. The Secretary-General of the United Nations shall prepare a list in alphabetical order of the persons thus nominated and shall submit it to the States Parties to the present Covenant. The election to fill the vacancy shall then take place in accordance with the relevant provisions of this part of the present Covenant.

3. A member of the Committee elected to fill a vacancy declared in accordance with article 33 shall hold office for the remainder of the term of the member who vacated the seat on the Committee under the provisions of that article.

Article 35

The members of the Committee shall, with the approval of the General Assembly of the United Nations, receive emoluments from United Nations resources on such terms and conditions as the General Assembly may decide, having regard to the importance of the Committee's responsibilities.

Article 36

The Secretary-General of the United Nations shall provide the necessary staff and facilities for the effective performance of the functions of the Committee under the present Covenant.

Article 37

1. The Secretary-General of the United Nations shall convene the initial meeting of the Committee at the Headquarters of the United Nations.

2. After its initial meeting, the Committee shall meet at such times as shall be provided in its rules of procedure.

3. The Committee shall normally meet at the Headquarters of the United Nations or at the United Nations Office at Geneva.

Article 38

Every member of the Committee shall, before taking up his duties, make a solemn declaration in open committee that he will perform his functions impartially and conscientiously.

Article 39

1. The Committee shall elect its officers for a term of two years. They may be re-elected.

2. The Committee shall establish its own rules of procedure, but these rules shall provide, *inter alia,* that:

    (a)   twelve members shall constitute a quorum;

    (b)   decisions of the Committee shall be made by a majority vote of the members present.

Article 40

1. The States Parties to the present Covenant undertake to submit reports on the measures they have adopted which give effect to the rights recognized herein and on the progress made in the enjoyment of those rights:

    (a)   within one year of the entry into force of the present Covenant for the States Parties concerned;

    (b)   thereafter whenever the Committee so requests.

2.   All reports shall be submitted to the Secretary-General of the United Nations, who shall transmit them to the Committee for consideration. Reports shall indicate the factors and difficulties, if any, affecting the implementation of the present Covenant.

3.   The Secretary-General of the United Nations may, after consultation with the Committee, transmit to the specialized agencies concerned copies of such parts of the reports as may fall within their field of competence.

4.   The Committee shall study the reports submitted by the States Parties to the present Covenant. It shall transmit its reports, and such general comments as it may consider appropriate, to the States Parties. The Committee may also transmit to the Economic and Social Council these comments along with the copies of the reports it has received from States Parties to the present Covenant.

5.   The States Parties to the present Covenant may submit to the Committee observations on any comments that may be made in accordance with paragraph 4 of this article.

Article 41

1.   A State Part to the present Covenant may at any time declare under this article that it recognizes the competence of the Committee to receive and consider communications to the effect that a State Party claims that another State Party is not fulfilling its obligations under the present Covenant. Communications under this article may be received and considered only if submitted by a State Party which has made a declaration recognizing in regard to itself the competence of the Committee. No communication shall be received by the Committee if it concerns a State Party which has not made such a declaration. Communications received under this article shall be dealt with in accordance with the following procedure:

(a)   If a State Party to the present Covenant considers that another State Party is not giving effect to the provisions of the present Covenant, it may, by written communication, bring the matter to the attention of that State Party. Within three months after the receipt of the communication, the receiving State shall afford the State which sent the communication an explanation or any other statement in writing clarifying the matter, which should include, to the extent possible and pertinent, reference to domestic procedures and remedies taken, pending, or available in the matter.

(b)   If the matter is not adjusted to the satisfaction of both States Parties concerned within six months after the receipt by the receiving State of the initial communication, either State shall have the right to refer the matter to the Committee, by notice given to the Committee and to the other State.

(c)   The Committee shall deal with a matter referred to it only after it has ascertained that all available domestic remedies have been invoked and exhausted in the matter, in conformity with the generally recognized principles of international law. This shall not be the rule where the application of the remedies is unreasonably prolonged.

(d)   The Committee shall hold closed meetings when examining communications under this article.

(e)   Subject to the provisions of subparagraph (c), the Committee shall make available its good offices to the States Parties concerned with a view to a friendly solution of the matter on the basis of respect for human rights and fundamental freedoms as recognized in the present Covenant.

(f)   In any matter referred to it, the Committee may call upon the States Parties concerned, referred to in subparagraph (b), to supply any relevant information.

(g)   The States Parties concerned, referred to in subparagraph (b), shall have the right to be represented when the matter is being considered in the Committee and to make submissions orally and/or in writing.

(h)   The Committee shall, within twelve months after the date of receipt of notice under subparagraph (b), submit a report:

(i)   if a solution within the terms of subparagraph (e) is reached, the Committee shall confine its report to a brief statement of the facts and of the solution reached;

(ii)   if a solution within the terms of subparagraph (e) is not reached, the Committee shall confine its report to a brief statement of the facts; the written submissions and record of the oral submissions made by the States Parties concerned shall be attached to the report.

In every matter, the report shall be communicated to the States Parties concerned.

2.   The provisions of this article shall come into force when ten States Parties to the present Covenant have made declarations under paragraph 1 of this article. Such declarations shall be deposited by the States Parties with the Secretary-General of the United Nations, who shall transmit copies thereof to the other States Parties. A declaration may be withdrawn at any time by notification to the Secretary-General. Such a withdrawal shall not prejudice the consideration of any matter which is the subject of a communication already transmitted under this article; no further communication by any State Party shall be received after the notification of withdrawal of the declaration has been received by the Secretary-General, unless the State Party concerned has made a new declaration.

Article 42

1.(a)   If a matter referred to the Committee in accordance with article 41 is not resolved to the satisfaction of the States Parties concerned, the Committee may, with the prior consent of the States Parties concerned, appoint an *ad hoc* Conciliation Commission (hereinafter referred to as the Commission). The good offices of the Commission shall be made available to the States Parties concerned with a view to an amicable solution of the matter on the basis of respect for the present Covenant;

(b)   The Commission shall consist of five persons acceptable to the States Parties concerned. If the States Parties concerned fail to reach agreement within three months on all or part of the composition of the Commission, the members of the Commission concerning whom no agreement has been reached shall be elected by secret ballot by a two-thirds majority vote of the Committee from among its members.

2.   The members of the Commission shall serve in their personal capacity. They shall not be nationals of the States Parties concerned, or of a State not party to the present Covenant, or of a State Party which has not made a declaration under article 41.

3.   The Commission shall elect its own Chairman and adopt its own rules of procedure.

4.   The meetings of the Commission shall normally be held at the Headquarters of the United Nations or at the United Nations Office at Geneva. However, they may be held at such other convenient places as the Commission may determine in consultation with the Secretary-General of the United Nations and the States Parties concerned.

5.   The secretariat provided in accordance with article 36 shall also service the commissions appointed under this article.

6.   The information received and collated by the Committee shall be made available to the Commission and the Commission may call upon the States Parties concerned to supply any other relevant information.

7.   When the Commission has fully considered the matter, but in any event not later than twelve months after having been seized of the matter, it shall submit to the Chairman of the Committee a report for communication to the States Parties concerned:

(a)   if the Commission is unable to complete its consideration of the matter within twelve months, it shall confine its report to a brief statement of the status of its consideration of the matter;

(b)   if an amicable solution to the matter on the basis of respect for human rights as recognized in the present Covenant is reached, the Commission shall confine its report to a brief statement of the facts and of the solution reached;

(c)   if a solution within the terms of subparagraph (b) is not reached, the Commission's report shall embody its findings on all questions of fact relevant to the issues between the States Parties concerned, and its views on the possibilities of an amicable solution of the matter. This report shall also contain the written submissions and a record of the oral submissions made by the States Parties concerned;

(d)   if the Commission's report is submitted under subparagraph (c), the States Parties concerned shall, within three months of the receipt of the report, notify the Chairman of the Committee whether or not they accept the contents of the report of the Commission.

8.   The provisions of this article are without prejudice to the responsibilities of the Committee under article 41.

9.   The States Parties concerned shall share equally all the expenses of the members of the Commission in accordance with estimates to be provided by the Secretary-General of the United Nations.

10.   The Secretary-General of the United Nations shall be empowered to pay the expenses of the members of the Commission, if necessary, before reimbursement by the States Parties concerned, in accordance with paragraph 9 of this article.

Article 43
The members of the Committee, and of the *ad hoc* conciliation commissions which may be appointed under article 42, shall be entitled to the facilities, privileges and immunities of experts on mission for the United Nations as laid down in the relevant sections of the Convention on the Privileges and Immunities of the United Nations.

Article 44
The provisions for the implementation of the present Covenant shall apply without prejudice to the procedures prescribed in the field of human rights by or under the constituent instruments and the conventions of the United Nations and of the specialized agencies and shall not prevent the States Parties to the present Covenant from having recourse to other procedures for settling a dispute in accordance with general or special international agreements in force between them.

Article 45
The Committee shall submit to the General Assembly of the United Nations, through the Economic and Social Council, an annual report on its activities.

PART V

Article 46
Nothing in the present Covenant shall be interpreted as impairing the provisions of the Charter of the United Nations and of the constitutions of the specialized agencies which define the respective responsibilities of the various organs of the United Nations and of the specialized agencies in regard to the matters dealt with in the present Covenant.

Article 47
Nothing in the present Covenant shall be interpreted as impairing the inherent right of all peoples to enjoy and utilize fully and freely their natural wealth and resources.

PART VI

Article 48

1.   The present Covenant is open for signature by any State Member of the United Nations or member of any of its specialized agencies, by any State Party to the Statute of the International Court of Justice, and by any other State which has been invited by the General Assembly of the United Nations to become a party to the present Covenant.

2.   The present Covenant is subject to ratification. Instruments of ratification shall be deposited with the Secretary-General of the United Nations.

3.   The present Covenant shall be open to accession by any State referred to in paragraph 1 of this article.

4.   Accession shall be effected by the deposit of an instrument of accession with the Secretary-General of the United Nations.

5.   The Secretary-General of the United Nations shall inform all States which have signed this Covenant or acceded to it of the deposit of each instrument of ratification or accession.

Article 49

1.   The present Covenant shall enter into force three months after the date of the deposit with the Secretary-General of the United Nations of the thirty-fifth instrument of ratification or instrument of accession.

2.   For each State ratifying the present Covenant or acceding to it after the deposit of the thirty-fifth instrument of ratification or instrument of accession, the present Covenant shall enter into force three months after the date of the deposit of its own instrument of ratification or instrument of accession.

Article 50

The provisions of the present Covenant shall extend to all parts of federal States without any limitations or exceptions.

Article 51

1.   Any State Party to the present Covenant may propose an amendment and file it with the Secretary-General of the United Nations. The Secretary-General of the United Nations shall thereupon communicate any proposed amendments to the States Parties to the present Covenant with a request that they notify him whether they favour a conference of States Parties for the purpose of considering and voting upon the proposals. In the event that at least one third of the States Parties favours such a conference, the Secretary-General shall convene the conference under the auspices of the United Nations. Any amendment adopted by a majority of the States Parties present and voting at the conference shall be submitted to the General Assembly of the United Nations for approval.

2.   Amendments shall come into force when they have been approved by the General Assembly of the United Nations and accepted by a two-thirds majority of the States Parties to the present Covenant in accordance with their respective constitutional processes.

3.   When amendments come into force, they shall be binding on those States Parties which have accepted them, other States Parties still being bound by the provisions of the present Covenant and any earlier amendment which they have accepted.

Article 52

Irrespective of the notifications made under article 48, paragraph 5, the Secretary-General of the United Nations shall inform all States referred to in paragraph 1 of the same article of the following particulars:

(a)   signatures, ratifications and accessions under article 48;

(b)   the date of the entry into force of the present Covenant under article 49 and the date of the entry into force of any amendments under article 51.

Article 53

1.   The present Covenant, of which the Chinese, English, French, Russian and Spanish texts are equally authentic, shall be deposited in the archives of the United Nations.

2.   The Secretary-General of the United Nations shall transmit certified copies of the present Covenant to all States referred to in article 48.

(FIRST) OPTIONAL PROTOCOL TO THE INTERNATIONAL COVENANT ON CIVIL AND POLITICAL RIGHTS (1966)

The States Parties to the Present Protocol,

Considering that in order further to achieve the purposes of the Covenant on Civil and Political Rights (hereinafter referred to as the Covenant) and the implementation of its provisions it would be appropriate to enable the Human Rights Committee set up in part IV of the Covenant (hereinafter referred to as the Committee) to receive and consider, as provided in the present Protocol, communications from individuals claiming to be victims of violations of any of the rights set forth in the Covenant,

Have agreed as follows:

Article 1

A State Party to the Covenant that becomes a party to the present Protocol recognizes the competence of the Committee to receive and consider communications from individuals subject to its jurisdiction who claim to be victims of a violation by that State Party of any of the rights set forth in the Covenant. No communication shall be received by the Committee if it concerns a State Party to the Covenant which is not a party to the present Protocol.

Article 2

Subject to the provisions of article 1, individuals who claim that any of their rights enumerated in the Covenant have been violated and who have exhausted all available domestic remedies may submit a written communication to the Committee for consideration.

Article 3

The Committee shall consider inadmissible any communication under the present Protocol which is anonymous, or which it considers to be an abuse of the right of submission of such communications or to be incompatible with the provisions of the Covenant.

Article 4

1.   Subject to the provisions of article 3, the Committee shall bring any communications submitted to it under the present Protocol to the attention of the State Party to the present Protocol alleged to be violating any provision of the Covenant.

2.   Within six months, the receiving State shall submit to the Committee written explanations or statements clarifying the matter and the remedy, if any, that may have been taken by that State.

Article 5

1.   The Committee shall consider communications received under the present Protocol in the light of all written information made available to it by the individual and by the State Party concerned.

2. The Committee shall not consider any communication from an individual unless it has ascertained that:

(a) the same matter is not being examined under another procedure of international investigation or settlement;

(b) the individual has exhausted all available domestic remedies. This shall not be the rule where the application of the remedies is unreasonably prolonged.

3. The Committee shall hold closed meetings when examining communications under the present Protocol.

4. The Committee shall forward its views to the State Party concerned and to the individual.

Article 6
The Committee shall include in its annual report under article 45 of the Covenant a summary of its activities under the present Protocol.

Article 7
Pending the achievement of the objectives of resolution 1514(XV) adopted by the General Assembly of the United Nations on 14 December 1960 concerning the Declaration on the Granting of Independence to Colonial Countries and Peoples, the provisions of the present Protocol shall in no way limit the right of petition granted to these peoples by the Charter of the United Nations and other international conventions and instruments under the United Nations and its specialized agencies.

Article 8
1. The present Protocol is open for signature by any State which has signed the Covenant.

2. The present Protocol is subject to ratification by any State which has ratified or acceded to the Covenant. Instruments of ratification shall be deposited with the Secretary-General of the United Nations.

3. The present Protocol shall be open to accession by any State which has ratified or acceded to the Covenant.

4. Accession shall be effected by the deposit of an instrument of accession with the Secretary-General of the United Nations.

5. The Secretary-General of the United Nations shall inform all States which have signed the present Protocol or acceded to it of the deposit of each instrument of ratification or accession.

Article 9
1. Subject to the entry into force of the Covenant, the present Protocol shall enter into force three months after the date of the deposit with the Secretary-General of the United Nations of the tenth instrument of ratification or instrument of accession.

2. For each State ratifying the present Protocol or acceding to it after the deposit of the tenth instrument of ratification or instrument of accession, the present Protocol shall enter into force three months after the date of the deposit of its own instrument of ratification or instrument of accession.

Article 10
The provisions of the present Protocol shall extend to all parts of federal States without any limitations or exceptions.

Article 11
1. Any State Party to the present Protocol may propose an amendment and file it with the Secretary-General of the United Nations. The Secretary-General shall thereupon communicate any proposed amendments to the States Parties to the present Protocol with a request that they notify him whether they favour a conference of States Parties for the purpose of considering and voting upon the proposal. In the

event that at least one third of the States Parties favours such a conference, the Secretary-General shall convene the conference under the auspices of the United Nations. Any amendment adopted by a majority of the States Parties present and voting at the conference shall be submitted to the General Assembly of the United Nations for approval.

2.   Amendments shall come into force when they have been approved by the General Assembly of the United Nations and accepted by a two-thirds majority of the States Parties to the present Protocol in accordance with their respective constitutional processes.

3.   When amendments come into force, they shall be binding on those States Parties which have accepted them, other States Parties still being bound by the provisions of the present Protocol and any earlier amendment which they have accepted.

Article 12

1.   Any State Party may denounce the present Protocol at any time by written notification addressed to the Secretary-General of the United Nations. Denunciation shall take effect three months after the date of receipt of the notification by the Secretary-General.

2.   Denunciation shall be without prejudice to the continued application of the provisions of the present Protocol to any communication submitted under article 2 before the effective date of denunciation.

Article 13

Irrespective of the notifications made under article 8, paragraph 5, of the present Protocol, the Secretary-General of the United Nations shall inform all States referred to in article 48, paragraph 1, of the Covenant of the following particulars:

(a)   signatures, ratifications and accessions under article 8;

(b)   the date of the entry into force of the present Protocol under article 9 and the date of the entry into force of any amendments under article 11;

(c)   denunciations under article 12.

Article 14

1.   The present Protocol, of which the Chinese, English, French, Russian and Spanish texts are equally authentic, shall be deposited in the archives of the United Nations.

2.   The Secretary-General of the United Nations shall transmit certified copies of the present Protocol to all States referred to in article 48 of the Covenant.

SECOND OPTIONAL PROTOCOL TO THE INTERNATIONAL COVENANT ON CIVIL AND POLITICAL RIGHTS, AIMING AT THE ABOLITION OF THE DEATH PENALTY (1990)

The States parties to the present Protocol,

Believing that abolition of the death penalty contributes to enhancement of human dignity and progressive development of human rights,

Recalling article 3 of the Universal Declaration of Human Rights adopted on 10 December 1948 and article 6 of the International Covenant on Civil and Political Rights adopted on 16 December 1966,

Noting that article 6 of the International Covenant on Civil and Political Rights refers to abolition of the death penalty in terms that strongly suggest that abolition is desirable,

Convinced that all measures of abolition of the death penalty should be considered as progress in the enjoyment of the right to life,

Desirous to undertake hereby an international commitment to abolish the death penalty,

Have agreed as follows:

Article 1

1.   No one within the jurisdiction of a State party to the present Optional Protocol shall be executed.

2.   Each State party shall take all necessary measures to abolish the death penalty within its jurisdiction.

Article 2

1.   No reservation is admissible to the present Protocol, except for a reservation made at the time of ratification or accession that provides for the application of the death penalty in time of war pursuant to a conviction for a most serious crime of a military nature committed during wartime.

2.   The State party making such a reservation shall at the time of ratification or accession communicate to the Secretary-General of the United Nations the relevant provisions of its national legislation applicable during wartime.

3.   The State party having made such a reservation shall notify the Secretary-General of the United Nations of any beginning or ending of a state of war applicable to its territory.

Article 3

The States parties to the present Protocol shall include in the reports they submit to the Human Rights Committee, in accordance with article 40 of the Covenant, information on the measures that they have adopted to give effect to the present Protocol.

Article 4

With respect to the States parties to the Covenant that have made a declaration under article 41, the competence of the Human Rights Committee to receive and consider communications when a State party claims that another State party is not fulfilling its obligations shall extend to the provisions of the present Protocol, unless the State party concerned has made a statement to the contrary at the moment of ratification or accession.

Article 5

With respect to the States parties to the (First) Optional Protocol to the International Covenant on Civil and Political Rights adopted on 16 December 1966, the competence of the Human Rights Committee to receive and consider communications from individuals subject to its jurisdiction shall extend to the provisions of the present Protocol, unless the State party concerned has made a statement to the contrary at the moment of ratification or accession.

Article 6

1.   The provisions of the present Protocol shall apply as additional provisions to the Covenant.

2.   Without prejudice to the possibility of a reservation under article 2 of the present Protocol, the right guaranteed in article 1, paragraph 1, of the present Protocol shall not be subject to any derogation under article 4 of the Covenant.

Article 7

1.   The present Protocol is open for signature by any State that has signed the Covenant.

2.   The present Protocol is subject to ratification by any State that has ratified the Covenant or acceded to it. Instruments of ratification shall be deposited with the Secretary-General of the United Nations.

3. The present Protocol shall be open to accession by any State that has ratified the Covenant or acceded to it.

4. Accession shall be effected by the deposit of an instrument of accession with the Secretary-General of the United Nations.

5. The Secretary-General of the United Nations shall inform all States that have signed the present Protocol or acceded to it of the deposit of each instrument of ratification or accession.

Article 8

1. The present Protocol shall enter into force three months after the date of the deposit with the Secretary-General of the United Nations of the tenth instrument of ratification or accession.

2. For each State ratifying the present Protocol or acceding to it after the deposit of the tenth instrument of ratification or accession, the present Protocol shall enter into force three months after the date of the deposit of its own instrument of ratification or accession.

Article 9

The provisions of the present Protocol shall extend to all parts of federal States without any limitations or exceptions.

Article 10

The Secretary-General of the United Nations shall inform all States referred to in article 48, paragraph 1, of the Covenant of the following particulars:

(a) reservations, communications and notifications under article 2 of the present Protocol;

(b) statements made under its articles 4 or 5;

(c) signatures, ratifications and accessions under its article 7;

(d) the date of the entry into force of the present Protocol under its article 8.

Article 11

1. The present Protocol, of which the Arabic, Chinese, English, French, Russian and Spanish texts are equally authentic, shall be deposited in the archives of the United Nations.

2. The Secretary-General of the United Nations shall transmit certified copies of the present Protocol to all States referred to in article 48 of the Covenant.

INTERNATIONAL COVENANT ON ECONOMIC, SOCIAL AND CULTURAL RIGHTS (1966)

PREAMBLE

The States Parties to the Present Covenant,

Considering that, in accordance with the principles proclaimed in the Charter of the United Nations, recognition of the inherent dignity and of the equal and inalienable rights of all members of the human family is the foundation of freedom, justice and peace in the world,

Recognizing that these rights derive from the inherent dignity of the human person,

Recognizing that, in accordance with the Universal Declaration of Human Rights, the ideal of free human beings enjoying freedom from fear and want can only be achieved if conditions are created whereby everyone may enjoy his economic, social and cultural rights, as well as his civil and political rights,

Considering the obligation of States under the Charter of the United Nations to promote universal respect for, and observance of, human rights and freedoms,

Realizing that the individual, having duties to other individuals and to community to which he belongs, is under a responsibility to strive for the promotion and observance of the rights recognized in the present Covenant,

Agree upon the following articles:

PART I

Article 1

1. All peoples have the right of self-determination. By virtue of that right they freely determine their political status and freely pursue their economic, social and cultural development.

2. All peoples may, for their own ends, freely dispose of their natural wealth and resources without prejudice to any obligations arising out of international economic co-operation, based upon the principle of mutual benefit, and international law. In no case may a people be deprived of its own means of subsistence.

3. The States Parties to the present Covenant, including those having responsibility for the administration of Non-Self-Governing and Trust Territories, shall promote the realization of the right of self-determination, and shall respect that right, in conformity with the provisions of the Charter of the United Nations.

PART II

Article 2

1. Each State Party to the present Covenant undertakes to take steps, individually and through international assistance and co-operation, especially economic and technical, to the maximum of its available resources, with a view to achieving progressively the full realization of the rights recognized in the present Covenant by all appropriate means, including particularly the adoption of legislative measures.

2. The States Parties to the present Covenant undertake to guarantee that the rights enunciated in the present Covenant will be exercised without discrimination of any kind as to race, colour, sex, language, religion, political or other opinion, national or social origin, property, birth or other status.

3. Developing countries, with due regard to human rights and their national economy, may determine to what extent they would guarantee the economic rights recognized in the present Covenant to non-nationals.

Article 3

The States Parties to the present Covenant undertake to ensure the equal right of men and women to the enjoyment of all economic, social and cultural rights set forth in the present Covenant.

Article 4

The States Parties to the present Covenant recognize that, in the enjoyment of those rights provided by the State in conformity with the present Covenant, the State may subject such rights only to such limitations as are determined by law only in so far as this may be compatible with the nature of these rights and solely for the purpose of promoting the general welfare in a democratic society.

Article 5

1. Nothing in the present Covenant may be interpreted as implying for any State, group or person any right to engage in any activity or to perform any act aimed at the destruction of any of the rights or freedoms recognized herein, or at their limitation to a greater extent than is provided for in the present Covenant.

2. No restriction upon or derogation from any of the fundamental human rights recognized or existing in any country in virtue of law, conventions, regulations or custom shall be admitted on the pretext that the present Covenant does not recognize such rights or that it recognizes them to a lesser extent.

PART III

Article 6

1. The States Parties to the present Covenant recognize the right to work, which includes the right of everyone to the opportunity to gain his living by work which he freely chooses or accepts, and will take appropriate steps to safeguard this right.

2. The steps to be taken by a State Party to the present Covenant to achieve the full realization of this right shall include technical and vocational guidance and training programmes, policies and techniques to achieve steady economic, social and cultural development and full and productive employment under conditions safeguarding fundamental political and economic freedoms to the individual.

Article 7

The States Parties to the present Covenant recognize the right of everyone to the enjoyment of just and favourable conditions of work which ensure, in particular:

(a) remuneration which provides all workers, as a minimum, with:

(i) fair wages and equal remuneration for work of equal value without distinction of any kind, in particular women being guaranteed conditions of work not inferior to those enjoyed by men, with equal pay for equal work;

(ii) a decent living for themselves and their families in accordance with the provisions of the present Covenant;

(b) safe and healthy working conditions;

(c) equal opportunity for everyone to be promoted in his employment to an appropriate higher level, subject to no considerations other than those of seniority and competence;

(d) rest, leisure and reasonable limitation of working hours and periodic holidays with pay, as well as remuneration for public holidays.

Article 8

1. The States Parties to the present Covenant undertake to ensure:

(a) the right of everyone to form trade unions and join the trade union of his choice, subject only to the rules of the organization concerned, for the promotion and protection of his economic and social interests. No restrictions may be placed on the exercise of this right other than those prescribed by law and which are necessary in a democratic society in the interests of national security or public order or for the protection of the rights and freedoms of others;

(b) the right of trade unions to establish national federations or confederations and the right of the latter to form or join international trade-union organizations;

(c) the right of trade unions to function freely subject to no limitations other than those prescribed by law and which are necessary in a democratic society in the interests of national security or public order or for the protection of the rights and freedoms of others;

(d) the right to strike, provided that it is exercised in conformity with the laws of the particular country.

2. This article shall not prevent the imposition of lawful restrictions on the exercise of these rights by members of the armed forces or of the police or of the administration of the State.

3. Nothing in this article shall authorize States Parties to the International Labour Organisation Convention of 1948 concerning Freedom of Association and Protection of the Right to Organise to take legislative measures which would prejudice, or apply the law in such a manner as would prejudice, the guarantees provided for in that Convention.

Article 9

The States Parties to the present Covenant recognize the right of everyone to social security, including social insurance.

Article 10
The States Parties to the present Covenant recognize that:

1. The widest possible protection and assistance should be accorded to the family, which is the natural and fundamental group unit of society, particularly for its establishment and while it is responsible for the care and education of dependent children. Marriage must be entered into with the free consent of the intending spouses.

2. Special protection should be accorded to mothers during a reasonable period before and after childbirth. During such period working mothers should be accorded paid leave or leave with adequate social security benefits.

3. Special measures of protection and assistance should be taken on behalf of all children and young persons without any discrimination for reasons of parentage or other conditions. Children and young persons should be protected from economic and social exploitation. Their employment in work harmful to their morals or health or dangerous to life or likely to hamper their normal development should be punishable by law. States should also set age limits below which the paid employment of child labour should be prohibited and punishable by law.

Article 11

1. The States Parties to the present Convenant recognize the right of everyone to an adequate standard of living for himself and his family, including adequate food, clothing and housing, and to the continuous improvement of living conditions. The States Parties will take appropriate steps to ensure the realization of this right, recognizing to this effect the essential importance of international co-operation based on free consent.

2. The States Parties to the present Covenant, recognizing the fundamental right of everyone to be free from hunger, shall take, individually and through international co-operation, the measures, including specific programmes, which are needed:

(a)   to improve methods of production, conservation and distribution of food by making full use of technical and scientific knowledge, by disseminating knowledge of the principles of nutrition and by developing or reforming agrarian systems in such a way as to achieve the most efficient development and utilization of natural resources;

(b)   taking into account the problems of both food-importing and food-exporting countries, to ensure an equitable distribution of world food supplies in relation to need.

Article 12

1. The States Parties to the present Covenant recognize the right of everyone to the enjoyment of the highest attainable standard of physical and mental health.

2. The steps to be taken by the States Parties to the present Covenant to achieve the full realization of this right shall include those necessary for:

(a)   the provision for the reduction of the stillbirth-rate and of infant mortality and for the healthy development of the child;

(b)   the improvement of all aspects of environmental and industrial hygiene;

(c)   the prevention, treatment and control of epidemic, endemic, occupational and other diseases;

(d)   the creation of conditions which would assure to all medical service and medical attention in the event of sickness.

Article 13

1. The States Parties to the present Covenant recognize the right of everyone to education. They agree that education shall be directed to the full development of the human personality and the sense of its dignity, and shall strengthen the respect for human rights and fundamental freedoms. They further agree that education shall

enable all persons to participate effectively in a free society, promote understanding, tolerance and friendship among all nations and all racial, ethnic or religious groups, and further the activities of the United Nations for the maintenance of peace.

2. The States Parties to the present Covenant recognize that, with a view to achieving the full realization of this right:

(a)   primary education shall be compulsory and available free to all;

(b)   secondary education in its different forms, including technical and vocational secondary education, shall be made generally available and accessible to all by every appropriate means, and in particular by the progressive introduction of free education;

(c)   higher education shall be made equally accessible to all, on the basis of capacity, by every appropriate means, and in particular by the progressive introduction of free education;

(d)   fundamental education shall be encouraged or intensified as far as possible for those persons who have not received or completed the whole period of their primary education;

(e)   the development of a system of schools at all levels shall be actively pursued, an adequate fellowship system shall be established, and the material conditions of teaching staff shall be continuously improved.

3. The States Parties to the present Covenant undertake to have respect for the liberty of parents and, when applicable, legal guardians to choose for their children schools, other than those established by the public authorities, which conform to such minimum educational standards as may be laid down or approved by the State and to ensure the religious and moral education of their children in conformity with their own convictions.

4. No part of this article shall be construed so as to interfere with the liberty of individuals and bodies to establish and direct educational institutions, subject always to the observance of the principles set forth in paragraph 1 of this article and to the requirement that the education given in such institutions shall conform to such minimum standards as may be laid down by the State.

Article 14

Each State Party to the present Covenant which, at the time of becoming a Party, has not been able to secure in its metropolitan territory or other territories under its jurisdiction compulsory primary education, free of charge, undertakes, within two years, to work out and adopt a detailed plan of action for the progressive implementation, within a reasonable number of years, to be fixed in the plan, of the principle of compulsory education free of charge for all.

Article 15

1. The States Parties to the present Covenant recognize the right of everyone:

(a)   to take part in cultural life;

(b)   to enjoy the benefits of scientific progress and its applications;

(c)   to benefit from the protection of the moral and material interests resulting from any scientific, literary or artistic production of which he is the author.

2. The steps to be taken by the States Parties to the present Covenant to achieve the full realization of this right shall include those necessary for the conservation, the development and the diffusion of science and culture.

3. The States Parties to the present Covenant undertake to respect the freedom indispensable for scientific research and creative activity.

4. The States Parties to the present Covenant recognize the benefits to be derived from the encouragement and development of international contacts and co-operation in the scientific and cultural fields.

PART IV

Article 16

1.   The States Parties to the present Covenant undertake to submit in conformity with this part of the Covenant reports on the measures which they have adopted and the progress made in achieving the observance of the rights recognized herein.

2.(a)   All reports shall be submitted to the Secretary-General of the United Nations, who shall transmit copies to the Economic and Social Council for consideration in accordance with the provisions of the present Covenant;

(b)   The Secretary-General of the United Nations shall also transmit to the specialized agencies copies of the reports, or any relevant parts therefrom, from States Parties to the present Covenant which are also members of these specialized agencies in so far as these reports, or parts therefrom, relate to any matters which fall within the responsibilities of the said agencies in accordance with their constitutional instruments.

Article 17

1.   The States Parties to the present Covenant shall furnish their reports in stages, in accordance with a programme to be established by the Economic and Social Council within one year of the entry into force of the present Covenant after consultation with the States Parties and the specialized agencies concerned.

2.   Reports may indicate factors and difficulties affecting the degree of fulfilment of obligations under the present Covenant.

3.   Where relevant information has previously been furnished to the United Nations or to any specialized agency by any State Party to the present Covenant, it will not be necessary to reproduce that information, but a precise reference to the information so furnished will suffice.

Article 18

Pursuant to its responsibilities under the Charter of the United Nations in the field of human rights and fundamental freedoms, the Economic and Social Council may make arrangements with the specialized agencies in respect of their reporting to it on the progress made in achieving the observance of the provisions of the present Covenant falling within the scope of their activities. These reports may include particulars of decisions and recommendations on such implementation adopted by their competent organs.

Article 19

The Economic and Social Council may transmit to the Commission on Human Rights for study and general recommendation or, as appropriate, for information the reports concerning human rights submitted by States in accordance with articles 16 and 17, and those concerning human rights submitted by the specialized agencies in accordance with article 18.

Article 20

The States Parties to the present Covenant and the specialized agencies concerned may submit comments to the Economic and Social Council on any general recommendation under article 19 or reference to such general recommendation in any report of the Commission on Human Rights or any documentation referred to therein.

Article 21

The Economic and Social Council may submit from time to time to the General Assembly reports with recommendations of a general nature and a summary of the information received from the States Parties to the present Covenant and the specialized agencies on the measures taken and the progress made in achieving general observance of the rights recognized in the present Covenant.

Article 22
The Economic and Social Council may bring to the attention of other organs of the United Nations, their subsidiary organs and specialized agencies concerned with furnishing technical assistance any matters arising out of the reports referred to in this part of the present Covenant which may assist such bodies in deciding, each within its field of competence, on the advisability of international measures likely to contribute to the effective progressive implementation of the present Covenant.

Article 23
The States Parties to the present Covenant agree that international action for the achievement of the rights recognized in the present Covenant includes such methods as the conclusion of conventions, the adoption of recommendations, the furnishing of technical assistance and the holding of regional meetings and technical meetings for the purpose of consultation and study organized in conjunction with the Governments concerned.

Article 24
Nothing in the present Covenant shall be interpreted as impairing the provisions of the Charter of the United Nations and of the constitutions of the specialized agencies which define the respective responsibilities of the various organs of the United Nations and of the specialized agencies in regard to the matters dealt with in the present Covenant.

Article 25
Nothing in the present Covenant shall be interpreted as impairing the inherent right of all peoples to enjoy and utilize fully and freely their natural wealth and resources.

PART V

Article 26
1. The present Covenant is open for signature by any State Member of the United Nations or member of any of its specialized agencies, by any State Party to the Statute of the International Court of Justice, and by any other State which has been invited by the General Assembly of the United Nations to become a party to the present Covenant.
2. The present Covenant is subject to ratification. Instruments of ratification shall be deposited with the Secretary-General of the United Nations.
3. The present Covenant shall be open to accession by any State referred to in paragraph 1 of this article.
4. Accession shall be effected by the deposit of an instrument of accession with the Secretary-General of the United Nations.
5. The Secretary-General of the United Nations shall inform all States which have signed the present Covenant or acceded to it of the deposit of each instrument of ratification or accession.

Article 27
1. The present Covenant shall enter into force three months after the date of the deposit with the Secretary-General of the United Nations of the thirty-fifth instrument of ratification or instrument of accession.
2. For each State ratifying the present Covenant or acceding to it after the deposit of the thirty-fifth instrument of ratification or instrument of accession, the present Covenant shall enter into force three months after the date of the deposit of its own instrument of ratification or instrument of accession.

Article 28
The provisions of the present Covenant shall extend to all parts of federal States without any limitations or exceptions.

Article 29

1.   Any State Party to the present Covenant may propose an amendment and file it with the Secretary-General of the United Nations. The Secretary-General shall thereupon communicate any proposed amendments to the States Parties to the present Covenant with a request that they notify him whether they favour a conference of States Parties for the purpose of considering and voting upon the proposals. In the event that at least one third of the States Parties favours such a conference, the Secretary-General shall convene the conference under the auspices of the United Nations. Any amendment adopted by a majority of the States Parties present and voting at the conference shall be submitted to the General Assembly of the United Nations for approval.

2.   Amendments shall come into force when they have been approved by the General Assembly of the United Nations and accepted by a two-thirds majority of the States Parties to the present Covenant in accordance with their respective constitutional processes.

3.   When amendments come into force they shall be binding on those States Parties which have accepted them, other States Parties still being bound by the provisions of the present Covenant and any earlier amendment which they have accepted.

Article 30

Irrespective of the notifications made under article 26, paragraph 5, the Secretary-General of the United Nations shall inform all States referred to in paragraph 1 of the same article of the following particulars:

(a)   signatures, ratifications and accessions under article 26;

(b)   the date of the entry into force of the present Covenant under article 27 and the date of the entry into force of any amendments under article 29.

Article 31

1.   The present Covenant, of which the Chinese, English, French, Russian and Spanish texts are equally authentic, shall be deposited in the archives of the United Nations.

2.   The Secretary-General of the United Nations shall transmit certified copies of the present Covenant to all States referred to in article 26.

DECLARATION ON THE ELIMINATION OF DISCRIMINATION AGAINST WOMEN (1967)

The General Assembly

Considering that the peoples of the United Nations have, in the Charter, reaffirmed their faith in fundamental human rights, in the dignity and worth of the human person and in the equal rights of men and women,

Considering that the Universal Declaration on Human Rights asserts the principle of non-discrimination and proclaims that all human beings are born free and equal in dignity and rights and that everyone is entitled to all the rights and freedoms set forth therein without distinction of any kind, including any distinction as to sex,

Taking into account the resolutions, declarations, conventions and recommendations of the United Nations and the specialized agencies designed to eliminate all forms of discrimination and to promote equal rights for men and women,

Concerned that, despite the Charter of the United Nations, the Universal Declaration of Human Rights, the International Covenants on Human Rights and other instruments of the United Nations and the specialized agencies and despite the progress made in the matter of equality of rights, there continues to exist considerable discrimination against women,

Considering that discrimination against women is incompatible with human dignity and with the welfare of the family and of society, prevents their participation, on equal terms with men, in the political, social, economic and cultural life of their countries and is an obstacle to the full development of the potentialities of women in the service of their countries and of humanity,

Bearing in mind the great contribution made by women to social, political, economic and cultural life and the part they play in the family and particularly in the rearing of children,

Convinced that the full and complete development of a country, the welfare of the world and the cause of peace require the maximum participation of women as well as men in all fields,

Considering that it is necessary to ensure the universal recognition in law and in fact of the principle of equality of men and women,

Solemnly proclaims this Declaration:

Article 1

Discrimination against women, denying or limiting as it does their equality of rights with men, is fundamentally unjust and constitutes an offence against human dignity.

Article 2

All appropriate measures shall be taken to abolish existing laws, customs, regulations and practices which are discriminatory against women, and to establish adequate legal protection for equal rights of men and women, in particular:

(a)   The principle of equality of rights shall be embodied in the constitution or otherwise guaranteed by law;

(b)   The international instruments of the United Nations and the specialized agencies relating to the elimination of discrimination against women shall be ratified or acceded to and fully implemented as soon as practicable.

Article 3

All appropriate measures shall be taken to educate public opinion and to direct national aspirations towards the eradication of prejudice and the abolition of customary and all other practices which are based on the idea of the inferiority of women.

Article 4

All appropriate measures shall be taken to ensure to women on equal terms with men, without any discrimination:

(a)   The right to vote in all elections and be eligible for election to all publicly elected bodies;

(b)   The right to vote in all public referenda;

(c)   The right to hold public office and to exercise all public functions. Such rights shall be guaranteed by legislation.

Article 5

Women shall have the same rights as men to acquire, change or retain their nationality. Marriage to an alien shall not automatically affect the nationality of the wife either by rendering her stateless or by forcing upon her the nationality of her husband.

Article 6

1.   Without prejudice to the safeguarding of the unity and the harmony of the family, which remains the basic unit of any society, all appropriate measures, particularly legislative measures, shall be taken to ensure to women, married or unmarried, equal rights with men in the field of civil law, and in particular:

(a)   The right to acquire, administer, enjoy, dispose of and inherit property, including property acquired during marriage;

(b)   The right to equality in legal capacity and the exercise thereof;

(c)   The same rights as men with regard to the law on the movement of persons.

2.   All appropriate measures shall be taken to ensure the principle of equality of status of the husband and wife, and in particular:

(a)   Women shall have the same right as men to free choice of a spouse and to enter into marriage only with their free and full consent;

(b)   Women shall have equal rights with men during marriage and at its dissolution. In all cases the interest of the children shall be paramount;

(c)   Parents shall have equal rights and duties in matters relating to their children. In all cases the interest of the children shall be paramount.

3.   Child marriage and the betrothal of young girls before puberty shall be prohibited, and effective action, including legislation, shall be taken to specify a minimum age for marriage and to make the registration of marriages in an official registry compulsory.

Article 7

All provisions of penal codes which constitute discrimination against women shall be repealed.

Article 8

All appropriate measures, including legislation, shall be taken to combat all forms of traffic in women and exploitation of prostitution of women.

Article 9

All appropriate measures shall be taken to ensure to girls and women, married or unmarried, equal rights with men in education at all levels, and in particular:

(a)   Equal conditions of access to, and study in, educational institutions of all types, including universities and vocational, technical and professional schools;

(b)   The same choice of curricula, the same examinations, teaching staff with qualifications of the same standard, and school premises and equipment of the same quality, whether the institutions are co-educational or not;

(c)   Equal opportunities to benefit from scholarships and other study grants;

(d)   Equal opportunities for access to programmes of continuing education, including adult literacy programmes;

(e)   Access to educational information to help in ensuring the health and well-being of families.

Article 10

1.   All appropriate measures shall be taken to ensure to women, married or unmarried, equal rights with men in the field of economic and social life, and in particular:

(a)   The right, without discrimination on grounds of marital status or any other grounds, to receive vocational training, to work, to free choice of profession and employment, and to professional and vocational advancement;

(b)   The right to equal remuneration with men and to equality of treatment in respect of work of equal value;

(c)   The right to leave with pay, retirement privileges and provision for security in respect of unemployment, sickness, old age or other incapacity to work;

(d)   The right to receive family allowances on equal terms with men.

2.   In order to prevent discrimination against women on account of marriage or maternity and to ensure their effective right to work, measures shall be taken to prevent their dismissal in the event of marriage or maternity and to provide paid maternity leave, with the guarantee of returning to former employment, and to provide the necessary social services, including child-care facilities.

3.   Measures taken to protect women in certain types of work, for reasons inherent in their physical nature, shall not be regarded as discriminatory.

Article 11

1. The principle of equality of rights of men and women demands implementation in all States in accordance with the principles of the Charter of the United Nations and of the Universal Declaration of Human Rights.

2. Governments, non-governmental organizations and individuals are urged, therefore, to do all in their power to promote the implementation ofthe principles contained in this Declaration.

INTERNATIONAL CONVENTION ON THE SUPPRESSION AND PUNISHMENT OF THE CRIME OF APARTHEID (1973)

The States Parties to the present Convention,

Recalling the provisions of the Charter of the United Nations, in which all Members pledged themselves to take joint and separate action in co-operation with the Organization for the achievement of universal respect for, and observance of, human rights and fundamental freedoms for all without distinction as to race, sex, language or religion,

Considering the Universal Declaration of Human Rights, which states that all human beings are born free and equal in dignity and rights and that everyone is entitled to all the rights and freedoms set forth in the Declaration, without distinction of any kind, such as race, colour or national origin,

Considering the Declaration on the Granting of Independence to Colonial Countries and Peoples, in which the General Assembly stated that the process of liberation is irresistible and irreversible and that, in the interests of human dignity, progress and justice, an end must be put to colonialism and all practices of segregation and discrimination associated therewith,

Observing that, in accordance with the International Convention on the Elimination of All Forms of Racial Discrimination, States particularly condemn racial segregation and *apartheid* and undertake to prevent, prohibit and eradicate all practices of this nature in territories under their jurisdiction,

Observing that, in the Convention on the Prevention and Punishment of the Crime of Genocide, certain acts which may also be qualified as acts of *apartheid* constitute a crime under international law,

Observing that, in the Convention on the Non-Applicability of Statutory Limitations to War Crimes and Crimes Against Humanity, 'inhuman acts resulting from the policy of *apartheid*' are qualified as crimes against humanity,

Observing that the General Assembly of the United Nations has adopted a number of resolutions in which the policies and practices of *apartheid* are condemned as a crime against humanity,

Observing that the Security Council has emphasized that *apartheid*, its continued intensification and expansion, seriously disturbs and threatens international peace and security,

Convinced that an International Convention on the Suppression and Punishment of the Crime of *Apartheid* would make it possible to take more effective measures at the international and national levels with a view to the suppression and punishment of the crime of *apartheid*,

Have agreed as follows:

Article I

1. The States Parties to the present Convention declare that *apartheid* is a crime against humanity and that inhuman acts resulting from the policies and practices of *apartheid* and similar policies and practices of racial segregation and discrimination, as defined in article II of the Convention, are crimes violating the principles of

international law, in particular the purposes and principles of the Charter of the United Nations, and constituting a serious threat to international peace and security.

2.   The States Parties to the present Convention declare criminal those organizations, institutions and individuals committing the crime of *apartheid*.

Article II

For the purpose of the present Convention, the term 'the crime of *apartheid*', which shall include similar policies and practices of racial segregation and discrimination as practised in southern Africa, shall apply to the following inhuman acts committed for the purpose of establishing and maintaining domination by one racial group of persons over any other racial group of persons and systematically oppressing them:

(a)   denial to a member or members of a racial group or groups of the right to life and liberty of person:

(i)   by murder of members of a racial group or groups;

(ii)   by the infliction upon the members of a racial group or groups of serious bodily or mental harm by the infringement of their freedom or dignity, or by subjecting them to torture or to cruel, inhuman or degrading treatment or punishment;

(iii) by arbitrary arrest and illegal imprisonment of the members of a racial group or groups;

(b)   deliberate imposition on a racial group or groups of living conditions calculated to cause its or their physical destruction in whole or in part;

(c)   any legislative measures and other measures calculated to prevent a racial group or groups from participation in the political, social, economic and cultural life of the country and the deliberate creation of conditions preventing the full development of such a group or groups, in particular by denying to members of a racial group or groups basic human rights and freedoms, including the right to work, the right to form recognized trade unions, the right to education, the right to leave and to return to their country, the right to a nationality, the right to freedom of movement and residence, the right to freedom of opinion and expression, and the right to freedom of peaceful assembly and association;

(d)   any measures, including legislative measures, designed to divide the population along racial lines by the creation of separate reserves and ghettos for the members of a racial group or groups, the prohibition of mixed marriages among members of various racial groups, the expropriation of landed property belonging to a racial group or groups or to members thereof;

(e)   exploitation of the labour of the members of a racial group or groups, in particular by submitting them to forced labour;

(f)   persecution of organizations and persons, by depriving them of fundamental rights and freedoms, because they oppose *apartheid*.

Article III

International criminal responsibility shall apply, irrespective of the motive involved, to individuals, members of organizations and institutions and representatives of the State, whether residing in the territory of the State in which the acts are perpetrated or in some other State, whenever they:

(a)   commit, participate in, directly incite or conspire in the commission of the acts mentioned in article II of the present Convention;

(b)   directly abet, encourage or co-operate in the commission of the crime of *apartheid*.

Article IV

The States Parties to the present Convention undertake:

(a)   to adopt any legislative or other measures necessary to suppress as well as to prevent any encouragement of the crime of *apartheid* and similar segregationist policies or their manifestations and to punish persons guilty of that crime;

(b)   to adopt legislative, judicial and administrative measures to prosecute, bring to trial and punish in accordance with their jurisdiction persons responsible for, or accused of, the acts defined in article II of the present Convention, whether or not such persons reside in the territory of the State in which the acts are committed or are nationals of that State or of some other State or are stateless persons.

Article V
Persons charged with the acts enumerated in article II of the present Convention may be tried by a competent tribunal of any State Party to the Convention which may acquire jurisdiction over the person of the accused or by an international penal tribunal having jurisdiction with respect to those States Parties which shall have accepted its jurisdiction.

Article VI
The States Parties to the present Convention undertake to accept and carry out in accordance with the Charter of the United Nations the decisions taken by the Security Council aimed at the prevention, suppression and punishment of the crime of *apartheid,* and to co-operate in the implementation of decisions adopted by other competent organs of the United Nations with a view to achieving the purposes of the Convention.

Article VII
1.   The States Parties to the present Convention undertake to submit periodic reports to the group established under article IX on the legislative, judicial, administrative or other measures that they have adopted and that give effect to the provisions of the Convention.

2.   Copies of the reports shall be transmitted through the Secretary-General of the United Nations to the Special Committee on *Apartheid.*

Article VIII
Any State Party to the present Convention may call upon any competent organ of the United Nations to take such action under the Charter of the United Nations as it considers appropriate for the prevention and suppression of the crime of *apartheid.*

Article IX
1.   The Chairman of the Commission on Human Rights shall appoint a group consisting of three members of the Commission on Human Rights, who are also representatives of States Parties to the present Convention, to consider reports submitted by States Parties in accordance with article VII.

2.   If, among the members of the Commission on Human Rights, there are no representatives of States Parties to the present Convention or if there are fewer than three such representatives, the Secretary-General of the United Nations shall, after consulting all States Parties to the Convention, designate a representative of the State Party or representatives of the States Parties which are not members of the Commission on Human Rights to take part in the work of the group established in accordance with paragraph 1 of this article, until such time as representatives of the States Parties to the Convention are elected to the Commission on Human Rights.

3.   The group may meet for a period of not more than five days, either before the opening or after the closing of the session of the Commission on Human Rights, to consider the reports submitted in accordance with article VII.

Article X
1.   The States Parties to the present Convention empower the Commission on Human Rights:

(a)   to request United Nations organs, when transmitting copies of petitions under article 15 of the International Convention on the Elimination of All Forms of

Racial Discrimination, to draw its attention to complaints concerning acts which are enumerated in article II of the present Convention;

　(b)　to prepare, on the basis of reports from competent organs of the United Nations and periodic reports from States Parties to the present Convention, a list of individuals, organizations, institutions and representatives of States which are alleged to be responsible for the crimes enumerated in article II of the Convention, as well as those against whom legal proceedings have been undertaken by States Parties to the Convention;

　(c)　to request information from the competent United Nations organs concerning measures taken by the authorities responsible for the administration of Trust and Non-Self-Governing Territories, and all other Territories to which General Assembly resolution 1514 (XV) of 14 December 1960 applies, with regard to such individuals alleged to be responsible for crimes under article II of the Convention who are believed to be under their territorial and administrative jurisdiction.

　2.　Pending the achievement of the objectives of the Declaration on the Granting of Independence to Colonial Countries and Peoples, contained in General Assembly resolution 1514 (XV), the provisions of the present Convention shall in no way limit the right of petition granted to those peoples by other international instruments or by the United Nations and its specialized agencies.

Article XI

　1.　Acts enumerated in article II of the present Convention shall not be considered political crimes for the purpose of extradition.

　2.　The States Parties to the present Convention undertake in such cases to grant extradition in accordance with their legislation and with the treaties in force.

Article XII

Disputes between States Parties arising out of the interpretation, application or implementation of the present Convention which have not been settled by negotiation shall, at the request of the States Parties to the dispute, be brought before the International Court of Justice, save where the parties to the dispute have agreed on some other form of settlement.

Article XIII

The present Convention is open for signature by all States. Any State which does not sign the Convention before its entry into force may accede to it.

Article XIV

　1.　The present Convention is subject to ratification. Instruments of ratification shall be deposited with the Secretary-General of the United Nations.

　2.　Accession shall be effected by the deposit of an instrument of accession with the Secretary-General of the United Nations.

Article XV

　1.　The present Convention shall enter into force on the thirtieth day after the date of the deposit with the Secretary-General of the United Nations of the twentieth instrument of ratification or accession.

　2.　For each State ratifying the present Convention or acceding to it after the deposit of the twentieth instrument of ratification or instrument of accession the Convention shall enter into force on the thirtieth day after the date of the deposit of its own instrument of ratification or instrument of accession.

Article XVI

A State Party may denounce the present Convention by written notification to the Secretary-General of the United Nations. Denunciation shall take effect one year after the date of receipt of the notification by the Secretary-General.

Article XVII

1.   A request for the revision of this Convention may be made at any time by any State Party by means of a notification in writing addressed to the Secretary-General of the United Nations.

2.   The General Assembly of the United Nations shall decide upon the steps, if any, to be taken in respect of such request.

Article XVIII

The Secretary-General of the United Nations shall inform all States of the following particulars:

(a)   signatures, ratifications and accessions under articles XIII and XIV;
(b)   the date of entry into force of the present Convention under article XV;
(c)   denunciations under article XVI;
(d)   notifications under article XVII.

Article XIX

1.   The present Convention, of which the Chinese, English, French, Russian and Spanish texts are equally authentic, shall be deposited in the archives of the United Nations.

2.   The Secretary-General of the United Nations shall transmit certified copies of the present Convention to all States.

CONVENTION ON THE ELIMINATION OF ALL FORMS OF DISCRIMINATION AGAINST WOMEN (1979)

The States Parties to the present Convention,

Noting that the Charter of the United Nations reaffirms faith in fundamental human rights, in the dignity and worth of the human person and in the equal rights of men and women,

Noting that the Universal Declaration of Human Rights affirms the principle of the inadmissibility of discrimination and proclaims that all human beings are born free and equal in dignity and rights and that everyone is entitled to all the rights and freedoms set forth therein, without distinction of any kind, including distinction based on sex,

Noting that the States Parties to the International Covenants on Human Rights have the obligation to ensure the equal right of men and women to enjoy all economic, social, cultural, civil and political rights,

Considering the international conventions concluded under the auspices of the United Nations and the specialized agencies promoting equality of rights of men and women,

Noting also the resolutions, declarations and recommendations adopted by the United Nations and the specialized agencies promoting equality of rights of men and women,

Concerned, however, that despite these various instruments extensive discrimination against women continues to exist,

Recalling that discrimination against women violates the principles of equality of rights and respect for human dignity, is an obstacle to the participation of women, on equal terms with men, in the political, social, economic and cultural life of their countries, hampers the growth of the prosperity of society and the family and makes more difficult the full development of the potentialities of women in the service of their countries and of humanity,

Concerned that in situations of poverty women have the least access to food, health, education, training and opportunities for employment and other needs,

Convinced that the establishment of the new international economic order based on equity and justice will contribute significantly towards the promotion of equality between men and women,

Emphasizing that the eradication of *apartheid*, of all forms of racism, racial discrimi-nation, colonialism, neo-colonialism, aggression, foreign occupation and domination and interference in the internal affairs of States is essential to the full enjoyment of the rights of men and women,

Affirming that the strengthening of international peace and security, relaxation of international tension, mutual co-operation among all States irrespective of their social and economic systems, general and complete disarmament, and in particular nuclear disarmament under strict and effective international control, the affirmation of the principles of justice, equality and mutual benefit in relations among countries and the realization of the right of peoples under alien and colonial domination and foreign occupation to self-determination and independence, as well as respect for national sovereignty and territorial integrity, will promote social progress and development and as a consequence will contribute to the attainment of full equality between men and women,

Convinced that the full and complete development of a country, the welfare of the world and the cause of peace require the maximum participation of women on equal terms with men in all fields,

Bearing in mind the great contribution of women to the welfare of the family and to the development of society, so far not fully recognized, the social significance of maternity and the role of both parents in the family and in the upbringing of children, and aware that the role of women in procreation should not be a basis for discrimi-nation but that the upbringing of children requires a sharing of responsibility between men and women and society as a whole,

Aware that a change in the traditional role of men as well as the role of women in society and in the family is needed to achieve full equality between men and women,

Determined to implement the principles set forth in the Declaration on the Elimin-ation of Discrimination against Women and, for that purpose, to adopt the measures required for the elimination of such discrimination in all its forms and manifestations,

Have agreed on the following:

PART I

Article 1
For the purposes of the present Convention, the term 'discrimination against women' shall mean any distinction, exclusion or restriction made on the basis of sex which has the effect or purpose of impairing or nullifying the recognition, enjoyment or exercise by women, irrespective of their marital status, on a basis of equality of men and women, of human rights and fundamental freedoms in the political, economic, social, cultural, civil or any other field.

Article 2
States Parties condemn discrimination against women in all its forms, agree to pursue by all appropriate means and without delay a policy of eliminating discrimination against women and, to this end, undertake:

(a)   To embody the principle of the equality of men and women in their national constitutions or other appropriate legislation if not yet incorporated therein and to ensure, through law and other appropriate means, the practical realization of this principle;

(b)   To adopt appropriate legislative and other measures, including sanctions where appropriate, prohibiting all discrimination against women;

(c)   To establish legal protection of the rights of women on an equal basis with men and to ensure through competent national tribunals and other public institutions the effective protection of women against any act of discrimination;

(d)   To refrain from engaging in any act or practice of discrimination against women and to ensure that public authorities and institutions shall act in conformity with this obligation;

(e) To take all appropriate measures to eliminate discrimination against women by any person, organization or enterprise;

(f) To take all appropriate measures, including legislation, to modify or abolish existing laws, regulations, customs and practices which constitute discrimination against women;

(g) To repeal all national penal provisions which constitute discrimination against women.

Article 3
States Parties shall take in all fields, in particular in the political, social, economic and cultural fields, all appropriate measures, including legislation, to ensure the full development and advancement of women, for the purpose of guaranteeing them the exercise and enjoyment of human rights and fundamental freedoms on a basis of equality with men.

Article 4
1. Adoption by States Parties of temporary special measures aimed at accelerating *de facto* equality between men and women shall not be considered discrimination as defined in the present Convention, but shall in no way entail as a consequence the maintenance of unequal or separate standards; these measures shall be discontinued when the objectives of equality of opportunity and treatment have been achieved.

2. Adoption by States Parties of special measures, including those measures contained in the present Convention, aimed at protecting maternity shall not be considered discriminatory.

Article 5
States Parties shall take all appropriate measures:

(a) To modify the social and cultural patterns of conduct of men and women, with a view to achieving the elimination of prejudices and customary and all other practices which are based on the idea of the inferiority or the superiority of either of the sexes or on stereotyped roles for men and women;

(b) To ensure that family education includes a proper understanding of maternity as a social function and the recognition of the common responsibility of men and women in the upbringing and development of their children, it being understood that the interest of the children is the primordial consideration in all cases.

Article 6
States Parties shall take all appropriate measures, including legislation, to suppress all forms of traffic in women and exploitation of prostitution of women.

PART II

Article 7
States Parties shall take all appropriate measures to eliminate discrimination against women in the political and public life of the country and, in particular, shall ensure to women, on equal terms with men, the right:

(a) To vote in all elections and public referenda and to be eligible for election to all publicly elected bodies;

(b) To participate in the formulation of government policy and the implementation thereof and to hold public office and perform all public functions at all levels of government;

(c) To participate in non-governmental organizations and associations concerned with the public and political life of the country.

Article 8
States Parties shall take all appropriate measures to ensure to women, on equal terms with men and without any discrimination, the opportunity to represent their

Governments at the international level and to participate in the work of international organizations.

Article 9

1. States Parties shall grant women equal rights with men to acquire, change or retain their nationality. They shall ensure in particular that neither marriage to an alien nor change of nationality by the husband during marriage shall automatically change the nationality of the wife, render her stateless or force upon her the nationality of the husband.

2. States Parties shall grant women equal rights with men with respect to the nationality of their children.

PART III

Article 10

States Parties shall take all appropriate measures to eliminate discrimination against women in order to ensure to them equal rights with men in the field of education and in particular to ensure, on a basis of equality of men and women:

(a) The same conditions for career and vocational guidance, for access to studies and for the achievement of diplomas in educational establishments of all categories in rural as well as in urban areas; this equality shall be ensured in pre-school, general, technical, professional and higher technical education, as well as in all types of vocational training;

(b) Access to the same curricula, the same examinations, teaching staff with qualifications of the same standard and school premises and equipment of the same quality;

(c) The elimination of any stereotyped concept of the roles of men and women at all levels and in all forms of education by encouraging coeducation and other types of education which will help to achieve this aim and, in particular, by the revision of textbooks and school programmes and the adaptation of teaching methods;

(d) The same opportunities to benefit from scholarships and other study grants;

(e) The same opportunities for access to programmes of continuing education, including adult and functional literacy programmes, particularly those aimed at reducing, at the earliest possible time, any gap in education existing between men and women;

(f) The reduction of female student drop-out rates and the organization of programmes for girls and women who have left school prematurely;

(g) The same opportunities to participate actively in sports and physical education;

(h) Access to specific educational information to help to ensure the health and well-being of families, including information and advice on family planning.

Article 11

1. States Parties shall take all appropriate measures to eliminate discrimination against women in the field of employment in order to ensure, on a basis of equality of men and women, the same rights, in particular:

(a) The right to work as an inalienable right of all human beings;

(b) The right to the same employment opportunities, including the application of the same criteria for selection in matters of employment;

(c) The right to free choice of profession and employment, the right to promotion, job security and all benefits and conditions of service and the right to receive vocational training and retraining, including apprenticeships, advanced vocational training and recurrent training;

(d) The right to equal remuneration, including benefits, and to equal treatment in respect of work of equal value, as well as equality of treatment in the evaluation of the quality of work;

(e)   The right to social security, particularly in cases of retirement, unemployment, sickness, invalidity and old age and other incapacity to work, as well as the right to paid leave;

(f)   The right to protection of health and to safety in working conditions, including the safeguarding of the function of reproduction.

2.   In order to prevent discrimination against women on the grounds of marriage or maternity and to ensure their effective right to work, States Parties shall take appropriate measures:

(a)   To prohibit, subject to the imposition of sanctions, dismissal on the grounds of pregnancy or of maternity leave and discrimination in dismissals on the basis of marital status;

(b)   To introduce maternity leave with pay or with comparable social benefits without loss of former employment, seniority or social allowances;

(c)   To encourage the provision of the necessary supporting social services to enable parents to combine family obligations with work responsibilities and participation in public life, in particular through promoting the establishment and development of a network of child-care facilities;

(d)   To provide special protection to women during pregnancy in types of work proved to be harmful to them.

3.   Protective legislation relating to matters covered in this article shall be reviewed periodically in the light of scientific and technological knowledge and shall be revised, repealed or extended as necessary.

Article 12

1.   States Parties shall take all appropriate measures to eliminate discrimination against women in the field of health care in order to ensure, on a basis of equality of men and women, access to health care services, including those related to family planning.

2.   Notwithstanding the provisions of paragraph 1 of this article, States Parties shall ensure to women appropriate services in connexion with pregnancy, confinement and the post-natal period, granting free services where necessary, as well as adequate nutrition during pregnancy and lactation.

Article 13

States Parties shall take all appropriate measures to eliminate discrimination against women in other areas of economic and social life in order to ensure, on a basis of equality of men and women, the same rights, in particular:

(a)   The right to family benefits;

(b)   The right to bank loans, mortgages and other forms of financial credit;

(c)   The right to participate in recreational activities, sports and all aspects of cultural life.

Article 14

1.   States Parties shall take into account the particular problems faced by rural women and the significant roles which rural women play in the economic survival of their families, including their work in the non-monetized sectors of the economy, and shall take all appropriate measures to ensure the application of the provisions of this Convention to women in rural areas.

2.   States Parties shall take all appropriate measures to eliminate discrimination against women in rural areas in order to ensure, on a basis of equality of men and women, that they participate in and benefit from rural development and, in particular, shall ensure to such women the right:

(a)   To participate in the elaboration and implementation of development planning at all levels;

(b)   To have access to adequate health care facilities, including information, counselling and services in family planning;

(c)   To benefit directly from social security programmes;

(d)   To obtain all types of training and education, formal and non-formal, including that relating to functional literacy, as well as, *inter alia*, the benefit of all community and extension services, in order to increase their technical proficiency;

(e)   To organize self-help groups and co-operatives in order to obtain equal access to economic opportunities through employment or self-employment;

(f)   To participate in all community activities;

(g)   To have access to agricultural credit and loans, marketing facilities, appropriate technology and equal treatment in land and agrarian reform as well as in land resettlement schemes;

(h)   To enjoy adequate living conditions, particularly in relation to housing, sanitation, electricity and water supply, transport and communications.

PART IV

Article 15

1.   States Parties shall accord to women equality with men before the law.

2.   States Parties shall accord to women, in civil matters, a legal capacity identical to that of men and the same opportunities to exercise that capacity. In particular, they shall give women equal rights to conclude contracts and to administer property and shall treat them equally in all stages of procedure in courts and tribunals.

3.   States Parties agree that all contracts and all other private instruments of any kind with a legal effect which is directed at restricting the legal capacity of women shall be deemed null and void.

4.   States Parties shall accord to men and women the same rights with regard to the law relating to the movement of persons and the freedom to choose their residence and domicile.

Article 16

1.   States Parties shall take all appropriate measures to eliminate discrimination against women in all matters relating to marriage and family relations and in particular shall ensure, on a basis of equality of men and women:

(a)   The same right to enter into marriage;

(b)   The same right freely to choose a spouse and to enter into marriage only with their free and full consent;

(c)   The same rights and responsibilities during marriage and at its dissolution;

(d)   The same rights and responsibilities as parents, irrespective of their marital status, in matters relating to their children; in all cases the interests of the children shall be paramount;

(e)   The some rights to decide freely and responsibly on the number and spacing of their children and to have access to the information, education and means to enable them to exercise these rights;

(f)   The same rights and responsibilities with regard to guardianship, wardship, trusteeship and adoption of children, or similar institutions where these concepts exist in national legislation; in all cases the interests of the children shall be paramount;

(g)   The same personal rights as husband and wife, including the right to choose a family name, a profession and an occupation;

(h)   The same rights for both spouses in respect of the ownership, acquisition, management, administration, enjoyment and disposition of property, whether free of charge or for a valuable consideration.

2.   The betrothal and the marriage of a child shall have no legal effect, and all necessary action, including legislation, shall be taken to specify a minimum age for marriage and to make the registration of marriages in an official registry compulsory.

PART V

Article 17

1. For the purpose of considering the progress made in the implementation of the present Convention, there shall be established a Committee on the Elimination of Discrimination against Women (hereinafter referred to as the Committee) consisting, at the time of entry into force of the Convention, of eighteen and, after ratification of or accession to the Convention by the thirty-fifth State Party, of twenty-three experts of high moral standing and competence in the field covered by the Convention. The experts shall be elected by States Parties from among their nationals and shall serve in their personal capacity, consideration being given to equitable geographical distribution and to the representation of the different forms of civilization as well as the principal legal systems.

2. The members of the Committee shall be elected by secret ballot from a list of persons nominated by States Parties. Each State Party may nominate one person from among its own nationals.

3. The initial election shall be held six months after the date of the entry into force of the present Convention. At least three months before the date of each election the Secretary-General of the United Nations shall address a letter to the States Parties inviting them to submit their nominations within two months. The Secretary-General shall prepare a list in alphabetical order of all persons thus nominated, indicating the States Parties which have nominated them, and shall submit it to the States Parties.

4. Elections of the members of the Committee shall be held at a meeting of States Parties convened by the Secretary-General at United Nations Headquarters. At that meeting, for which two thirds of the States Parties shall constitute a quorum, the persons elected to the Committee shall be those nominees who obtain the largest number of votes and an absolute majority of the votes of the representatives of States Parties present and voting.

5. The members of the Committee shall be elected for a term of four years. However, the terms of nine of the members elected at the first election shall expire at the end of two years; immediately after the first election the names of these nine members shall be chosen by lot by the Chairman of the Committee.

6. The election of the five additional members of the Committee shall be held in accordance with the provisions of paragraphs 2, 3 and 4 of this article, following the thirty-fifth ratification or accession. The terms of two of the additional members elected on this occasion shall expire at the end of two years, the names of these two members having been chosen by lot by the Chairman of the Committee.

7. For the filling of casual vacancies, the State Party whose expert has ceased to function as a member of the Committee shall appoint another expert from among its nationals, subject to the approval of the Committee.

8. The members of the Committee shall, with the approval of the General Assembly, receive emoluments from United Nations resources on such terms and conditions as the Assembly may decide, having regard to the importance of the Committee's responsibilities.

9. The Secretary-General of the United Nations shall provide the necessary staff and facilities for the effective performance of the functions of the Committee under the present Convention.

Article 18

1. States Parties undertake to submit to the Secretary-General of the United Nations, for consideration by the Committee, a report on the legislative, judicial, administrative or other measures which they have adopted to give effect to the provisions of the present Convention and on the progress made in this respect:

    (a) Within one year after the entry into force for the State concerned; and

(b)   Thereafter at least every four years and further whenever the Committee so requests.

2.   Reports may indicate factors and difficulties affecting the degree of fulfilment of obligations under the present Convention.

Article 19
1.   The Committee shall adopt its own rules of procedure.
2.   The Committee shall elect its officers for a term of two years.

Article 20
1.   The Committee shall normally meet for a period of not more than two weeks annually in order to consider the reports submitted in accordance with article 18 of the present Convention.
2.   The meetings of the Committee shall normally be held at United Nations Headquarters or at any other convenient place as determined by the Committee.

Article 21
1.   The Committee shall, through the Economic and Social Council, report annually to the General Assembly of the United Nations on its activities and may make suggestions and general recommendations based on the examination of reports and information received from the States Parties. Such suggestions and general recommendations shall be included in the report of the Committee together with comments, if any, from States Parties.
2.   The Secretary-General shall transmit the reports of the Committee to the Commission on the Status of Women for its information.

Article 22
The specialized agencies shall be entitled to be represented at the consideration of the implementation of such provisions of the present Convention as fall within the scope of their activities. The Committee may invite the specialized agencies to submit reports on the implementation of the Convention in areas falling within the scope of their activities.

PART VI

Article 23
Nothing in this Convention shall affect any provisions that are more conducive to the achievement of equality between men and women which may be contained:
(a)   In the legislation of a State Party; or
(b)   In any other international convention, treaty or agreement in force for that State.

Article 24
States Parties undertake to adopt all necessary measures at the national level aimed at achieving the full realization of the rights recognized in the present Convention.

Article 25
1.   The present Convention shall be open for signature by all States.
2.   The Secretary-General of the United Nations is designated as the depositary of the present Convention.
3.   The present Convention is subject to ratification. Instruments of ratification shall be deposited with the Secretary-General of the United Nations.
4.   The present Convention shall be open to accession by all States. Accession shall be effected by the deposit of an instrument of accession with the Secretary-General of the United Nations.

Article 26

1.   A request for the revision of the present Convention may be made at any time by any State Party by means of a notification in writing addressed to the Secretary-General of the United Nations.

2.   The General Assembly of the United Nations shall decide upon the steps, if any, to be taken in respect of such a request.

Article 27

1.   The present Convention shall enter into force on the thirtieth day after the date of deposit with the Secretary-General of the United Nations of the twentieth instrument of ratification or accession.

2.   For each State ratifying the present Convention or acceding to it after the deposit of the twentieth instrument of ratification or accession, the Convention shall enter into force on the thirtieth day after the date of the deposit of its own instrument of ratification or accession.

Article 28

1.   The Secretary-General of the United Nations shall receive and circulate to all States the text of reservations made by States at the time of ratification or accession.

2.   A reservation incompatible with the object and purpose of the present Convention shall not be permitted.

3.   Reservations may be withdrawn at any time by notification to this effect addressed to the Secretary-General of the United Nations, who shall then inform all States thereof. Such notification shall take effect on the date on which it is received.

Article 29

1.   Any dispute between two or more States Parties concerning the interpretation or application of the present Convention which is not settled by negotiation shall, at the request of one of them, be submitted to arbitration. If within six months from the date of the request for arbitration the parties are unable to agree on the organization of the arbitration, any one of those parties may refer the dispute to the International Court of Justice by request in conformity with the Statute of the Court.

2.   Each State Party may at the time of signature or ratification of this Convention or accession thereto declare that it does not consider itself bound by paragraph 1 of this article. The other States Parties shall not be bound by that paragraph with respect to any State Party which has made such a reservation.

3.   Any State Party which has made a reservation in accordance with paragraph 2 of this article may at any time withdraw that reservation by notification to the Secretary-General of the United Nations.

Article 30

The present Convention, the Arabic, Chinese, English, French, Russian and Spanish texts of which are equally authentic, shall be deposited with the Secretary-General of the United Nations.

IN WITNESS WHEREOF the undersigned, duly authorized, have signed the present Convention.

DECLARATION ON THE ELIMINATION OF ALL FORMS OF INTOLERANCE AND OF DISCRIMINATION BASED ON RELIGION OR BELIEF (1981)

The General Assembly,

Considering that one of the basic principles of the Charter of the United Nations is that of the dignity and equality inherent in all human beings, and that all Member

States have pledged themselves to take joint and separate action in co-operation with the Organization to promote and encourage universal respect for and observance of human rights and fundamental freedoms for all, without distinction as to race, sex, language or religion,

Considering that the Universal Declaration of Human Rights and the International Covenants on Human Rights proclaim the principles of non-discrimination and equality before the law and the right to freedom of thought, conscience, religion and belief,

Considering that the disregard and infringement of human rights and fundamental freedoms, in particular of the right to freedom of thought, conscience, religion or whatever belief, have brought, directly or indirectly, wars and great suffering to mankind, especially where they serve as a means of foreign interference in the internal affairs of other States and amount to kindling hatred between peoples and nations,

Considering that religion or belief, for anyone who professes either, is one of the fundamental elements in his conception of life and that freedom of religion or belief should be fully respected and guaranteed,

Considering that it is essential to promote understanding, tolerance and respect in matters relating to freedom of religion and belief and to ensure that the use of religion or belief for ends inconsistent with the Charter of the United Nations, other relevant instruments of the United Nations and the purposes and principles of the present Declaration is inadmissible,

Convinced that freedom of religion and belief should also contribute to the attainment of the goals of world peace, social justice and friendship among peoples and to the elimination of ideologies or practices of colonialism and racial discrimination,

Noting with satisfaction the adoption of several, and the coming into force of some, conventions, under the aegis of the United Nations and of the specialized agencies, for the elimination of various forms of discrimination,

Concerned by manifestations of intolerance and by the existence of discrimination in matters of religion or belief still in evidence in some areas of the world,

Resolved to adopt all necessary measures for the speedy elimination of such intolerance in all its forms and manifestations and to prevent and combat discrimination on the ground of religion or belief,

Proclaims this Declaration on the Elimination of All Forms of Intolerance and of Discrimination Based on Religion or Belief:

Article 1

1.   Everyone shall have the right to freedom of thought, conscience and religion. This right shall include freedom to have a religion or whatever belief of his choice, and freedom, either individually or in community with others and in public or private, to manifest his religion or belief in worship, observance, practice and teaching.

2.   No one shall be subject to coercion which would impair his freedom to have a religion or belief of his choice.

3.   Freedom to manifest one's religion or belief may be subject only to such limitations as are prescribed by law and are necessary to protect public safety, order, health or morals or the fundamental rights and freedoms of others.

Article 2

1.   No one shall be subject to discrimination by any State, institution, group of persons, or person on the grounds of religion or other belief.

2.   For the purposes of the present Declaration, the expression 'intolerance and discrimination based on religion or belief' means any distinction, exclusion, restriction or preference based on religion or belief and having as its purpose or as its effect nullification or impairment of the recognition, enjoyment or exercise of human rights and fundamental freedoms on an equal basis.

Article 3
Discrimination between human beings on the grounds of religion or belief constitutes an affront to human dignity and a disavowal of the principles of the Charter of the United Nations, and shall be condemned as a violation of the human rights and fundamental freedoms proclaimed in the Universal Declaration of Human Rights and enunciated in detail in the International Covenants on Human Rights, and as an obstacle to friendly and peaceful relations between nations.

Article 4
1. All States shall take effective measures to prevent and eliminate discrimination on the grounds of religion or belief in the recognition, exercise and enjoyment of human rights and fundamental freedoms in all fields of civil, economic, political, social and cultural life.
2. All States shall make all efforts to enact or rescind legislation where necessary to prohibit any such discrimination, and to take all appropriate measures to combat intolerance on the grounds of religion or other beliefs in this matter.

Article 5
1. The parents or, as the case may be, the legal guardians of the child have the right to organize the life within the family in accordance with their religion or belief and bearing in mind the moral education in which they believe the child should be brought up.
2. Every child shall enjoy the right to have access to education in the matter of religion or belief in accordance with the wishes of his parents or, as the case may be, legal guardians, and shall not be compelled to receive teaching on religion or belief against the wishes of his parents or legal guardians, the best interests of the child being the guiding principle.
3. The child shall be protected from any form of discrimination on the ground of religion or belief. He shall be brought up in a spirit of understanding, tolerance, friendship among peoples, peace and universal brotherhood, respect for freedom of religion or belief of others, and in full consciousness that his energy and talents should be devoted to the service of his fellow men.
4. In the case of a child who is not under the care either of his parents or of legal guardians, due account shall be taken of their expressed wishes or of any other proof of their wishes in the matter of religion or belief, the best interests of the child being the guiding principle.
5. Practices of a religion or belief in which a child is brought up must not be injurious to his physical or mental health or to his full development, taking into account article 1, paragraph 3, of the present Declaration.

Article 6
In accordance with article 1 of the present Declaration, and subject to the provisions of article 1, paragraph 3, the right to freedom of thought, conscience, religion or belief shall include, *inter alia*, the following freedoms:
(a) To worship or assemble in connection with a religion or belief, and to establish and maintain places for these purposes;
(b) To establish and maintain appropriate charitable or humanitarian institutions;
(c) To make, acquire and use to an adequate extent the necessary articles and materials related to the rites or customs of a religion or belief;
(d) To write, issue and disseminate relevant publications in these areas;
(e) To teach a religion or belief in places suitable for these purposes;
(f) To solicit and receive voluntary financial and other contributions from individuals and institutions;

(g)   To train, appoint, elect or designate by succession appropriate leaders called for by the requirements and standards of any religion or belief;

(h)   To observe days of rest and to celebrate holidays and ceremonies in accordance with the precepts of one's religion or belief;

(i)   To establish and maintain communications with individuals and communities in matters of religion and belief at the national and international levels.

Article 7

The rights and freedoms set forth in the present Declaration shall be accorded in national legislation in such a manner that everyone shall be able to avail himself of such rights and freedoms in practice.

Article 8

Nothing in the present Declaration shall be construed as restricting or derogating from any right defined in the Universal Declaration of Human Rights and the International Covenants on Human Rights.

CONVENTION AGAINST TORTURE AND OTHER CRUEL, INHUMAN OR DEGRADING TREATMENT OR PUNISHMENT (1984)

The States Parties to this Convention,

Considering that, in accordance with the principles proclaimed in the Charter of the United Nations, recognition of the equal and inalienable rights of all members of the human family is the foundation of freedom, justice and peace in the world,

Recognizing that those rights derive from the inherent dignity of the human person,

Considering the obligation of States under the Charter, in particular Article 55, to promote universal respect for, and observance of, human rights and fundamental freedoms,

Having regard to article 5 of the Universal Declaration of Human Rights and article 7 of the International Covenant on Civil and Political Rights, both of which provide that no one shall be subjected to torture or to cruel, inhuman or degrading treatment or punishment,

Having regard also to the Declaration on the Protection of All Persons from Being Subjected to Torture and Other Cruel, Inhuman or Degrading Treatment or Punishment, adopted by the General Assembly on 9 December 1975,

Desiring to make more effective the struggle against torture and other cruel, inhuman or degrading treatment or punishment throughout the world,

Have agreed as follows:

PART I

Article 1

1.   For the purposes of this Convention, the term 'torture' means any act by which severe pain or suffering, whether physical or mental, is intentionally inflicted on a person for such purposes as obtaining from him or a third person information or a confession, punishing him for an act he or a third person has committed or is suspected of having committed, or intimidating or coercing him or a third person, or for any reason based on discrimination of any kind, when such pain or suffering is inflicted by or at the instigation of or with the consent or acquiescence of a public official or other person acting in an official capacity. It does not include pain or suffering arising only from, inherent in or incidental to lawful sanctions.

2.   This article is without prejudice to any international instrument or national legislation which does or may contain provisions of wider application.

Article 2
1.   Each State Party shall take effective legislative, administrative, judicial or other measures to prevent acts of torture in any territory under its jurisdiction.
2.   No exceptional circumstances whatsoever, whether a state of war or a threat of war, internal political instability or any other public emergency, may be invoked as a justification of torture.
3.   An order from a superior officer or a public authority may not be invoked as a justification of torture.

Article 3
1.   No State Party shall expel, return (*'refouler'*) or extradite a person to another State where there are substantial grounds for believing that he would be in danger of being subjected to torture.
2.   For the purpose of determining whether there are such grounds, the competent authorities shall take into account all relevant considerations including, where applicable, the existence in the State concerned of a consistent pattern of gross, flagrant or mass violations of human rights.

Article 4
1.   Each State Party shall ensure that all acts of torture are offences under its criminal law. The same shall apply to an attempt to commit torture and to an act by any person which constitutes complicity or participation in torture.
2.   Each State Party shall make these offences punishable by appropriate penalties which take into account their grave nature.

Article 5
1.   Each State Party shall take such measures as may be necessary to establish its jurisdiction over the offences referred to in article 4 in the following cases:
    (a)   when the offences are committed in any territory under its jurisdiction or on board a ship or aircraft registered in that State;
    (b)   when the alleged offender is a national of that State;
    (c)   when the victim is a national of that State if that State considers it appropriate.
2.   Each State Party shall likewise take such measures as may be necessary to establish its jurisdiction over such offences in cases where the alleged offender is present in any territory under its jurisdiction and it does not extradite him pursuant to article 8 to any of the States mentioned in paragraph 1 of this article.
3.   This Convention does not exclude any criminal jurisdiction exercised in accordance with internal law.

Article 6
1.   Upon being satisfied, after an examination of information available to it, that the circumstances so warrant, any State Party in whose territory a person alleged to have committed any offence referred to in article 4 is present shall take him into custody or take other legal measures to ensure his presence. The custody and other legal measures shall be as provided in the law of that State but may be continued only for such time as is necessary to enable any criminal or extradition proceedings to be instituted.
2.   Such State shall immediately make a preliminary inquiry into the facts.
3.   Any person in custody pursuant to paragraph 1 of this article shall be assisted in communicating immediately with the nearest appropriate representative of the State of which he is a national, or, if he is a stateless person, with the representative of the State where he usually resides.
4.   When a State, pursuant to this article, has taken a person into custody, it shall immediately notify the States referred to in article 5, paragraph 1, of the fact that such

person is in custody and of the circumstances which warrant his detention. The State which makes the preliminary inquiry contemplated in paragraph 2 of this article shall promptly report its findings to the said States and shall indicate whether it intends to exercise jurisdiction.

Article 7

1. The State Party in the territory under whose jurisdiction a person alleged to have committed any offence referred to in article 4 is found shall in the cases contemplated in article 5, if it does not extradite him, submit the case to its competent authorities for the purpose of prosecution.

2. These authorities shall take their decision in the same manner as in the case of any ordinary offence of a serious nature under the law of that State. In the cases referred to in article 5, paragraph 2, the standards of evidence required for prosecution and conviction shall in no way be less stringent than those which apply in the cases referred to in article 5, paragraph 1.

3. Any person regarding whom proceedings are brought in connection with any of the offences referred to in article 4 shall be guaranteed fair treatment at all stages of the proceedings.

Article 8

1. The offences referred to in article 4 shall be deemed to be included as extraditable offences in any extradition treaty existing between States Parties. States Parties undertake to include such offences as extraditable offences in every extradition treaty to be concluded between them.

2. If a State Party which makes extradition conditional on the existence of a treaty receives a request for extradition from another State Party with which it has no extradition treaty, it may consider this Convention as the legal basis for extradition in respect of such offences. Extradition shall be subject to the other conditions provided by the law of the requested State.

3. States Parties which do not make extradition conditional on the existence of a treaty shall recognize such offences as extraditable offences between themselves subject to the conditions provided by the law of the requested State.

4. Such offences shall be treated, for the purpose of extradition between States Parties, as if they had been committed not only in the place in which they occurred but also in the territories of the States required to establish their jurisdiction in accordance with article 5, paragraph 1.

Article 9

1. States Parties shall afford one another the greatest measure of assistance in connection with criminal proceedings brought in respect of any of the offences referred to in article 4, including the supply of all evidence at their disposal necessary for the proceedings.

2. States Parties shall carry out their obligations under paragraph 1 of this article in conformity with any treaties on mutual judicial assistance that may exist between them.

Article 10

1. Each State Party shall ensure that education and information regarding the prohibition against torture are fully included in the training of law enforcement personnel, civil or military, medical personnel, public officials and other persons who may be involved in the custody, interrogation or treatment of any individual subjected to any form of arrest, detention or imprisonment.

2. Each State Party shall include this prohibition in the rules or instructions issued in regard to the duties and functions of any such persons.

Article 11
Each State Party shall keep under systematic review interrogation rules, instructions, methods and practices as well as arrangements for the custody and treatment of persons subjected to any form of arrest, detention or imprisonment in any territory under its jurisdiction, with a view to preventing any cases of torture.

Article 12
Each State Party shall ensure that its competent authorities proceed to a prompt and impartial investigation, wherever there is reasonable ground to believe that an act of torture has been committed in any territory under its jurisdiction.

Article 13
Each State Party shall ensure that any individual who alleges he has been subjected to torture in any territory under its jurisdiction has the right to complain to, and to have his case promptly and impartially examined by, its competent authorities. Steps shall be taken to ensure that the complainant and witnesses are protected against all ill-treatment or intimidation as a consequence of his complaint or any evidence given.

Article 14
1. Each State Party shall ensure in its legal system that the victim of an act of torture obtains redress and has an enforceable right to fair and adequate compensation, including the means for as full rehabilitation as possible. In the event of the death of the victim as a result of an act of torture, his dependants shall be entitled to compensation.
2. Nothing in this article shall affect any right of the victim or other persons to compensation which may exist under national law.

Article 15
Each State Party shall ensure that any statement which is established to have been made as a result of torture shall not be invoked as evidence in any proceedings, except against a person accused of torture as evidence that the statement was made.

Article 16
1. Each State Party shall undertake to prevent in any territory under its jurisdiction other acts of cruel, inhuman or degrading treatment or punishment which do not amount to torture as defined in article 1, when such acts are committed by or at the instigation of or with the consent or acquiescence of a public official or other person acting in an official capacity. In particular, the obligations contained in articles 10, 11, 12 and 13 shall apply with the substitution for references to torture of references to other forms of cruel, inhuman or degrading treatment or punishment.
2. The provisions of this Convention are without prejudice to the provisions of any other international instrument or national law which prohibits cruel, inhuman or degrading treatment or punishment or which relates to extradition or expulsion.

PART II

Article 17
1. There shall be established a Committee against Torture (hereinafter referred to as the Committee) which shall carry out the functions hereinafter provided. The Committee shall consist of ten experts of high moral standing and recognized competence in the field of human rights, who shall serve in their personal capacity. The experts shall be elected by the States Parties, consideration being given to equitable geographical distribution and to the usefulness of the participation of some persons having legal experience.
2. The members of the Committee shall be elected by secret ballot from a list of persons nominated by States Parties. Each State Party may nominate one person from

among its own nationals. States Parties shall bear in mind the usefulness of nominating persons who are also members of the Human Rights Committee established under the International Covenant on Civil and Political Rights and who are willing to serve on the Committee against Torture.

3.   Elections of the members of the Committee shall be held at biennial meetings of States Parties convened by the Secretary-General of the United Nations. At those meetings, for which two thirds of the States Parties shall constitute a quorum, the persons elected to the Committee shall be those who obtain the largest number of votes and an absolute majority of the votes of the representatives of States Parties present and voting.

4.   The initial election shall be held no later that six months after the date of the entry into force of this Convention. At least four months before the date of each election, the Secretary-General of the United Nations shall address a letter to the States Parties inviting them to submit their nominations within three months. The Secretary-General shall prepare a list in alphabetical order of all persons thus nominated, indicating the States Parties which have nominated them, and shall submit it to the States Parties.

5.   The members of the Committee shall be elected for a term of four years. They shall be eligible for re-election if renominated. However, the term of five of the members elected at the first election shall expire at the end of two years; immediately after the first election the names of these five members shall be chosen by lot by the chairman of the meeting referred to in paragraph 3 of this article.

6.   If a member of the Committee dies or resigns or for any other cause can no longer perform his Committee duties, the State Party which nominated him shall appoint another expert from among its nationals to serve for the remainder of his term, subject to the approval of the majority of the States Parties. The approval shall be considered given unless half or more of the States Parties respond negatively within six weeks after having been informed by the Secretary-General of the United Nations of the proposed appointment.

7.   States Parties shall be responsible for the expenses of the members of the Committee while they are in performance of Committee duties.

Article 18

1.   The Committee shall elect its officers for a term of two years. They may be re-elected.

2.   The Committee shall establish its own rules of procedure, but these rules shall provide, *inter alia,* that:

(a)   six members shall constitute a quorum;

(b)   decisions of the Committee shall be made by a majority vote of the members present.

3.   The Secretary-General of the United Nations shall provide the necessary staff and facilities for the effective performance of the functions of the Committee under this Convention.

4.   The Secretary-General of the United Nations shall convene the initial meeting of the Committee. After its initial meeting, the Committee shall meet at such times as shall be provided in its rules of procedure.

5.   The States Parties shall be responsible for expenses incurred in connection with the holding of meetings of the States Parties and of the Committee, including reimbursement to the United Nations for any expenses, such as the cost of staff and facilities, incurred by the United Nations pursuant to paragraph 3 of this article.

Article 19

1.   The States Parties shall submit to the Committee, through the Secretary-General of the United Nations, reports on the measures they have taken to give effect

to their undertakings under this Convention, within one year after the entry into force of the Convention for the State Party concerned. Thereafter the States Parties shall submit supplementary reports every four years on any new measures taken and such other reports as the Committee may request.

2.   The Secretary-General of the United Nations shall transmit the reports to all States Parties.

3.   Each report shall be considered by the Committee which may make such general comments on the report as it may consider appropriate and shall forward these to the State Party concerned. That State Party may respond with any observations it chooses to the Committee.

4.   The Committee may, at its discretion, decide to include any comments made by it in accordance with paragraph 3 of this article, together with the observations thereon received from the State Party concerned, in its annual report made in accordance with article 24. If so requested by the State Party concerned, the Committee may also include a copy of the report submitted under paragraph 1 of this article.

Article 20

1.   If the Committee receives reliable information which appears to it to contain well-founded indications that torture is being systematically practised in the territory of a State Party, the Committee shall invite that State Party to co-operate in the examination of the information and to this end to submit observations with regard to the information concerned.

2.   Taking into account any observations which may have been submitted by the State Party concerned, as well as any other relevant information available to it, the Committee may, if it decides that this is warranted, designate one or more of its members to make a confidential inquiry and to report to the Committee urgently.

3.   If an inquiry is made in accordance with paragraph 2 of this article, the Committee shall seek the co-operation of the State Party concerned. In agreement with that State Party, such an inquiry may include a visit to its territory.

4.   After examining the findings of its member or members submitted in accordance with paragraph 2 of this article, the Committee shall transmit these findings to the State Party concerned together with any comments or suggestions which seem appropriate in view of the situation.

5.   All the proceedings of the Committee referred to in paragraphs 1 to 4 of this article shall be confidential, and at all stages of the proceedings the co-operation of the State Party shall be sought. After such proceedings have been completed with regard to an inquiry made in accordance with paragraph 2, the Committee may, after consultations with the State Party concerned, decide to include a summary account of the results of the proceedings in its annual report made in accordance with article 24.

Article 21

1.   A State Party to this Convention may at any time declare under this article that it recognizes the competence of the Committee to receive and consider communications to the effect that a State Party claims that another State Party is not fulfilling its obligations under this Convention. Such communications may be received and considered according to the procedures laid down in this article only if submitted by a State Party which has made a declaration recognizing in regard to itself the competence of the Committee. No communication shall be dealt with by the Committee under this article if it concerns a State Party which has not made such a declaration. Communications received under this article shall be dealt with in accordance with the following procedure:

(a)   if a State Party considers that another State Party is not giving effect to the provisions of this Convention, it may, by written communication, bring the matter to the attention of that State Party. Within three months after the receipt of the communication the receiving State shall afford the State which sent the communication an explanation or any other statement in writing clarifying the matter, which should include, to the extent possible and pertinent, reference to domestic procedures and remedies taken, pending or available in the matter;

(b) if the matter is not adjusted to the satisfaction of both States Parties concerned within six months after the receipt by the receiving State of the initial communication, either State shall have the right to refer the matter to the Committee, by notice given to the Committee and to the other State;

(c) the Committee shall deal with a matter referred to it under this article only after it has ascertained that all domestic remedies have been invoked and exhausted in the matter, in conformity with the generally recognized principles of international law. This shall not be the rule where the application of the remedies is unreasonably prolonged or is unlikely to bring effective relief to the person who is the victim of the violation of this Convention;

(d) the Committee shall hold closed meetings when examining communications under this article;

(e) subject to the provisions of subparagraph (c), the Committee shall make available its good offices to the States Parties concerned with a view to a friendly solution of the matter on the basis of respect for the obligations provided for in this Convention. For this purpose, the Committee may, when appropriate, set up an *ad hoc* conciliation commission;

(f) in any matter referred to it under this article, the Committee may call upon the States Parties concerned, referred to in subparagraph (b), to supply any relevant information;

(g) the States Parties concerned, referred to in subparagraph (b) shall have the right to be represented when the matter is being considered by the Committee and to make submissions orally and/or in writing;

(h) the Committee shall, within twelve months after the date of receipt of notice under subparagraph (b), submit a report:

(i) if a solution within the terms of subparagraph (e) is reached, the Committee shall confine its report to a brief statement of the facts and of the solution reached;

(ii) if a solution within the terms of subparagraph (e) is not reached the Committee shall confine its report to a brief statement of the facts; the written submissions and record of the oral submissions made by the States Parties concerned shall be attached to the report.

In every matter, the report shall be communicated to the States Parties concerned.

2. The provisions of this article shall come into force when five States Parties to this Convention have made declarations under paragraph 1 of this article. Such declarations shall be deposited by the States Parties with the Secretary-General of the United Nations, who shall transmit copies thereof to the other States Parties. A declaration may be withdrawn at any time by notification to the Secretary-General. Such a withdrawal shall not prejudice the consideration of any matter which is the subject of a communication already transmitted under this article; no further communication by any State Party shall be received under this article after the notification of withdrawal of the declaration has been received by the Secretary-General, unless the State Party concerned has made a new declaration.

Article 22

1. A State Party to this Convention may at any time declare under this article that it recognizes the competence of the Committee to receive and consider communications from or on behalf of individuals subject to its jurisdiction who claim to be

victims of a violation by a State Party of the provisions of the Convention. No communication shall be received by the Committee if it concerns a State Party which has not made such a declaration.

2.   The Committee shall consider inadmissible any communication under this article which is anonymous or which it considers to be an abuse of the right of submission of such communications or to be incompatible with the provisions of this Convention.

3.   Subject to the provisions of paragraph 2, the Committee shall bring any communications submitted to it under this article to the attention of the State Party to this Convention which has made a declaration under paragraph 1 and is alleged to be violating any provisions of the Convention. Within six months, the receiving State shall submit to the Committee written explanations or statements clarifying the matter and the remedy, if any, that may have been taken by that State.

4.   The Committee shall consider communications received under this article in the light of all information made available to it by or on behalf of the individual and by the State Party concerned.

5.   The Committee shall not consider any communications from an individual under this article unless it has ascertained that:

(a)   the same matter has not been, and is not being, examined under another procedure of international investigation or settlement;

(b)   the individual has exhausted all available domestic remedies; this shall not be the rule where the application of the remedies is unreasonably prolonged or is unlikely to bring effective relief to the person who is the victim of the violation of this Convention.

6.   The Committee shall hold closed meetings when examining communications under this article.

7.   The Committee shall forward its views to the State Party concerned and to the individual.

8.   The provisions of this article shall come into force when five States Parties to this Convention have made declarations under paragraph 1 of this article. Such declarations shall be deposited by the States Parties with the Secretary-General of the United Nations, who shall transmit copies thereof to the other States Parties. A declaration may be withdrawn at any time by notification to the Secretary-General. Such a withdrawal shall not prejudice the consideration of any matter which is the subject of a communication already transmitted under this article, no further communication by or on behalf of an individual shall be received under this article after the notification of withdrawal of the declaration has been received by the Secretary-General, unless the State Party has made a new declaration.

Article 23
The members of the Committee and of the *ad hoc* conciliation commissions which may be appointed under article 21, paragraph 1(e), shall be entitled to the facilities, privileges and immunities of experts on mission for the United Nations as laid down in the relevant sections of the Convention on the Privileges and Immunities of the United Nations.

Article 24
The Committee shall submit an annual report on its activities under this Convention to the States Parties and to the General Assembly of the United Nations.

PART III

Article 25
1.   This Convention is open for signature by all States.

2.   This Convention is subject to ratification. Instruments of ratification shall be deposited with the Secretary-General of the United Nations.

Article 26
This Convention is open to accession by all States. Accession shall be effected by the deposit of an instrument of accession with the Secretary-General of the United Nations.

Article 27
1. This Convention shall enter into force on the thirtieth day after the date of the deposit with the Secretary-General of the United Nations of the twentieth instrument of ratification or accession.

2. For each State ratifying this Convention or acceding to it after the deposit of the twentieth instrument of ratification or accession, the Convention shall enter into force on the thirtieth day after the date of the deposit of its own instrument of ratification or accession.

Article 28
1. Each State may, at the time of signature or ratification of this Convention or accession thereto, declare that it does not recognize the competence of the Committee provided for in article 20.

2. Any State Party having made a reservation in accordance with paragraph 1 of this article may, at any time, withdraw this reservation by notification to the Secretary-General of the United Nations.

Article 29
1. Any State Party to this Convention may propose an amendment and file it with the Secretary-General of the United Nations. The Secretary-General shall thereupon communicate the proposed amendment to the States Parties with a request that they notify him whether they favour a conference of States Parties for the purpose of considering and voting upon the proposal. In the event that within four months from the date of such communication at least one third of the States Parties favours such a conference, the Secretary-General shall convene the conference under the auspices of the United Nations. Any amendment adopted by a majority of the States Parties present and voting at the conference shall be submitted by the Secretary-General to all the States Parties for acceptance.

2. An amendment adopted in accordance with paragraph 1 of this article shall enter into force when two thirds of the States Parties to this Convention have notified the Secretary-General of the United Nations that they have accepted it in accordance with their respective constitutional processes.

3. When amendments enter into force, they shall be binding on those States Parties which have accepted them, other States Parties still being bound by the provisions of this Convention and any earlier amendments which they have accepted.

Article 30
1. Any dispute between two or more States Parties concerning the interpretation or application of this Convention which cannot be settled through negotiation shall, at the request of one of them, be submitted to arbitration. If within six months from the date of the request for arbitration the Parties are unable to agree on the organization of the arbitration, any one of those Parties may refer the dispute to the International Court of Justice by request in conformity with the Statute of the Court.

2. Each State may, at the time of signature or ratification of this Convention or accession thereto, declare that it does not consider itself bound by paragraph 1 of this article. The other States Parties shall not be bound by paragraph 1 of this article with respect to any State Party having made such a reservation.

3. Any State Party having made a reservation in accordance with paragraph 2 of this article may at any time withdraw this reservation by notification to the Secretary-General of the United Nations.

Article 31
1. A State Party may denounce this Convention by written notification to the Secretary-General of the United Nations. Denunciation becomes effective one year after the date of receipt of the notification by the Secretary-General.
2. Such a denunciation shall not have the effect of releasing the State Party from its obligations under this Convention in regard to any act or omission which occurs prior to the date at which the denunciation becomes effective, nor shall denunciation prejudice in any way the continued consideration of any matter which is already under consideration by the Committee prior to the date at which the denunciation becomes effective.
3. Following the date at which the denunciation of a State Party becomes effective, the Committee shall not commence consideration of any new matter regarding that State.

Article 32
The Secretary-General of the United Nations shall inform all States Members of the United Nations and all States which have signed this Convention or acceded to it of the following:
    (a)   signatures, ratifications and accessions under articles 25 and 26;
    (b)   the date of entry into force of this Convention under article 27 and the date of the entry into force of any amendments under article 29;
    (c) denunciations under article 31.

Article 33
1. This Convention, of which the Arabic, Chinese, English, French, Russian and Spanish texts are equally authentic, shall be deposited with the Secretary-General of the United Nations.
2. The Secretary-General of the United Nations shall transmit certified copies of this Convention to all States.

UNITED NATIONS CONVENTION ON THE RIGHTS OF THE CHILD
(1989)

PREAMBLE

The States Parties to the present Convention,
    Considering that, in accordance with the principles proclaimed in the Charter of the United Nations, recognition of the inherent dignity and of the equal and inalienable rights of all members of the human family is the foundation of freedom, justice and peace in the world,
    Bearing in mind that the peoples of the United Nations have, in the Charter, reaffirmed their faith in fundamental human rights and in the dignity and worth of the human person, and have determined to promote social progress and better standards of life in larger freedom,
    Recognizing that the United Nations has, in the Universal Declaration of Human Rights and in the International Covenants on Human Rights, proclaimed and agreed that everyone is entitled to all the rights and freedoms set forth therein, without distinction of any kind, such as race, colour, sex, language, religion, political or other opinion, national or social origin, property, birth or other status,
    Recalling that, in the Universal Declaration of Human Rights, the United Nations has proclaimed that childhood is entitled to special care and assistance,
    Convinced that the family, as the fundamental group of society and the natural environment for the growth and well-being of all its members and particularly children, should be afforded the necessary protection and assistance so that it can fully assume its responsibilities within the community,

Recognizing that the child, for the full and harmonious development of his or her personality, should grow up in a family environment, in an atmosphere of happiness, love and understanding,

Considering that the child should be fully prepared to live an individual life in society, and brought up in the spirit of the ideals proclaimed in the Charter of the United Nations, and in particular in the spirit of peace, dignity, tolerance, freedom, equality and solidarity,

Bearing in mind that the need to extend particular care to the child has been stated in the Geneva Declaration of the Rights of the Child of 1924 and in the Declaration of the Rights of the Child adopted by the General Assembly on 20 November 1959 and recognized in the Universal Declaration of Human Rights, in the International Covenant on Civil and Political Rights (in particular in articles 23 and 24), in the International Covenant on Economic, Social and Cultural Rights (in particular in article 10) and in the statutes and relevant instruments of specialized agencies and international organizations concerned with the welfare of children,

Bearing in mind that, as indicated in the Declaration of the Rights of the Child, 'the child, by reason of his physical and mental immaturity, needs special safeguards and care, including appropriate legal protection, before as well as after birth',

Recalling the provisions of the Declaration on Social and Legal Principles relating to the Protection and Welfare of Children, with Special Reference to Foster Placement and Adoption Nationally and Internationally; the United Nations Standard Minimum Rules for the Administration of Juvenile Justice (The Beijing Rules); and the Declaration on the Protection of Women and Children in Emergency and Armed Conflict,

Recognizing that, in all countries in the world, there are children living in exceptionally difficult conditions, and that such children need special consideration,

Taking due account of the importance of the traditions and cultural values of each people for the protection and harmonious development of the child,

Recognizing the importance of international co-operation for improving the living conditions of children in every country, in particular in the developing countries,

Have agreed as follows:

PART I

Article 1
For the purposes of the present Convention, a child means every human being below the age of eighteen years unless, under the law applicable to the child, majority is attained earlier.

Article 2
1. States Parties shall respect and ensure the rights set forth in the present Convention to each child within their jurisdiction without discrimination of any kind, irrespective of the child's or his or her parent's or legal guardian's race, colour, sex, language, religion, political or other opinion, national, ethnic or social origin, property, disability, birth or other status.

2. States Parties shall take all appropriate measures to ensure that the child is protected against all forms of discrimination or punishment on the basis of the status, activities, expressed opinions, or beliefs of the child's parents, legal guardians, or family members.

Article 3
1. In all actions concerning children, whether undertaken by public or private social welfare institutions, courts of law, administrative authorities or legislative bodies, the best interests of the child shall be a primary consideration.

2. States Parties undertake to ensure the child such protection and care as is necessary for his or her well-being, taking into account the rights and duties of his or

her parents, legal guardians, or other individuals legally responsible for him or her, and, to this end, shall take all appropriate legislative and administrative measures.

3. States Parties shall ensure that the institutions, services and facilities responsible for the care or protection of children shall conform with the standards established by competent authorities, particularly in the areas of safety, health, in the number and suitability of their staff, as well as competent supervision.

Article 4
States Parties shall undertake all appropriate legislative, administrative, and other measures for the implementation of the rights recognized in the present Convention. With regard to economic, social and cultural rights, States Parties shall undertake such measures to the maximum extent of their available resources and, where needed, within the framework of international co-operation.

Article 5
States Parties shall respect the responsibilities, rights and duties of parents or, where applicable, the members of the extended family or community as provided for by local custom, legal guardians or other persons legally responsible for the child, to provide, in a manner consistent with the evolving capacities of the child, appropriate direction and guidance in the exercise by the child of the rights recognized in the present Convention.

Article 6
1. States Parties recognize that every child has the inherent right to life.

2. States Parties shall ensure to the maximum extent possible the survival and development of the child.

Article 7
1. The child shall be registered immediately after birth and shall have the right from birth to a name, the right to acquire a nationality and, as far as possible, the right to know and be cared for by his or her parents.

2. States Parties shall ensure the implementation of these rights in accordance with their national law and their obligations under the relevant international instruments in this field, in particular where the child would otherwise be stateless.

Article 8
1. States Parties undertake to respect the right of the child to preserve his or her identity, including nationality, name and family relations as recognized by law without unlawful interference.

2. Where a child is illegally deprived of some or all of the elements of his or her identity, States Parties shall provide appropriate assistance and protection, with a view to speedily re-establishing his or her identity.

Article 9
1. States Parties shall ensure that a child shall not be separated from his or her parents against their will, except when competent authorities subject to judicial review determine, in accordance with applicable law and procedures, that such separation is necessary for the best interests of the child. Such determination may be necessary in a particular case such as one involving abuse or neglect of the child by the parents, or one where the parents are living separately and a decision must be made as to the child's place of residence.

2. In any proceedings pursuant to paragraph 1 of the present article, all interested parties shall be given an opportunity to participate in the proceedings and make their views known.

3. States Parties shall respect the right of the child who is separated from one or both parents to maintain personal relations and direct contact with both parents on a regular basis, except if it is contrary to the child's best interests.

4.   Where such separation results from any action initiated by a State Party, such as the detention, imprisonment, exile, deportation or death (including death arising from any cause while the person is in the custody of the State) of one or both parents or of the child, that State Party shall, upon request, provide the parents, the child or, if appropriate, another member of the family with the essential information concerning the whereabouts of the absent member(s) of the family unless the provision of the information would be detrimental to the well-being of the child. States Parties shall further ensure that the submission of such a request shall of itself entail no adverse consequences for the person(s) concerned.

Article 10

1.   In accordance with the obligation of States Parties under article 9, paragraph 1, applications by a child or his or her parents to enter or leave a State Party for the purpose of family reunification shall be dealt with by State Parties in a positive, humane and expeditious manner. States Parties shall further ensure that the submission of such a request shall entail no adverse consequences for the applicants and for the members of their family.

2.   A child whose parents reside in different States shall have the right to maintain on a regular basis, save in exceptional circumstances personal relations and direct contacts with both parents. Towards that end and in accordance with the obligation of States Parties under article 9, paragraph 2, States Parties shall respect the right of the child and his or her parents to leave any country, including their own, and to enter their own country. The right to leave any country shall be subject only to such restrictions as are prescribed by law and which are necessary to protect the national security, public order (*ordre public*), public health or morals or the rights and freedoms of others and are consistent with the other rights recognized in the present Convention.

Article 11

1.   States Parties shall take measures to combat the illicit transfer and non-return of children abroad.

2.   To this end, States Parties shall promote the conclusion of bilateral or multilateral agreements or accession to existing agreements.

Article 12

1.   States Parties shall assure to the child who is capable of forming his or her own views the right to express those views freely in all matters affecting the child, the views of the child being given due weight in accordance with the age and maturity of the child.

2.   For this purpose, the child shall in particular be provided the opportunity to be heard in any judicial and administrative proceedings affecting the child, either directly, or through a representative or an appropriate body, in a manner consistent with the procedural rules of national law.

Article 13

1.   The child shall have the right to freedom of expression; this right shall include freedom to seek, receive and impart information and ideas of all kinds, regardless of frontiers, either orally, in writing or in print, in the form of art, or through any other media of the child's choice.

2.   The exercise of this right may be subject to certain restrictions, but these shall only be such as are provided by law and are necessary:

(a)   for respect of the rights or reputations of others; or

(b)   for the protection of national security or of public order (*ordre public*), or of public health or morals.

Article 14
1.   States Parties shall respect the right of the child to freedom of thought, conscience and religion.
2.   States Parties shall respect the rights and duties of the parents and, when applicable, legal guardians, to provide direction to the child in the exercise of his or her right in a manner consistent with the evolving capacities of the child.
3.   Freedom to manifest one's religion or beliefs may be subject only to such limitations as are prescribed by law and are necessary to protect public safety, order, health or morals, or the fundamental rights and freedoms of others.

Article 15
1.   States Parties recognize the rights of the child to freedom of association and to freedom of peaceful assembly.
2.   No restrictions may be placed on the exercise of these rights other than those imposed in conformity with the law and which are necessary in a democratic society in the interests of national security or public safety, public order (*ordre public*), the protection of public health or morals or the protection of the rights and freedoms of others.

Article 16
1.   No child shall be subjected to arbitrary or unlawful interference with his or her privacy, family, home or correspondence, nor to unlawful attacks on his or her honour and reputation.
2.   The child has the right to the protection of the law against such interference or attacks.

Article 17
States Parties recognize the important function performed by the mass media and shall ensure that the child has access to information and material from a diversity of national and international sources, especially those aimed at the promotion of his or her social, spiritual and moral well-being and physical and mental health. To this end, States Parties shall:
(a)   encourage the mass media to disseminate information and material of social and cultural benefit to the child and in accordance with the spirit of article 29;
(b)   encourage international co-operation in the production, exchange and dissemination of such information and material from a diversity of cultural, national and international sources;
(c)   encourage the production and dissemination of children's books,
(d)   encourage the mass media to have particular regard to the linguistic needs of the child who belongs to a minority group or who is indigenous;
(e)   encourage the development of appropriate guidelines for the protection of the child from information and material injurious to his or her well-being, bearing in mind the provisions of articles 13 and 18.

Article 18
1.   States Parties shall use their best efforts to ensure recognition of the principle that both parents have common responsibilities for the upbringing and development of the child. Parents or, as the case may be, legal guardians, have the primary responsibility for the upbringing and development of the child. The best interests of the child will be their basic concern.
2.   For the purpose of guaranteeing and promoting the rights set forth in the present Convention, States Parties shall render appropriate assistance to parents and legal guardians in the performance of their child-rearing responsibilities and shall ensure the development of institutions, facilities and services for the care of children.

3.   States Parties shall take all appropriate measures to ensure that children of working parents have the right to benefit from child-care services and facilities for which they are eligible.

Article 19

1.   States Parties shall take all appropriate legislative, administrative, social and educational measures to protect the child from all forms of physical or mental violence, injury or abuse, neglect or negligent treatment, maltreatment or exploitation, including sexual abuse, while in the care of parent(s), legal guardian(s) or any other person who has the care of the child.

2.   Such protective measures should, as appropriate, include effective procedures for the establishment of social programmes to provide necessary support for the child and for those who have the care of the child, as well as for other forms of prevention and for identification, reporting, referral, investigation, treatment and follow-up of instances of child maltreatment described heretofore, and, as appropriate, for judicial involvement.

Article 20

1.   A child temporarily or permanently deprived of his or her family environment, or in whose own best interests cannot be allowed to remain in that environment, shall be entitled to special protection and assistance provided by the State.

2.   States Parties shall in accordance with their national laws ensure alternative care for such a child.

3.   Such care could include, *inter alia,* foster placement, *kafalah* of Islamic law, adoption or if necessary placement in suitable institutions for the care of children. When considering solutions, due regard shall be paid to the desirability of continuity in a child's upbringing and to the child's ethnic, religious, cultural and linguistic background.

Article 21

States Parties that recognize and/or permit the system of adoption shall ensure that the best interests of the child shall be the paramount consideration and they shall:

(a)   ensure that the adoption of a child is authorized only by competent authorities who determine, in accordance with applicable law and procedures and on the basis of all pertinent and reliable information, that the adoption is permissible in view of the child's status concerning parents, relatives and legal guardians and that, if required, the persons concerned have given their informed consent to the adoption on the basis of such counselling as may be necessary;

(b)   recognize that inter-country adoption may be considered as an alternative means of child's care, if the child cannot be placed in a foster or an adoptive family or cannot in any suitable manner be cared for in the child's country of origin;

(c)   ensure that the child concerned by inter-country adoption enjoys safeguards and standards equivalent to those existing in the case of national adoption;

(d)   take all appropriate measures to ensure that, in inter-country adoption, the placement does not result in improper financial gain for those involved in it;

(e)   promote, where appropriate, the objectives of the present article by concluding bilateral or multilateral arrangements or agreements, and endeavour, within this framework, to ensure that the placement of the child in another country is carried out by competent authorities or organs.

Article 22

1.   States Parties shall take appropriate measures to ensure that a child who is seeking refugee status or who is considered a refugee in accordance with applicable international or domestic law and procedures shall, whether unaccompanied or accompanied by his or her parents or by any other person, receive appropriate protection and humanitarian assistance in the enjoyment of applicable rights set forth

in this Convention and in other international human rights or humanitarian instruments to which the said States are Parties.

2.   For this purpose, States Parties shall provide, as they consider appropriate, co-operation in any efforts by the United Nations and other competent intergovernmental organizations or non-governmental organizations co-operating with the United Nations to protect and assist such a child and to trace the parents or other members of the family of any refugee child in order to obtain information necessary for reunification with his or her family. In cases where no parents or other members of the family can be found, the child shall be accorded the same protection as any other child permanently or temporarily deprived of his or her family environment for any reason, as set forth in the present Convention.

Article 23

1.   States Parties recognize that a mentally or physically disabled child should enjoy a full and decent life, in conditions which ensure dignity, promote self-reliance and facilitate the child's active participation in the community.

2.   States Parties recognize the right of the disabled child to special care and shall encourage and ensure the extension, subject to available resources, to the eligible child and those responsible for his or her care, of assistance for which application is made and which is appropriate to the child's condition and to the circumstances of the parents or others caring for the child.

3.   Recognizing the special needs of a disabled child, assistance extended in accordance with paragraph 2 of the present article shall be provided free of charge, whenever possible, taking into account the financial resources of the parents or others caring for the child, and shall be designed to ensure that the disabled child has effective access to and receives education, training, health care services, rehabilitation services, preparation for employment and recreation opportunities in a manner conducive to the child's achieving the fullest possible social integration and individual development, including his or her cultural and spiritual development.

4.   States Parties shall promote, in the spirit of international co-operation, the exchange of appropriate information in the field of preventive health care and of medical, psychological and functional treatment of disabled children, including dissemination of and access to information concerning methods of rehabilitation, education and vocational services, with the aim of enabling States Parties to improve their capabilities and skills and to widen their experience in these areas. In this regard, particular account shall be taken of the needs of developing countries.

Article 24

1.   States Parties recognize the right of the child to the enjoyment of the highest attainable standard of health and to facilities for the treatment of illness and rehabilitation of health. States Parties shall strive to ensure that no child is deprived of his or her right of access to such health care services.

2.   States Parties shall pursue full implementation of this right and, in particular, shall take appropriate measures:

(a)   to diminish infant and child mortality;

(b)   to ensure the provision of necessary medical assistance and health care to all children with emphasis on the development of primary health care;

(c)   to combat disease and malnutrition, including within the framework of primary health care, through, *inter alia,* the application of readily available technology and through the provision of adequate nutritious foods and clean drinking-water, taking into consideration the dangers and risks of environmental pollution;

(d)   to ensure appropriate prenatal and post-natal health care for mothers;

(e)   to ensure that all segments of society, in particular parents and children, are informed, have access to education and are supported in the use of basic knowledge of child health and nutrition, the advantages of breast-feeding, hygiene and environmental sanitation and the prevention of accidents;

(f)   to develop preventive health care, guidance for parents and family planning education and services.

3.   States Parties shall take all effective and appropriate measures with a view to abolishing traditional practices prejudicial to the health of children.

4.   States Parties undertake to promote and encourage international co-operation with a view to achieving progressively the full realization of the right recognized in the present article. In this regard, particular account shall be taken of the needs of developing countries.

Article 25

States Parties recognize the right of a child who has been placed by the competent authorities for the purposes of care, protection or treatment of his or her physical or mental health, to a periodic review of the treatment provided to the child and all other circumstances relevant to his or her placement.

Article 26

1.   States Parties shall recognize for every child the right to benefit from social security, including social insurance, and shall take the necessary measures to achieve the full realization of this right in accordance with their national law.

2.   The benefits should, where appropriate, be granted, taking into account the resources and the circumstances of the child and persons having responsibility for the maintenance of the child, as well as any other consideration relevant to an application for benefits made by or on behalf of the child.

Article 27

1.   States Parties recognize the right of every child to a standard of living adequate for the child's physical, mental, spiritual, moral and social development.

2.   The parent(s) or others responsible for the child have the primary responsibility to secure, within their abilities and financial capacities, the conditions of living necessary for the child's development.

3.   States Parties, in accordance with national conditions and within their means, shall take appropriate measures to assist parents and others responsible for the child to implement this right and shall in case of need provide material assistance and support programmes, particularly with regard to nutrition, clothing and housing.

4.   States Parties shall take all appropriate measures to secure the recovery of maintenance for the child from the parents or other persons having financial responsibility for the child, both within the State Party and from abroad. In particular, where the person having financial responsibility for the child lives in a State different from that of the child, States Parties shall promote the accession to international agreements or the conclusion of such agreements, as well as the making of other appropriate arrangements.

Article 28

1.   States Parties recognize the right of the child to education, and with a view to achieving this right progressively and on the basis of equal opportunity, they shall, in particular:

(a)   make primary education compulsory and available free to all;

(b)   encourage the development of different forms of secondary education, including general and vocational education, make them available and accessible to every child, and take appropriate measures such as the introduction of free education and offering financial assistance in case of need;

(c)   make higher education accessible to all on the basis of capacity by every appropriate means;

(d)   make educational and vocational information and guidance available and accessible to all children;

(e)   take measures to encourage regular attendance at schools and the reduction of drop-out rates.

2.   States Parties shall take all appropriate measures to ensure that school discipline is administered in a manner consistent with the child's human dignity and in conformity with the present Convention.

3.   States Parties shall promote and encourage international co-operation in matters relating to education, in particular with a view to contributing to the elimination of ignorance and illiteracy throughout the world and facilitating access to scientific and technical knowledge and modern teaching methods. In this regard, particular account shall be taken of the needs of developing countries.

Article 29

1.   States Parties agree that the education of the child shall be directed to:

(a)   the development of the child's personality, talents and mental and physical abilities to their fullest potential;

(b)   the development of respect for human rights and fundamental freedoms, and for the principles enshrined in the Charter of the United Nations;

(c)   the development of respect for the child's parents, his or her own cultural identity, language and values, for the national values of the country in which the child is living, the country from which he or she may originate, and for civilizations different from his or her own;

(d)   the preparation of the child for responsible life in a free society, in the spirit of understanding, peace, tolerance, equality of sexes, and friendship among all peoples, ethnic, national and religious groups and persons of indigenous origin;

(e)   the development of respect for the natural environment.

2.   No part of the present article or article 28 shall be construed so as to interfere with the liberty of individuals and bodies to establish and direct educational institutions, subject always to the observance of the principles set forth in paragraph 1 of the present article and to the requirements that the education given in such institutions shall conform to such minimum standards as may be laid down by the State.

Article 30

In those States in which ethnic, religious or linguistic minorities or persons of indigenous origin exist, a child belonging to such a minority or who is indigenous shall not be denied the right, in community with other members of his or her group, to enjoy his or her own culture, to profess and practise his or her own religion, or to use his or her own language.

Article 31

1.   States Parties recognize the right of the child to rest and leisure, to engage in play and recreational activities appropriate to the age of the child and to participate freely in cultural life and the arts.

2.   States Parties shall respect and promote the right of the child to participate fully in cultural and artistic life and shall encourage the provision of appropriate and equal opportunities for cultural, artistic, recreational and leisure activity.

Article 32

1.   States Parties recognize the right of the child to be protected from economic exploitation and from performing any work that is likely to be hazardous or to interfere with the child's education, or to be harmful to the child's health or physical, mental, spiritual, moral or social development.

2.   States Parties shall take legislative, administrative, social and educational measures to ensure the implementation of the present article. To this end, and having

regard to the relevant provisions of other international instruments, States Parties shall in particular:

(a)   provide for a minimum age or minimum ages for admission to employment;

(b)   provide for appropriate regulation of the hours and conditions of employment;

(c)   provide for appropriate penalties or other sanctions to ensure the effective enforcement of the present article.

Article 33
States Parties shall take all appropriate measures, including legislative, administrative, social and educational measures, to protect children from the illicit use of narcotic drugs and psychotropic substances as defined in the relevant international treaties, and to prevent the use of children in the illicit production and trafficking of such substances.

Article 34
States Parties undertake to protect the child from all forms of sexual exploitation and sexual abuse. For these purposes, States Parties shall in particular take all appropriate national, bilateral and multilateral measures to prevent:

(a)   the inducement or coercion of a child to engage in any unlawful sexual activity;

(b)   the exploitative use of children in prostitution or other unlawful sexual practices;

(c)   the exploitative use of children in pornographic performances and materials.

Article 35
States Parties shall take all appropriate national, bilateral and multilateral measures to prevent the abduction of, the sale of or traffic in children for any purpose or in any form.

Article 36
States Parties shall protect the child against all other forms of exploitation prejudicial to any aspects of the child's welfare.

Article 37
States Parties shall ensure that:

(a)   no child shall be subjected to torture or other cruel, inhuman or degrading treatment or punishment. Neither capital punishment nor life imprisonment without possibility of release shall be imposed for offences committed by persons below eighteen years of age;

(b)   no child shall be deprived of his or her liberty unlawfully or arbitrarily. The arrest, detention or imprisonment of a child shall be in conformity with the law and shall be used only as a measure of last resort and for the shortest appropriate period of time;

(c)   every child deprived of liberty shall be treated with humanity and respect for the inherent dignity of the human person, and in a manner which takes into account the needs of persons of his or her age. In particular, every child deprived of liberty shall be separated from adults unless it is considered in the child's best interest not to do so and shall have the right to maintain contact with his or her family through correspondence and visits, save in exceptional circumstances;

(d)   every child deprived of his or her liberty shall have the right to prompt access to legal and other appropriate assistance, as well as the right to challenge the legality of the deprivation of his or her liberty before a court or other competent, independent and impartial authority, and to a prompt decision on any such action.

Article 38

1. States Parties undertake to respect and to ensure respect for rules of international humanitarian law applicable to them in armed conflicts which are relevant to the child.

2. States Parties shall take all feasible measures to ensure that persons who have not attained the age of fifteen years do not take a direct part in hostilities.

3. States Parties shall refrain from recruiting any person who has not attained the age of fifteen years into their armed forces. In recruiting among those persons who have attained the age of fifteen years but who have not attained the age of eighteen years, States Parties shall endeavour to give priority to those who are oldest.

4. In accordance with their obligations under international humanitarian law to protect the civilian population in armed conflicts, States Parties shall take all feasible measures to ensure protection and care of children who are affected by an armed conflict.

Article 39

States Parties shall take all appropriate measures to promote physical and psychological recovery and social reintegration of a child victim of: any form of neglect, exploitation, or abuse; torture or any other form of cruel, inhuman or degrading treatment or punishment; or armed conflicts. Such recovery and reintegration shall take place in an environment which fosters the health, self-respect and dignity of the child.

Article 40

1. States Parties recognize the right of every child alleged as, accused of, or recognized as having infringed the penal law to be treated in a manner consistent with the promotion of the child's sense of dignity and worth, which reinforces the child's respect for the human rights and fundamental freedoms of others and which takes into account the child's age and the desirability of promoting the child's reintegration and the child's assuming a constructive role in society.

2. To this end, and having regard to the relevant provisions of international instruments, States Parties shall, in particular, ensure that:

(a) no child shall be alleged as, be accused of, or recognized as having infringed the penal law by reason of acts or omissions that were not prohibited by national or international law at the time they were committed;

(b) every child alleged as or accused of having infringed the penal law has at least the following guarantees:

(i) to be presumed innocent until proven guilty according to law;

(ii) to be informed promptly and directly of the charges against him or her, and, if appropriate, through his or her parents or legal guardians, and to have legal or other appropriate assistance in the preparation and presentation of his or her defence;

(iii) to have the matter determined without delay by a competent, independent and impartial authority or judicial body in a fair hearing according to law, in the presence of legal or other appropriate assistance and, unless it is considered not to be in the best interest of the child, in particular, taking into account his or her age or situation, his or her parents or legal guardians;

(iv) not to be compelled to give testimony or to confess guilt; to examine or have examined adverse witnesses and to obtain the participation and examination of witnesses on his or her behalf under conditions of equality;

(v) if considered to have infringed the penal law, to have this decision and any measures imposed in consequence thereof reviewed by a higher competent, independent and impartial authority or judicial body according to law;

(vi) to have the free assistance of an interpreter if the child cannot understand or speak the language used;

(vii)   to have his or her privacy fully respected at all stages of the proceedings.

3.   States Parties shall seek to promote the establishment of laws, procedures, authorities and institutions specifically applicable to children alleged as, accused of, or recognized as having infringed the penal law, and, in particular:

(a)   the establishment of a minimum age below which children shall be presumed not to have the capacity to infringe the penal law;

(b)   whenever appropriate and desirable, measures for dealing with such children without resorting to judicial proceedings, providing that human rights and legal safeguards are fully respected.

4.   A variety of dispositions, such as care, guidance and supervision orders; counselling; probation; foster care; education and vocational training programmes and other alternatives to institutional care shall be available to ensure that children are dealt with in a manner appropriate to their well-being and proportionate both to their circumstances and the offence.

Article 41

Nothing in the present Convention shall affect any provisions which are more conducive to the realization of the rights of the child and which may be contained in:

(a)   the law of a State Party; or

(b)   international law in force for that State.

PART II

Article 42

States Parties undertake to make the principles and provisions of the Convention widely known, by appropriate and active means, to adults and children alike.

Article 43

1.   For the purpose of examining the progress made by States Parties in achieving the realization of the obligations undertaken in the present Convention, there shall be established a Committee on the Rights of the Child, which shall carry out the functions hereinafter provided.

2.   The Committee shall consist of ten experts of high moral standing and recognized competence in the field covered by this Convention. The members of the Committee shall be elected by States Parties from among their nationals and shall serve in their personal capacity, consideration being given to equitable geographical distribution, as well as to the principal legal systems.

3.   The members of the Committee shall be elected by secret ballot from a list of persons nominated by States Parties. Each State Party may nominate one person from among its own nationals.

4.   The initial election to the Committee shall be held no later than six months after the date of the entry into force of the present Convention and thereafter every second year. At least four months before the date of each election, the Secretary-General of the United Nations shall address a letter to States Parties inviting them to submit their nominations within two months. The Secretary-General shall subsequently prepare a list in alphabetical order of all persons thus nominated, indicating States Parties which have nominated them, and shall submit it to the States Parties to the present Convention.

5.   The elections shall be held at meetings of States Parties convened by the Secretary-General at United Nations Headquarters. At those meetings, for which two thirds of States Parties shall constitute a quorum, the persons elected to the Committee shall be those who obtain the largest number of votes and an absolute majority of the votes of the representatives of States Parties present and voting.

6.   The members of the Committee shall be elected for a term of four years. They shall be eligible for re-election if renominated. The term of five of the members elected

at the first election shall expire at the end of two years; immediately after the first election, the names of these five members shall be chosen by lot by the Chairman of the meeting.

7.   If a member of the Committee dies or resigns or declares that for any other cause he or she can no longer perform the duties of the Committee, the State Party which nominated the member shall appoint another expert from among its nationals to serve for the remainder of the term, subject to the approval of the Committee.

8.   The Committee shall establish its own rules of procedure.

9.   The Committee shall elect its officers for a period of two years.

10.   The meetings of the Committee shall normally be held at United Nations Headquarters or at any other convenient place as determined by the Committee. The Committee shall normally meet annually. The duration of the meetings of the Committee shall be determined, and reviewed, if necessary, by a meeting of the States Parties to the present Convention, subject to the approval of the General Assembly.

11.   The Secretary-General of the United Nations shall provide the necessary staff and facilities for the effective performance of the functions of the Committee under the present Convention.

12.   With the approval of the General Assembly, the members of the Committee established under the present Convention shall receive emoluments from United Nations resources on such terms and conditions as the Assembly may decide.

Article 44

1.   States Parties undertake to submit to the Committee, through the Secretary-General of the United Nations, reports on the measures they have adopted which give effect to the rights recognized herein and on the progress made on the enjoyment of those rights:

(a)   within two years of the entry into force of the Convention for the State Party concerned;

(b)   thereafter every five years.

2.   Reports made under the present article shall indicate factors and difficulties, if any, affecting the degree of fulfilment of the obligations under the present Convention. Reports shall also contain sufficient information to provide the Committee with a comprehensive understanding of the implementation of the Convention in the country concerned.

3.   A State Party which has submitted a comprehensive initial report to the Committee need not, in its subsequent reports submitted in accordance with paragraph 1 (b) of the present article, repeat basic information previously provided.

4.   The Committee may request from States Parties further information relevant to the implementation of the Convention.

5.   The Committee shall submit to the General Assembly, through the Economic and Social Council, every two years, reports on its activities.

6.   States Parties shall make their reports widely available to the public in their own countries.

Article 45

In order to foster the effective implementation of the Convention and to encourage international co-operation in the field covered by the Convention:

(a)   the specialized agencies, the United Nations Children's Fund, and other United Nations organs shall be entitled to be represented at the consideration of the implementation of such provisions of the present Convention as fall within the scope of their mandate. The Committee may invite the specialized agencies, the United Nations Children's Fund and other competent bodies as it may consider appropriate to provide expert advice on the implementation of the Convention in areas falling within the scope of their respective mandates. The Committee may invite the specialized agencies, the United Nations Children's Fund, and other United Nations organs to submit reports on the implementation of the Convention in areas falling within the scope of their activities;

(b)   the Committee shall transmit, as it may consider appropriate, to the specialized agencies, the United Nations Children's Fund and other competent bodies, any reports from States Parties that contain a request, or indicate a need, for technical advice or assistance, along with the Committee's observations and suggestions, if any, on these requests or indications;

(c)   the Committee may recommend to the General Assembly to request the Secretary-General to undertake on its behalf studies on specific issues relating to the rights of the child;

(d)   the Committee may make suggestions and general recommendations based on information received pursuant to articles 44 and 45 of the present Convention. Such suggestions and general recommendations shall be transmitted to any State Party concerned and reported to the General Assembly, together with comments, if any, from States Parties.

PART III

Article 46
The present Convention shall be open for signature by all States.

Article 47
The present Convention is subject to ratification. Instruments of ratification shall be deposited with the Secretary-General of the United Nations.

Article 48
The present Convention shall remain open for accession by any State. The instruments of accession shall be deposited with the Secretary-General of the United Nations.

Article 49
1.   The present Convention shall enter into force on the thirtieth day following the date of deposit with the Secretary-General of the United Nations of the twentieth instrument of ratification or accession.

2.   For each State ratifying or acceding to the Convention after the deposit of the twentieth instrument of ratification or accession, the Convention shall enter into force on the thirtieth day after the deposit by such State of its instrument of ratification or accession.

Article 50
1.   Any State Party may propose an amendment and file it with the Secretary-General of the United Nations. The Secretary-General shall thereupon communicate the proposed amendment to States Parties, with a request that they indicate whether they favour a conference of States Parties for the purpose of considering and voting upon the proposals. In the event that, within four months from the date of such communication, at least one third of the States Parties favour such a conference, the Secretary-General shall convene the conference under the auspices of the United Nations. Any amendment adopted by a majority of States Parties present and voting at the conference shall be submitted to the General Assembly for approval.

2.   An amendment adopted in accordance with paragraph 1 of the present article shall enter into force when it has been approved by the General Assembly of the United Nations and accepted by a two-thirds majority of States Parties.

3.   When an amendment enters into force, it shall be binding on those States Parties which have accepted it, other States Parties still being bound by the provisions of the present Convention and any earlier amendments which they have accepted.

Article 51
1.   The Secretary-General of the United Nations shall receive and circulate to all States the text of reservations made by States at the time of ratification or accession.
2.   A reservation incompatible with the object and purpose of the present Convention shall not be permitted.
3.   Reservations may be withdrawn at any time by notification to that effect addressed to the Secretary-General of the United Nations, who shall then inform all States. Such notification shall take effect on the date on which it is received by the Secretary-General.

Article 52
A State Party may denounce the present Convention by written notification to the Secretary-General of the United Nations. Denunciation becomes effective one year after the date of receipt of the notification by the Secretary-General.

Article 53
The Secretary-General of the United Nations is designated as the depositary of the present Convention.

Article 54
The original of the present Convention, of which the Arabic, Chinese, English, French, Russian and Spanish texts are equally authentic, shall be deposited with the Secretary-General of the United Nations.
   In witness thereof the undersigned plenipotentiaries, being duly authorized thereto by their respective Governments, have signed the present Convention.

DECLARATION ON THE RIGHTS OF PERSONS BELONGING TO NATIONAL OR ETHNIC, RELIGIOUS AND LINGUISTIC MINORITIES (1992)

The General Assembly,
   Reaffirming that one of the basic aims of the United Nations, as proclaimed in the Charter, is to promote and encourage respect for human rights and for fundamental freedoms for all, without distinction as to race, sex, language or religion,
   Reaffirming faith in fundamental human rights, in the dignity and worth of the human person, in the equal rights of men and women and of nations large and small,
   Desiring to promote the realization of the principles contained in the Charter, the Universal Declaration of Human Rights, the Convention on the Prevention and Punishment of the Crime of Genocide, the International Convention on the Elimination of All Forms of Racial Discrimination, the International Covenant on Civil and Political Rights, the International Covenant on Economic, Social and Cultural Rights, the Declaration on the Elimination of All Forms of Intolerance and of Discrimination Based on Religion or Belief, and the Convention on the Rights of the Child, as well as other relevant international instruments that have been adopted at the universal or regional level and those concluded between individual States Members of the United Nations,
   Inspired by the provisions of article 27 of the International Covenant on Civil and Political Rights concerning the rights of persons belonging to ethnic, religious or linguistic minorities,
   Considering that the promotion and protection of the rights of persons belonging to national or ethnic, religious and linguistic minorities contribute to the political and social stability of States in which they live,
   Emphasizing that the constant promotion and realization of the rights of persons belonging to national or ethnic, religious and linguistic minorities, as an integral part

of the development of society as a whole and within a democratic framework based on the rule of law, would contribute to the strengthening of friendship and cooperation among peoples and States,

Considering that the United Nations has an important role to play regarding the protection of minorities,

Bearing in mind the work done so far within the United Nations system, in particular by the Commission on Human Rights, the Subcommission on Prevention of Discrimination and Protection of Minorities and the bodies established pursuant to the International Covenants on Human Rights and other relevant international human rights instruments in promoting and protecting the rights of persons belonging to national or ethnic, religious and linguistic minorities,

Taking into account the important work which is done by intergovernmental and non-governmental organizations in protecting minorities and in promoting and protecting the rights of persons belonging to national or ethnic, religious and linguistic minorities,

Recognizing the need to ensure even more effective implementation of international human rights instruments with regard to the rights of persons belonging to national or ethnic, religious and linguistic minorities,

Proclaims this Declaration on the Rights of Persons Belonging to National or Ethnic, Religious and Linguistic Minorities:

Article 1

1.   States shall protect the existence and the national or ethnic, cultural, religious and linguistic identity of minorities within their respective territories and shall encourage conditions for the promotion of that identity.

2.   States shall adopt appropriate legislative and other measures to achieve those ends.

Article 2

1.   Persons belonging to national or ethnic, religious and linguistic minorities (hereinafter referred to as persons belonging to minorities) have the right to enjoy their own culture, to profess and practise their own religion, and to use their own language, in private and in public, freely and without interference or any form of discrimination.

2.   Persons belonging to minorities have the right to participate effectively in cultural, religious, social, economic and public life.

3.   Persons belonging to minorities have the right to participate effectively in decisions on the national and, where appropriate, regional level concerning the minority to which they belong or the regions in which they live, in a manner not incompatible with national legislation.

4.   Persons belonging to minorities have the right to establish and maintain their own associations.

5.   Persons belonging to minorities have the right to establish and maintain, without any discrimination, free and peaceful contacts with other members of their group and with persons belonging to other minorities, as well as contacts across frontiers with citizens of other States to whom they are related by national or ethnic, religious or linguistic ties.

Article 3

1.   Persons belonging to minorities may exercise their rights, including those set forth in the present Declaration, individually as well as in community with other members of their group, without any discrimination.

2.   No disadvantage shall result for any person belonging to a minority as the consequence of the exercise or non-exercise of the rights set forth in the present Declaration.

Article 4

1. States shall take measures where required to ensure that persons belonging to minorities may exercise fully and effectively all their human rights and fundamental freedoms without any discrimination and in full equality before the law.

2. States shall take measures to create favourable conditions to enable persons belonging to minorities to express their characteristics and to develop their culture, language, religion, traditions and customs, except where specific practices are in violation of national law and contrary to international standards.

3. States should take appropriate measures so that, wherever possible, persons belonging to minorities may have adequate opportunities to learn their mother tongue or to have instruction in their mother tongue.

4. States should, where appropriate, take measures in the field of education, in order to encourage knowledge of the history, traditions, language and culture of the minorities existing within their territory. Persons belonging to minorities should have adequate opportunities to gain knowledge of the society as a whole.

5. States should consider appropriate measures so that persons belonging to minorities may participate fully in the economic progress and development in their country.

Article 5

1. National policies and programmes shall be planned and implemented with due regard for the legitimate interests of persons belonging to minorities.

2. Programmes of cooperation and assistance among States should be planned and implemented with due regard for the legitimate interests of persons belonging to minorities.

Article 6

States should cooperate on questions relating to persons belonging to minorities, *inter alia*, exchanging information and experiences, in order to promote mutual understanding and confidence.

Article 7

States should cooperate in order to promote respect for the rights set forth in the present Declaration.

Article 8

1. Nothing in the present Declaration shall prevent the fulfilment of international obligations of States in relation to persons belonging to minorities. In particular, States shall fulfil in good faith the obligations and commitments they have assumed under international treaties and agreements to which they are parties.

2. The exercise of the rights set forth in the present Declaration shall not prejudice the enjoyment by all persons of universally recognized human rights and fundamental freedoms.

3. Measures taken by States to ensure the effective enjoyment of the rights set forth in the present Declaration shall not *prima facie* be considered contrary to the principle of equality contained in the Universal Declaration of Human Rights.

4. Nothing in the present Declaration may be construed as permitting any activity contrary to the purposes and principles of the United Nations, including sovereign equality, territorial integrity and political independence of States.

Article 9

The specialized agencies and other organizations of the United Nations system shall contribute to the full realization of the rights and principles set forth in the present Declaration, within their respective fields of competence.

UNITED NATIONS PROCEDURE FOR HANDLING HUMAN RIGHTS COMPLAINTS

RESOLUTION 728 F (XXVIII) OF THE ECONOMIC AND SOCIAL COUNCIL

COMMUNICATIONS CONCERNING HUMAN RIGHTS

The Economic and Social Council,

Having considered chapter V of the report of the Commission on Human Rights at its first session, concerning communications, and chapter IX of the report of the Commission on its fifteenth session,

1. *Approves* the statement that the Commission on Human Rights recognizes that it has no power to take any action in regard to any complaints concerning human rights;

2. *Requests* the Secretary-General:

(a) To compile and distribute to members of the Commission on Human Rights before each session a non-confidential list containing a brief indication of the substance of each communication, however addressed, which deals with the principles involved in the promotion of universal respect for, and observance of, human rights and to divulge the identity of the authors of such communications unless they indicate that they wish their names to remain confidential;

(b) To compile before each session of the Commission a confidential list containing a brief indication of the substance of other communications concerning human rights, however addressed, and to furnish this list to members of the Commission, in private meeting, without divulging the identity of the authors of communications except in cases where the authors state that they have already divulged or intend to divulge their names or that they have no objection to their names being divulged;

(c) To enable the members of the Commission, upon request, to consult the originals of communications dealing with the principles involved in the promotion of universal respect for, and observance of, human rights;

(d) To inform the writers of all communications concerning human rights, however addressed, that their communications will be handled in accordance with this resolution, indicating that the Commission has no power to take any action in regard to any complaint concerning human rights;

(e) To furnish each Member State concerned with a copy of any communication concerning human rights which refers explicitly to that State or to territories under its jurisdiction, without divulging the identity of the author, except as provided for in sub-paragraph (b) above;

(f) To ask Governments sending replies to communications brought to their attention in accordance with sub-paragraph (e) whether they wish their replies to be presented to the Commission in summary form or in full;

3. *Resolves* to give members of the Sub-Commission on Prevention of Discrimination and Protection of Minorities, with respect to communications dealing with discrimination and minorities, the same facilities as are enjoyed by members of the Commission on Human Rights under the present resolution;

4. *Suggests* to the Commission on Human Rights that it should at each session appoint an *ad hoc* committee to meet shortly before its next session for the purpose of reviewing the list of communications prepared by the Secretary-General under paragraph 2 (a) above and of recommending which of these communications, in

original, should, in accordance with paragraph 2 (c) above, be made available to members of the Commission on request.

1088 plenary meeting,
30 July 1959.

RESOLUTION 1235 (XLII) OF THE ECONOMIC AND SOCIAL COUNCIL

Question of the violation of human rights and fundamental freedoms, including policies of racial discrimination and segregation and of apartheid, in all countries, with particular reference to colonial and other dependent countries and territories
The Economic and Social Council,
    Noting resolutions 8 (XXIII) and 9 (XXIII) of the Commission on Human Rights,
    1. *Welcomes* the decision of the Commission on Human Rights to give annual consideration to the item entitled 'Question of the violation of human rights and fundamental freedoms, including policies of racial discrimination and segregation and of apartheid, in all countries, with particular reference to colonial and other dependent countries and territories,' without prejudice to the functions and powers of organs already in existence or which may be established within the framework of measures of implementation included in international covenants and conventions on the protection of human rights and fundamental freedoms, and concurs with the requests for assistance addressed to the Sub-Commission on Prevention of Discrimination and Protection of Minorities and to the Secretary-General;
    2. *Authorizes* the Commission on Human Rights and the Sub-Commission on Prevention of Discrimination and Protection of Minorities, in conformity with the provisions of paragraph 1 of the Commission's resolution 8 (XXIII), to examine information relevant to gross violations of human rights and fundamental freedoms, as exemplified by the policy of apartheid as practised in the Republic of South Africa and the Territory of South West Africa under the direct responsibility of the United Nations and now illegally occupied by the Government of South Africa, and to racial discrimination as practised notably in Southern Rhodesia, contained in the communications listed by the Secretary-General pursuant to Economic and Social Council resolution 728 F (XXVIII) of 30 July 1959;
    3. *Decides* that the Commission on Human Rights may, in appropriate cases, and after careful consideration of the information thus made available to it, in conformity with the provisions of paragraph 1 above, make a thorough study of situations which reveal a consistent pattern of violations of human rights, as exemplified by the policy of apartheid as practised in the Republic of South Africa and the Territory of South West Africa under the direct responsibility of the United Nations and now illegally occupied by the Government of South Africa, and racial discrimination as practised notably in Southern Rhodesia, and report, with recommendations thereon, to the Economic and Social Council;
    4. *Decides* to review the provisions of paragraphs 2 and 3 of the present resolution after the entry into force of the International Covenants on Human Rights;
    5. *Takes note* of the fact that the Commission on Human Rights, in its resolution 6 (XXIII), has instructed an *ad hoc* study group to study in all its aspects the question of the ways and means by which the Commission might be enabled or assisted to discharge functions in relation to violations of human rights and fundamental freedoms, whilst maintaining and fulfilling its other functions;
    6. *Requests* the Commission on Human Rights to report to it on the result of this study after having given consideration to the conclusions of the *ad hoc* study group referred to in paragraph 5 above.

1479th plenary meeting,
6 June 1967

RESOLUTION 1503 (XLVIII) OF THE ECONOMIC AND SOCIAL COUNCIL

PROCEDURE FOR DEALING WITH COMMUNICATIONS RELATING TO VIOLATIONS OF HUMAN RIGHTS AND FUNDAMENTAL FREEDOMS

The Economic and Social Council,

Noting resolutions 7 (XXVI) and 17 (XXV) of the Commission on Human Rights and resolution 2 (XXI) of the Sub-Commission on Prevention of Discrimination and Protection of Minorities,

1. *Authorizes* the Sub-Commission on Prevention of Discrimination and Protection of Minorities to appoint a working group consisting of not more than five of its members, with due regard to geographical distribution, to meet once a year in private meetings for a period not exceeding ten days immediately before the sessions of the Sub-Commission to consider all communications, including replies of Governments thereon, received by the Secretary-General under Council resolution 728 F (XXVIII) of 30 July 1959 with a view to bringing to the attention of the Sub-Commission those communications, together with replies of Governments, if any, which appear to reveal a consistent pattern of gross and reliably attested violations of human rights and fundamental freedoms within the terms of reference of the Sub-Commission;

2. *Decides* that the Sub-Commission on Prevention of Discrimination and Protection of Minorities should, as the first stage in the implementation of the present resolution, devise at its twenty-third session appropriate procedures for dealing with the question of admissibility of communications received by the Secretary-General under Council resolution 728 F (XXVIII) and in accordance with Council resolution 1235 (XLII) of 6 June 1967;

3. *Requests* the Secretary-General to prepare a document on the question of admissibility of communications for the Sub-Commission's consideration at its twenty-third session;

4. *Further requests* the Secretary-General:

(a) To furnish to the members of the Sub-Commission every month a list of communications prepared by him in accordance with Council resolution 728 F (XXVIII) and a brief description of them, together with the text of any replies received from Governments;

(b) To make available to the members of the working group at their meetings the originals of such communications listed as they may request, having due regard to the provisions of paragraph 2 (*b*) of Council resolution 728 F (XXVIII) concerning the divulging of the identity of the authors of communications;

(c) To circulate to the members of the Sub-Commission, in the working languages, the originals of such communications as are referred to the Sub-Commission by the working group;

5. *Requests* the Sub-Commission on Prevention of Discrimination and Protection of Minorities to consider in private meetings, in accordance with paragraph 1 above, the communications brought before it in accordance with the decision of a majority of the members of the working group and any replies of Governments relating thereto and other relevant information, with a view to determining whether to refer to the Commission on Human Rights particular situations which appear to reveal a consistent pattern of gross and reliably attested violations of human rights requiring consideration by the Commission;

6. *Requests* the Commission on Human Rights after it has examined any situation referred to it by the Sub-Commission to determine:

(a) Whether it requires a thorough study by the Commission and a report and recommendations thereon to the Council in accordance with paragraph 3 of Council resolution 1235 (XLII);

(b)   Whether it may be a subject of an investigation by an *ad hoc* committee to be appointed by the Commission which shall be undertaken only with the express consent of the State concerned and shall be conducted in constant co-operation with that State and under conditions determined by agreement with it. In any event, the investigation may be undertaken only if:

(i)   All available means at the national level have been resorted to and exhausted;

(ii)   The situation does not relate to a matter which is being dealt with under other procedures prescribed in the constituent instruments of, or conventions adopted by, the United Nations and the specialized agencies, or in regional conventions, or which the State concerned wishes to submit to other procedures in accordance with general or special international agreements to which it is a party.

7.   *Decides* that if the Commission on Human Rights appoints an *ad hoc* committee to carry on an investigation with the consent of the State concerned:

(a)   The composition of the committee shall be determined by the Commission. The members of the committee shall be independent persons whose competence and impartiality is beyond question. Their appointment shall be subject to the consent of the Government concerned;

(b)   The committee shall establish its own rules of procedure. It shall be subject to the quorum rule. It shall have authority to receive communications and hear witnesses, as necessary. The investigation shall be conducted in co-operation with the Government concerned;

(c)   The committee's procedure shall be confidential, its proceedings shall be conducted in private meetings and its communications shall not be publicized in any way;

(d)   The committee shall strive for friendly solutions before, during and even after the investigation;

(e)   The committee shall report to the Commission on Human Rights with such observations and suggestions as it may deem appropriate;

8.   *Decides* that all actions envisaged in the implementation of the present resolution by the Sub-Commission on Prevention of Discrimination and Protection of Minorities or the Commission on Human Rights shall remain confidential until such time as the Commission may decide to make recommendations to the Economic and Social Council;

9.   *Decides* to authorize the Secretary-General to provide all facilities which may be required to carry out the present resolution, making use of the existing staff of the Division of Human Rights of the United Nations Secretariat;

10.   *Decides* that the procedure set out in the present resolution for dealing with communications relating to violations of human rights and fundamental freedoms should be reviewed if any new organ entitled to deal with such communications should be established within the United Nations or by international agreement.

1693rd plenary meeting,
27 May 1970.

RESOLUTION 1 (XXIV) OF THE SUB-COMMISSION ON PREVENTION OF DISCRIMINATION AND PROTECTION OF MINORITIES

QUESTION OF THE VIOLATION OF HUMAN RIGHTS AND FUNDAMENTAL FREEDOMS, INCLUDING POLICIES OF RACIAL DISCRIMINATION AND SEGREGATION AND OF APARTHEID IN ALL COUNTRIES, WITH PARTICULAR REFERENCE TO COLONIAL AND OTHER DEPENDENT COUNTRIES AND TERRITORIES

The Sub-Commission on Prevention of Discrimination and Protection of Minorities

Considering that the Economic and Social Council, by its resolution 1503 (XLVIII), decided that the Sub-Commission should devise appropriate procedures for dealing with the question of admissibility of communications received by the Secretary-General under Council resolution 728 F (XXVIII) of 30 July 1959 and in accordance with Council resolution 1235 (XLII) of 6 June 1967,

Adopts the following provisional procedures for dealing with the question of admissibility of communications referred to above:

1. *Standards and criteria*

(a) The object of the communication must not be inconsistent with the relevant principles of the Charter, of the Universal Declaration of Human Rights and of the other applicable instruments in the field of human rights.

(b) Communications shall be admissible only if, after consideration thereof, together with the replies if any of the Governments concerned, there are reasonable grounds to believe that they may reveal a consistent pattern of gross and reliably attested violations of human rights and fundamental freedoms, including policies of racial discrimination and segregation and of *apartheid* in any country, including colonial and other dependent countries and peoples.

2. *Source of communications*

(a) Admissible communications may originate from a person or group of persons who, it can be reasonably presumed, are victims of the violations referred to in subparagraph 1. (b) above, any person or group of persons who have direct and reliable knowledge of those violations, or non-governmental organizations acting in good faith in accordance with recognized principles of human rights, not resorting to politically motivated stands contrary to the provisions of the Charter of the United Nations and having direct and reliable knowledge of such violations.

(b) Anonymous communications shall be inadmissible; subject to the requirements of subparagraph 2. (b) of resolution 728 F (XXVIII) of the Economic and Social Council, the author of a communication, whether an individual, a group of individuals or an organization, must be clearly identified.

(c) Communications shall not be inadmissible solely because the knowledge of the individual authors is second-hand, provided that they are accompanied by clear evidence.

3. *Contents of communications and nature of allegations*

(a) The communication must contain a description of the facts and must indicate the purpose of the petition and the rights that have been violated.

(b) Communications shall be inadmissible if their language is essentially abusive and in particular if they contain insulting references to the State against which the complaint is directed. Such communications may be considered if they meet the other criteria for admissibility after deletion of the abusive language.

(c) A communication shall be inadmissible if it has manifestly political motivations and its subject is contrary to the provisions of the Charter of the United Nations.

(d) A communication shall be inadmissible if it appears that it is based exclusively on reports disseminated by mass media.

4. *Existence of other remedies*

(a) Communications shall be inadmissible if their admission would prejudice the functions of the specialized agencies of the United Nations system.

(b) Communications shall be inadmissible if domestic remedies have not been exhausted, unless it appears that such remedies would be ineffective or unreasonably prolonged. Any failure to exhaust remedies should be satisfactorily established.

(c) Communications relating to cases which have been settled by the States concerned in accordance with the principles set forth in the Universal Declaration of Human Rights and other applicable documents in the field of human rights will not be considered.

5. *Timeliness*

A communication shall be inadmissible if it is not submitted to the United Nations within a reasonable time after the exhaustion of the domestic remedies as provided above.

627th meeting,
13 August 1971

REGIONAL INSTRUMENTS

EUROPE

CONVENTION FOR THE PROTECTION OF HUMAN RIGHTS AND FUNDAMENTAL FREEDOMS (1950)[1]

The Governments signatory hereto, being Members of the Council of Europe,
Considering the Universal Declaration of Human Rights proclaimed by the General Assembly of the United Nations on 10th December 1948;
Considering that this Declaration aims at securing the universal and effective recognition and observance of the rights therein declared;
Considering that the aim of the Council of Europe is the achievement of greater unity between its members and that one of the methods by which that aim is to be pursued is the maintenance and further realisation of human rights and fundamental freedoms;
Reaffirming their profound belief in those fundamental freedoms which are the foundation of justice and peace in the world and are best maintained on the one hand by an effective political democracy and on the other by a common understanding and observance of the human rights upon which they depend;
Being resolved, as the governments of European countries which are likeminded and have a common heritage of political traditions, ideals, freedom and the rule of law to take the first steps for the collective enforcement of certain of the rights stated in the Universal Declaration,
Have agreed as follows;

Article 1   Obligation to respect human rights
The High Contracting Parties shall secure to everyone within their jurisdiction the rights and freedoms defined in Section I of this Convention.

SECTION I   RIGHTS AND FREEDOMS

Article 2   Right to life
1.   Everyone's right to life shall be protected by law. No one shall be deprived of his life intentionally save in the execution of a sentence of a court following his conviction of a crime for which this penalty is provided by law.
2.   Deprivation of life shall not be regarded as inflicted in contravention of this Article when it results from the use of force which is no more than absolutely necessary:
   (a)   in defence of any person from unlawful violence;
   (b)   in order to effect a lawful arrest or to prevent the escape of a person lawfully detained;
   (c)   in action lawfully taken for the purpose of quelling a riot or insurrection.

Article 3   Prohibition of torture
No one shall be subjected to torture or to inhuman or degrading treatment or punishment.

Article 4   Prohibition of slavery and forced labour
1.   No one shall be held in slavery or servitude.
2.   No one shall be required to perform forced or compulsory labour.
3.   For the purpose of this Article the term 'forced or compulsory labour' shall not include:

---

[1]As amended by Protocols Nos. 3, 5, 8 and 11 the first three of which entered into force on 21 September 1970, 20 December 1971 and 1 January 1990 respectively. Protocol No. 11 was concluded on 11 May 1994.

(a)   any work required to be done in the ordinary course of detention imposed according to the provisions of Article 5 of this Convention or during conditional release from such detention;

(b)   any service of a military character or, in case of conscientious objectors in countries where they are recognised, service exacted instead of compulsory military service;

(c)   any service exacted in case of an emergency or calamity threatening the life or well-being of the community;

(d)   any work or service which forms part of normal civic obligations.

Article 5   Right to liberty and security

1.   Everyone has the right to liberty and security of person. No one shall be deprived of his liberty save in the following cases and in accordance with a procedure prescribed by law:

(a)   the lawful detention of a person after conviction by a competent court;

(b)   the lawful arrest or detention of a person for non-compliance with the lawful order of a court or in order to secure the fulfilment of any obligation prescribed by law;

(c)   the lawful arrest or detention of a person effected for the purpose of bringing him before the competent legal authority on reasonable suspicion of having committed an offence or when it is reasonably considered necessary to prevent his committing an offence or fleeing after having done so;

(d)   the detention of a minor by lawful order for the purpose of educational supervision or his lawful detention for the purpose of bringing him before the competent legal authority;

(e)   the lawful detention of persons for the prevention of the spreading of infectious diseases, of persons of unsound mind, alcoholics or drug addicts or vagrants;

(f)   the lawful arrest or detention of a person to prevent his effecting an unauthorised entry into the country or of a person against whom action is being taken with a view to deportation or extradition.

2.   Everyone who is arrested shall be informed promptly, in a language which he understands, of the reasons for his arrest and of any charge against him.

3.   Everyone arrested or detained in accordance with the provisions of paragraph 1 (c) of this Article shall be brought promptly before a judge or other officer authorised by law to exercise judicial power and shall be entitled to trial within a reasonable time or to release pending trial. Release may be conditioned by guarantees to appear for trial.

4.   Everyone who is deprived of his liberty by arrest or detention shall be entitled to take proceedings by which the lawfulness of his detention shall be decided speedily by a court and his release ordered if the detention is not lawful.

5.   Everyone who has been the victim of arrest or detention in contravention of the provisions of this Article shall have an enforceable right to compensation.

Article 6   Right to a fair trial

1.   In the determination of his civil rights and obligations or of any criminal charge against him, everyone is entitled to a fair and public hearing within a reasonable time by an independent and impartial tribunal established by law. Judgment shall be pronounced publicly but the press and public may be excluded from all or part of the trial in the interests of morals, public order or national security in a democratic society, where the interests of juveniles or the protection of the private life of the parties so require, or to the extent strictly necessary in the opinion of the court in special circumstances where publicity would prejudice the interests of justice.

2.   Everyone charged with a criminal offence shall be presumed innocent until proved guilty according to law.

3.   Everyone charged with a criminal offence has the following minimum rights:
   (a)   to be informed promptly, in a language which he understands and in detail, of the nature and cause of the accusation against him;
   (b)   to have adequate time and facilities for the preparation of his defence;
   (c)   to defend himself in person or through legal assistance of his own choosing or, if he has not sufficient means to pay for legal assistance, to be given it free when the interests of justice so require;
   (d)   to examine or have examined witnesses against him and to obtain the attendance and examination of witnesses on his behalf under the same conditions as witnesses against him;
   (e)   to have the free assistance of an interpreter if he cannot understand or speak the language used in court.

Article 7   No punishment without law

1.   No one shall be held guilty of any criminal offence on account of any act or omission which did not constitute a criminal offence under national or international law at the time when it was committed. Nor shall a heavier penalty be imposed than the one that was applicable at the time the criminal offence was committed.

2.   This Article shall not prejudice the trial and punishment of any person for any act or omission which, at the time when it was committed, was criminal according to the general principles of law recognised by civilised nations.

Article 8   Right to respect for family and private life

1.   Everyone has the right to respect for his private and family life, his home and his correspondence.

2.   There shall be no interference by a public authority with the exercise of this right except such as is in accordance with the law and is necessary in a democratic society in the interests of national security, public safety or the economic well-being of the country, for the prevention of disorder or crime, for the protection of health or morals, or for the protection of the rights and freedoms of others.

Article 9   Freedom of thought, conscience and religion

1.   Everyone has the right to freedom of thought, conscience and religion; this right includes freedom to change his religion or belief and freedom, either alone or in community with others and in public or private, to manifest his religion or belief, in worship, teaching, practice and observance.

2.   Freedom to manifest one's religion or beliefs shall be subject only to such limitations as are prescribed by law and are necessary in a democratic society in the interests of public safety, for the protection of public order, health or morals, or for the protection of the rights and freedoms of others.

Article 10   Freedom of expression

1.   Everyone has the right to freedom of expression. This right shall include freedom to hold opinions and to receive and impart information and ideas without interference by public authority and regardless of frontiers. This Article shall not prevent States from requiring the licensing of broadcasting, television or cinema enterprises.

2.   The exercise of these freedoms, since it carries with it duties and responsibilities, may be subject to such formalities, conditions, restrictions or penalties as are prescribed by law and are necessary in a democratic society, in the interests of national security, territorial integrity or public safety, for the prevention of disorder or crime, for the protection of health or morals, for the protection of the reputation or rights of others, for preventing the disclosure of information received in confidence, or for maintaining the authority and impartiality of the judiciary.

Article 11   Freedom of assembly and association

1.   Everyone has the right to freedom of peaceful assembly and to freedom of association with others, including the right to form and to join trade unions for the protection of his interests.

2.   No restrictions shall be placed on the exercise of these rights other than such as are prescribed by law and are necessary in a democratic society in the interests of national security or public safety, for the prevention of disorder or crime, for the protection of health or morals or for the protection of the rights and freedoms of others. This Article shall not prevent the imposition of lawful restrictions on the exercise of these rights by members of the armed forces, of the police or of the administration of the State.

Article 12   Right to marry

Men and women of marriageable age have the right to marry and to found a family, according to the national laws governing the exercise of this right.

Article 13   Right to an effective remedy

Everyone whose rights and freedoms as set forth in this Convention are violated shall have an effective remedy before a national authority notwithstanding that the violation has been committed by persons acting in an official capacity.

Article 14   Prohibition of discrimination

The enjoyment of the rights and freedoms set forth in this Convention shall be secured without discrimination on any ground such as sex, race, colour, language, religion, political or other opinion, national or social origin, association with a national minority, property, birth or other status.

Article 15   Derogation in time of emergency

1.   In time of war or other public emergency threatening the life of the nation any High Contracting Party may take measures derogating from its obligations under this Convention to the extent strictly required by the exigencies of the situation, provided that such measures are not inconsistent with its other obligations under international law.

2.   No derogation from Article 2, except in respect of deaths resulting from lawful acts of war, or from Articles 3, 4 (paragraph 1) and 7 shall be made under this provision.

3.   Any High Contracting Party availing itself of this right of derogation shall keep the Secretary-General of the Council of Europe fully informed of the measures which it has taken and the reasons therefor. It shall also inform the Secretary-General of the Council of Europe when such measures have ceased to operate and the provisions of the Convention are again being fully executed.

Article 16   Restrictions on political activity of aliens

Nothing in Articles 10, 11 and 14 shall be regarded as preventing the High Contracting Parties from imposing restrictions on the political activity of aliens.

Article 17   Prohibition of abuse of rights

Nothing in this Convention may be interpreted as implying for any State, group or person any right to engage in any activity or perform any act aimed at the destruction of any of the rights and freedoms set forth herein or at their limitation to a greater extent than is provided for in the Convention.

Article 18   Limitation on use of restrictions on rights

The restrictions permitted under this Convention to the said rights and freedoms shall not be applied for any purpose other than those for which they have been prescribed.

SECTION II   EUROPEAN COURT OF HUMAN RIGHTS

Article 19   Establishment of the Court
To ensure the observance of the engagements undertaken by the High Contracting Parties in the Convention and the protocols thereto, there shall be set up a European Court of Human Rights, hereinafter referred to as 'the Court'. It shall function on a permanent basis.

Article 20   Number of judges
The Court shall consist of a number of judges equal to that of the High Contracting Parties.

Article 21   Criteria for office
1.   The judges shall be of high moral character and must either possess the qualifications required for appointment to high judicial office or be jurisconsults of recognised competence.
2.   The judges shall sit on the Court in their individual capacity.
3.   During their term of office the judges shall not engage in any activity which is incompatible with their independence, impartiality or with the demands of a full-time office; all questions arising from the application of this paragraph shall be decided by the Court.

Article 22   Election of judges
1.   The judges shall be elected by the Parliamentary Assembly with respect to each High Contracting Party by a majority of votes cast from a list of three candidates nominated by the High Contracting Party.
2.   The same procedure shall be followed to complete the Court in the event of the accession of new High Contracting Parties and in filling casual vacancies.

Article 23   Terms of office
1.   The judges shall be elected for a period of six years. They may be re-elected. However, the terms of office of one-half of the judges elected at the first election shall expire at the end of three years.
2.   The judges whose terms of office are to expire at the end of the initial period of three years shall be chosen by lot by the Secretary-General of the Council of Europe immediately after their election.
3.   In order to ensure that, as far as possible, the terms of office of one-half of the judges are renewed every three years, the Parliamentary Assembly may decide, before proceeding to any subsequent election, that the term or terms of office of one or more judges to be elected shall be for a period other than six years but not more than nine and not less than three years.
4.   In cases where more than one term of office is involved and where the Parliamentary Assembly applies the preceding paragraph, the allocation of the terms of office shall be effected by a drawing of lots by the Secretary-General of the Council of Europe immediately after the election.
5.   A judge elected to replace a judge whose term of office has not expired shall hold office for the remainder of his predecessor's term.
6.   The terms of office of judges shall expire when they reach the age of 70.
7.   The judges shall hold office until replaced. They shall, however, continue to deal with such cases as they already have under consideration.

Article 24   Dismissal
No judge may be dismissed from his office unless the other judges decide by a majority of two-thirds that he has ceased to fulfil the required conditions.

Article 25   Registry and legal secretaries
The Court shall have a registry, the functions and organisation of which shall be laid down in the rules of the Court. The Court shall be assisted by legal secretaries.

Article 26   Plenary Court
The plenary Court shall:
  (a)   elect its President and one or two Vice-Presidents for a period of three years; they may be re-elected;
  (b)   set up Chambers, constituted for a fixed period of time;
  (c)   elect the Presidents of the Chambers of the Court; they may be re-elected;
  (d)   adopt the rules of the Court; and
  (e)   elect the Registrar and one or more Deputy Registrars.

Article 27   Committees, Chambers and Grand Chamber
  1.   To consider cases brought before it, the Court shall sit in committees of three judges, in Chambers of seven judges and in a Grand Chamber of seventeen judges. The Court's Chambers shall set up committees for a fixed period of time.
  2.   There shall sit as an *ex officio* member of the Chamber and the Grand Chamber the judge elected in respect of the State Party concerned or, if there is none or if he is unable to sit, a person of its choice who shall sit in the capacity of judge.
  3.   The Grand Chamber shall also include the President of the Court, the Vice-Presidents, the Presidents of the Chambers and other judges chosen in accordance with the rules of the Court. When a case is referred to the Grand Chamber under Article 43, no judge from the Chamber which rendered the judgment shall sit in the Grand Chamber, with the exception of the President of the Chamber and the judge who sat in respect of the State Party concerned.

Article 28   Declarations of inadmissibility by committees
A committee may, by a unanimous vote, declare inadmissible or strike out of its list of cases an individual application submitted under Article 34 where such a decision can be taken without further examination. The decision shall be final.

Article 29   Decisions by Chambers on admissibility and merits
  1.   If no decision is taken under Article 28, a Chamber shall decide on the admissibility and merits of individual applications submitted under Article 34.
  2.   A Chamber shall decide on the admissibility and merits of inter-State applications submitted under Article 33.
  3.   The decision on admissibility shall be taken separately unless the Court, in exceptional cases, decides otherwise.

Article 30   Relinquishment of jurisdiction to the Grand Chamber
Where a case pending before a Chamber raises a serious question affecting the interpretation of the Convention or the protocols thereto or where the resolution of a question before it might have a result inconsistent with a judgment previously delivered by the Court, the Chamber may, at any time before it has rendered its judgment, relinquish jurisdiction in favour of the Grand Chamber, unless one of the parties to the case objects.

Article 31   Powers of the Grand Chamber
The Grand Chamber shall:
  (a)   determine applications submitted either under Article 33 or Article 34 when a Chamber has relinquished jurisdiction under Article 30 or when the case has been referred to it under Article 43; and
  (b)   consider requests for advisory opinions submitted under Article 47.

Article 32   Jurisdiction of the Court

1.   The jurisdiction of the Court shall extend to all matters concerning the interpretation and application of the Convention and the protocols thereto which are referred to it as provided in Articles 33, 34 and 47.

2.   In the event of dispute as to whether the Court has jurisdiction, the Court shall decide.

Article 33   Inter-State cases

Any High Contracting Party may refer to the Court any alleged breach of the provisions of the Convention and the protocols thereto by another High Contracting Party.

Article 34   Individual applications

The Court may receive applications from any person, non-governmental organization or group of individuals claiming to be the victim of a violation by one of the High Contracting Parties of the rights set forth in the Convention or the protocols thereto. The High Contracting Parties undertake not to hinder in any way the effective exercise of this right.

Article 35   Admissibility criteria

1.   The Court may only deal with the matter after all domestic remedies have been exhausted, according to the generally recognised rules of international law, and within a period of six months from the date on which the final decision was taken.

2.   The Court shall not deal with any individual application submitted under Article 34 that:

    (a)   is anonymous; or

    (b)   is substantially the same as a matter that has already been examined by the Court or has already been submitted to another procedure of international investigation or settlement and contains no relevant new information.

3.   The Court shall declare inadmissible any individual application submitted under Article 34 which it considers incompatible with the provisions of the Convention or the protocols thereto, manifestly ill-founded, or an abuse of the right of application.

4.   The Court shall reject any application which it considers inadmissible under this Article. It may do so at any stage of the proceedings.

Article 36   Third-party intervention

1.   In all cases before a Chamber or the Grand Chamber, a High Contracting Party one of whose nationals is an applicant shall have the right to submit written comments and to take part in hearings.

2.   The President of the Court may, in the interest of the proper administration of justice, invite any High Contracting Party which is not a party to the proceedings or any person concerned who is not the applicant to submit written comments or take part in hearings.

Article 37   Striking out applications

1.   The Court may at any stage of the proceedings decide to strike an application out of its list of cases where the circumstances lead to the conclusion that:

    (a)   the applicant does not intend to pursue his application; or

    (b)   the matter has been resolved; or

    (c)   for any other reason established by the Court, it is no longer justified to continue the examination of the application.

However, the Court shall continue the examination of the application if respect for human rights as defined in the Convention and the protocols thereto so requires.

2.   The Court may decide to restore an application to its list of cases if it considers that the circumstances justify such a course.

Article 38   Examination of the case and friendly settlement proceedings
1.   If the Court declares the application admissible, it shall:
   (a)   pursue the examination of the case, together with the representatives of the parties, and if need be, undertake an investigation, for the effective conduct of which the States concerned shall furnish all necessary facilities;
   (b)   place itself at the disposal of the parties concerned with a view to securing a friendly settlement of the matter on the basis of respect for human rights as defined in the Convention and the protocols thereto.
2.   Proceedings conducted under paragraph 1(b) shall be confidential.

Article 39   Finding of a friendly settlement
If a friendly settlement is effected, the Court shall strike the case out of its list by means of a decision which shall be confined to a brief statement of the facts and of the solution reached.

Article 40   Public hearings and access to documents
1.   Hearings shall be public unless the Court in exceptional circumstances decides otherwise.
2.   Documents deposited with the Registrar shall be accessible to the public unless the President of the Court decides otherwise.

Article 41   Just satisfaction
If the Court finds that there has been a violation of the Convention or the protocols thereto, and if the internal law of the High Contracting Party concerned allows only partial reparation to be made, the Court shall, if necessary, afford just satisfaction to the injured party.

Article 42   Judgments of Chambers
Judgments of Chambers shall become final in accordance with the provisions of Article 44, paragraph 2.

Article 43   Referral to the Grand Chamber
1.   Within a period of three months from the date of the judgment of the Chamber, any party to the case may, in exceptional cases, request that the case be referred to the Grand Chamber.
2.   A panel of five judges of the Grand Chamber shall accept the request if the case raises a serious question affecting the interpretation or application of the Convention or the protocols thereto, or a serious issue of general importance.
3.   If the panel accepts the request, the Grand Chamber shall decide the case by means of a judgment.

Article 44   Final judgments
1.   The judgment of the Grand Chamber shall be final.
2.   The judgment of a Chamber shall become final:
   (a)   when the parties declare that they will not request that the case be referred to the Grand Chamber; or
   (b)   three months after the date of the judgment, if reference of the case to the Grand Chamber has not been requested; or
   (c)   when the panel of the Grand Chamber rejects the request to refer under Article 43.
3.   The final judgment shall be published.

Article 45   Reasons for judgments and decisions
1.   Reasons shall be given for judgments as well as for decisions declaring applications admissible or inadmissible.
2.   If a judgment does not represent, in whole or in part, the unanimous opinion of the judges, any judge shall be entitled to deliver a separate opinion.

Article 46   Binding force and execution of judgments
1.   The High Contracting Parties undertake to abide by the final judgment of the Court in any case to which they are parties.
2.   The final judgment of the Court shall be transmitted to the Committee of Ministers, which shall supervise its execution.

Article 47   Advisory opinions
1.   The Court may, at the request of the Committee of Ministers, give advisory opinions on legal questions concerning the interpretation of the Convention and the protocols thereto.
2.   Such opinions shall not deal with any question relating to the content or scope of the rights or freedoms defined in Section I of the Convention and the protocols thereto, or with any other question which the Court or the Committee of Ministers might have to consider in consequence of any such proceedings as could be instituted in accordance with the Convention.
3.   Decisions of the Committee of Ministers to request an advisory opinion of the Court shall require a majority vote of the representatives entitled to sit on the Committee.

Article 48   Advisory jurisdiction of the Court
The Court shall decide whether a request for an advisory opinion submitted by the Committee of Ministers is within its competence as defined in Article 47.

Article 49   Reasons for advisory opinions
1.   Reasons shall be given for advisory opinions of the Court.
2.   If the advisory opinion does not represent, in whole or in part, the unanimous opinion of the judges, any judge shall be entitled to deliver a separate opinion.
3.   Advisory opinions of the Court shall be communicated to the Committee of Ministers.

Article 50   Expenditure on the Court
The expenditure on the Court shall be borne by the Council of Europe.

Article 51   Privileges and immunities of judges
The judges shall be entitled, during the exercise of their functions, to the privileges and immunities provided for in Article 40 of the Statute of the Council of Europe and in the agreements made thereunder.

SECTION III   MISCELLANEOUS PROVISIONS

Article 52   Enquiries by the Secretary-General
On receipt of a request from the Secretary-General of the Council of Europe any High Contracting Party shall furnish an explanation of the manner in which its internal law ensures the effective implementation of any of the provisions of this Convention.

Article 53   Safeguard for existing human rights
Nothing in this Convention shall be construed as limiting or derogating from any of the human rights and fundamental freedoms which may be ensured under the laws of any High Contracting Party or under any other agreement to which it is a Party.

Article 54   Powers of the Committee of Ministers
Nothing in this Convention shall prejudice the powers conferred on the Committee of Ministers by the Statute of the Council of Europe.

Article 55   Exclusion of other means of dispute settlement
The High Contracting Parties agree that, except by special agreement, they will not avail themselves of treaties, conventions or declarations in force between them for the purpose of submitting, by way of petition, a dispute arising out of the interpretation

or application of this Convention to a means of settlement other than those provided for in this Convention.

Article 56   Territorial application

1.   Any State may at the time of its ratification or at any time thereafter declare by notification addressed to the Secretary-General of the Council of Europe that the present Convention shall, subject to paragraph 4 of this Article, extend to all or any of the territories for whose international relations it is responsible.

2.   The Convention shall extend to the territory or territories named in the notification as from the thirtieth day after the receipt of this notification by the Secretary-General of the Council of Europe.

3.   The provisions of this Convention shall be applied in such territories with due regard, however, to local requirements.

4.   Any State which has made a declaration in accordance with paragraph 1 of this Article may at any time thereafter declare on behalf of one or more of the territories to which the declaration relates that it accepts the competence of the Court to receive applications from individuals, non-governmental organisations or groups of individuals as provided in Article 34 of the Convention.

Article 57   Reservations

1.   Any State may, when signing this Convention or when depositing its instrument of ratification, make a reservation in respect of any particular provision of the Convention to the extent that any law then in force in its territory is not in conformity with the provision. Reservations of a general character shall not be permitted under this Article.

2.   Any reservation made under this Article shall contain a brief statement of the law concerned.

Article 58   Denunciation

1.   A High Contracting Party may denounce the present Convention only after the expiry of five years from the date on which it became a Party to it and after six months' notice contained in a notification addressed to the Secretary-General of the Council of Europe, who shall inform the other High Contracting Parties.

2.   Such a denunciation shall not have the effect of releasing the High Contracting Party concerned from its obligations under this Convention in respect of any act which, being capable of constituting a violation of such obligations, may have been performed by it before the date at which the denunciation became effective.

3.   Any High Contracting Party which shall cease to be a Member of the Council of Europe shall cease to be a Party to this Convention under the same conditions.

4.   The Convention may be denounced in accordance with the provisions of the preceding paragraphs in respect of any territory to which it has been declared to extend under the terms of Article 56.

Article 59   Signature and ratification

1.   This Convention shall be open to the signature of the members of the Council of Europe. It shall be ratified. Ratifications shall be deposited with the Secretary-General of the Council of Europe.

2.   The present Convention shall come into force after the deposit of ten instruments of ratification.

3.   As regards any signatory ratifying subsequently, the Convention shall come into force at the date of the deposit of its instrument of ratification.

4.   The Secretary-General of the Council of Europe shall notify all the members of the Council of Europe of the entry into force of the Convention, the names of the High Contracting Parties who have ratified it, and the deposit of all instruments of ratification which may be effected subsequently.

Done at Rome this 4th day of November 1950, in English and French, both texts being equally authentic, in a single copy which shall remain deposited in the archives of the Council of Europe. The Secretary-General shall transmit certified copies to each of the signatories.

FIRST PROTOCOL (1952)

The Governments signatory hereto, being members of the Council of Europe,

Being resolved to take steps to ensure the collective enforcement of certain rights and freedoms other than those already included in Section I of the Convention for the Protection of Human Rights and Fundamental Freedoms signed at Rome on 4th November, 1950 (hereinafter referred to as 'the Convention').

Have agreed as follows:

Article 1   Protection of property

Every natural or legal person is entitled to the peaceful enjoyment of his possessions. No one shall be deprived of his possessions except in the public interest and subject to the conditions provided for by law and by the general principles of international law.

The preceding provisions shall not, however, in any way impair the right of a State to enforce such laws as it deems necessary to control the use of property in accordance with the general interest or to secure the payment of taxes or other contributions or penalties.

Article 2   Right to education

No person shall be denied the right to education. In the exercise of any functions which it assumes in relation to education and to teaching, the State shall respect the right of parents to ensure such education and teaching in conformity with their own religious and philosophical convictions.

Article 3   Right to free elections

The High Contracting Parties undertake to hold free elections at reasonable intervals by secret ballot, under conditions which will ensure the free expression of the opinion of the people in the choice of the legislature.

Article 4   Territorial application

Any High Contracting Party may at the time of signature or ratification or at any time thereafter communicate to the Secretary-General of the Council of Europe a declaration stating the extent to which it undertakes that the provisions of the present Protocol shall apply to such of the territories for the international relations of which it is responsible as are named therein.

Any High Contracting Party which has communicated a declaration in virtue of the preceding paragraph may from time to time communicate a further declaration modifying the terms of any former declaration or terminating the application of the provisions of this Protocol in respect of any territory.

A declaration made in accordance with this Article shall be deemed to have been made in accordance with paragraph (1) of Article 56 of the Convention.

Article 5   Relationship to the Convention

As between the High Contracting Parties the provisions of Articles 1, 2, 3 and 4 of this Protocol shall be regarded as additional Articles to the Convention and all the provisions of the Convention shall apply accordingly.

Article 6   Signature and ratification

This Protocol shall be open for signature by the Members of the Council of Europe, who are the signatories of the Convention: it shall be ratified at the same time as or after the ratification of the Convention. It shall enter into force after the deposit of ten instruments of ratification. As regards any signatory ratifying subsequently, the Protocol shall enter into force at the date of the deposit of its instrument of ratification.

The instruments of ratification shall be deposited with the Secretary-General of the Council of Europe, who will notify all Members of the names of those who have ratified.

Done at Paris on the 20th day of March 1952, in English and French, both texts being equally authentic, in a single copy which shall remain deposited in the archives of the Council of Europe. The Secretary-General shall transmit certified copies to each of the signatory Governments.

FOURTH PROTOCOL (1963)
[Securing certain rights and freedoms other than those already included in the Convention and in the first Protocol thereto]

The Governments signatory hereto, being members of the Council of Europe,

Being resolved to take steps to ensure the collective enforcement of certain rights and freedoms other than those already included in Section I of the Convention for the Protection of Human Rights and Fundamental Freedoms signed at Rome on 4th November 1950 (hereinafter referred to as 'the Convention') and in Articles 1 to 3 of the First Protocol to the Convention, signed at Paris on 20th March 1952,

Have agreed as follows:

Article 1   Prohibition of imprisonment for debt
No one shall be deprived of his liberty merely on the ground of inability to fulfil a contractual obligation.

Article 2   Freedom of movement
1.   Everyone lawfully within the territory of a State shall, within that territory, have the right to liberty of movement and freedom to choose his residence.

2.   Everyone shall be free to leave any country, including his own.

3.   No restrictions shall be placed on the exercise of these rights other than such as are in accordance with law and are necessary in a democratic society in the interests of national security or public safety, for the maintenance of *ordre public,* for the prevention of crime, for the protection of health or morals, or for the protection of the rights and freedoms of others.

4.   The rights set forth in paragraph 1 may also be subject, in particular areas, to restrictions imposed in accordance with law and justified by the public interest in a democratic society.

Article 3   Prohibition of expulsion of nationals
1.   No one shall be expelled, by means either of an individual or of a collective measure, from the territory of the State of which he is a national.

2.   No one shall be deprived of the right to enter the territory of the State of which he is a national.

Article 4   Prohibition of collective expulsion of aliens
Collective expulsion of aliens is prohibited.

Article 5   Territorial application
1.   Any High Contracting Party may, at the time of signature or ratification of this Protocol, or at any time thereafter, communicate to the Secretary-General of the Council of Europe a declaration stating the extent to which it undertakes that the provisions of this Protocol shall apply to such of the territories for the international relations of which it is responsible as are named therein.

2. Any High Contracting Party which has communicated a declaration in virtue of the preceding paragraph may, from time to time, communicate a further declaration modifying the terms of any former declaration or terminating the application of the provisions of this Protocol in respect of any territory.

3. A declaration made in accordance with this Article shall be deemed to have been made in accordance with paragraph 1 of Article 56 of the Convention.

4. The territory of any State to which this Protocol applies by virtue of ratification or acceptance by that State, and each territory to which this Protocol is applied by virtue of a declaration by that State under this Article, shall be treated as separate territories for the purpose of the references in Articles 2 and 3 to the territory of a State.

5. Any State which has made a declaration in accordance with paragraph 1 or 2 of this Article may at any time thereafter declare on behalf of one or more of the territories to which the declaration relates that it accepts the competence of the Court to receive applications from individuals, non-governmental organizations or groups of individuals as provided in Article 34 of the Convention in respect of all or any of Articles 1 to 4 of this Protocol.

Article 6   Relationship to the Convention
As between the High Contracting Parties the provisions of Articles 1 to 5 of this Protocol shall be regarded as additional Articles to the Convention, and all the provisions of the Convention shall apply accordingly.

Article 7   Signature and ratification
1. This Protocol shall be open for signature by the members of the Council of Europe who are the signatories of the Convention; it shall be ratified at the same time as or after the ratification of the Convention. It shall enter into force after the deposit of five instruments of ratification. As regards any signatory ratifying subsequently, the Protocol shall enter into force at the date of the deposit of its instrument of ratification.

2. The instruments of ratification shall be deposited with the Secretary-General of the Council of Europe, who will notify all members of the names of those who have ratified.

In witness whereof, the undersigned, being duly authorised thereto, have signed this Protocol.

Done at Strasbourg, this 16th day of September 1963, in English and in French, both texts being equally authoritative, in a single copy which shall remain deposited in the archives of the Council of Europe. The Secretary-General shall transmit certified copies to each of the signatory States.

SIXTH PROTOCOL (1983)
[Concerning the abolition of the death penalty]

The member States of the Council of Europe, signatory to this Protocol to the Convention for the Protection of Human Rights and Fundamental Freedoms, signed at Rome on 4 November 1950 (hereinafter referred to as 'the Convention'),

Considering that the evolution that has occurred in several member States of the Council of Europe expresses a general tendency in favour of abolition of the death penalty,

Have agreed as follows:

Article 1   Abolition of the death penalty
The death penalty shall be abolished. No one shall be condemned to such penalty or executed.

Article 2   Death penalty in time of war
A State may make provision in its law for the death penalty in respect of acts committed in time of war or of imminent threat of war; such penalty shall be applied only in the instances laid down in the law and in accordance with its provisions. The State shall communicate to the Secretary of the Council of Europe the relevant provisions of that law.

Article 3   Prohibition of derogations
No derogation from the provisions of this Protocol shall be made under Article 15 of the Convention.

Article 4   Prohibition of reservations
No reservation may be made under Article 57 of the Convention in respect of the provisions of this Protocol.

Article 5   Territorial application
1. Any State may at the time of signature or when depositing its instrument of ratification, acceptance or approval, specify the territory or territories to which this Protocol shall apply.
2. Any State may at any later date, by a declaration addressed to the Secretary-General of the Council of Europe, extend the application of this Protocol to any other territory specified in the declaration. In respect of such territory the Protocol shall enter into force on the first day of the month following the date of receipt of such a declaration by the Secretary-General.
3. Any declaration made under the two preceding paragraphs may, in respect of any territory specified in such declaration, be withdrawn by a notification addressed to the Secretary-General. The withdrawal shall become effective on the first day of the month following the date of receipt of such notification by the Secretary-General.

Article 6   Relationship to the Convention
As between the States Parties the provisions of Articles 1 to 5 of this Protocol shall be regarded as additional articles to the Convention and all the provisions of the Convention shall apply accordingly.

Article 7   Signature and ratification
This Protocol shall be open for signature by the member States of the Council of Europe, signatories to the Convention. It shall be subject to ratification, acceptance or approval. A member State of the Council of Europe may not ratify, accept or approve this Protocol unless it has, simultaneously or previously, ratified the Convention. Instruments of ratification, acceptance or approval shall be deposited with the Secretary-General of the Council of Europe.

Article 8   Entry into force
1. This Protocol shall enter into force on the first day of the month following the date on which five member States of the Council of Europe have expressed their consent to be bound by the Protocol in accordance with the provisions of Article 7.
2. In respect of any member State which subsequently expresses its consent to be bound by it, the Protocol shall enter into force on the first day of the month following the date of the deposit of the instrument of ratification, acceptance or approval.

Article 9   Depositary functions
The Secretary-General of the Council of Europe shall notify the member States of the Council of:
    (a)   any signature;
    (b)   the deposit of any instrument of ratification, acceptance or approval;
    (c)   any date of entry into force of this Protocol in accordance with Articles 5 and 8;

(d)   any other act, notification or communication relating to this Protocol.

In witness whereof the undersigned, being duly authorised thereto, have signed this Protocol.

Done at Strasbourg, this 28th day of April 1983, in English and French, both texts being equally authentic, in a single copy which shall be deposited in the archives of the Council of Europe. The Secretary-General of the Council of Europe shall transmit certified copies to each member State of the Council of Europe.

SEVENTH PROTOCOL (1984)

The member States of the Council of Europe signatory hereto,

Being resolved to take further steps to ensure the collective enforcement of certain rights and freedoms by means of the Convention for the Protection of Human Rights and Fundamental Freedoms signed at Rome on 4 November 1950 (hereinafter referred to as 'the Convention'),

Have agreed as follows:

Article 1   Procedural safeguards relating to expulsion of aliens

1.   An alien lawfully resident in the territory of a State shall not be expelled therefrom except in pursuance of a decision reached in accordance with law and shall be allowed:

(a)   to submit reasons against his expulsion;

(b)   to have his case reviewed; and

(c)   to be represented for these purposes before the competent authority or a person or persons designated by that authority.

2.   An alien may be expelled before the exercise of his rights under paragraph 1 (a), (b) and (c) of this Article, when such expulsion is necessary in the interests of public order or is grounded on reasons of national security.

Article 2   Right of appeal in criminal matters

1.   Everyone convicted of a criminal offence by a tribunal shall have the right to have conviction or sentence reviewed by a higher tribunal. The exercise of this right, including the grounds on which it may be exercised, shall be governed by law.

2.   This right may be subject to exceptions in regard to offences of a minor character, as prescribed by law, or in cases in which the person concerned was tried in the first instance by the highest tribunal or was convicted following an appeal against acquittal.

Article 3   Compensation for wrongful conviction

When a person has by a final decision been convicted of a criminal offence and when subsequently his conviction has been reversed, or he has been pardoned, on the ground that a new or newly discovered fact shows conclusively that there has been a miscarriage of justice, the person who has suffered punishment as a result of such conviction shall be compensated according to the law or the practice of the State concerned, unless it is proved that the non-disclosure of the unknown fact in time is wholly or partly attributable to him.

Article 4   Right not to be tried or punished twice

1.   No one shall be liable to be tried or punished again in criminal proceedings under the jurisdiction of the same State for an offence for which he has already been finally acquitted or convicted in accordance with the law and penal procedure of that State.

2.   The provisions of the preceding paragraph shall not prevent the re-opening of the case in accordance with the law and penal procedure of the State concerned, if

there is evidence of new or newly discovered facts, or if there has been a fundamental defect in the previous proceedings, which could affect the outcome of the case.

3.   No derogation from this Article shall be made under Article 15 of the Convention.

Article 5   Equality between spouses

1.   Spouses shall enjoy equality of rights and responsibilities of a private law character between them, and in their relations with their children, as to marriage, during marriage and in the event of its dissolution. This Article shall not prevent States from taking such measures as are necessary in the interests of the children.

Article 6   Territorial applications

1.   Any State may at the time of signature or when depositing its instrument of ratification, acceptance or approval, specify the territory or territories to which this Protocol shall apply and state the extent to which it undertakes that the provisions of this Protocol shall apply to this or these territories.

2.   Any State may at any later date, by a declaration addressed to the Secretary-General of the Council of Europe, extend the application of this Protocol to any other territory specified in the declaration. In respect of such territory the Protocol shall enter into force on the first day of the month following the expiration of a period of two months after the date of receipt by the Secretary-General of such declaration.

3.   Any declaration made under the two preceding paragraphs may, in respect of any territory specified in such declaration, be withdrawn or modified by a notification addressed to the Secretary-General. The withdrawal or modification shall become effective on the first day of the month following the expiration of a period of two months after the date of receipt of such notification by the Secretary-General.

4.   A declaration made in accordance with this Article shall be deemed to have been made in accordance with paragraph 1 of Article 56 of the Convention.

5.   The territory of any State to which this Protocol applies by virtue of ratification, acceptance or approval by that State, and each territory to which this Protocol is applied by virtue of a declaration by that State under this Article, may be treated as separate territories for the purpose of the reference in Article 1 to the territory of a State.

6.   Any State which has made a declaration in accordance with paragraph 1 or 2 of this Article may at any time thereafter declare on behalf of one or more of the territories to which the declaration relates that it accepts the competence of the Court to receive applications from individuals, non-governmental organizations or groups of individuals as provided in Article 34 of the Convention in respect of Articles 1 to 5 of this Protocol.

Article 7   Relationship to the Convention

As between the States Parties, the provisions of Articles 1 to 6 of this Protocol shall be regarded as additional Articles to the Convention, and all the provisions of the Convention shall apply accordingly.

Article 8   Signature and ratification

This Protocol shall be open for signature by member States of the Council of Europe which have signed the Convention. It is subject to ratification, acceptance or approval. A member State of the Council of Europe may not ratify, accept or approve this Protocol without previously or simultaneously ratifying the Convention. Instruments of ratification, acceptance or approval shall be deposited with the Secretary-General of the Council of Europe.

Article 9   Entry into force

1.   This Protocol shall enter into force on the first day of the month following the expiration of a period of two months after the date on which seven member States of

the Council of Europe have expressed their consent to be bound by the Protocol in accordance with the provisions of Article 8.

2.   In respect of any member State which subsequently expresses its consent to be bound by it, the Protocol shall enter into force on the first day of the month following the expiration of a period of two months after the date of the deposit of the instrument of ratification, acceptance or approval.

Article 10   Depository functions

The Secretary-General of the Council of Europe shall notify all the member States of the Council of:

(a)   any signature;

(b)   the deposit of any instrument of ratification, acceptance or approval;

(c)   any date of entry into force of this Protocol in accordance with Articles 6 and 9;

(d)   any other act, notification or declaration relating to this Protocol.

In witness whereof the undersigned, being duly authorised thereto, have signed this Protocol.

Done at Strasbourg, this 22nd day of November 1984, in English and French, both texts being equally authentic, in a single copy which shall be deposited in the archives of the Council of Europe. The Secretary-General of the Council of Europe shall transmit certified copies to each member State of the Council.

EUROPEAN CONVENTION FOR THE PREVENTION OF TORTURE AND INHUMAN OR DEGRADING TREATMENT OR PUNISHMENT (1987)

The member States of the Council of Europe, signatory hereto,

Having regard to the provisions of the Convention for the Protection of Human Rights and Fundamental Freedoms,

Recalling that, under Article 3 of the same Convention, 'no one shall be subjected to torture or to inhuman or degrading treatment or punishment';

Noting that the machinery provided for in that Convention operates in relation to persons who allege that they are victims of violations of Article 3;

Convinced that the protection of persons deprived of their liberty against torture and inhuman or degrading treatment or punishment could be strengthened by non-judicial means of a preventive character based on visits,

Have agreed as follows:

CHAPTER I

Article 1

There shall be established a European Committee for the Prevention of Torture and Inhuman or Degrading Treatment or Punishment (hereinafter referred to as 'the Committee'). The Committee shall, by means of visits, examine the treatment of persons deprived of their liberty with a view to strengthening, if necessary, the protection of such persons from torture and from inhuman or degrading treatment or punishment.

Article 2

Each Party shall permit visits, in accordance with this Convention, to any place within its jurisdiction where persons are deprived of their liberty by a public authority.

Article 3

In the application of this Convention, the Committee and the competent national authorities of the Party concerned shall co-operate with each other.

CHAPTER II

Article 4

1. The Committee shall consist of a number of members equal to that of the Parties.

2. The members of the Committee shall be chosen from among persons of high moral character, known for their competence in the field of human rights or having professional experience in the areas covered by this Convention.

3. No two members of the Committee may be nationals of the same State.

4. The members shall serve in their individual capacity, shall be independent and impartial, and shall be available to serve the Committee effectively.

Article 5

1. The members of the Committee shall be elected by the Committee of Ministers of the Council of Europe by an absolute majority of votes, from a list of names drawn up by the Bureau of the Consultative Assembly of the Council of Europe; each national delegation of the Parties in the Consultative Assembly shall put forward three candidates, of whom two at least shall be its nationals.

2. The same procedure shall be followed in filling casual vacancies.

3. The members of the Committee shall be elected for a period of four years. They may only be re-elected once. However, among the members elected at the first election, the terms of three members shall expire at the end of two years. The members whose terms are to expire at the end of the initial period of two years shall be chosen by lot by the Secretary-General of the Council of Europe immediately after the first election has been completed.

Article 6

1. The Committee shall meet in camera. A quorum shall be equal to the majority of its members. The decisions of the Committee shall be taken by a majority of the members present, subject to the provisions of Article 10, paragraph 2.

2. The Committee shall draw up its own rules of procedure.

3. The Secretariat of the Committee shall be provided by the Secretary-General of the Council of Europe.

CHAPTER III

Article 7

1. The Committee shall organise visits to places referred to in Article 2. Apart from periodic visits, the Committee may organise such other visits as appear to it to be required in the circumstances.

2. As a general rule, the visits shall be carried out by at least two members of the Committee. The Committee may, if it considers it necessary, be assisted by experts and interpreters.

Article 8

1. The Committee shall notify the Government of the Party concerned of its intention to carry out a visit. After such notification, it may at any time visit any place referred to in Article 2.

2. A Party shall provide the Committee with the following facilities to carry out its task:

    (a)   access to its territory and the right to travel without restriction;

    (b)   full information on the places where persons deprived of their liberty are being held;

    (c)   unlimited access to any place where persons are deprived of their liberty, including the right to move inside such places without restriction;

    (d)   other information available to the Party which is necessary for the Committee to carry out its task. In seeking such information, the Committee shall have regard to applicable rules of national law and professional ethics.

3. The Committee may interview in private persons deprived of their liberty.

4. The Committee may communicate freely with any person whom it believes can supply relevant information.

5. If necessary, the Committee may immediately communicate observations to the competent authorities of the Party concerned.

Article 9

1. In exceptional circumstances, the competent authorities of the Party concerned may make representations to the Committee against a visit at the time or to the particular place proposed by the Committee. Such representations may only be made on grounds of national defence, public safety, serious disorder in places where persons are deprived of their liberty, the medical condition of a person or that an urgent interrogation relating to a serious crime is in progress.

2. Following such representations, the Committee and the Party shall immediately enter into consultations in order to clarify the situation and seek agreement on arrangements to enable the Committee to exercise its functions expeditiously. Such arrangements may include the transfer to another place of any person whom the Committee proposed to visit. Until the visit takes place, the Party shall provide information to the Committee about any person concerned.

Article 10

1. After each visit, the Committee shall draw up a report on the facts found during the visit, taking account of any observations which may have been submitted by the Party concerned. It shall transmit to the latter its report containing any recommendations it considers necessary. The Committee may consult with the Party with a view to suggesting, if necessary, improvements in the protection of persons deprived of their liberty.

2. If the Party fails to co-operate or refuses to improve the situation in the light of the Committee's recommendations, the Committee may decide, after the Party has had an opportunity to make known its views, by a majority of two-thirds of its members to make a public statement on the matter.

Article 11

1. The information gathered by the Committee in relation to a visit, its report and its consultations with the Party concerned shall be confidential.

2. The Committee shall publish its report, together with any comments of the Party concerned, whenever requested to do so by that Party.

3. However, no personal data shall be published without the express consent of the person concerned.

Article 12

Subject to the rules of confidentiality in Article 11, the Committee shall every year submit to the Committee of Ministers a general report on its activities which shall be transmitted to the Consultative Assembly and made public.

Article 13

The members of the Committee, experts and other persons assisting the Committee are required, during and after their terms of office, to maintain the confidentiality of the facts or information of which they have become aware during the discharge of their functions.

Article 14

1. The names of persons assisting the Committee shall be specified in the notification under Article 8, paragraph 1.

2. Experts shall act on the instructions and under the authority of the Committee. They shall have particular knowledge and experience in the areas covered by this

Convention and shall be bound by the same duties of independence, impartiality and availability as the members of the Committee.

3.   A Party may exceptionally declare that an expert or other person assisting the Committee may not be allowed to take part in a visit to a place within its jurisdiction.

CHAPTER IV

Article 15

Each Party shall inform the Committee of the name and address of the authority competent to receive notifications to its Government, and of any liaison officer it may appoint.

Article 16

The Committee, its members and experts referred to in Article 7, paragraph 2, shall enjoy the privileges and immunities set out in the annex to this Convention.

Article 17

1.   This Convention shall not prejudice the provisions of domestic law or any international agreement which provide greater protection for persons deprived of their liberty.

2.   Nothing in this Convention shall be construed as limiting or derogating from the competence of the organs of the European Convention on Human Rights or from the obligations assumed by the Parties under that Convention.

3.   The Committee shall not visit places which representatives or delegates of protecting powers or the International Committee of the Red Cross effectively visit on a regular basis by virtue of the Geneva Conventions of 12 August 1949 and the Additional Protocols of 8 June 1977 thereto.

CHAPTER V

Article 18

This Convention shall be open for signature by the member States of the Council of Europe. It is subject to ratification, acceptance or approval. Instruments of ratification, acceptance or approval shall be deposited with the Secretary-General of the Council of Europe.

Article 19

1.   This Convention shall enter into force on the first day of the month following the expiration of a period of three months after the date on which seven member States of the Council of Europe have expressed their consent to be bound by the Convention in accordance with the provisions of Article 18.

2.   In respect of any member State which subsequently expresses its consent to be bound by it, the Convention shall enter into force on the first day of the month following the expiration of a period of three months after the date of the deposit of the instrument of ratification, acceptance or approval.

Article 20

1.   Any State may at the time of signature or when depositing its instrument of ratification, acceptance or approval, specify the territory or territories to which this Convention shall apply.

2.   Any State may at any later date, by a declaration addressed to the Secretary-General of the Council of Europe, extend the application of this Convention to any other territory specified in the declaration. In respect of such territory the Convention shall enter into force on the first day of the month following the expiration of a period of three months after the date of receipt of such declaration by the Secretary-General.

3.   Any declaration made under the two preceding paragraphs may, in respect of any territory specified in such declaration, be withdrawn by a notification addressed

to the Secretary-General. The withdrawal shall become effective on the first day of the month following the expiration of a period of three months after the date of receipt of such notification by the Secretary-General.

Article 21
No reservation may be made in respect of the provisions of this Convention.

Article 22
1.   Any Party may, at any time, denounce this Convention by means of a notification addressed to the Secretary-General of the Council of Europe.
2.   Such denunciation shall become effective on the first day of the month following the expiration of a period of twelve months after the date of receipt of the notification by the Secretary-General.

Article 23
The Secretary-General of the Council of Europe shall notify the member States of the Council of Europe of:
    (a)   any signature;
    (b)   the deposit of any instrument of ratification, acceptance or approval;
    (c)   any date of entry into force of this Convention in accordance with Articles 19 and 20;
    (d)   any other act, notification or communication relating to this Convention, except for action taken in pursuance of Articles 8 and 10.

In witness whereof, the undersigned, being duly authorised thereto, have signed this Convention.

Done at Strasbourg, the 26 November 1987, in English and French, both texts being equally authentic, in a single copy which shall be deposited in the archives of the Council of Europe. The Secretary-General of the Council of Europe shall transmit certified copies to each member State of the Council of Europe.

Annex
PRIVILEGES AND IMMUNITIES
(ARTICLE 16)

1.   For the purpose of this annex, references to members of the Committee shall be deemed to include references to experts mentioned in Article 7, paragraph 2.
2.   The members of the Committee shall, while exercising their functions and during journeys made in the exercise of their functions, enjoy the following privileges and immunities:
    (a)   immunity from personal arrest or detention and from seizure of their personal baggage and, in respect of words spoken or written and all acts done by them in their official capacity, immunity from legal process of every kind;
    (b)   exemption from any restrictions on their freedom of movement: on exit from and return to their country of residence, and entry into and exit from the country in which they exercise their functions, and from alien registration in the country which they are visiting or through which they are passing in the exercise of their functions.
3.   In the course of journeys undertaken in the exercise of their functions, the members of the Committee shall, in the matter of customs and exchange control, be accorded:
    (a)   by their own government, the same facilities as those accorded to senior officials travelling abroad on temporary official duty;
    (b)   by the governments of other Parties, the same facilities as those accorded to representatives of foreign governments on temporary official duty.
4.   Documents and papers of the Committee, insofar as they relate to the business of the Committee, shall be inviolable.

The official correspondence and other official communications of the Committee may not be held up or subjected to censorship.

5. In order to secure for the members of the Committee complete freedom of speech and complete independence in the discharge of their duties, the immunity from legal process in respect of words spoken or written and all acts done by them in discharging their duties shall continue to be accorded, notwithstanding that the persons concerned are no longer engaged in the discharge of such duties.

6. Privileges and immunities are accorded to the members of the Committee, not for the personal benefit of the individuals themselves but in order to safeguard the independent exercise of their functions. The Committee alone shall be competent to waive the immunity of its members; it has not only the right, but is under a duty, to waive the immunity of one of its members in any case where, in its opinion, the immunity would impede the course of justice, and where it can be waived without prejudice to the purpose for which the immunity is accorded.

FIRST PROTOCOL (1993)

The member States of the Council of Europe, signatories to this Protocol to the European Convention for the Prevention of Torture and Inhuman or Degrading Treatment or Punishment, signed at Strasbourg on 26 November 1987 (hereinafter referred to as 'the Convention'),

Considering that non-member States of the Council of Europe should be allowed to accede to the Convention at the invitation of the Committee of Ministers,

Have agreed as follows:

Article 1
A sub-paragraph shall be added to Article 5, paragraph 1, of the Convention as follows:

'Where a member is to be elected to the Committee in respect of a non-member State of the Council of Europe, the Bureau of the Consultative Assembly shall invite the Parliament of that State to put forward three candidates, of whom two at least shall be its nationals. The election by the Committee of Ministers shall take place after consultation with the Party concerned.'

Article 2
Article 12 of the Convention shall read as follows:

'Subject to the rules of confidentiality in Article 11, the committee shall every year submit to the Committee of Ministers a general report on its activities which shall be transmitted to the consultative Assembly and to any non-member State of the Council of Europe which is a party to the Convention, and made public.'

Article 3
The text of Article 18 of the Convention shall become paragraph 1 of that article and shall be supplemented by the following second paragraph:

'2. The Committee of Ministers of the Council of Europe may invite any non-member State of the Council of Europe to accede to the Convention.'

Article 8
This Protocol shall enter into force on the first day of the month following the expiration of a period of three months after the date on which all Parties to the Convention have expressed their consent to be bound by the Protocol, in accordance with the provisions of Article 7.

SECOND PROTOCOL (1993)

The States, signatories to this Protocol to the European Convention for the Prevention of Torture and Inhuman or Degrading Treatment or Punishment, signed at Strasbourg on 26 November 1987 (hereinafter referred to as 'the Convention'),

Convinced of the advisability of enabling members of the European Committee for the Prevention of Torture and Inhuman and Degrading Treatment (hereinafter referred to as 'the Committee') to be re-elected twice;

Also considering the need to guarantee an orderly renewal of the membership of the Committee,

Have agreed as follows:

Article 1

1.   In Article 5, paragraph 3, the second sentence shall read as follows:
'They may be re-elected twice.'

2.   Article 5 of the Convention shall be supplemented by the following paragraphs 4 and 5:

'4.   In order to ensure that, as far as possible, one half of the membership of the Committee shall be renewed every two years, the Committee of Ministers may decide, before proceeding to any subsequent election, that the term or terms of office of one or more members to be elected shall be for a period other than four years but not more than six and not less than two years.

5.   In cases where more than one term of office is involved and the Committee of Ministers applies the preceding paragraph, the allocation of the terms of office shall be effected by the drawing of lots by the Secretary-General, immediately after the election.'

Article 3

This Protocol shall enter into force on the first day of the month following the expiration of a period of three months after the date on which all Parties to the Convention have expressed their consent to be bound by the Protocol, in accordance with the provisions of Article 2.

AMERICA

AMERICAN CONVENTION ON HUMAN RIGHTS ('PACT OF SAN JOSÉ, COSTA RICA') (1969)

PREAMBLE

The American States signatory to the present Convention,

Reaffirming their intention to consolidate in this hemisphere, within the framework of democratic institutions, a system of personal liberty and social justice based on respect for the essential rights of man;

Recognizing that the essential rights of man are not derived from one's being a national of a certain state, but are based upon attributes of the human personality, and that they therefore justify international protection in the form of a convention reinforcing or complementing the protection provided by the domestic law of the American states;

Considering that these principles have been set forth in the Charter of the Organization of American States, in the American Declaration of the Rights and Duties of Man, and in the Universal Declaration of Human Rights, and that they have been reaffirmed and refined in other international instruments, worldwide as well as regional in scope;

Reiterating that, in accordance with the Universal Declaration of Human Rights, the ideal of free men enjoying freedom from fear and want can be achieved only if conditions are created whereby everyone may enjoy his economic, social, and cultural rights, as well as his civil and political rights; and

Considering that the Third Special Inter-American Conference (Buenos Aires, 1967) approved the incorporation into the Charter of the Organization itself of broader standards with respect to economic, social, and educational rights and resolved that an inter-American convention on human rights should determine the structure, competence, and procedure of the organs responsible for these matters,
Have agreed upon the following:

PART I
STATE OBLIGATIONS AND RIGHTS PROTECTED
CHAPTER I   GENERAL OBLIGATIONS

Article 1   Obligation to respect rights
1.   The States Parties to this Convention undertake to respect the rights and freedoms recognized herein and to ensure to all persons subject to their jurisdiction the free and full exercise of those rights and freedoms, without any discrimination for reasons of race, color, sex, language, religion, political or other opinion, national or social origin, economic status, birth, or any other social condition.
2.   For the purposes of this Convention, 'person' means every human being.

Article 2   Domestic legal effects
Where the exercise of any of the rights or freedoms referred to in Article 1 is not already ensured by legislative or other provisions, the States Parties undertake to adopt, in accordance with their constitutional processes and the provisions of this Convention, such legislative or other measures as may be necessary to give effect to those rights or freedoms.

CHAPTER II   CIVIL AND POLITICAL RIGHTS

Article 3   Right to juridical personality
Every person has the right to recognition as a person before the law.

Article 4   Right to life
1.   Every person has the right to have his life respected. This right shall be protected by law, and, in general, from the moment of conception. No one shall be arbitrarily deprived of his life.
2.   In countries that have not abolished the death penalty, it may be imposed only for the most serious crimes and pursuant to a final judgment rendered by a competent court and in accordance with a law establishing such punishment, enacted prior to the commission of the crime. The application of such punishment shall not be extended to crimes to which it does not presently apply.
3.   The death penalty shall not be reestablished in states that have abolished it.
4.   In no case shall capital punishment be inflicted for political offenses or related common crimes.
5.   Capital punishment shall not be imposed upon persons who, at the time the crime was committed, were under 18 years of age or over 70 years of age; nor shall it be applied to pregnant women.
6.   Every person condemned to death shall have the right to apply for amnesty, pardon, or commutation of sentence, which may be granted in all cases. Capital punishment shall not be imposed while such a petition is pending decision by the competent authority.

Article 5   Right to humane treatment
1.   Every person has the right to have his physical, mental, and moral integrity respected.
2.   No one shall be subjected to torture or to cruel, inhuman, or degrading punishment or treatment. All persons deprived of their liberty shall be treated with respect for the inherent dignity of the human person.

3.   Punishment shall not be extended to any person other than the criminal.

4.   Accused persons shall, save in exceptional circumstances, be segregated from convicted persons, and shall be subject to separate treatment appropriate to their status as unconvicted persons.

5.   Minors while subject to criminal proceedings shall be separated from adults and brought before specialized tribunals, as speedily as possible, so that they may be treated in accordance with their status as minors.

6.   Punishments consisting of deprivation of liberty shall have as an essential aim the reform and social readaptation of the prisoners.

Article 6   Freedom from slavery

1.   No one shall be subject to slavery or to involuntary servitude, which are prohibited in all their forms, as are the slave trade and traffic in women.

2.   No one shall be required to perform forced or compulsory labor. This provision shall not be interpreted to mean that, in those countries in which the penalty established for certain crimes is deprivation of liberty at forced labor, the carrying out of such a sentence imposed by a competent court is prohibited. Forced labor shall not adversely affect the dignity or the physical or intellectual capacity of the prisoner.

3.   For the purposes of this article the following do not constitute forced or compulsory labor:

(a)   work or service normally required of a person imprisoned in execution of a sentence or formal decision passed by the competent judicial authority. Such work or service shall be carried out under the supervision and control of public authorities, and any persons performing such work or service shall not be placed at the disposal of any private party, company, or juridical person;

(b)   military service and, in countries in which conscientious objectors are recognized, national service that the law may provide for in lieu of military service;

(c)   service exacted in time of danger or calamity that threatens the existence or the well-being of the community; or

(d)   work or service that forms part of normal civic obligations.

Article 7   Right to personal liberty

1.   Every person has the right to personal liberty and security.

2.   No one shall be deprived of his physical liberty except for the reasons and under the conditions established beforehand by the constitution of the State Party concerned or by a law established pursuant thereto.

3.   No one shall be subject to arbitrary arrest or imprisonment.

4.   Anyone who is detained shall be informed of the reasons for his detention and shall be promptly notified of the charge or charges against him.

5.   Any person detained shall be brought promptly before a judge or other officer authorized by law to exercise judicial power and shall be entitled to trial within a reasonable time or to be released without prejudice to the continuation of the proceedings. His release may be subject to guarantees to assure his appearance for trial.

6.   Anyone who is deprived of his liberty shall be entitled to recourse to a competent court, in order that the court may decide without delay on the lawfulness of his arrest or detention and order his release if the arrest or detention is unlawful. In States Parties whose laws provide that anyone who believes himself to be threatened with deprivation of his liberty is entitled to recourse to a competent court in order that it may decide on the lawfulness of such threat, this remedy may not be restricted or abolished. The interested party or another person in his behalf is entitled to seek these remedies.

7.   No one shall be detained for debt. This principle shall not limit the orders of a competent judicial authority issued for nonfulfillment of duties of support.

Article 8   Right to a fair trial

1.   Every person has the right to a hearing, with due guarantees and within a reasonable time, by a competent, independent, and impartial tribunal, previously established by law, in the substantiation of any accusation of a criminal nature made against him or for the determination of his rights and obligations of a civil, labor, fiscal, or any other nature.

2.   Every person accused of a criminal offense has the right to be presumed innocent so long as his guilt has not been proven according to law. During the proceedings, every person is entitled, with full equality, to the following minimum guarantees:

(a)   the right of the accused to be assisted without charge by a translator or interpreter, if he does not understand or does not speak the language of the tribunal or court;

(b)   prior notification in detail to the accused of the charges against him;

(c)   adequate time and means for the preparation of his defense;

(d)   the right of the accused to defend himself personally or to be assisted by legal counsel of his own choosing, and to communicate freely and privately with his counsel;

(e)   the inalienable right to be assisted by counsel provided by the state, paid or not as the domestic law provides, if the accused does not defend himself personally or engage his own counsel within the time period established by law;

(f)   the right of the defense to examine witnesses present in the court and to obtain the appearance, as witnesses, of experts or other persons who may throw light on the facts;

(g)   the right not to be compelled to be a witness against himself or to plead guilty; and

(h)   the right to appeal the judgment to a higher court.

3.   A confession of guilt by the accused shall be valid only if it is made without coercion of any kind.

4.   An accused person acquitted by a nonappealable judgment shall not be subjected to a new trial for the same cause.

5.   Criminal proceedings shall be public, except insofar as may be necessary to protect the interests of justice.

Article 9   Freedom from ex post facto laws

No one shall be convicted of any act or omission that did not constitute a criminal offense, under the applicable law, at the time it was committed. A heavier penalty shall not be imposed than the one that was applicable at the time the criminal offense was committed. If subsequent to the commission of the offense the law provides for the imposition of a lighter punishment, the guilty person shall benefit therefrom.

Article 10   Right to compensation

Every person has the right to be compensated in accordance with the law in the event he has been sentenced by a final judgment through a miscarriage of justice.

Article 11   Right to privacy

1.   Everyone has the right to have his honor respected and his dignity recognized.

2.   No one may be the object of arbitrary or abusive interference with his private life, his family, his home, or his correspondence, or of unlawful attacks on his honor or reputation.

3.   Everyone has the right to the protection of the law against such interference or attacks.

Article 12   Freedom of conscience and religion

1.   Everyone has the right to freedom of conscience and of religion. This includes freedom to maintain or to change one's religion or beliefs, and freedom to profess or

disseminate one's religion or beliefs either individually or together with others, in public or in private.

2. No one shall be subject to restrictions that might impair his freedom to maintain or to change his religion or beliefs.

3. Freedom to manifest one's religion and beliefs may be subject only to the limitations prescribed by law that are necessary to protect public safety, order, health, or morals, or the rights or freedoms of others.

4. Parents or guardians, as the case may be, have the right to provide for the religious and moral education of their children or wards that is in accord with their own convictions.

Article 13   Freedom of thought and expression

1. Everyone shall have the right to freedom of thought and expression. This right shall include freedom to seek, receive, and impart information and ideas of all kinds, regardless of frontiers, either orally, in writing, in print, in the form of art, or through any other medium of one's choice.

2. The exercise of the right provided for in the foregoing paragraph shall not be subject to prior censorship but shall be subject to subsequent imposition of liability, which shall be expressly established by law to the extent necessary in order to ensure:

(a)   respect for the rights or reputations of others; or

(b)   the protection of national security, public order, or public health or morals.

3. The right of expression may not be restricted by indirect methods or means, such as the abuse of government or private controls over newsprint, radio broadcasting frequencies, or equipment used in the dissemination of information, or by any other means tending to impede the communication and circulation of ideas and opinions.

4. Notwithstanding the provisions of paragraph 2 above, public entertainments may be subject by law to prior censorship for the sole purpose of regulating access to them for the moral protection of childhood and adolescence.

5. Any propaganda for war and any advocacy of national, racial, or religious hatred that constitute incitements to lawless violence or to any other similar illegal action against any person or group of persons on any grounds including those of race, color, religion, language, or national origin shall be considered as offenses punishable by law.

Article 14   Right of reply

1. Anyone injured by inaccurate or offensive statements or ideas disseminated to the public in general by a legally regulated medium of communication has the right to reply or make a correction using the same communications outlet, under such conditions as the law may establish.

2. The correction or reply shall not in any case remit other legal liabilities that may have been incurred.

3. For the effective protection of honor and reputation, every publisher, and every newspaper, motion picture, radio, and television company, shall have a person responsible, who is not protected by immunities or special privileges.

Article 15   Right of assembly

The right of peaceful assembly, without arms, is recognized. No restrictions may be placed on the exercise of this right other than those imposed in conformity with the law and necessary in a democratic society in the interest of national security, public safety or public order, or to protect public health or morals or the rights or freedoms of others.

Article 16   Freedom of association

1. Everyone has the right to associate freely for ideological, religious, political, economic, labor, social, cultural, sports, or other purposes.

2. The exercise of this right shall be subject only to such restrictions established by law as may be necessary in a democratic society, in the interest of national security, public safety or public order, or to protect public health or morals or the rights and freedoms of others.

3. The provisions of this article do not bar the imposition of legal restrictions, including even deprivation of the exercise of the right of association, on members of the armed forces and the police.

Article 17 Rights of the family

1. The family is the natural and fundamental group unit of society and is entitled to protection by society and the state.

2. The right of men and women of marriageable age to marry and to raise a family shall be recognized, if they meet the conditions required by domestic laws, insofar as such conditions do not affect the principle of nondiscrimination established in this Convention.

3. No marriage shall be entered into without the free and full consent of the intending spouses.

4. The States Parties shall take appropriate steps to ensure the equality of rights and the adequate balancing of responsibilities of the spouses as to marriage, during marriage, and in the event of its dissolution. In case of dissolution, provision shall be made for the necessary protection of any children solely on the basis of their own best interests.

5. The law shall recognize equal rights for children born out of wedlock and those born in wedlock.

Article 18 Right to a name

Every person has the right to a given name and to the surnames of his parents or that of one of them. The law shall regulate the manner in which this right shall be ensured for all, by the use of assumed names if necessary.

Article 19 Rights of the child

Every minor child has the right to the measures of protection required by his condition as a minor on the part of his family, society, and the state.

Article 20 Right to nationality

1. Every person has the right to a nationality.

2. Every person has the right to the nationality of the state in whose territory he was born if he does not have the right to any other nationality.

3. No one shall be arbitrarily deprived of his nationality or of the right to change it.

Article 21 Right to property

1. Everyone has the right to the use and enjoyment of his property. The law may subordinate such use and enjoyment to the interest of society.

2. No one shall be deprived of his property except upon payment of just compensation, for reasons of public utility or social interest, and in the cases and according to the forms established by law.

3. Usury and any other form of exploitation of man by man shall be prohibited by law.

Article 22 Freedom of movement and residence

1. Every person lawfully in the territory of a State Party has the right to move about in it and to reside in it subject to the provisions of the law.

2. Every person has the right to leave any country freely, including his own.

3. The exercise of the foregoing rights may be restricted only pursuant to a law to the extent necessary in a democratic society to prevent crime or to protect national

security, public safety, public order, public morals, public health, or the rights or freedoms of others.

4. The exercise of the rights recognized in paragraph 1 may also be restricted by law in designated zones for reasons of public interest.

5. No one can be expelled from the territory of the state of which he is a national or be deprived of the right to enter it.

6. An alien lawfully in the territory of a State Party to this Convention may be expelled from it only pursuant to a decision reached in accordance with law.

7. Every person has the right to seek and be granted asylum in a foreign territory, in accordance with the legislation of the state and international conventions, in the event he is being pursued for political offenses or related common crimes.

8. In no case may an alien be deported or returned to a country, regardless of whether or not it is his country of origin, if in that country his right to life or personal freedom is in danger of being violated because of his race, nationality, religion, social status, or political opinions.

9. The collective expulsion of aliens is prohibited.

Article 23   Right to participate in government

1. Every citizen shall enjoy the following rights and opportunities:

(a)   to take part in the conduct of public affairs, directly or through freely chosen representatives;

(b)   to vote and to be elected in genuine periodic elections, which shall be by universal and equal suffrage and by secret ballot that guarantees the free expression of the will of the voters; and

(c)   to have access, under general conditions of equality, to the public service of his country.

2. The law may regulate the exercise of the rights and opportunities referred to in the preceding paragraph only on the basis of age, nationality, residence, language, education, civil and mental capacity, or sentencing by a competent court in criminal proceedings.

Article 24   Right to equal protection

All persons are equal before the law. Consequently, they are entitled, without discrimination, to equal protection of the law.

Article 25   Right to judicial protection

1. Everyone has the right to simple and prompt recourse, or any other effective recourse, to a competent court or tribunal for protection against acts that violate his fundamental rights recognized by the constitution or laws of the state concerned or by this Convention, even though such violation may have been committed by persons acting in the course of their official duties.

2. The States Parties undertake:

(a)   to ensure that any person claiming such remedy shall have his rights determined by the competent authority provided for by the legal system of the state;

(b)   to develop the possibilities of judicial remedy; and

(c)   to ensure that the competent authorities shall enforce such remedies when granted.

CHAPTER III   ECONOMIC, SOCIAL, AND CULTURAL RIGHTS

Article 26   Progressive development

The States Parties undertake to adopt measures, both internally and through international co-operation, especially those of an economic and technical nature, with a view to achieving progressively, by legislation or other appropriate means, the full realization of the rights implicit in the economic, social, educational, scientific, and cultural standards set forth in the Charter of the Organization of American States as amended by the Protocol of Buenos Aires.

CHAPTER IV SUSPENSION OF GUARANTEES, INTERPRETATION, AND APPLICATION

Article 27 Suspension of guarantees

1. In time of war, public danger, or other emergency that threatens the independence or security of a State Party, it may take measures derogating from its obligations under the present Convention to the extent and for the period of time strictly required by the exigencies of the situation, provided that such measures are not inconsistent with its other obligations under international law and do not involve discrimination on the ground of race, color, sex, language, religion, or social origin.

2. The foregoing provision does not authorize any suspension of the following articles: Article 3 (Right to Juridical Personality), Article 4 (Right to Life), Article 5 (Right to Humane Treatment), Article 6 (Freedom from Slavery), Article 9 (Freedom from *Ex Post Facto* Laws), Article 12 (Freedom of Conscience and Religion), Article 17 (Rights of the Family), Article 18 (Right to a Name), Article 19 (Rights of the Child), Article 20 (Right to Nationality), and Article 23 (Right to Participate in Government), or of the judicial guarantees essential for the protection of such rights.

3. Any State Party availing itself of the right of suspension shall immediately inform the other States Parties, through the Secretary-General of the Organization of American States, of the provisions the application of which it has suspended, the reasons that gave rise to the suspension, and the date set for the termination of such suspension.

Article 28 Federal clause

1. Where a State Party is constituted as a federal state, the national government of such State Party shall implement all the provisions of the Convention over whose subject matter it exercises legislative and judicial jurisdiction.

2. With respect to the provisions over whose subject matter the constituent units of the federal state have jurisdiction, the national government shall immediately take suitable measures, in accordance with its constitution and its laws, to the end that the competent authorities of the constituent units may adopt appropriate provisions for the fulfillment of this Convention.

3. Whenever two or more States Parties agree to form a federation or other type of association they shall take care that the resulting federal or other compact contains the provisions necessary for continuing and rendering effective the standards of this Convention in the new state that is organized.

Article 29 Restrictions regarding interpretation

No provision of this Convention shall be interpreted as:

(a) permitting any State Party, group, or person to suppress the enjoyment or exercise of the rights and freedoms recognized in this Convention or to restrict them to a greater extent than is provided for herein;

(b) restricting the enjoyment or exercise of any right or freedom recognized by virtue of the laws of any State Party or by virtue of another convention to which one of the said states is a party;

(c) precluding other rights or guarantees that are inherent in the human personality or derived from representative democracy as a form of government; or

(d) excluding or limiting the effect that the American Declaration of the Rights and Duties of Man and other international acts of the same nature may have.

Article 30 Scope of restrictions

The restrictions that, pursuant to this Convention, may be placed on the enjoyment or exercise of the rights or freedoms recognized herein may not be applied except in accordance with the laws enacted for reasons of general interest and in accordance with the purpose for which such restrictions have been established.

Article 31   Recognition of other rights
Other rights and freedoms recognized in accordance with the procedures established in Articles 76 and 77 may be included in the system of protection of this Convention.

CHAPTER V   PERSONAL RESPONSIBILITIES

Article 32   Relationship between duties and rights
1.   Every person has responsibilities to his family, his community, and mankind.
2.   The rights of each person are limited by the rights of others, by the security of all, and by the just demands of the general welfare, in a democratic society.

PART II
MEANS OF PROTECTION
CHAPTER VI   COMPETENT ORGANS

Article 33
The following organs shall have competence with respect to matters relating to the fulfillment of the commitments made by the States Parties to this Convention:
      (a)   the Inter-American Commission on Human Rights, referred to as 'The Commission'; and
      (b)   the Inter-American Court of Human Rights, referred to as 'The Court'.

CHAPTER VII   INTER-AMERICAN COMMISSION ON HUMAN RIGHTS
SECTION I   ORGANIZATION

Article 34
The Inter-American Commission on Human Rights shall be composed of seven members, who shall be persons of high moral character and recognized competence in the field of human rights.

Article 35
The Commission shall represent all the member countries of the Organization of American States.

Article 36
1.   The members of the Commission shall be elected in a personal capacity by the General Assembly of the Organization from a list of candidates proposed by the governments of the member states.
2.   Each of those governments may propose up to three candidates, who may be nationals of the states proposing them or of any other member state of the Organization of American States. When a slate of three is proposed, at least one of the candidates shall be a national of a state other than the one proposing the slate.

Article 37
1.   The members of the Commission shall be elected for a term of four years and may be reelected only once, but the terms of three of the members chosen in the first election shall expire at the end of two years. Immediately following that election the General Assembly shall determine the names of those three members by lot.
2.   No two nationals of the same state may be members of the Commission.

Article 38
Vacancies that may occur on the Commission for reasons other than the normal expiration of a term shall be filled by the Permanent Council of the Organization in accordance with the provisions of the Statute of the Commission.

Article 39
The Commission shall prepare its Statute, which it shall submit to the General Assembly for approval. It shall establish its own Regulations.

Article 40
Secretariat services for the Commission shall be furnished by the appropriate specialized unit of the General Secretariat of the Organization. This unit shall be provided with the resources required to accomplish the tasks assigned to it by the Commission.

SECTION 2   FUNCTIONS

Article 41
The main functions of the Commission shall be to promote respect for and defense of human rights. In the exercise of its mandate, it shall have the following functions and powers:

(a)   to develop an awareness of human rights among the peoples of America;

(b)   to make recommendations to the governments of the member states, when it considers such action advisable, for the adoption of progressive measures in favor of human rights within the framework of their domestic law and constitutional provisions as well as appropriate measures to further the observance of those rights;

(c)   to prepare such studies or reports as it considers advisable in the performance of its duties;

(d)   to request the governments of the member states to supply it with information on the measures adopted by them in matters of human rights;

(e)   to respond, through the General Secretariat of the Organization of American States, to inquiries made by the member states on matters related to human rights and, within the limits of its possibilities, to provide those states with the advisory services they request;

(f)   to take action on petitions and other communications pursuant to its authority, under the provisions of Articles 44 through 51 of this Convention; and

(g)   to submit an annual report to the General Assembly of the Organization of American States.

Article 42
The States Parties shall transmit to the Commission a copy of each of the reports and studies that they submit annually to the Executive Committees of the Inter-American Economic and Social Council and the Inter-American Council for Education, Science, and Culture, in their respective fields, so that the Commission may watch over the promotion of the rights implicit in the economic, social, educational, scientific, and cultural standards set forth in the Charter of the Organization of American States as amended by the Protocol of Buenos Aires.

Article 43
The States Parties undertake to provide the Commission with such information as it may request of them as to the manner in which their domestic law ensures the effective application of any provisions of this Convention.

SECTION 3   COMPETENCE

Article 44
Any person or group of persons, or any nongovernmental entity legally recognized in one or more member states of the Organization, may lodge petitions with the Commission containing denunciations or complaints of violation of this Convention by a State Party.

Article 45
1.   Any State Party may, when it deposits its instrument of ratification of or adherence to this Convention, or at any later time, declare that it recognizes the

competence of the Commission to receive and examine communications in which a State Party alleges that another State Party has committed a violation of a human right set forth in this Convention.

2.	Communications presented by virtue of this article may be admitted and examined only if they are presented by a State Party that has made a declaration recognizing the aforementioned competence of the Commission. The Commission shall not admit any communication against a State Party that has not made such a declaration.

3.	A declaration concerning recognition of competence may be made to be valid for an indefinite time, for a specified period, or for a specific case.

4.	Declarations shall be deposited with the General Secretariat of the Organization of American States, which shall transmit copies thereof to the member states of that Organization.

Article 46

1.	Admission by the Commission of a petition or communication lodged in accordance with Articles 44 or 45 shall be subject to the following requirements:

(a)	that the remedies under domestic law have been pursued and exhausted in accordance with generally recognized principles of international law;

(b)	that the petition or communication is lodged within a period of six months from the date on which the party alleging violation of his rights was notified of the final judgment;

(c)	that the subject of the petition or communication is not pending before another international procedure for settlement; and

(d)	that, in the case of Article 44, the petition contains the name, nationality, profession, domicile, and signature of the person or persons or of the legal representative of the entity lodging the petition.

2.	The provisions of paragraphs 1 (a) and 1 (b) of this article shall not be applicable when:

(a)	the domestic legislation of the state concerned does not afford due process of law for the protection of the right or rights that have allegedly been violated;

(b)	the party alleging violation of his rights has been denied access to the remedies under domestic law or has been prevented from exhausting them; or

(c)	there has been unwarranted delay in rendering a final judgment under the aforementioned remedies.

Article 47

The Commission shall consider inadmissible any petition or communication submitted under Articles 44 or 45 if:

(a)	any of the requirements indicated in Article 46 has not been met;

(b)	the petition or communication does not state facts that tend to establish a violation of the rights guaranteed by this Convention;

(c)	the statements of the petitioner or of the state indicate that the petition or communication is manifestly groundless or obviously out of order; or

(d)	the petition or communication is substantially the same as one previously studied by the Commission or by another international organization.

SECTION 4 PROCEDURE

Article 48

1.	When the Commission receives a petition or communication alleging violation of any of the rights protected by this Convention, it shall proceed as follows:

(a)	If it considers the petition or communication admissible, it shall request information from the government of the state indicated as being responsible for the alleged violations and shall furnish that government a transcript of the pertinent portions of the petition or communication. This information shall be submitted within a reasonable period to be determined by the Commission in accordance with the circumstances of each case.

(b) After the information has been received, or after the period established has elapsed and the information has not been received, the Commission shall ascertain whether the grounds for the petition or communication still exist. If they do not, the Commission shall order the record to be closed.

(c) The Commission may also declare the petition or communication inadmissible or out of order on the basis of information or evidence subsequently received.

(d) If the record has not been closed, the Commission shall, with the knowledge of the parties, examine the matter set forth in the petition or communication in order to verify the facts. If necessary and advisable, the Commission shall carry out an investigation, for the effective conduct of which it shall request, and the states concerned shall furnish to it, all necessary facilities.

(e) The Commission may request the states concerned to furnish any pertinent information and, if so requested, shall hear oral statements or receive written statements from the parties concerned.

(f) The Commission shall place itself at the disposal of the parties concerned with a view to reaching a friendly settlement of the matter on the basis of respect for the human rights recognized in this Convention.

2. However, in serious and urgent cases, only the presentation of a petition or communication that fulfills all the formal requirements of admissibility shall be necessary in order for the Commission to conduct an investigation with the prior consent of the state in whose territory a violation has allegedly been committed.

Article 49

If a friendly settlement has been reached in accordance with paragraph 1 (f) of Article 48, the Commission shall draw up a report, which shall be transmitted to the petitioner and to the States Parties to this Convention, and shall then be communicated to the Secretary-General of the Organization of American States for publication. This report shall contain a brief statement of the facts and of the solution reached. If any party in the case so requests, the fullest possible information shall be provided to it.

Article 50

1. If a settlement is not reached, the Commission shall, within the time limit established by its Statute, draw up a report setting forth the facts and stating its conclusions. If the report, in whole or in part, does not represent the unanimous agreement of the members of the Commission, any member may attach to it a separate opinion. The written and oral statements made by the parties in accordance with paragraph 1 (e) of Article 48 shall also be attached to the report.

2. The report shall be transmitted to the states concerned, which shall not be at liberty to publish it.

3. In transmitting the report, the Committee may make such proposals and recommendations as it sees fit.

Article 51

1. If, within a period of three months from the date of the transmittal of the report of the Commission to the states concerned, the matter has not either been settled or submitted by the Commission or by the state concerned to the Court and its jurisdiction accepted, the Commission may, by the vote of an absolute majority of its members, set forth its opinion and conclusions concerning the question submitted for its consideration.

2. Where appropriate, the Commission shall make pertinent recommendations and shall prescribe a period within which the state is to take the measures that are incumbent upon it to remedy the situation examined.

3. When the prescribed period has expired, the Commission shall decide by the vote of an absolute majority of its members whether the state has taken adequate measures and whether to publish its report.

CHAPTER VIII   INTER-AMERICAN COURT OF HUMAN RIGHTS
SECTION I   ORGANIZATION

Article 52

1. The Court shall consist of seven judges, nationals of the member states of the Organization, elected in an individual capacity from among jurists of the highest moral authority and of recognized competence in the field of human rights, who possess the qualifications required for the exercise of the highest judicial functions in conformity with the law of the state of which they are nationals or of the state that proposes them as candidates.

2. No two judges may be nationals of the same state.

Article 53

1. The judges of the Court shall be elected by secret ballot by an absolute majority vote of the States Parties to the Convention in the General Assembly of the Organization, from a panel of candidates proposed by those states.

2. Each of the States Parties may propose up to three candidates, nationals of the state that proposes them or of any other member state of the Organization of American States. When a slate of three is proposed, at least one of the candidates shall be a national of a state other than the one proposing the slate.

Article 54

1. The judges of the Court shall be elected for a term of six years and may be reelected only once. The term of three of the judges chosen in the first election shall expire at the end of three years. Immediately after the election, the names of the three judges shall be determined by lot in the General Assembly.

2. A judge elected to replace a judge whose term has not expired shall complete the term of the latter.

3. The judges shall continue in office until the expiration of their term. However, they shall continue to serve with regard to cases that they have begun to hear and that are still pending, for which purposes they shall not be replaced by the newly elected judges.

Article 55

1. If a judge is a national of any of the States Parties to a case submitted to the Court, he shall retain his right to hear that case.

2. If one of the judges called upon to hear a case should be a national of one the States Parties to the case, any other State Party in the case may appoint a person of its choice to serve on the Court as an *ad hoc* judge.

3. If among the judges called upon to hear a case none is a national of any of the States Parties to the case, each of the latter may appoint an *ad hoc* judge.

4. An *ad hoc* judge shall possess the qualifications indicated in Article 52.

5. If several States Parties to the Convention should have the same interest in a case, they shall be considered as a single party for purposes of the above provisions. In case of doubt, the Court shall decide.

Article 56

Five judges shall constitute a quorum for the transaction of business by the Court.

Article 57
The Commission shall appear in all cases before the Court.

Article 58
1. The Court shall have its seat at the place determined by the States Parties to the Convention in the General Assembly of the Organization; however, it may convene in the territory of any member state of the Organization of American States when a majority of the Court consider it desirable, and with the prior consent of the state concerned.
The seat of the Court may be changed by the States Parties to the Convention in the General Assembly by a two thirds vote.
2. The Court shall appoint its own Secretary.
3. The Secretary shall have his office at the place where the Court has its seat and shall attend the meetings that the Court may hold away from its seat.

Article 59
The Court shall establish its Secretariat, which shall function under the direction of the Secretary of the Court, in accordance with the administrative standards of the General Secretariat of the Organization in all respects not incompatible with the independence of the Court. The staff of the Court's Secretariat shall be appointed by the Secretary-General of the Organization, in consultation with the Secretary of the Court.

Article 60
The Court shall draw up its Statute, which it shall submit to the General Assembly for approval. It shall adopt its own Rules of Procedure.

SECTION 2 JURISDICTION AND FUNCTIONS

Article 61
1. Only the States Parties and the Commission shall have the right to submit a case to the Court.
2. In order for the Court to hear a case, it is necessary that the procedures set forth in Articles 48 to 50 shall have been completed.

Article 62
1. A State Party may, upon depositing its instrument of ratification or adherence to this Convention, or at any subsequent time, declare that it recognizes as binding, *ipso facto*, and not requiring special agreement, the jurisdiction of the Court on all matters relating to the interpretation or application of this Convention.
2. Such declaration may be made unconditionally, on the condition of reciprocity, for a specified period, or for specific cases. It shall be presented to the Secretary-General of the Organization, who shall transmit copies thereof to the other member states of the Organization and to the Secretary of the Court.
3. The jurisdiction of the Court shall comprise all cases concerning the interpretation and application of the provisions of this Convention that are submitted to it, provided that the States Parties to the case recognize or have recognized such jurisdiction, whether by special declaration pursuant to the preceding paragraphs, or by a special agreement.

Article 63
1. If the Court finds that there has been a violation of a right or freedom protected by this Convention, the Court shall rule that the injured party be ensured the enjoyment of his right or freedom that was violated. It shall also rule, if appropriate, that the consequences of the measure or situation that constituted the breach of such right or freedom be remedied and that fair compensation be paid to the injured party.

2.   In cases of extreme gravity and urgency, and when necessary to avoid irreparable damage to persons, the Court shall adopt such provisional measures as it deems pertinent in matters it has under consideration. With respect to a case not yet submitted to the Court, it may act at the request of the Commission.

Article 64

1.   The member states of the Organization may consult the Court regarding the interpretation of this Convention or of other treaties concerning the protection of human rights in the American states. Within their spheres of competence, the organs listed in Chapter X of the Charter of the Organization of American States, as amended by the Protocol of Buenos Aires, may in like manner consult the Court.

2.   The Court, at the request of a member state of the Organization, may provide that state with opinions regarding the compatibility of any of its domestic laws with the aforesaid international instruments.

Article 65

To each regular session of the General Assembly of the Organization of American States the Court shall submit, for the Assembly's consideration, a report on its work during the previous year. It shall specify, in particular, the cases in which a state has not complied with its judgments, making any pertinent recommendations.

SECTION 3   PROCEDURE

Article 66

1.   Reasons shall be given for the judgment of the Court.

2.   If the judgment does not represent in whole or in part the unanimous opinion of the judges, any judge shall be entitled to have his dissenting or separate opinion attached to the judgment.

Article 67

The judgment of the Court shall be final and not subject to appeal. In case of disagreement as to the meaning or scope of the judgment, the Court shall interpret it at the request of any of the parties, provided the request is made within ninety days from the date of notification of the judgment.

Article 68

1.   The States Parties to the Convention undertake to comply with the judgment of the Court in any case to which they are parties.

2.   That part of a judgment that stipulates compensatory damages may be executed in the country concerned in accordance with domestic procedure governing the execution of judgments against the state.

Article 69

The parties to the case shall be notified of the judgment of the Court and it shall be transmitted to the States Parties to the Convention.

CHAPTER IX   COMMON PROVISIONS

Article 70

1.   The judges of the Court and the members of the Commission shall enjoy, from the moment of their election and throughout their term of office, the immunities extended to diplomatic agents in accordance with international law. During the exercise of their official function they shall, in addition, enjoy the diplomatic privileges necessary for the performance of their duties.

2.   At no time shall the judges of the Court or the members of the Commission be held liable for any decisions or opinions issued in the exercise of their functions.

Article 71
The position of judge of the Court or member of the Commission is incompatible with any other activity that might affect the independence or impartiality of such judge or member, as determined in the respective statutes.

Article 72
The judges of the Court and the members of the Commission shall receive emoluments and travel allowances in the form and under the conditions set forth in their statutes, with due regard for the importance and independence of their office. Such emoluments and travel allowances shall be determined in the budget of the Organization of American States, which shall also include the expenses of the Court and its Secretariat. To this end, the Court shall draw up its own budget and submit it for approval to the General Assembly through the General Secretariat. The latter may not introduce any changes in it.

Article 73
The General Assembly may, only at the request of the Commission or the Court, as the case may be, determine sanctions to be applied against members of the Commission or judges of the Court when there are justifiable grounds for such action as set forth in the respective statutes. A vote of a two-thirds majority of the member states of the Organization shall be required for a decision in the case of members of the Commission and, in the case of judges of the Court, a two-thirds majority vote of the States Parties to the Convention shall also be required.

PART III
GENERAL AND TRANSITORY PROVISIONS
CHAPTER X SIGNATURE, RATIFICATION, RESERVATIONS, AMENDMENTS, PROTOCOLS, AND DENUNCIATION

Article 74
1. This Convention shall be open for signature and ratification by or adherence of any member state of the Organization of American States.
2. Ratification of or adherence to this Convention shall be made by the deposit of an instrument of ratification or adherence with the General Secretariat of the Organization of American States. As soon as eleven states have deposited their instruments of ratification or adherence, the Convention shall enter into force. With respect to any state that ratifies or adheres thereafter, the Convention shall enter into force on the date of the deposit of its instrument of ratification or adherence.
3. The Secretary-General shall inform all member states of the Organization of the entry into force of the Convention.

Article 75
This Convention shall be subject to reservations only in conformity with the provisions of the Vienna Convention on the Law of Treaties signed on May 23, 1969.

Article 76
1. Proposals to amend this Convention may be submitted to the General Assembly for the action it deems appropriate by any State Party directly, and by the Commission or the Court through the Secretary-General.
2. Amendments shall enter into force for the states ratifying them on the date when two thirds of the States Parties to this Convention have deposited their respective instruments of ratification. With respect to the other States Parties, amendments shall enter into force on the dates on which they deposit their respective instruments of ratification.

Article 77

1. In accordance with Article 31, any State Party and the Commission may submit proposed protocols to this Convention for consideration by the States Parties at the General Assembly with a view to gradually including other rights and freedoms within its system of protection.

2. Each Protocol shall determine the manner of its entry into force and shall be applied only among the States Parties to it.

Article 78

1. The States Parties may denounce this Convention at the expiration of a five-year period starting from the date of its entry into force and by means of notice given one year in advance. Notice of the denunciation shall be addressed to the Secretary-General of the Organization, who shall inform the other States Parties.

2. Such a denunciation shall not have the effect of releasing the State Party concerned from the obligations contained in this Convention with respect to any act that may constitute a violation of those obligations and that has been taken by that state prior to the effective date of denunciation.

CHAPTER XI   TRANSITORY PROVISIONS
SECTION I   INTER-AMERICAN COMMISSION ON HUMAN RIGHTS

Article 79

Upon the entry into force of this Convention, the Secretary-General shall, in writing, request each member state of the Organization to present, within ninety days, its candidates for membership on the Inter-American Commission on Human Rights. The Secretary-General shall prepare a list in alphabetical order of the candidates presented, and transmit it to the member states of the Organization at least thirty days prior to the next session of the General Assembly.

Article 80

The members of the Commission shall be elected by secret ballot of the General Assembly from the list of candidates referred to in Article 79. The candidates who obtain the largest number of votes and an absolute majority of the votes of the representatives of the member states shall be declared elected. Should it become necessary to have several ballots in order to elect all the members of the Commission, the candidates who receive the smallest number of votes shall be eliminated successively, in the manner determined by the General Assembly.

SECTION 2   INTER-AMERICAN COURT OF HUMAN RIGHTS

Article 81

Upon the entry into force of this Convention, the Secretary-General shall, in writing, request each State Party to present, within ninety days, its candidates for membership on the Inter-American Court of Human Rights. The Secretary-General shall prepare a list in alphabetical order of the candidates presented and transmit it to the States Parties at least thirty days prior to the next session of the General Assembly.

Article 82

The judges of the Court shall be elected from the list of candidates referred to in Article 81, by secret ballot of the States Parties to the Convention in the General Assembly. The candidates who obtain the largest number of votes and an absolute majority of the votes of the representatives of the States Parties shall be declared elected. Should it become necessary to have several ballots in order to elect all the judges of the Court, the candidates who receive the smallest number of votes shall be eliminated successively, in the manner determined by the States Parties.

IN WITNESS WHEREOF, the undersigned Plenipotentiaries, whose full powers were found in good and due form, sign this Convention, which shall be called 'PACT OF SAN JOSE, COSTA RICA', (in the city of San José, Costa Rica, this twenty-second day of November, nineteen hundred and sixty-nine).

ADDITIONAL PROTOCOL TO THE AMERICAN CONVENTION ON HUMAN RIGHTS IN THE AREA OF ECONOMIC, SOCIAL AND CULTURAL RIGHTS 'PROTOCOL OF SAN SALVADOR' (1988)

PREAMBLE

The States Parties to the American Convention on Human Rights 'Pact San José, Costa Rica,'

Reaffirming their intention to consolidate in this hemisphere, within the framework of democratic institutions, a system of personal liberty and social justice based on respect for the essential rights of man;

Recognizing that the essential rights of man are not derived from one's being a national of a certain State, but are based upon attributes of the human person, for which reason they merit international protection in the form of a convention reinforcing or complementing the protection provided by the domestic law of the American States;

Considering the close relationship that exists between economic, social and cultural rights, and civil and political rights, in that the different categories of rights constitute an indivisible whole based on the recognition of the dignity of the human person, for which reason both require permanent protection and promotion if they are to be fully realized, and the violation of some rights in favor of the realization of others can never be justified;

Recognizing the benefits that stem from the promotion and development of cooperation among States and international relations;

Recalling that, in accordance with the Universal Declaration of Human Rights and the American Convention on Human Rights, the ideal of free human beings enjoying freedom from fear and want can only be achieved if conditions are created whereby everyone may enjoy his economic, social and cultural rights as well as his civil and political rights;

Bearing in mind that, although fundamental economic, social and cultural rights have been recognized in earlier international instruments of both world and regional scope, it is essential that those rights be reaffirmed, developed, perfected and protected in order to consolidate in America, on the basis of full respect for the rights of the individual, the democratic representative form of government as well as the right of its peoples to development, self-determination, and the free disposal of their wealth and natural resources, and

Considering that the American Convention on Human Rights provides that draft additional protocols to that Convention may be submitted for consideration to the States Parties, meeting together on the occasion of the General Assembly of the Organization of American States, for the purpose of gradually incorporating other rights and freedoms into the protective system thereof,

Have agreed upon the following Additional Protocol to the American Convention on Human Rights 'Protocol of San Salvador:'

Article 1   Obligation to Adopt Measures

The States Parties to this Additional Protocol to the American Convention on Human Rights undertake to adopt the necessary measures, both domestically and through international cooperation, especially economic and technical, to the extent allowed by their available resources, and taking into account their degree of development, for the purpose of achieving progressively and pursuant to their internal legislations, the full observance of the rights recognized in this Protocol.

Article 2   Obligation to Enact Domestic Legislation
If the exercise of the rights set forth in this Protocol is not already guaranteed by legislative or other provisions, the States Parties undertake to adopt, in accordance with their constitutional processes and the provisions of this Protocol, such legislative or other measures as may be necessary for making those rights a reality.

Article 3   Obligation of nondiscrimination
The States Parties to this Protocol undertake to guarantee the exercise of the rights set forth herein without discrimination of any kind for reasons related to race, color, sex, language, religion, political or other opinions, national or social origin, economic status, birth or any other social condition.

Article 4   Inadmissibility of Restrictions
A right which is recognized or in effect in a State by virtue of its internal legislation or international conventions may not be restricted or curtailed on the pretext that this Protocol does not recognize the right or recognizes it to a lesser degree.

Article 5   Scope of Restrictions and Limitations
The States Parties may establish restrictions and limitations on the enjoyment and exercise of the rights established herein by means of laws promulgated for the purpose of preserving the general welfare in a democratic society only to the extent that they are not incompatible with the purpose and reason underlying those rights.

Article 6   Right to Work
1.   Everyone has the right to work, which includes the opportunity to secure the means for living a dignified and decent existence by performing a freely elected or accepted lawful activity.

2.   The States Parties undertake to adopt measures that will make the right to work fully effective, especially with regard to the achievement of full employment, vocational guidance, and the development of technical and vocational training projects, in particular those directed to the disabled. The States Parties also undertake to implement and strengthen programs that help to ensure suitable family care, so that women may enjoy a real opportunity to exercise the right to work.

Article 7   Just, Equitable, and Satisfactory Conditions of Work
The States Parties to this Protocol recognize that the right to work to which the foregoing article refers presupposes that everyone shall enjoy that right under just, equitable, and satisfactory conditions, which the States Parties undertake to guarantee in their internal legislation, particularly with respect to:

(a)   Remuneration which guarantees, as a minimum, to all workers dignified and decent living conditions for them and their families and fair and equal wages for equal work, without distinction;

(b)   The right of every worker to follow his vocation and to devote himself to the activity that best fulfills his expectations and to change employment in accordance with the pertinent national regulations;

(c)   The right of every worker to promotion or upward mobility in his employment, for which purpose account shall be taken of his qualifications, competence, integrity and seniority;

(d)   Stability of employment, subject to the nature of each industry and occupation and the causes for just separation. In cases of unjustified dismissal, the worker shall have the right to indemnity or to reinstatement on the job or any other benefits provided by domestic legislation;

(e)   Safety and hygiene at work;

(f)   The prohibition of night work or unhealthy or dangerous working conditions and, in general, of all work which jeopardizes health, safety, or morals, for persons under 18 years of age. As regards minors under the age of 16, the work day shall be subordinated to the provisions regarding compulsory education and in no case shall work constitute an impediment to school attendance or a limitation on benefiting from education received;

(g)   A reasonable limitation of working hours, both daily and weekly. The days shall be shorter in the case of dangerous or unhealthy work or of night work;

(h)   Rest, leisure and paid vacations as well as remuneration for national holidays.

Article 8   Trade Union Rights

1.   The States Parties shall ensure:

(a)   The right of workers to organize trade unions and to join the union of their choice for the purpose of protecting and promoting their interests. As an extension of that right, the States Parties shall permit trade unions to establish national federations or confederations, or to affiliate with those that already exist, as well as to form international trade union organizations and to affiliate with that of their choice. The States Parties shall also permit trade unions, federations and confederations to function freely;

(b)   The right to strike.

2.   The exercise of the rights set forth above may be subject only to restrictions established by law, provided that such restrictions are characteristic of a democratic society and necessary for safeguarding public order or for protecting public health or morals or the rights and freedoms of others. Members of the armed forces and the police and of other essential public services shall be subject to limitations and restrictions established by law.

3.   No one may be compelled to belong to a trade union.

Article 9   Right to Social Security

1.   Everyone shall have the right to social security protecting him from the consequences of old age and of disability which prevents him, physically or mentally, from securing the means for a dignified and decent existence. In the event of the death of a beneficiary, social security benefits shall be applied to his dependents.

2.   In the case of persons who are employed, the right to social security shall cover at least medical care and an allowance or retirement benefit in the case of work accidents or occupational disease and, in the case of women, paid maternity leave before and after childbirth.

Article 10   Right to Health

1.   Everyone shall have the right to health, understood to mean the enjoyment of the highest level of physical, mental and social well-being.

2.   In order to ensure the exercise of the right to health, the States Parties agree to recognize health as a public good and, particularly, to adopt the following measures to ensure that right:

(a)   Primary health care, that is, essential health care made available to all individuals and families in the community;

(b)   Extension of the benefits of health services to all individuals subject to the State's jurisdiction;

(c)   Universal immunization against the principal infectious diseases;

(d)   Prevention and treatment of endemic, occupational and other diseases;

(e)   Education of the population on the prevention and treatment of health problems, and

(f)   Satisfaction of the health needs of the highest risk groups and of those whose poverty makes them the most vulnerable.

Article 11   Right to a Healthy Environment

1.   Everyone shall have the right to live in a healthy environment and to have access to basic public services.

2.   The States Parties shall promote the protection, preservation, and improvement of the environment.

Article 12   Right to Food

1.   Everyone has the right to adequate nutrition which guarantees the possibility of enjoying the highest level of physical, emotional and intellectual development.

2.   In order to promote the exercise of this right and eradicate malnutrition, the States Parties undertake to improve methods of production, supply and distribution of food, and to this end, agree to promote greater international cooperation in support of the relevant national policies.

Article 13   Right to Education

1.   Everyone has the right to education.

2.   The States Parties to this Protocol agree that education should be directed towards the full development of the human personality and human dignity and should strengthen respect for human rights, ideological pluralism, fundamental freedoms, justice and peace. They further agree that education ought to enable everyone to participate effectively in a democratic and pluralistic society and achieve a decent existence and should foster understanding, tolerance and friendship among all nations and all racial, ethnic or religious groups and promote activities for the maintenance of peace.

3.   The States Parties to this Protocol recognize that in order to achieve the full exercise of the right to education:

  (a)   Primary education should be compulsory and accessible to all without cost;

  (b)   Secondary education in its different forms, including technical and vocational secondary education, should be made generally available and accessible to all by every appropriate means, and in particular, by the progressive introduction of free education;

  (c)   Higher education should be made equally accessible to all, on the basis of individual capacity, by every appropriate means, and in particular, by the progressive introduction of free education;

  (d)   Basic education should be encouraged or intensified as far as possible for those persons who have not received or completed the whole cycle of primary instruction;

  (e)   Programs of special education should be established for the handicapped, so as to provide special instruction and training to persons with physical disabilities or mental deficiencies.

4.   In conformity with the domestic legislation of the States Parties, parents should have the right to select the type of education to be given to their children, provided that it conforms to the principles set forth above.

5.   Nothing in this Protocol shall be interpreted as a restriction of the freedom of individuals and entities to establish and direct educational institutions in accordance with the domestic legislation of the States Parties.

Article 14   Right to the Benefits of Culture

1.   The States Parties to this Protocol recognize the right of everyone:

  (a)   To take part in the cultural and artistic life of the community;

  (b)   To enjoy the benefits of scientific and technological progress;

  (c)   To benefit from the protection of moral and material interests deriving from any scientific, literary or artistic production of which he is the author.

2. The steps to be taken by the States Parties to this Protocol to ensure the full exercise of this right shall include those necessary for the conservation, development and dissemination of science, culture and art.

3. The States Parties to this Protocol undertake to respect the freedom indispensable for scientific research and creative activity.

4. The States Parties to this Protocol recognize the benefits to be derived from the encouragement and development of international cooperation and relations in the fields of science, arts and culture, and accordingly agree to foster greater international cooperation in these fields.

Article 15   Right to the Formation and the Protection of Families

1. The family is the natural and fundamental element of society and ought to be protected by the State, which should see to the improvement of its spiritual and material conditions.

2. Everyone has the right to form a family, which shall be exercised in accordance with the provisions of the pertinent domestic legislation.

3. The States Parties hereby undertake to accord adequate protection to the family unit and in particular:

   (a)   To provide special care and assistance to mothers during a reasonable period before and after childbirth;

   (b)   To guarantee adequate nutrition for children at the nursing stage and during school attendance years;

   (c)   To adopt special measures for the protection of adolescents in order to ensure the full development of their physical, intellectual and moral capacities;

   (d)   To undertake special programs of family training so as to help create a stable and positive environment in which children will receive and develop the values of understanding, solidarity, respect and responsibility.

Article 16   Rights of Children

Every child, whatever his parentage, has the right to the protection that his status as a minor requires from his family, society and the State. Every child has the right to grow under the protection and responsibility of his parents; save in exceptional, judicially-recognized circumstances, a child of young age ought not to be separated from his mother. Every child has the right to free and compulsory education, at least in the elementary phase, and to continue his training at higher levels of the educational system.

Article 17   Protection of the Elderly

Everyone has the right to special protection in old age. With this in view the States Parties agree to take progressively the necessary steps to make this right a reality and, particularly, to:

   (a)   Provide suitable facilities, as well as food and specialized medical care, for elderly individuals who lack them and are unable to provide them for themselves;

   (b)   Undertake work programs specifically designed to give the elderly the opportunity to engage in a productive activity suited to their abilities and consistent with their vocations or desires;

   (c)   Foster the establishment of social organizations aimed at improving the quality of life for the elderly.

Article 18   Protection of the Handicapped

Everyone affected by a diminution of his physical or mental capacities is entitled to receive special attention designed to help him achieve the greatest possible development of his personality. The States Parties agree to adopt such measures as may be necessary for this purpose and, especially, to:

   (a)   Undertake programs specifically aimed at providing the handicapped with the resources and environment needed for attaining this goal, including work programs consistent with their possibilities and freely accepted by them or their legal representatives, as the case may be;

    (b)   Provide special training to the families of the handicapped in order to help them solve the problems of coexistence and convert them into active agents in the physical, mental and emotional development of the latter;

    (c)   Include the consideration of solutions to specific requirements arising from needs of this group as a priority component of their urban development plans;

    (d)   Encourage the establishment of social groups in which the handicapped can be helped to enjoy a fuller life.

Article 19   Means of Protection

1.   Pursuant to the provisions of this article and the corresponding rules to be formulated for this purpose by the General Assembly of the Organization of American States, the States Parties to this Protocol undertake to submit periodic reports on the progressive measures they have taken to ensure due respect for the rights set forth in this Protocol.

2.   All reports shall be submitted to the Secretary General of the OAS, who shall transmit them to the Inter-American Economic and Social Council and the Inter-American Council for Education, Science and Culture so that they may examine them in accordance with the provisions of this article. The Secretary General shall send a copy of such reports to the Inter-American Commission on Human Rights.

3.   The Secretary General of the Organization of American States shall also transmit to the specialized organizations of the inter-American system of which the States Parties to the present Protocol are members, copies or pertinent portions of the reports submitted, insofar as they relate to matters within the purview of those organizations, as established by their constituent instruments.

4.   The specialized organizations of the inter-American system may submit reports to the Inter-American Economic and Social Council and the Inter-American Council for Education, Science and Culture relative to compliance with the provisions of the present Protocol in their fields of activity.

5.   The annual reports submitted to the General Assembly by the Inter-American Economic and Social Council and the Inter-American Council for Education, Science and Culture shall contain a summary of the information received from the States Parties to the present Protocol and the specialized organizations concerning the progressive measures adopted in order to ensure respect for the rights acknowledged in the Protocol itself and the general recommendations they consider to be appropriate in this respect.

6.   Any instance in which the rights established in paragraph a) of Article 8 and in Article 13 are violated by action directly attributable to a State Party to this Protocol may give rise, through participation of the Inter-American Commission on Human Rights and, when applicable, of the Inter-American Court of Human Rights, to application of the system of individual petitions governed by Article 44 through 51 and 61 through 69 of the American Convention on Human Rights.

7.   Without prejudice to the provisions of the preceding paragraph, the Inter-American Commission on Human Rights may formulate such observations and recommendations as it deems pertinent concerning the status of the economic, social and cultural rights established in the present Protocol in all or some of the States Parties, which it may include in its Annual Report to the General Assembly or in a special report, whichever it considers more appropriate.

8.   The Councils and the Inter-American Commission on Human Rights, in discharging the functions conferred upon them in this article, shall take into account the progressive nature of the observance of the rights subject to protection by this Protocol.

Article 20   Reservations

The States Parties may, at the time of approval, signature, ratification or accession, make reservations to one or more specific provisions of this Protocol, provided that such reservations are not incompatible with the object and purpose of the Protocol.

Article 21   Signature, Ratification or Accession. Entry into Effect

1.   This Protocol shall remain open to signature and ratification or accession by any State Party to the American Convention on Human Rights.

2.   Ratification of or accession to this Protocol shall be effected by depositing an instrument of ratification or accession with the General Secretariat of the Organization of American States.

3.   The Protocol shall enter into effect when eleven States have deposited their respective instruments of ratification or accession.

4.   The Secretary General shall notify all the member states of the Organization of American States of the entry of the Protocol into effect.

Article 22   Inclusion of other Rights and Expansion of those Recognized

1.   Any State Party and the Inter-American Commission on Human Rights may submit for the consideration of the States Parties meeting on the occasion of the General Assembly proposed amendments to include the recognition of other rights or freedoms or to extend or expand rights or freedoms recognized in this Protocol.

2.   Such amendments shall enter into effect for the States that ratify them on the date of deposit of the instrument of ratification corresponding to the number representing two thirds of the States Parties to this Protocol. For all other States Parties they shall enter into effect on the date on which they deposit their respective instrument of ratification.

PROTOCOL TO THE AMERICAN CONVENTION ON HUMAN RIGHTS TO ABOLISH THE DEATH PENALTY (1990)

PREAMBLE

THE STATES PARTIES TO THIS PROTOCOL,
CONSIDERING:

That Article 4 of the American Convention on Human Rights recognizes the right to life and restricts the application of the death penalty;

That everyone has the inalienable right to respect for his life, a right that cannot be suspended for any reason;

That the tendency among the American States is to be in favor of abolition of the death penalty;

That application of the death penalty has irrevocable consequences, forecloses the correction of judicial error, and precludes any possibility of changing or rehabilitating those convicted;

That the abolition of the death penalty helps to ensure more effective protection of the right to life;

That an international agreement must be arrived at that will entail a progressive development of the American Convention on Human Rights, and

That States Parties to the American Convention on Human Rights have expressed their intention to adopt an international agreement with a view to consolidating the practice of not applying the death penalty in the Americas,

HAVE AGREED TO SIGN THE FOLLOWING
PROTOCOL TO THE AMERICAN CONVENTION ON HUMAN RIGHTS
TO ABOLISH THE DEATH PENALTY

Article 1

The States Parties to this Protocol shall not apply the death penalty in their territory to any person subject to their jurisdiction.

Article 2

1. No reservations may be made to this Protocol. However, at the time of ratification or accession, the States Parties to this instrument may declare that they reserve the right to apply the death penalty in wartime in accordance with international law, for extremely serious crimes of a military nature.

2. The State Party making this reservation shall, upon ratification or accession, inform the Secretary General of the Organization of American States of the pertinent provisions of its national legislation applicable in wartime, as referred to in the preceding paragraph.

3. Said State Party shall notify the Secretary General of the Organization of American States of the beginning or end of any state of war in effect in its territory.

Article 3

1. This Protocol shall be open for signature and ratification or accession by any State Party to the American Convention on Human Rights.

2. Ratification of this Protocol or accession thereto shall be made through the deposit of an instrument of ratification or accession with the General Secretariat of the Organization of American States.

Article 4

This Protocol shall enter into force among the States that ratify or accede to it when they deposit their respective instruments of ratification or accession with the General Secretariat of the Organization of American States.

INTER-AMERICAN CONVENTION TO PREVENT AND PUNISH TORTURE (1985)

The American States signatory to the present Convention,

Aware of the provision of the American Convention on Human Rights that no one shall be subjected to torture or to cruel, inhuman, or degrading punishment or treatment;

Reaffirming that all acts of torture or any other cruel, inhuman, or degrading treatment or punishment constitute an offense against human dignity and a denial of the principles set forth in the Charter of the Organization of American States and in the Charter of the United Nations and are violations of the fundamental human rights and freedoms proclaimed in the American Declaration of the Rights and Duties of Man and the Universal Declaration of Human Rights;

Noting that, in order for the pertinent rules contained in the aforementioned global and regional instruments to take effect, it is necessary to draft an Inter-American Convention that prevents and punishes torture;

Reaffirming their purpose of consolidating in this hemisphere the conditions that make for recognition of and respect for the inherent dignity of man, and ensure the full exercise of his fundamental rights and freedoms,

Have agreed upon the following:

Article 1

The State Parties undertake to prevent and punish torture in accordance with the terms of this Convention.

Article 2

For the purposes of this Convention, torture shall be understood to be any act intentionally performed whereby physical or mental pain or suffering is inflicted on a person for purposes of criminal investigation, as a means of intimidation, as personal punishment, as a preventive measure, as a penalty, or for any other purpose. Torture shall also be understood to be the use of methods upon a person intended to obliterate the personality of the victim or to diminish his physical or mental capacities, even if they do not cause physical pain or mental anguish.

The concept of torture shall not include physical or mental pain or suffering that is inherent in or solely the consequence of lawful measures, provided that they do not include the performance of the acts or use of the methods referred to in this article.

Article 3

The following shall be held guilty of the crime of torture:

(a) A public servant or employee who acting in that capacity orders, instigates or induces the use of torture, or who directly commits it or who, being able to prevent it, fails to do so.

(b) A person who at the instigation of a public servant or employee mentioned in subparagraph (a) orders, instigates or induces the use of torture, directly commits it or is an accomplice thereto.

Article 4

The fact of having acted under orders of a superior shall not provide exemption from the corresponding criminal liability.

Article 5

The existence of circumstances such as a state of war, threat of war, state of siege or of emergency, domestic disturbance or strife, suspension of constitutional guarantees, domestic political instability, or other public emergencies or disasters shall not be invoked or admitted as justification for the crime of torture.

Neither the dangerous character of the detainee or prisoner, nor the lack of security of the prison establishment or penitentiary shall justify torture.

Article 6

In accordance with the terms of Article 1, the States Parties shall take effective measures to prevent and punish torture within their jurisdiction.

The States Parties shall ensure that all acts of torture and attempts to commit torture are offenses under their criminal law and shall make such acts punishable by severe penalties that take into account their serious nature.

The States Parties likewise shall take effective measures to prevent and punish other cruel, inhuman, or degrading treatment or punishment within their jurisdiction.

Article 7

The States Parties shall take measures so that, in the training of police officers and other public officials responsible for the custody of persons temporarily or definitively deprived of their freedom, special emphasis shall be put on the prohibition of the use of torture in interrogation, detention, or arrest.

The States Parties likewise shall take similar measures to prevent other cruel, inhuman, or degrading treatment or punishment.

Article 8

The States Parties shall guarantee that any person making an accusation of having been subjected to torture within their jurisdiction shall have the right to an impartial examination of his case.

Likewise, if there is an accusation or well-grounded reason to believe that an act of torture has been committed within their jurisdiction, the States Parties shall guarantee that their respective authorities will proceed properly and immediately to conduct an investigation into the case and to initiate, whenever appropriate, the corresponding criminal process.

After all the domestic legal procedures of the respective State and the corresponding appeals have been exhausted, the case may be submitted to the international fora whose competence has been recognized by that State.

Article 9
The States Parties undertake to incorporate into their national laws regulations guaranteeing suitable compensation for victims of torture.

None of the provisions of this article shall affect the right to receive compensation that the victim or other persons may have by virtue of existing national legislation.

Article 10
No statement that is verified as having been obtained through torture shall be admissible as evidence in a legal proceeding, except in a legal action taken against a person or persons accused of having elicited it through acts of torture, and only as evidence that the accused obtained such statement by such means.

Article 11
The States Parties shall take the necessary steps to extradite anyone accused of having committed the crime of torture or sentenced for commission of that crime, in accordance with their respective national laws on extradition and their international commitments on this matter.

Article 12
Every State Party shall take the necessary measures to establish its jurisdiction over the crime described in this Convention in the following cases:

    (a) When torture has been committed within its jurisdiction;

    (b) When the alleged criminal is a national of that State; or

    (c) When the victim is a national of that State and it so deems appropriate.

Every State Party shall also take the necessary measures to establish its jurisdiction over the crime described in this Convention when the alleged criminal is within the area under its jurisdiction and it is not appropriate to extradite him in accordance with Article 11.

This Convention does not exclude criminal jurisdiction exercised in accordance with domestic law.

Article 13
The crime referred to in Article 2 shall be deemed to be included among the extraditable crimes in every extradition treaty entered into between States Parties. The States Parties undertake to include the crime of torture as an extraditable offence in every extradition treaty to be concluded between them.

Every State Party that makes extradition conditional on the existence of a treaty may, if it receives a request for extradition from another State Party with which it has no extradition treaty, consider this Convention as the legal basis for extradition in respect of the crime of torture. Extradition shall be subject to the other conditions that may be required by the law of the requested State.

States Parties which do not make extradition conditional on the existence of a treaty shall recognize such crimes as extraditable offences between themselves, subject to the conditions required by the law of the requested State.

Extradition shall not be granted nor shall the person sought be returned when there are grounds to believe that his life is in danger, that he will be subjected to torture or to cruel, inhuman or degrading treatment, or that he will be tried by special or ad hoc courts in the requesting State.

Article 14
When a State Party does not grant the extradition, the case shall be submitted to its competent authorities as if the crime had been committed within its jurisdiction, for the purposes of investigation, and when appropriate, for criminal action, in accordance with its national law. Any decision adopted by these authorities shall be communicated to the State that has requested the extradition.

Article 15
No provision of this Convention may be interpreted as limiting the right of asylum, when appropriate, nor as altering the obligations of the States Parties in the matter of extradition.

Article 16
This Convention shall not limit the provisions of the American Convention on Human Rights, other conventions on the subject, or the Statutes of the Inter-American Commission on Human Rights, with respect to the crime of torture.

Article 17
The States Parties undertake to inform the Inter-American Commission on Human Rights of any legislative, judicial, administrative, or other measures they adopt in application of this Convention.

In keeping with its duties and responsibilities, the Inter-American Commission on Human Rights will endeavor in its annual report to analyze the existing situation in the member states of the Organization of American States in regard to the prevention and elimination of torture.

Article 18
This Convention is open to signature by the member states of the Organization of American States.

Article 19
This Convention is subject to ratification. The instruments of ratification shall be deposited with the General Secretariat of the Organization of American States.

Article 20
This Convention is open to accession by any other American state. The instruments of accession shall be deposited with the General Secretariat of the Organization of American States.

Article 21
The States Parties may, at the time of approval, signature, ratification, or accession, make reservations to this Convention, provided that such reservations are not incompatible with the object and purpose of the Convention and concern one or more specific provisions.

Article 22
This Convention shall enter into force on the thirtieth day following the date on which the second instrument of ratification is deposited. For each State ratifying or acceding to the Convention after the second instrument of ratification has been deposited, the Convention shall enter into force on the thirtieth day following the date on which that State deposits its instrument of ratification or accession.

Article 23
This Convention shall remain in force indefinitely, but may be denounced by any State Party. The instrument of denunciation shall be deposited with the General Secretariat of the Organization of American States. After one year from the date of deposit of the instrument of denunciation, this Convention shall cease to be in effect for the denouncing State but shall remain in force for the remaining States Parties.

Article 24
The original instrument of this Convention, the English, French, Portuguese, and Spanish texts of which are equally authentic, shall be deposited with the General Secretariat of the Organization of American States, which shall send a certified copy to the Secretariat of the United Nations for registration and publication, in accordance

with the provisions of Article 102 of the United Nations Charter. The General Secretariat of the Organization of American States shall notify the member states of the Organization and the States that have acceded to the Convention of signatures and of deposits of instruments of ratification, accession, and denunciation, as well as reservations, if any.

AFRICA

AFRICAN CHARTER ON HUMAN AND PEOPLES' RIGHTS (1981)

PREAMBLE

The African States members of the Organization of African Unity, parties to the present convention entitled 'African Charter on Human and Peoples' Rights';

Recalling Decision 115 (XVI) of the Assembly of Heads of State and Government at its Sixteenth Ordinary Session held in Monrovia, Liberia, from 17 to 20 July 1979 on the preparation of 'a preliminary draft on an African Charter on Human and Peoples' Rights providing *inter alia* for the establishment of bodies to promote and protect human and peoples' rights';

Considering the Charter of the Organization of African Unity, which stipulates that 'freedom, equality, justice and dignity are essential objectives for the achievement of the legitimate aspirations of the African peoples';

Reaffirming the pledge they solemnly made in Article 2 of the said Charter to eradicate all forms of colonialism from Africa, to co-ordinate and intensify their co-operation and efforts to achieve a better life for the peoples of Africa and to promote international co-operation, having due regard to the Charter of the United Nations and the Universal Declaration of Human Rights;

Taking into consideration the virtues of their historical tradition and the values of African civilization which should inspire and characterize their reflection on the concept of human and peoples' rights;

Recognizing on the one hand, that fundamental human rights stem from the attributes of human beings, which justifies their international protection and on the other hand, that the reality and respect of peoples' rights should necessarily guarantee human rights;

Considering that the enjoyment of rights and freedoms also implies the performance of duties on the part of everyone;

Convinced that it is henceforth essential to pay particular attention to the right to development and that civil and political rights cannot be dissociated from economic, social and cultural rights in their conception as well as universality and that the satisfaction of economic, social and cultural rights is a guarantee for the enjoyment of civil and political rights;

Conscious of their duty to achieve the total liberation of Africa, the peoples of which are still struggling for their dignity and genuine independence, and undertaking to eliminate colonialism, neo-colonialism, apartheid, zionism, and to dismantle aggressive foreign military bases and all forms of discrimination, particularly those based on race, ethnic group, colour, sex, language, religion or political opinion;

Reaffirming their adherence to the principles of human and peoples' rights and freedoms contained in the declarations, conventions and other instruments adopted by the Organization of African Unity, the Movement of Non-Aligned Countries and the United Nations;

Firmly convinced of their duty to promote and protect human and peoples' rights and freedoms taking into account the importance traditionally attached to these rights and freedoms in Africa;

HAVE AGREED AS FOLLOWS:

PART I
RIGHTS AND DUTIES
CHAPTER I   HUMAN AND PEOPLES' RIGHTS

Article 1
The Member States of the Organization of African Unity parties to the present Charter shall recognize the rights, duties and freedoms enshrined in this Charter and shall undertake to adopt legislative or other measures to give effect to them.

Article 2
Every individual shall be entitled to the enjoyment of the rights and freedoms recognized and guaranteed in the present Charter without distinction of any kind such as race, ethnic group, colour, sex, language, religion, political or any other opinion, national and social origin, fortune, birth or other status.

Article 3
1. Every individual shall be equal before the law.
2. Every individual shall be entitled to equal protection of the law.

Article 4
Human beings are inviolable. Every human being shall be entitled to respect for his life and the integrity of his person. No one may be arbitrarily deprived of this right.

Article 5
Every individual shall have the right to the respect of the dignity inherent in a human being and to the recognition of his legal status. All forms of exploitation and degradation of man particularly slavery, slave trade, torture, cruel, inhuman or degrading punishment and treatment shall be prohibited.

Article 6
Every individual shall have the right to liberty and to the security of his person. No one may be deprived of his freedom except for reasons and conditions previously laid down by law. In particular, no one may be arbitrarily arrested or detained.

Article 7
1. Every individual shall have the right to have his cause heard. This comprises:
    (a)   the right to an appeal to competent national organs against acts violating his fundamental rights as recognized and guaranteed by conventions, laws, regulations and customs in force;
    (b)   the right to be presumed innocent until proved guilty by a competent court or tribunal;
    (c)   the right to defence, including the right to be defended by counsel of his choice;
    (d)   the right to be tried within a reasonable time by an impartial court or tribunal.
2. No one may be condemned for an act or omission which did not constitute a legally punishable offence at the time it was committed. No penalty may be inflicted for an offence for which no provision was made at the time it was committed. Punishment is personal and can be imposed only on the offender.

Article 8
Freedom of conscience, the profession and free practice of religion shall be guaranteed. No one may, subject to law and order, be submitted to measures restricting the exercise of these freedoms.

Article 9
1. Every individual shall have the right to receive information.
2. Every individual shall have the right to express and disseminate his opinions within the law.

Article 10
1. Every individual shall have the right to free association provided that he abides by the law.
2. Subject to the obligation of solidarity provided for in Article 29 no one may be compelled to join an association.

Article 11
Every individual shall have the right to assemble freely with others. The exercise of this right shall be subject only to necessary restrictions provided for by law in particular those enacted in the interest of national security, the safety, health, ethics and rights and freedoms of others.

Article 12
1. Every individual shall have the right to freedom of movement and residence within the borders of a State provided he abides by the law.
2. Every individual shall have the right to leave any country including his own, and to return to his country. This right may only be subject to restrictions, provided for by law for the protection of national security, law and order, public health or morality.
3. Every individual shall have the right, when persecuted, to seek and obtain asylum in other countries in accordance with the laws of those countries and international conventions.
4. A non-national legally admitted in a territory of a State party to the present Charter, may only be expelled from it by virtue of a decision taken in accordance with the law.
5. The mass expulsion of non-nationals shall be prohibited. Mass expulsion shall be that which is aimed at national, racial, ethnic or religious groups.

Article 13
1. Every citizen shall have the right to participate freely in the government of his country, either directly or through freely chosen representatives in accordance with the provisions of the law.
2. Every citizen shall have the right of equal access to the public service of his country.
3. Every individual shall have the right of access to public property and services in strict equality of all persons before the law.

Article 14
The right to property shall be guaranteed. It may only be encroached upon in the interest of public need or in the general interest of the community and in accordance with the provisions of appropriate laws.

Article 15
Every individual shall have the right to work under equitable and satisfactory conditions, and shall receive equal pay for equal work.

Article 16
1. Every individual shall have the right to enjoy the best attainable state of physical and mental health.
2. States parties to the present Charter shall take the necessary measures to protect the health of their people and to ensure that they receive medical attention when they are sick.

Article 17
1. Every individual shall have the right to education.
2. Every individual may freely take part in the cultural life of his community.
3. The promotion and protection of morals and traditional values recognized by the community shall be the duty of the State.

Article 18
1. The family shall be the natural unit and basis of society. It shall be protected by the State which shall take care of its physical and moral health.
2. The State shall have the duty to assist the family which is the custodian of morals and traditional values recognized by the community.
3. The State shall ensure the elimination of every discrimination against women and also ensure the protection of the rights of the woman and the child as stipulated in international declarations and conventions.
4. The aged and the disabled shall also have the right to special measures of protection in keeping with their physical or moral needs.

Article 19
All peoples shall be equal; they shall enjoy the same respect and shall have the same rights. Nothing shall justify the domination of a people by another.

Article 20
1. All peoples shall have right to existence. They shall have the unquestionable and inalienable right to self-determination. They shall freely determine their political status and shall pursue their economic and social development according to the policy they have freely chosen.
2. Colonized or oppressed peoples shall have the right to free themselves from the bonds of domination by resorting to any means recognized by the international community.
3. All peoples shall have the right to the assistance of the States parties to the present Charter in their liberation struggle against foreign domination, be it political, economic or cultural.

Article 21
1. All peoples shall freely dispose of their wealth and natural resources. This right shall be exercised in the exclusive interest of the people. In no case shall a people be deprived of it.
2. In case of spoliation the dispossessed people shall have the right to the lawful recovery of its property as well as to an adequate compensation.
3. The free disposal of wealth and natural resources shall be exercised without prejudice to the obligation of promoting international economic co-operation based on mutual respect, equitable exchange and the principles of international law.
4. States parties to the present Charter shall individually and collectively exercise the right to free disposal of their wealth and natural resources with a view to strengthening African unity and solidarity.
5. States parties to the present Charter shall undertake to eliminate all forms of foreign economic exploitation particularly that practised by international monopolies so as to enable their peoples to fully benefit from the advantages derived from their national resources.

Article 22
1. All peoples shall have the right to their economic, social and cultural development with due regard to their freedom and identity and in the equal enjoyment of the common heritage of mankind.
2. States shall have the duty, individually or collectively, to ensure the exercise of the right to development.

Article 23

1.   All peoples shall have the right to national and international peace and security. The principles of solidarity and friendly relations implicitly affirmed by the Charter of the United Nations and reaffirmed by that of the Organization of African Unity shall govern relations between States.

2.   For the purpose of strengthening peace, solidarity and friendly relations, States parties to the present Charter shall ensure that:

(a)   any individual enjoying the right of asylum under Article 12 of the present Charter shall not engage in subversive activities against his country of origin or any other State party to the present Charter;

(b)   their territories shall not be used as bases for subversive or terrorist activities against the people of any other State party to the present Charter.

Article 24

All people shall have the right to a general satisfactory environment favourable to their development.

Article 25

States parties to the present Charter shall have the duty to promote and ensure through teaching, education and publication, the respect of the rights and freedoms contained in the present Charter and to see to it that these freedoms and rights as well as corresponding obligations and duties are understood.

Article 26

States parties to the present Charter shall have the duty to guarantee the independence of the Courts and shall allow the establishment and improvement of appropriate national institutions entrusted with the promotion and protection of the rights and freedoms guaranteed by the present Charter.

CHAPTER II   DUTIES

Article 27

1.   Every individual shall have duties towards his family and society, the State and other legally recognized communities and the international community.

2.   The rights and freedoms of each individual shall be exercised with due regard to the rights of others, collective security, morality and common interest.

Article 28

Every individual shall have the duty to respect and consider his fellow beings without discrimination, and to maintain relations aimed at promoting, safeguarding and reinforcing mutual respect and tolerance.

Article 29

The individual shall also have the duty:

1.   To preserve the harmonious development of the family and to work for the cohesion and respect of the family; to respect his parents at all times, to maintain them in case of need;

2.   To serve his national community by placing his physical and intellectual abilities at its service;

3.   Not to compromise the security of the State whose national or resident he is;

4.   To preserve and strengthen social and national solidarity, particularly when the latter is threatened;

5.   To preserve and strengthen the national independence and the territorial integrity of his country and to contribute to its defence in accordance with the law;

6.   To work to the best of his abilities and competence, and to pay taxes imposed by law in the interest of the society;

7. To preserve and strengthen positive African cultural values in his relations with other members of the society, in the spirit of tolerance, dialogue and consultation and, in general, to contribute to the promotion of the moral well-being of society;

8. To contribute to the best of his abilities, at all times and at all levels, to the promotion and achievement of African unity.

PART II
MEASURES OF SAFEGUARD
CHAPTER I ESTABLISHMENT AND ORGANIZATION OF THE AFRICAN
COMMISSION ON HUMAN AND PEOPLES' RIGHTS

Article 30
An African Commission on Human and Peoples' Rights, hereinafter called 'the Commission', shall be established within the Organization of African Unity to promote human and peoples' rights and ensure their protection in Africa.

Article 31
1. The Commission shall consist of eleven members chosen from amongst African personalities of the highest reputation, known for their high morality, integrity, impartiality and competence in matters of human and peoples' rights; particular consideration being given to persons having legal experience.
2. The members of the Commission shall serve in their personal capacity.

Article 32
The Commission shall not include more than one national of the same State.

Article 33
The members of the Commission shall be elected by secret ballot by the Assembly of Heads of State and Government, from a list of persons nominated by the States parties to the present Charter.

Article 34
Each State party to the present Charter may not nominate more than two candidates. The candidates must have the nationality of one of the States parties of the present Charter. When two candidates are nominated by a State, one of them may not be a national of that State.

Article 35
1. The Secretary-General of the Organization of African Unity shall invite States parties to the present Charter at least four months before the elections to nominate candidates.
2. The Secretary-General of the Organization of African Unity shall make an alphabetical list of the persons thus nominated and communicate it to the Heads of State and Government at least one month before the elections.

Article 36
The members of the Commission shall be elected for a six-year period and shall be eligible for re-election. However, the term of office of four of the members elected at the first election shall terminate after two years and the term of office of three others, at the end of four years.

Article 37
Immediately after the first election, the Chairman of the Assembly of Heads of State and Government of the Organization of African Unity shall draw lots to decide the names of those members referred to in Article 36.

Article 38
After their election, the members of the Commission shall make a solemn declaration to discharge their duties impartially and faithfully.

Article 39
1. In case of death or resignation of a member of the Commission, the Chairman of the Commission shall immediately inform the Secretary-General of the Organization of African Unity, who shall declare the seat vacant from the date of death or from the date on which the resignation takes effect.
2. If, in the unanimous opinion of other members of the Commission, a member has stopped discharging his duties for any reason other than a temporary absence, the Chairman of the Commission shall inform the Secretary-General of the Organization of African Unity, who shall then declare the seat vacant.
3. In each of the cases anticipated above, the Assembly of Heads of State and Government shall replace the member whose seat became vacant for the remaining period of his term unless the period is less than six months.

Article 40
Every member of the Commission shall be in office until the date his successor assumes office.

Article 41
The Secretary-General of the Organization of African Unity shall appoint the Secretary of the Commission. He shall also provide the staff and services necessary for the effective discharge of the duties of the Commission. The Organization of African Unity shall bear the cost of the staff and services.

Article 42
1. The Commission shall elect its Chairman and Vice-Chairman for a two-year period. They shall be eligible for re-election.
2. The Commission shall lay down its rules of procedure.
3. Seven members shall form the quorum.
4. In case of an equality of votes, the Chairman shall have a casting vote.
5. The Secretary-General may attend the meetings of the Commission. He shall neither participate in deliberations nor shall he be entitled to vote. The Chairman of the Commission may, however, invite him to speak.

Article 43
In discharging their duties, members of the Commission shall enjoy diplomatic privileges and immunities provided for in the General Convention on the Privileges and Immunities of the Organization of African Unity.

Article 44
Provision shall be made for the emoluments and allowances of the members of the Commission in the Regular Budget of the Organization of African Unity.

CHAPTER II   MANDATE OF THE COMMISSION

Article 45
The functions of the Commission shall be:
1. To promote Human and Peoples' Rights and in particular:
    (a) to collect documents, undertake studies and researches on African problems in the field of human and peoples' rights, organize seminars, symposia and conferences, disseminate information, encourage national and local institutions concerned with human and peoples' rights and, should the case arise, give its views or make recommendations to Governments;
    (b) to formulate and lay down, principles and rules aimed at solving legal problems relating to human and peoples' rights and fundamental freedoms upon which African Governments may base their legislations;

(c)   co-operate with other African and international institutions concerned with the promotion and protection of human and peoples' rights.

2.   Ensure the protection of human and peoples' rights under conditions laid down by the present Charter.

3.   Interpret all the provisions of the present Charter at the request of a State party, an institution of the Organization of African Unity or an African organization recognized by the Organization of African Unity.

4.   Perform any other tasks which may be entrusted to it by the Assembly of Heads of State and Government.

CHAPTER III   PROCEDURE OF THE COMMISSION

Article 46

The Commission may resort to any appropriate method of investigation; it may hear from the Secretary-General of the Organization of African Unity or any other person capable of enlightening it.

COMMUNICATION FROM STATES

Article 47

If a State Party to the present Charter has good reasons to believe that another State party to this Charter has violated the provisions of the Charter, it may draw, by written communication, the attention of that State to the matter. This communication shall also be addressed to the Secretary-General of the Organization of African Unity and to the Chairman of the Commission. Within three months of the receipt of the communication the State to which the communication is addressed shall give the enquiring State, written explanation or statement elucidating the matter. This should include as much as possible relevant information relating to the laws and rules of procedure applied and applicable and the redress already given or course of action available.

Article 48

If within three months from the date on which the original communication is received by the State to which it is addressed, the issue is not settled to the satisfaction of the two States involved through bilateral negotiation or by any other peaceful procedure, either State shall have the right to submit the matter to the Commission through the Chairman and shall notify the other State involved.

Article 49

Notwithstanding the provisions of Article 47, if a State party to the present Charter considers that another State party has violated the provisions of the Charter, it may refer the matter directly to the Commission by addressing a communication to the Chairman, to the Secretary-General of the Organization of African Unity and the State concerned.

Article 50

The Commission can only deal with a matter submitted to it after making sure that all local remedies, if they exist, have been exhausted, unless it is obvious to the Commission that the procedure of achieving these remedies would be unduly prolonged.

Article 51

1.   The Commission may ask the States concerned to provide it with all relevant information.

2.   When the Commission is considering the matter, States concerned may be represented before it and submit written or oral representations.

Article 52
After having obtained from the States concerned and from other sources all the information it deems necessary and after having tried all appropriate means to reach an amicable solution based on the respect of human and peoples' rights, the Commission shall prepare, within a reasonable period of time from the notification referred to in Article 48, a report stating the facts and its findings. This report shall be sent to the States concerned and communicated to the Assembly of Heads of State and Government.

Article 53
While transmitting its report, the Commission may make to the Assembly of Heads of State and Government such recommendations as it deems useful.

Article 54
The Commission shall submit to each Ordinary Session of the Assembly of Heads of State and Government a report on its activities.

OTHER COMMUNICATIONS

Article 55
1.   Before each session, the Secretary of the Commission shall make a list of the communications other than those of States parties to the present Charter and transmit them to the members of the Commission, who shall indicate which communications should be considered by the Commission.
2.   A communication shall be considered by the Commission if a simple majority of its members so decide.

Article 56
Communications relating to human and peoples' rights referred to in Article 55 received by the Commission, shall be considered if they:
1.   Indicate their authors even if the latter request anonymity;
2.   Are compatible with the Charter of the Organization of African Unity or with the present Charter;
3.   Are not written in disparaging or insulting language directed against the State concerned and its institutions or to the Organization of African Unity;
4.   Are not based exclusively on news disseminated through the mass media;
5.   Are sent after exhausting local remedies, if any, unless it is obvious that this procedure is unduly prolonged;
6.   Are submitted within a reasonable period from the time local remedies are exhausted or from the date the Commission is seized of the matter; and
7.   Do not deal with cases which have been settled by these States involved in accordance with the principles of the Charter of the United Nations, or the Charter of the Organization of African Unity or the provisions of the present Charter.

Article 57
Prior to any substantive consideration, all communications shall be brought to the knowledge of the State concerned by the Chairman of the Commission.

Article 58
1.   When it appears after deliberations of the Commission that one or more communications apparently relate to special cases which reveal the existence of a series of serious or massive violations of human and peoples' rights, the Commission shall draw the attention of the Assembly of Heads of State and Government to these special cases.
2.   The Assembly of Heads of State and Government may then request the Commission to undertake an in-depth study of these cases and make a factual report, accompanied by its finding and recommendations.

3. A case of emergency duly noticed by the Commission shall be submitted by the latter to the Chairman of the Assembly of Heads of State and Government who may request an in-depth study.

Article 59

1. All measures taken within the provisions of the present Charter shall remain confidential until such a time as the Assembly of Heads of State and Government shall otherwise decide.

2. However, the report shall be published by the Chairman of the Commission upon the decision of the Assembly of Heads of State and Government.

3. The report on the activities of the Commission shall be published by its Chairman after it has been considered by the Assembly of Heads of State and Government.

CHAPTER IV APPLICABLE PRINCIPLES

Article 60

The Commission shall draw inspiration from international law on human and peoples' rights, particularly from the provisions of various African instruments on human and peoples' rights, the Charter of the United Nations, the Charter of the Organization of African Unity, the Universal Declaration of Human Rights, other instruments adopted by the United Nations and by African countries in the field of human and peoples' rights as well as from the provisions of various instruments adopted within the Specialised Agencies of the United Nations of which the parties to the present Charter are members.

Article 61

The Commission shall also take into consideration, as subsidiary measures to determine the principles of law, other general or special international conventions, laying down rules expressly recognized by Member States of the Organization of African Unity, African practices consistent with international norms on human and peoples' rights, customs generally accepted as law, general principles of law recognized by African States as well as legal precedents and doctrine.

Article 62

Each State party shall undertake to submit every two years, from the date the present Charter comes into force, a report on the legislative or other measures taken with a view to giving effect to the rights and freedoms recognized and guaranteed by the present Charter.

Article 63

1. The present Charter shall be open to signature, ratification or adherence of the Member States of the Organization of African Unity.

2. The instruments of ratification or adherence to the present Charter shall be deposited with the Secretary-General of the Organization of African Unity.

3. The present Charter shall come into force three months after the reception by the Secretary-General of the instruments of ratification or adherence of a simple majority of the Member States of the Organization of African Unity.

PART III
GENERAL PROVISIONS

Article 64

1. After the coming into force of the present Charter, members of the Commission shall be elected in accordance with the relevant Articles of the present Charter.

2. The Secretary-General of the Organization of African Unity shall convene the first meeting of the Commission at the Headquarters of the Organization within three

months of the constitution of the Commission. Thereafter, the Commission shall be convened by its Chairman whenever necessary but at least once a year.

Article 65
For each of the States that will ratify or adhere to the present Charter after its coming into force, the Charter shall take effect three months after the date of the deposit by that State of its instrument of ratification or adherence.

Article 66
Special protocols or agreements may, if necessary, supplement the provisions of the present Charter.

Article 67
The Secretary-General of the Organization of African Unity shall inform Member States of the Organization of the deposit of each instrument of ratification or adherence.

Article 68
The present Charter may be amended if a State party makes a written request to that effect to the Secretary-General of the Organization of African Unity. The Assembly of Heads of State and Government may only consider the draft amendment after all the States parties have been duly informed of it and the Commission has given its opinion on it at the request of the sponsoring State. The amendment shall be approved by a simple majority of the States parties. It shall come into force for each State which has accepted it in accordance with its constitutional procedure three months after the Secretary-General has received notice of the acceptance.

CONFERENCE ON SECURITY AND COOPERATION IN EUROPE INSTRUMENTS

CONFERENCE ON SECURITY AND COOPERATION IN EUROPE: FINAL ACT, HELSINKI (1975)

The Conference on Security and Co-operation in Europe, which opened at Helsinki on 3 July 1973 and continued at Geneva from 18 September 1973 to 21 July 1975, was concluded at Helsinki on 1 August 1975 by the High Representatives of Austria, Belgium, Bulgaria, Canada, Cyprus, Czechoslovakia, Denmark, Finland, France, the German Democratic Republic, the Federal Republic of Germany, Greece, the Holy See, Hungary, Iceland, Ireland, Italy, Liechtenstein, Luxembourg, Malta, Monaco, the Netherlands, Norway, Poland, Portugal, Romania, San Marino, Spain, Sweden, Switzerland, Turkey, the Union of Soviet Socialist Republics, the United Kingdom, the United States of America and Yugoslavia.

During the opening and closing stages of the Conference the participants were addressed by the Secretary-General of the United Nations as their guest of honour. The Director-General of UNESCO and the Executive Secretary of the United Nations Economic Commission for Europe addressed the Conference during its second stage.

During the meetings of the second stage of the Conference, contributions were received, and statements heard, from the following non-participating Mediterranean States on various agenda items: the Democratic and Popular Republic of Algeria, the Arab Republic of Egypt, Israel, the Kingdom of Morocco, the Syrian Arab Republic, Tunisia.

Motivated by the political will, in the interest of peoples, to improve and intensify their relations and to contribute in Europe to peace, security, justice and co-operation as well as to rapprochement among themselves and with the other States of the world.

Determined, in consequence, to give full effect to the results of the Conference and to assure, among their States and throughout Europe, the benefits deriving from those results and thus to broaden, deepen and make continuing and lasting the process of detente.

The High Representatives of the participating States have solemnly adopted the following:

QUESTIONS RELATING TO SECURITY IN EUROPE

The States participating in the Conference on Security and Co-operation in Europe,

Reaffirming their objective of promoting better relations among themselves and ensuring conditions in which their people can live in true and lasting peace free from any threat to or attempt against their security;

Convinced of the need to exert efforts to make détente both a continuing and an increasingly viable and comprehensive process, universal in scope, and that the implementation of the results of the Conference on Security and Co-operation in Europe will be a major contribution to this process;

Considering that solidarity among peoples, as well as the common purpose of the participating States in achieving the aims as set forth by the Conference on Security and Co-operation in Europe, should lead to the development of better and closer relations among them in all fields and thus to overcoming the confrontation stemming from the character of their past relations, and to better mutual understanding;

Mindful of their common history and recognizing that the existence of elements common to their traditions and values can assist them in developing their relations, and desiring to search, fully taking into account the individuality and diversity of their positions and views, for possibilities of joining their efforts with a view to overcoming distrust and increasing confidence, solving the problems that separate them and co-operating in the interest of mankind;

Recognizing the indivisibility of security in Europe as well as their common interest in the development of co-operation throughout Europe and among themselves and expressing their intention to pursue efforts accordingly;

Recognizing the close link between peace and security in Europe and in the world as a whole and conscious of the need for each of them to make its contribution to the strengthening of world peace and security and to the promotion of fundamental rights, economic and social progress and well-being for all peoples;

Have adopted the following:

1. (a) Declaration on Principles Guiding Relations between Participating States

The participating States,

Reaffirming their commitment to peace, security and justice and the continuing development of friendly relations and co-operation;

Recognizing that this commitment, which reflects the interest and aspirations of peoples, constitutes for each participating State a present and future responsibility, heightened by experience of the past;

Reaffirming, in conformity with their membership in the United Nations and in accordance with the purposes and principles of the United Nations, their full and active support for the United Nations and for the enhancement of its role and effectiveness in strengthening international peace, security and justice, and in promoting the solution of international problems, as well as the development of friendly relations and co-operation among States;

Expressing their common adherence to the principles which are set forth below and are in conformity with the Charter of the United Nations, as well as their common will to act, in the application of these principles, in conformity with the purposes and principles of the Chapter of the United Nations;

Declare their determination to respect and put into practice, each of them in its relations with all other participating States, irrespective of their political, economic or social systems as well as of their size, geographical location or level of economic development, the following principles, which all are of primary significance, guiding their mutual relations:

I. *Sovereign equality, respect for the rights inherent in sovereignty*

The participating States will respect each other's sovereign equality and individuality as well as all the rights inherent in and encompassed by its sovereignty, including in particular the right of every State to juridical equality, to territorial integrity and to freedom and political independence. They will also respect each other's right freely to choose and develop its political, social, economic and cultural systems as well as its right to determine its laws and regulations.

Within the framework of international law, all the participating States have equal rights and duties. They will respect each other's right to define and conduct as it wishes its relations with other States in accordance with international law and in the spirit of the present Declaration. They consider that their frontiers can be changed, in accordance with international law, by peaceful means and by agreement. They also have the right to belong or not to belong to international organizations, to be or not to be a party to bilateral or multilateral treaties including the right to be or not to be a party to treaties of alliance; they also have the right to neutrality.

II. *Refraining from the threat or use of force*

The participating States will refrain in their mutual relations, as well as in their international relations in general, from the threat or use of force against the territorial integrity or political independence of any State, or in any other manner inconsistent with the purposes of the United Nations and with the present Declaration. No consideration may be invoked to serve to warrant resort to the threat or use of force in contravention of this principle.

Accordingly, the participating States will refrain from any acts constituting a threat of force or direct or indirect use of force against another participating State. Likewise they will refrain from any manifestation of force for the purpose of inducing another participating State to renounce the full exercise of its sovereign rights. Likewise they will also refrain in their mutual relations from any act of reprisal by force.

No such threat or use of force will be employed as a means of settling disputes, or questions likely to give rise to disputes, between them.

III. *Inviolability of frontiers*

The participating States regard as inviolable all one another's frontiers as well as the frontiers of all States in Europe and therefore they will refrain now and in the future from assaulting these frontiers.

Accordingly, they will also refrain from any demand for, or act of, seizure and usurpation of part or all of the territory of any participating State.

IV. *Territorial integrity of States*

The participating States will respect the territorial integrity of each of the participating States.

Accordingly, they will refrain from any action inconsistent with the purposes and principles of the Charter of the United Nations against the territorial integrity, political independence or the unity of any participating State, and in particular from any such action constituting a threat or use of force.

The participating States will likewise refrain from making each other's territory the object of military occupation or other direct or indirect measures of force in contravention of international law, or the object of acquisition by means of such measures or the threat of them. No such occupation or acquisition will be recognized as legal.

V. *Peaceful settlement of disputes*

The participating States will settle disputes among them by peaceful means in such a manner as not to endanger international peace and security, and justice.

They will endeavour in good faith and a spirit of cooperation to reach a rapid and equitable solution on the basis of international law.

For this purpose they will use such means as negotiation, enquiry, mediation, conciliation, arbitration, judicial settlement or other peaceful means of their own choice including any settlement procedure agreed to in advance of disputes to which they are parties.

In the event of failure to reach a solution by any of the above peaceful means, the parties to a dispute will continue to seek a mutually agreed way to settle the dispute peacefully.

Participating States, parties to a dispute among them, as well as other participating States, will refrain from any action which might aggravate the situation to such a degree as to endanger the maintenance of international peace and security and thereby make a peaceful settlement of the dispute more difficult.

VI. *Non-intervention in internal affairs*

The participating States will refrain from any intervention, direct or indirect, individual or collective, in the internal or external affairs falling within the domestic jurisdiction of another participating State, regardless of their mutual relations.

They will accordingly refrain from any form of armed intervention against another participating State.

They will likewise in all circumstances refrain from any other act of military, or of political, economic or other coercion designed to subordinate to their own interest the exercise by another participating State of the rights inherent in its sovereignty and thus to secure advantages of any kind.

Accordingly, they will, inter alia, refrain from direct or indirect assistance to terrorist activities, or to subversive or other activities directed towards the violent overthrow of the regime of another participating State.

VII. *Respect for human rights and fundamental freedoms, including the freedom of thought, conscience, religion or belief*

The participating States will respect human rights and fundamental freedoms, including the freedom of thought, conscience, religion or belief, for all without distinction as to race, sex, language or religion.

They will promote and encourage the effective exercise of civil, political, economic, social, cultural and other rights and freedoms all of which derive from the inherent dignity of the human person and are essential for his free and full development.

Within this framework the participating States will recognize and respect the freedom of the individual to profess and practise, alone or in community with others, religion or belief acting in accordance with the dictates of his own conscience.

The participating States on whose territory national minorities exist will respect the right of persons belonging to such minorities to equality before the law, will afford them the full opportunity for the actual enjoyment of human rights and fundamental freedoms and will, in this manner, protect their legitimate interests in this sphere.

The participating States recognize the universal significance of human rights and fundamental freedoms, respect for which is an essential factor for the peace, justice and well-being necessary to ensure the development of friendly relations and co-operation among themselves as among all States.

They will constantly respect these rights and freedoms in their mutual relations and will endeavour jointly and separately, including in cooperation with the United Nations, to promote universal and effective respect for them.

They confirm the right of the individual to know and act upon his rights and duties in this field.

In the field of human rights and fundamental freedoms, the participating States will act in conformity with the purposes and principles of the Charter of the United Nations and with the Universal Declaration of Human Rights. They will also fulfill their obligations as set forth in the international declarations and agreements in this field, including inter alia the International Covenants on Human Rights, by which they may be bound.

VIII. *Equal rights and self-determination of peoples*

The participating States will respect the equal rights of peoples and their right to self-determination, acting at all times in conformity with the purposes and principles of the Charter of the United Nations and with the relevant norms of international law, including those relating to territorial integrity of States.

By virtue of the principle of equal rights and self-determination of peoples, all peoples always have the right, in full freedom, to determine, when and as they wish, their internal and external political status, without external interference, and to pursue as they wish their political, economic, social and cultural development.

The participating States reaffirm the universal significance of respect for and effective exercise of equal rights and self-determination of peoples for the development of friendly relations among themselves as among all States; they also recall the importance of the elimination of any form of violation of this principle.

IX.   *Co-operation among States*

The participating States will develop their co-operation with one another and with all States in all fields in accordance with the purposes and principles of the Charter of the United Nations. In developing their co-operation the participating States will place special emphasis on the fields as set forth within the framework of the Conference on Security and Co-operation in Europe, with each of them making its contribution in conditions of full equality.

They will endeavour, in developing their co-operation as equals, to promote mutual understanding and confidence, friendly and good-neighbourly relations among themselves, international peace, security and justice. They will equally endeavour, in developing their co-operation, to improve the well-being of peoples and contribute to the fulfilment of their aspirations through, inter alia, the benefits resulting from increased mutual knowledge and from progress and achievement in the economic, scientific, technological, social, cultural and humanitarian fields. They will take steps to promote conditions favourable to making these benefits available to all; they will take into account the interest of all in the narrowing of differences in the levels of economic development, and in particular the interest of developing countries throughout the world.

They confirm that governments, institutions, organizations and persons have a relevant and positive role to play in contributing toward the achievement of these aims of their co-operation.

They will strive, in increasing their co-operation as set forth above, to develop closer relations among themselves on an improved and more enduring basis for the benefit of peoples.

X.   *Fulfilment in good faith of obligations under international law*

The participating States will fulfil in good faith their obligations under international law, both those obligations arising from the generally recognized principles and rules of international law and those obligations arising from treaties or other agreements, in conformity with international law, to which they are parties.

In exercising their sovereign rights, including the right to determine their laws and regulations, they will conform with their legal obligations under international law; they will furthermore pay due regard to and implement the provisions in the Final Act of the Conference on Security and Co-operation in Europe.

The participating States confirm that in the event of a conflict between the obligations of the members of the United Nations under the Charter of the United Nations and their obligations under any treaty or other international agreement, their obligations under the Charter will prevail, in accordance with Article 103 of the Charter of the United Nations.

All the principles set forth above are of primary significance and, accordingly, they will be equally and unreservedly applied, each of them being interpreted taking into account the others.

The participating States express their determination fully to respect and apply these principles, as set forth in the present Declaration, in all aspects, to their mutual relations and co-operation in order to ensure to each participating State the benefits resulting from the respect and application of these principles by all.

The participating States, paying due regard to the principles above and, in particular, to the first sentence of the tenth principle, 'Fulfilment in good faith of obligations under international law', note that the present Declaration does not affect their rights and obligations, nor the corresponding treaties and other agreements and arrangements.

The participating States express the conviction that respect for these principles will encourage the development of normal and friendly relations and the progress of co-operation among them in all fields. They also express the conviction that respect for these principles will encourage the development of political contacts among them which in turn would contribute to better mutual understanding of their positions and views.

The participating States declare their intention to conduct their relations with all other States in the spirit of the principles contained in the present Declaration.

(b) Matters related to giving effect to certain of the above Principles

(i) *The participating States,*

Reaffirming that they will respect and give effect to refraining from the threat or use of force and convinced of the necessity to make it an effective norm of international life,

Declare that they are resolved to respect and carry out, in their relations with one another, inter alia, the following provisions which are in conformity with the Declaration on Principles Guiding Relations between Participating States:

— To give effect and expression, by all the ways and forms which they consider appropriate, to the duty to refrain from the threat or use of force in their relations with one another.

— To refrain from any use of armed forces inconsistent with the purposes and principles of the Charter of the United Nations and the provisions of the Declaration on Principles Guiding Relations between Participating States, against another participating State, in particular from invasion of or attack on its territory.

— To refrain from any manifestations of force for the purpose of inducing another participating State to renounce the full exercise of its sovereign rights.

— To refrain from any act of economic coercion designated to subordinate to their own interest the exercise by another participating State of the rights inherent in its sovereignty and thus to secure advantages of any kind.

— To take effective measures which by their scope and by their nature constitute steps towards the ultimate achievement of general and complete disarmament under strict and effective international control.

— To promote, by all means which each of them considers appropriate, a climate of confidence and respect among peoples consonant with their duty to refrain from propaganda for wars of aggression or for any threat or use of force inconsistent with the purposes of the United Nations and with the Declaration on Principles Guiding Relations between Participating States, against another participating State.

— To make every effort to settle exclusively by peaceful means any dispute between them, the continuance of which is likely to endanger the maintenance of international peace and security in Europe, and to seek, first of all, a solution through the peaceful means set forth in Article 33 of the United Nations Charter.

To refrain from any action which could hinder the peaceful settlement of disputes between the participating States.

(ii) *The participating States,*

Reaffirming their determination to settle their disputes as set forth in the Principle of Peaceful Settlement of Disputes;

Convinced that the peaceful settlement of disputes is a complement to refraining from the threat or use of force, both being essential though not exclusive factors for the maintenance and consolidation of peace and security;

Desiring to reinforce and to improve the methods at their disposal for the peaceful settlement of disputes;

1.   Are resolved to pursue the examination and elaboration of a generally acceptable method for the peaceful settlement of disputes aimed at complementing existing methods, and to continue to this end to work upon the 'Draft Convention on a European System for the Peaceful Settlement of Disputes' submitted by Switzerland during the second stage of the Conference on Security and Co-operation in Europe, as well as other proposals relating to it and directed towards the elaboration of such a method.

2.   Decide that, on the invitation of Switzerland, a meeting of experts of all the participating States will be convoked in order to fulfill the mandate described in paragraph 1 above within the framework and under the procedures of the follow-up to the Conference laid down in the chapter 'Follow-up to the Conference.'

3.   This meeting of experts will take place after the meeting of the representatives appointed by the Ministers of Foreign Affairs of the participating States, scheduled according to the chapter 'Follow-up to the Conference' for 1977; the results of the work of this meeting of experts will be submitted to Governments.

2.   Document on confidence-building measures and certain aspects of security and disarmament

The participating States,

Desirous of eliminating the causes of tension that may exist among them and thus of contributing to the strengthening of peace and security in the world;

Determined to strengthen confidence among them and thus to contribute to increasing stability and security in Europe;

Determined further to refrain in their mutual relations, as well as in their international relations in general, from the threat or use of force against the territorial integrity or political independence of any State, or in any other manner inconsistent with the purposes of the United Nations and with the Declaration on Principles Guiding Relations between Participating States as adopted in this Final Act;

Recognizing the need to contribute to reducing the dangers of armed conflict and of misunderstanding or miscalculation of military activities which could give rise to apprehension, particularly in a situation where the participating States lack clear and timely information about the nature of such activities;

Taking into account considerations relevant to efforts aimed at lessening tension and promoting disarmament;

Recognizing that the exchange of observers by invitation at military manoeuvres will help to promote contacts and mutual understanding;

Having studied the question of prior notification of major military movements in the context of confidence-building;

Recognizing that there are other ways in which individual States can contribute further to their common objectives;

Convinced of the political importance of prior notification of major military manoeuvres for the promotion of mutual understanding and the strengthening of confidence, stability and security;

Accepting the responsibility of each of them to promote these objectives and to implement this measure, in accordance with the accepted criteria and modalities, as essentials for the realization of these objectives;

Recognizing that this measure deriving from political decision rests upon a voluntary basis;

Have adopted the following:

I. *Prior notification of major military manoeuvres*

They will notify their major military manoeuvres to all other participating States through usual diplomatic channels in accordance with the following provisions:

Notification will be given of major military manoeuvres exceeding a total of 25,000 troops, independently or combined with any possible air or naval components (in this context the word 'troops' includes amphibious and airborne troops). In the case of independent manoeuvres of amphibious or airborne troops, or of combined manoeuvres involving them, these troops will be included in the total. Furthermore, in the case of combined manoeuvres which do not reach the above total but which involve land forces together with significant numbers of either amphibious or airborne troops, or both, notification can also be given.

Notification will be given of major military manoeuvres which take place on the territory, in Europe, of any participating State as well as, if applicable, in the adjoining sea area and air space.

In the case of a participating State whose territory extends beyond Europe, prior notification need be given only of manoeuvres which take place in an area within 250 kilometres from its frontier facing or shared with any other European participating State, the participating State need not, however, give notification in cases in which that area is also contiguous to the participating State's frontier facing or shared with a non-European non-participating State.

Notification will be given 21 days or more in advance of the start of the manoeuvre or in the case of a manoeuvre arranged at shorter notice at the earliest possible opportunity prior to its starting date.

Notification will contain information of the designation, if any, the general purpose of and the States involved in the manoeuvre, the type or types and numerical strength of the forces engaged, the area and estimated time-frame of its conduct. The participating States will also, if possible, provide additional relevant information, particularly that related to the components of the forces engaged and the period of involvement of these forces.

Prior notification of other military manoeuvres

The participating States recognize that they can contribute further to strengthening confidence and increasing security and stability, and to this end may also notify smaller-scale military manoeuvres to other participating States, with special regard for those near the area of such manoeuvres.

To the same end, the participating States also recognize that they may notify other military manoeuvres conducted by them.

Exchange of observers

The participating States will invite other participating States, voluntarily and on a bilateral basis, in a spirit of reciprocity and goodwill towards all participating States, to send observers to attend military manoeuvres.

The inviting State will determine in each case the number of observers, the procedures and conditions of their participation, and give other information which it may consider useful. It will provide appropriate facilities and hospitality.

The invitation will be given as far ahead as is conveniently possible through usual diplomatic channels.

Prior notification of major military movements

In accordance with the Final Recommendations of the Helsinki Consultations the participating States studied the question of prior notification of major military movements as a measure to strengthen confidence.

Accordingly, the participating States recognize that they may, at their own dis-cretion and with a view to contributing to confidence-building, notify their major military movements.

In the same spirit, further consideration will be given by the States participating in the Conference on Security and Co-operation in Europe to the question of prior notification of major military movements, bearing in mind, in particular, the experience gained by the implementation of the measures which are set forth in this document.

Other confidence-building measures

The participating States recognize that there are other means by which their common objectives can be promoted.

In particular, they will, with due regard to reciprocity and with a view to better mutual understanding, promote exchanges by invitation among their military person-nel, including visits by military delegations.

In order to make a fuller contribution to their common objective of confidence-building, the participating States, when conducting their military activities in the area covered by the provisions for the prior notification of major military manoeuvres, will duly take into account and respect this objective.

They also recognize that the experience gained by the implementation of the provisions set forth above, together with further efforts, could lead to developing and enlarging measures aimed at strengthening confidence.

II   Questions relating to disarmament

The participating States recognize the interest of all of them in efforts aimed at lessening military confrontation and promoting disarmament which are designed to complement political détente in Europe and to strengthen their security. They are convinced of the necessity to take effective measures in these fields which by their scope and by their nature constitute steps towards the ultimate achievement of general and complete disarmament under strict and effective international control, and which should result in strengthening peace and security throughout the world.

III   General considerations

Having considered the views expressed on various subjects related to the strengthen-ing of security in Europe through joint efforts aimed at promoting détente and disarmament, the participating States, when engaged in such efforts, will, in this context, proceed, in particular, from the following essential considerations:

— The complementary nature of the political and military aspects of security;

— The interrelation between the security of each participating State and security in Europe as a whole and the relationship which exists, in the broader context of world security, between security in Europe and security in the Mediterranean area;

— Respect for the security interests of all States participating in the Conference on Security and Co-operation in Europe inherent in their sovereign equality;

— The importance that participants in negotiating fora see to it that information about relevant developments, progress and results is provided on an appropriate basis to other States participating in the Conference on Security and Co-operation in Europe and, in return, the justified interest of any of those States in having their views considered.

CO-OPERATION IN THE FIELD OF ECONOMICS, OF SCIENCE AND TECHNOLOGY AND OF THE ENVIRONMENT

The participating States,

Convinced that their efforts to develop co-operation in the fields of trade, industry, science and technology, the environment and other areas of economic activity contribute to the reinforcement of peace and security in Europe and in the world as a whole,

Recognizing that co-operation in these fields would promote economic and social progress and the improvement of the conditions of life,

Aware of the diversity of their economic and social systems,

Reaffirming their will to intensify such co-operation between one another, irrespective of their systems,

Recognizing that such co-operation, with due regard for the different levels of economic development, can be developed, on the basis of equality and mutual satisfaction of the partners, and of reciprocity permitting, as a whole, an equitable distribution of advantages and obligations of comparable scale, with respect for bilateral and multilateral agreements,

Taking into account the interests of the developing countries throughout the world, including those among the participating countries as long as they are developing from the economic point of view; reaffirming their will to co-operate for the achievement of the aims and objectives established by the appropriate bodies of the United Nations in the pertinent documents concerning development, it being understood that each participating State maintains the positions it has taken on them; giving special attention to the least developed countries,

Convinced that the growing world-wide economic interdependence calls for increasing common and effective efforts towards the solution of major world economic problems such as food, energy, commodities, monetary and financial problems, and therefore emphasizes the need for promoting stable and equitable international economic relations, thus contributing to the continuous and diversified economic development of all countries,

Having taken into account the work already undertaken by relevant international organizations and wishing to take advantage of the possibilities offered by these organizations, in particular by the United Nations Economic Commission for Europe, for giving effect to the provisions of the final documents of the Conference,

Considering that the guidelines and concrete recommendations contained in the following texts are aimed at promoting further development of their mutual economic relations, and convinced that their co-operation in this field should take place in full respect for the principles guiding relations among participating States as set forth in the relevant document,

Have adopted the following:

1.   Commercial Exchanges

General provisions

The participating States,

Conscious of the growing role of international trade as one of the most important factors in economic growth and social progress,

Recognizing that trade represents an essential sector of their co-operation, and bearing in mind that the provisions contained in the above preamble apply in particular to this sector,

Considering that the volume and structure of trade among the participating States do not in all cases correspond to the possibilities created by the current level of their economic, scientific and technological development,

are resolved to promote, on the basis of the modalities of their economic co-operation, the expansion of their mutual trade in goods and services, and to ensure conditions favourable to such development;

recognize the beneficial effects which can result for the development of trade from the application of most favoured nation treatment;

will encourage the expansion of trade on as broad a multilateral basis as possible, thereby endeavouring to utilize the various economic and commercial possibilities;

recognize the importance of bilateral and multilateral intergovernmental and other agreements for the long-term development of trade.

note the importance of monetary and financial questions for the development of international trade, and will endeavour to deal with them with a view to contributing to the continuous expansion of trade;

will endeavour to reduce or progressively eliminate all kinds of obstacles to the development of trade;

will foster a steady growth of trade while avoiding as far as possible abrupt fluctuations in their trade;

consider that their trade in various products should be conducted in such a way as not to cause or threaten to cause serious injury — and should the situation arise, market disruption — in domestic markets for these products and in particular to the detriment of domestic producers of like or directly competitive products; as regards the concept of market disruption, it is understood that it should not be invoked in a way inconsistent with the relevant provisions of their international agreements; if they resort to safeguard measures, they will do so in conformity with their commitments in this field arising from international agreements to which they are parties and will take account of the interests of the parties directly concerned;

will give due attention to measures for the promotion of trade and the diversification of its structure;

note that the growth and diversification of trade would contribute to widening the possibilities of choice of products;

consider it appropriate to create favourable conditions for the participation of firms, organizations and enterprises in the development of trade.

Business contacts and facilities

The participating States,

Conscious of the importance contribution which an improvement of business contacts, and the accompanying growth of confidence in business relationships, could make to the development of commercial and economic relations,

will take measures further to improve conditions for the expansion of contacts between representatives of official bodies, of the different organizations, enterprises, firms and banks concerned with foreign trade, in particular, where useful, between sellers and users of products and services, for the purpose of studying commercial possibilities, concluding contracts, ensuring their implementation and providing after-sales services;

will encourage organizations, enterprises and firms concerned with foreign trade to take measures to accelerate the conduct of business negotations;

will further take measures aimed at improving working conditions of representatives of foreign organizations, enterprises, firms and banks concerned with external trade, particularly as follows:

— by providing the necessary information, including information on legislation and procedures relating to the establishment and operation of permanent representation by the above mentioned bodies;

— by examining as favourably as possible requests for the establishment of permanent representation and of offices for this purpose, including, where appropriate, the opening of joint offices by two or more firms;

— by encouraging the provision, on conditions as favourable as possible and equal for all representatives of the above-mentioned bodies, of hotel accommodation, means of communication, and of other facilities normally required by them, as well as of suitable business and residential premises for purposes of permanent representation;

recognize the importance of such measures to encourage greater participation by small and medium sized firms in trade between participating States.

Economic and commercial information

The participating States,

Conscious of the growing role of economic and commercial information in the development of international trade,

Considering that economic information should be of such a nature as to allow adequate market analysis and to permit the preparation of medium and long term forecasts, thus contributing to the establishment of a continuing flow of trade and a better utilization of commercial possibilities,

Expressing their readiness to improve the quality and increase the quantity and supply of economic and relevant administrative information,

Considering that the value of statistical information on the international level depends to a considerable extent on the possibility of its comparability,

will promote the publication and dissemination of economic and commercial information at regular intervals and as quickly as possible, in particular:

— statistics concerning production, national income, budget, consumption and productivity;

— foreign trade statistics drawn up on the basis of comparable classification including breakdown by product with indication of volume and value, as well as country of origin or destination;

— laws and regulations concerning foreign trade;

— information allowing forecasts of development of the economy to assist in trade promotion, for example, information on the general orientation of national economic plans and programmes;

— other information to help businessmen in commercial contacts, for example, periodic directories, lists, and where possible, organizational charts of firms and organizations concerned with foreign trade;

will in addition to the above encourage the development of the exchange of economic and commercial information through, where appropriate, joint commissions for economic, scientific and technical co-operation, national and joint chambers of commerce, and other suitable bodies;

will support a study, in the framework of the United Nations Economic Commission for Europe, of the possibilities of creating a multilateral system of notification of laws and regulations concerning foreign trade and changes therein;

will encourage international work on the harmonization of statistical nomenclatures, notably in the United Nations Economic Commission for Europe.

Marketing

The participating States,

Recognizing the importance of adapting production to the requirements of foreign markets in order to ensure the expansion of international trade,

Conscious of the need of exporters to be as fully familiar as possible with and take account of the requirements of potential users,

will encourage organizations, enterprises and firms concerned with foreign trade to develop further the knowledge and techniques required for effective marketing;

will encourage the improvement of conditions for the implementation of measures to promote trade and to satisfy the needs of users in respect of imported products, in particular through market research and advertising measures as well as, where useful, the establishment of supply facilities, the furnishing of spare parts, the functioning of after sales services, and the training of the necessary local technical personnel;

will encourage international co-operation in the field of trade promotion, including marketing, and the work undertaken on these subjects within the international bodies, in particular the United Nations Economic Commission for Europe.

2. Industrial co-operation and projects of common interest

Industrial co-operation

The participating States,

Considering that industrial co-operation, being motivated by economic considerations, can

— create lasting ties thus strengthening long-term overall economic co-operation,

— contribute to economic growth as well as to the expansion and diversification of international trade and to a wider utilization of modern technology,

— lead to the mutually advantageous utilization of economic complementarities through better use of all factors of production, and

— accelerate the industrial development of all those who take part in such co-operation,

propose to encourage the development of industrial co-operation between the competent organizations, enterprises and firms of their countries;

consider that industrial co-operation may be facilitated by means of intergovernmental and other bilateral and multilateral agreements between the interested parties;

note that in promoting industrial co-operation they should bear in mind the economic structures and the development levels of their countries;

note that industrial co-operation is implemented by means of contracts concluded between competent organizations, enterprises and firms on the basis of economic considerations;

express their willingness to promote measures designed to create favourable conditions for industrial co-operation;

recognize that industrial co-operation covers a number of forms of economic relations going beyond the framework of conventional trade, and that in concluding contracts on industrial co-operation the partners will determine jointly the appropriate forms and conditions of co-operation, taking into account their mutual interests and capabilities;

recognize further that, if it is in their mutual interest, concrete forms such as the following may be useful for the development of industrial co-operation: joint production and sale, specialization in production and sale, construction, adaptation and modernization of industrial plants, co-operation for the setting up of complete industrial installations with a view to thus obtaining part of the resultant products, mixed companies, exchanges of 'knowhow', of technical information, of patents and of licenses, and joint industrial research within the framework of specific co-operation projects;

recognize that new forms of industrial co-operation can be applied with a view to meeting specific needs;

note the importance of economic, commercial, technical and administrative information such as to ensure the development of industrial co-operation;

Consider it desirable:

— to improve the quality and the quantity of information relevant to industrial co-operation, in particular the laws and regulations, including those relating to foreign exchange, general orientation of national economic plans and programmes as well as programme priorities and economic conditions of the market; and

— to disseminate as quickly as possible published documentation thereon;

will encourage all forms of exchange of information and communication of experience relevant to industrial co-operation, including through contacts between potential partners and, where appropriate, through joint commissions for economic, industrial, scientific and technical co-operation, national and joint chambers of commerce, and other suitable bodies;

consider it desirable, with a view to expanding industrial co-operation, to encourage the exploration of co-operation possibilities and the implementation of co-operation projects and will take measures to this end, *inter alia*, by facilitating and increasing organizations, enterprises and firms and between their respective qualified personnel;

note that the provisions adopted by the Conference relating to business contacts in the economic and commercial fields also apply to foreign organizations, enterprises and firms engaged in industrial co-operation, taking into account the specific conditions of this co-operation, and will endeavour to ensure, in particular, the existence of appropriate working conditions for personnel engaged in the implementation of co-operation projects;

consider it desirable that proposals for industrial co-operation projects should be sufficiently specific and should contain the necessary economic and technical data, in particular preliminary estimates of the cost of the project, information on the form of co-operation envisaged, and market possibilities, to enable potential partners to proceed with initial studies and to arrive at decisions in the shortest possible time;

will encourage the parties concerned with industrial co-operation to take measures to accelerate the conduct of negotiations for the conclusion of co-operation contracts;

recommend further the continued examination — for example within the framework of the United Nations Economic Commission for Europe — of means of improving the provision of information to those concerned on general conditions of industrial co-operation and guidance on the preparation of contracts in this field;

consider it desirable to further improve conditions for the implementation of industrial co-operation projects, in particular with respect to:

— the protection of the interests of the partners in industrial co-operation projects, including the legal protection of the various kinds of property involved;

— the consideration, in ways that are compatible with their economic systems, of the needs and possibilities of industrial co-operation within the frame-work of economic policy and particularly in national economic plans and programmes;

consider it desirable that the partners, when concluding industrial co-operation contracts, should devote due attention to provisions concerning the extension of the necessary mutual assistance and the provision of the necessary information during the implementation of these contracts, in particular with a view to attaining the required technical level and quality of the products resulting from such co-operation;

recognize the usefulness of an increased participation of small and medium sized firms in industrial co-operation projects.

Projects of common interest

The participating States,

Considering that their economic potential and their natural resources permit, through common efforts, long-term co-operation in the implementation, including at the regional or sub-regional level, of major projects of common interest, and that these may contribute to the speeding-up of the economic development of the countries participating therein,

Considering it desirable that the competent organizations, enterprises and firms of all countries should be given the possibility of indicating their interest in participating in such projects, and, in case of agreement, of taking part in their implementation,

Noting that the provisions adopted by the Conference relating to industrial co-operation are also applicable to projects *of common* interest,

regard it as necessary to encourage, where appropriate, the investigation by competent and interested organizations, enterprises and firms of the possibilities for the carrying out of projects of common interest in the fields of energy resources and of the exploitation of raw materials, as well as of transport and communications.

regard it as desirable that organizations, enterprises and firms exploring the possibilities of taking part in projects of common interest exchange with their potential partners, through the appropriate channels, the requisite economic, legal, financial and technical information pertaining to these projects;

consider that the fields of energy resources, in particular, petroleum, natural gas and coal, and extraction and processing of mineral raw materials, in particular, iron ore and bauxite, are suitable ones for strengthening long-term economic co-operation and for the development of trade which could result;

consider that possibilities for projects of common interest with a view to long-term economic co-operation also exist in the following fields:

— exchanges of electricity energy within Europe with a view to utilizing the capacity of the electrical power stations as rationally as possible;

— co-operation in research for new sources of energy and, in particular, in the field of nuclear energy;

— development of road networks and co-operation aimed at establishing a coherent navigable network in Europe;

— co-operation in research and the perfecting of equipment for multimodal transport operations and for the handling of containers;

recommended that the States interested in projects of common interest should consider under what conditions it would be possible to establish them, and if they so desire, create the necessary conditions for their actual implementation.

3. Provisions concerning trade and individual co-operation

Harmonization of standards

The participating States,

Recognizing the development of international harmonization of standards and technical regulations and of international co-operation in the field of certification as an important means of eliminating technical obstacles to international trade and industrial co-operation, thereby facilitating their development and increasing productivity;

reaffirm their interest to achieve the widest possible international harmonization of standards and technical regulations;

express their readiness to promote international agreements and other appropriate arrangements on acceptance of certificates of conformity with standards and technical regulations;

consider it desirable to increase international co-operation on standardization, in particular by supporting the activities of intergovernmental and other appropriate organizations in the field.

Arbitration

The participating States,

Considering that the prompt and equitable settlement of disputes which may arise from commercial transactions relating to goods and services and contracts for industrial co-operation would contribute to expanding and facilitating trade and co-operation.

Considering that arbitration is an appropriate means of settling such disputes.

recommend, where appropriate, to organizations, enterprises and firms in their countries, to include arbitration clauses in commercial contracts and industrial co-operation contracts, or in special agreement;

recommend that the provisions on arbitration should provide for arbitration under a mutually acceptable set of arbitration rules, and permit arbitration in a third country, taking into account existing intergovernmental and other agreements in this field.

Specific bilateral arrangements

The participating States,

Conscious of the need to facilitate trade and to promote the application of new forms of industrial co-operation,

will consider favourably the conclusion, in appropriate cases, of specific bilateral agreements concerning various problems of mutual interest in the fields of commercial exchanges and industrial cooperation, in particular with a view of avoiding double taxation and to facilitating the transfer of profits and the return of the value of the assets invested.

4. Science and technology

The participating States,

Convinced that scientific and technological cooperation constitutes an important contribution to the strengthening of security and co-operation among them, in that it assists the effective solution of problems of common interest and the improvement of the conditions of human life,

Considering that in developing such co-operation, it is important to promote the sharing of information and experience, facilitating the study and transfer of scientific and technology achievements, as well as the access to such achievements on a mutually advantageous basis and in fields of co-operation agreed between interested parties,

Considering that it is for the potential partners, i.e. the competent organizations, institutions, enterprises, scientists and technologists of the participating States to determine the opportunities for mutually beneficial co-operation and to develop its details,

Affirming that such co-operation can be developed and implemented bilaterally and multilaterally at the governmental and non-governmental levels, for example, through inter-governmental and other agreements, international programmes, co-operative projects and commercial channels, while utilizing also various forms of contacts, including direct and individual contacts,

Aware of the need to take measures further to improve scientific and technological co-operation between them,

Possibilities for improving co-operation

Recognize the possibilities exist for further improving scientific and technological co-operation, and to this end, express their intention to remove obstacles to such co-operation, in particular through:

— the improvement of opportunities for the exchange and dissemination of scientific and technological information among the parties interested in scientific and technological research and co-operation including information related to the organization and implementation of such co-operation;

— the expeditious implementation and improvement in organization, including programmes, of international visits of scientists and specialists in connexion with exchanges, conferences and co-operation;

— the wider use of commercial channels and activities for applied scientific and technological research and for the transfer of achievements obtained in this field while providing information on and protection of intellectual and industrial property rights;

Fields of co-operation

Consider that possibilities to expand co-operation exist within the areas given below as examples, noting that it is for potential partners in the participating countries to identify and develop projects and arrangements of mutual interest and benefit:

Agriculture
Research into new methods and technologies for increasing the productivity of crop cultivation and animal husbandry; the application of chemistry to agriculture; the design, construction and utilization of agricultural machinery; technologies of irrigation and other agricultural land improvement works;

Energy
New technologies of production, transport and distribution of energy aimed at improving the use of existing fuels and sources of hydroenergy, as well as research in the field of new energy sources, including nuclear, solar and geothermal energy;

New technologies, rational use of resources
Research on new technologies and equipment designed in particular to reduce energy consumption and to minimize or eliminate waste;

Transport technology
Research on the means of transport and the technology applied to the development and operation of international, national and urban transport networks including container transport as well as transport safety;

Physics
Study of problems in high energy physics and plasma physics; research in the field of theoretical and experimental nuclear physics;

Chemistry
Research on problems in electrochemistry and the chemistry of polymers, of natural products, and of metals and alloys, as well as the development of improved chemical technology, especially materials processing; practical application of the latest achievements of chemistry to industry, construction and other sectors of the economy;

Meteorology and hydrology
Meteorological and hydrological research, including methods of collection, evaluation and transmission of data and their utilization for weather forecasting and hydrology forecasting;

Oceanography
Oceanographic research, including the study of air/sea interactions;

Seismological research
Study and forecasting of earthquakes and associated geological changes; development and research of technology of seism-resisting constructions;

Research on glaciology, permafrost and problems of life under conditions of cold
Research on glaciology and permafrost; transportation and construction technologies; human adaptation to climatic extremes and changes in the living conditions of indigenous populations;

Computer, communication and information technologies
Development of computers as well as of telecommunications and information systems; technology associated with computers and telecommunications, including their use for management systems, for production processes, for automation, for the study of economic problems, in scientific research and for the collection, processing and dissemination of information;

Space research
Space exploration and the study of the earth's natural resources and the natural environment by remote sensing in particular with the assistance of satellites and rocket-probes;

Medicine and public health
Research on cardiovascular, tumour and virus diseases, molecular biology, neurophysiology; development and testing of new drugs; study of contemporary problems of pediatrics, gerontology and the organization and techniques of medical services;

Environmental research
Research on specific scientific and technological problems related to human environment.

Forms and methods of co-operation

Express their view that scientific and technological co-operation should, in particular, employ the following forms and methods:
— exchange and circulation of books, periodicals and other scientific and technological publications and papers among interested organizations, scientific and technological institutions, enterprises and scientists and technologists, as well as participation in international programmes for the abstracting and indexing of publications;
— exchanges and visits as well as other direct contacts and communications among scientists and technologists, on the basis of mutual agreement and other arrangements, for such purposes as consultations, lecturing and conducting research, including the use of laboratories, scientific libraries, and other documentation centres in connexion therewith;
— holding of international and national conferences, symposia, seminars, courses and other meetings of a scientific and technological character, which would include the participation of foreign scientists and technologists;
— joint preparation and implementation of programmes and projects of mutual interest on the basis of consultation and agreement among all parties concerned, including, where possible and appropriate, exchanges of experience and research results, and correlation of research programmes, between scientific and technological research institutions and organizations;
— use of commercial channels and methods for identifying and transferring technological and scientific developments, including the conclusion of mutually beneficial co-operation arrangements between firms and enterprises in fields agreed upon between them and for carrying out, where appropriate, joint research and development programmes and projects;
consider it desirable that periodic exchanges of views and information take place on scientific policy, in particular on general problems of orientation and administration of research and the question of a better use of large-scale scientific and experimental equipment on a co-operative basis;
recommend that, in developing co-operation in the field of science and technology, full use be made of existing practices of bilateral and multilateral co-operation, including that of a regional or sub-regional character, together with the forms and methods of co-operation described in this document;
recommend further that more effective utilization be made of the possibilities and capabilities of existing international organizations, intergovernmental and non-governmental, concerned with science and technology, for improving exchanges of information and experience, as well as for developing other forms of co-operation in fields of common interest, for example:
— in the United Nations Economic Commission for Europe, study of possibilities for expanding multilateral co-operation, taking into account models for projects and research used in various international organizations; and for sponsoring conferences, symposia, and study and working groups such as those which would bring together younger scientists and technologists with eminent specialists in their field;
— through their participation in particular international scientific and technological co-operation programmes, including those of UNESCO and other international

organizations, pursuit of continuing progress towards the objectives of such pro-grammes, notably those of UNISIST [World Science Information System] with particular respect to information policy guidance, technical advice, information contributions and data processing.

5. Environment

The participating States,

Affirming that the protection and improvement of the environment, as well as the protection of nature and the rational utilization of its resources in the interests of present and future generations, is one of the tasks of major importance to the well-being of peoples and the economic development of all countries and that many environmental problems, particularly in Europe, can be solved effectively only through close international co-operation,

Acknowledging that each of the participating States, in accordance with the prin-ciples of international law, ought to ensure, in a spirit of co-operation, that activities carried out on its territory do not cause degradation of the environment in another State or in areas lying beyond the limits of national jurisdiction,

Considering that the success of any environmental policy presupposes that all population groups and social forces, aware of their responsibilities, help to protect and improve the environment, which necessitates continued and thorough educative action, particularly with regard to youth,

Affirming that experience has shown that economic development and technological progress must be compatible with the protection of the environment and the preservation of historical and cultural values; that damage to the environment is best avoided by preventive measures; and that the ecological balance must be preserved in the exploitation and management of natural resources,

Aims of co-operation

Agree to the following aims of co-operation, in particular:

— to study, with a view to their solution, those environmental problems which, by their nature, are of a multilateral, bilateral, regional or sub-regional dimension; as well as to encourage the development of an interdisciplinary approach to environ-mental problems;

— to increase the effectiveness of national and international measures for the protection of the environment, by the comparison and, if appropriate, the harmoniz-ation of methods of gathering and analyzing facts, by improving the knowledge of pollution phenomena and rational utilization of natural resources, by the exchange of information, by the harmonization of definitions and the adoption, as far as possible, of a common terminology in the field of the environment;

— to take the necessary measures to bring environmental policies closer together and, where appropriate and possible, to harmonize them;

— to encourage, where possible and appropriate, national and international efforts by their interested organizations, enterprise and firms in the development, production and improvement of equipment designed for monitoring, protecting and enhancing the environment.

Fields of co-operation

To attain these aims, the participating States will make use of every suitable opportunity to co-operate in the field of environment and, in particular, within the areas described below as examples:

Control of air pollution

Desulphurization of fossil fuels and exhaust gases; pollution control of heavy metals, particles, aerosols, nitrogen oxides, in particular those emitted by transport, power stations, and other industrial plants; systems and methods of observation and control of air pollution and its effects, including long-range transport of air pollutants;

Water pollution control and fresh water utilization
Prevention and control of water pollution, in particular of transboundary rivers and international lakes; techniques for the improvement of the quality of water and further development of ways and means for industrial and municipal sewage effluent purification; methods of assessment of fresh water resources and the improvement of their utilization, in particular by developing methods of production which are less polluting and lead to less consumption of fresh water;

Protection of the marine environment
Protection of the marine environment of participating States, and especially the Mediterranean Sea, from pollutants emanating from land-based sources and those from ships and other vessels, notably the harmful substances listed in Annexes I and II to the London Convention on the Prevention of Marine Pollution by the Dumping of Wastes and Other Matters; problems of maintaining marine ecological balances and food chains, in particular such problems as may arise from the exploration and exploitation of biological and mineral resources of the seas and the sea-bed;

Land utilization and soils
Problems associated with more effective use of lands, including land amelioration, reclamation and recultivation; control of soil pollution, water and air erosion, as well as other forms of soil degradation; maintaining and increasing the productivity of soils with due regard for the possible negative effects of the application of chemical fertilizers and pesticides;

Nature conservation and nature reserves
Protection of nature and nature reserves; conservation and maintenance of existing genetic resources, especially rare animal and plant species; conservation of natural ecological systems; establishment of nature reserves and other protected landscapes and areas, including their use for research, tourism, recreation and other purposes;

Improvement of environmental conditions in areas of human settlement
Environmental conditions associated with transport, housing, working areas, urban development and planning, water supply and sewage disposal systems; assessment of harmful effects of noise, and noise control methods; collection, treatment and utilization of wastes, including the recovery and recycling of materials; research on substitutes for non-biodegradable substances;

Fundamental research, monitoring, forecasting and assessment of environment changes
Study of changes in climate, landscapes and ecological balances under the impact of both natural factors and human activities; forecasting of possible genetic changes in flora and fauna as a result of environmental pollution; harmonization of statistical data, development of scientific concepts and systems of monitoring networks, standardized methods of observation, measurement and assessment of changes in the biosphere; assessment of the effects of environmental pollution levels and degradation of the environment upon human health, study and development of criteria and standards for various environmental pollutants and regulation regarding production and use of various products;

Legal and administrative measures
Legal and administrative measures for the protection of the environment including procedures for establishing environmental impact assessments.

Forms and methods of co-operation
The participating States declare that problems relating to the protection and improvement of the environment will be solved on both a bilateral and a multilateral,
including regional and sub-regional, basis, making full use of existing patterns and
forms of co-operation. They will develop co-operation in the field of the environment
in particular by taking into consideration the Stockholm Declaration on the Human
Environment, relevant resolutions of the United Nations General Assembly and the
United Nations Economic Commission for Europe Prague symposium on environmental problems.

The participating States are resolved that co-operation in the field of the environment will be implemented in particular through:

— exchanges of scientific and technical information, documentation and research
results, including information on the means of determining the possible effects on the
environment of technical and economic activities;

— organization of conferences, symposia and meetings of experts;

— exchanges of scientists, specialists and trainees;

— joint preparation and implementation of programmes and projects for the study
and solution of various problems of environmental protection;

— harmonization, where appropriate and necessary, of environmental protection
standards and norms, in particular with the object of avoiding possible difficulties in
trade which may arise from efforts to resolve ecological problems of production
processes and which relate to the achievement of certain environmental qualities in
manufactured products;

— consultations on various aspects of environmental protection, as agreed upon
among countries concerned, especially in connexion with problems which could have
international consequences.

The participating States will further develop such co-operation by:

— promoting the progressive development, codification and implementation of
international law as one means of preserving and enhancing the human environment,
including principles and practices, as accepted by them, relating to pollution and other
environmental damage caused by activities within the jurisdiction or control of their
States affecting other countries and regions;

— supporting and promoting the implementation of relevant international Conventions to which they are parties, in particular those designed to prevent and combat
marine and fresh water pollution, recommending States to ratify Conventions which
have already been signed, as well as considering possibilities of accepting other
appropriate Conventions to which they are not parties at present;

— advocating the inclusion, where appropriate and possible, of the various areas
of co-operation into the programmes of work of the United Nations Economic
Commission for Europe, supporting such co-operation within the framework of the
Commission and of the United Nations Environment Programme, and taking into
account the work of other competent international organizations of which they are
members;

— making wider use, in all types of co-operation, of information already available
from national and international sources, including internationally agreed criteria, and
utilizing the possibilities and capabilities of various competent international organizations.

The participating States agree on the following recommendations on specific
measures:

— to develop through international co-operation an extensive programme for the
monitoring and evaluation of the long-range transport of air pollutants, starting with
sulphur dioxide and with possible extension to other pollutants, and to this end to
take into account basic elements of a co-operation programme which were identified

by the experts who met in Oslo in December 1974 at the invitation of the Norwegian Institute of Air Research;
— to advocate that within the framework of the United Nations Economic Commission for Europe a study be carried out of procedures and relevant experience relating to the activities of Governments in developing the capabilities of their countries to predict adequately environmental consequences of economic activities and technological development.

6. Co-operation in other areas

Development of transport

The participating States
Considering that the improvement of the conditions of transport constitutes one of the factors essential to the development of co-operation among them,
Considering that it is necessary to encourage the development of transport and the solution of existing problems by employing appropriate national and international means,
Taking into account the work being carried out on these subjects by existing international organizations, especially by the Inland Transport Committee of the United Nations Economic Commission for Europe,
note that the speed of technical progress in the various fields of transport makes desirable a development of co-operation and an increase in exchanges of information among them;
declare themselves in favour of a simplification and a harmonization of administrative formalities in the field of international transport, in particular at frontiers;
consider it desirable to promote, while allowing for their particular national circumstances in this sector, the harmonization of administrative and technical provisions concerning safety in road, rail, river, air and sea transport;
express their intention to encourage the development of international inland transport of passengers and goods as well as the possibilities of adequate participation in such transport on the basis of reciprocal advantage;
declare themselves in favour, with due respect for their rights and international commitments, of the elimination of disparities arising from the legal provisions applied to traffic on inland waterways which are subject to international conventions and, in particular, of the disparity in the application of those provisions; and to this end invite the member States of the Central Commission for the Navigation of the Rhine, of the Danube Commission and of other bodies to develop the work and studies now being carried out, in particular within the United Nations Economic Commission for Europe;
express their willingness, with a view of improving international rail transport and with due respect for their rights and international commitments, to work towards the elimination of difficulties arising from disparities in existing international legal provisions governing the reciprocal railway transport of passengers and goods between their territories;
express the desire for intensification of the work being carried out by existing international organizations in the field of transport, especially that of the Inland Transport Committee of the United Nations Economic Commission for Europe, and express their intention to contribute thereto by their efforts;
consider that examination by the participating States of the possibility of their accession to the different conventions or to membership of international organizations specializing in transport matters, as well as their efforts to implement conventions when ratified, could contribute to the strengthening of their co-operation in this field.

Promotion of tourism

The participating States,

Aware of the contribution made by international tourism to the development of mutual understanding among peoples, to increased knowledge of other countries' achievements in various fields, as well as to economic, social and cultural progress,

Recognizing the interrelationship between the development of tourism and measures taken in other areas of economic activity,

express their intention to encourage increased tourism on both an individual and group basis in particular by:

— encouraging the improvement of the tourist infrastructure and co-operation in this field;

— encouraging the carrying out of joint tourist projects including technical co-operation, particularly where this is suggested by territorial proximity and the convergence of tourist interests;

— encouraging the exchange of information, including relevant laws and regulations, studies, data and documentation relating to tourism, and by improving statistics with a view to facilitating their comparability;

— dealing in a positive spirit with questions connected with the allocation of financial means for tourist travel abroad, having regard to their economic possibilities, as well as with those connected with the formalities required for such travel, taking into account other provisions on tourism adopted by the Conference;

— facilitating the activities of foreign travel agencies and passenger transport companies in the promotion of international tourism;

— encouraging tourism outside the high season;

— examining the possibilities of exchanging specialists and students in the field of tourism, with a view to improving their qualifications;

— promoting conferences and symposia on the planning and development of tourism;

consider it desirable to carry out in the appropriate international framework, and with the co-operation of the relevant national bodies, detailed studies on tourism, in particular:

— a comparative study on the status and activities of travel agencies as well as on ways and means of achieving better cooperation among them;

— a study of the problems raised by the seasonal concentration of vacations, with the ultimate objective of encouraging tourism outside peak periods;

— studies of the problems arising in areas where tourism has injured the environment;

consider also that interested parties might wish to study the following questions:

— uniformity of hotel classification; and

— tourist routes comprising two or more countries;

— will endeavour, where possible, to ensure that the development of tourism does not injure the environment and the artistic, historic and cultural heritage in their respective countries;

will pursue their co-operation in the field of tourism bilaterally and multilaterally with a view to attaining the above objectives.

Economic and social aspects of migrant labour

The participating States,

Considering that the movements of migrant workers in Europe have reached substantial proportions, and that they constitute an important economic, social and human factor for host countries as well as for countries of origin,

Recognizing that workers' migrations have also given rise to a number of economic, social, human and other problems in both the receiving countries and the countries of origin,

Taking due account of the activities of the competent international organizations, more particularly the International Labour Organization, in this area,

are of the opinion that the problems arising bilaterally from the migration of workers in Europe as well as between the participating States should be dealt with by the parties directly concerned, in order to resolve these problems in their mutual interest, in the light of the concern of each State involved to take due account of the requirements resulting from its socio-economic situation, having regard to the obligation of each State to comply with the bilateral and multilateral agreements to which it is party, and with the following aims in view;

to encourage the efforts of the countries of origin directed towards increasing the possibilities of employment for their nationals in their own territories, in particular by developing economic co-operation appropriate for this purpose and suitable for the host countries and the countries of origin concerned;

to ensure, through collaboration between the host country and the country of origin, the conditions under which the orderly movement of workers might take place, while at the same time protecting their personal and social welfare and, if appropriate, to organize the recruitment of migrant workers and the provision of elementary language and vocational training;

to ensure equality of rights between migrant workers and nationals of the host countries with regard to conditions of employment and work and to social security, and to endeavour to ensure that migrant workers may enjoy satisfactory living conditions, especially housing conditions;

to endeavour to ensure, as far as possible, that migrant workers may enjoy the same opportunities as nationals of the host countries of finding other suitable employment in the event of unemployment;

to regard with favour the provision of vocational training to migrant workers and, as far as possible, free instruction in the language of the host country, in the framework of their employment;

to confirm the right of migrant workers to receive, as far as possible, regular information in their own language, covering both their country of origin and the host country;

to ensure that the children of migrant workers established in the host country have access to the education usually given there, under the same condition as the children of that country and, furthermore to permit them to receive supplementary education in their own language, national culture, history and geography;

to bear in mind that migrant workers, particularly those who have acquired qualifications, can be returning to their countries after a certain period of time help to remedy any deficiency of skilled labour in their country of origin;

to facilitate, as far as possible, the reuniting of migrant workers with their families;

to regard with favour the efforts of the countries of origin to attract the savings of migrant workers, with a view of increasing, within the framework of their economic development, appropriate opportunities for employment, thereby facilitating the reintegration of these workers on their return home.

Training of personnel

The participating States,

Conscious of the importance of the training and advanced training of professional staff and technicians for the economic development of every country,

declare themselves willing to encourage co-operation in this field notably by promoting exchange of information on the subject of institutions, programmes and methods of training and advanced training open to professional staff and technicians in the various sectors of economic activity and especially in those of management, public planning, agriculture and commercial and banking techniques;

consider that it is desirable to develop, under mutually acceptable conditions, exchanges of professional staff and technicians, particularly through training activities, of which it would be left to the competent and interested bodies in the participating States to discuss the modalities — duration, financing, education and qualification levels of potential participants;

declare themselves in favour of examining, through appropriate channels, the possibilities of co-operating on the organization and carrying out of vocational training on the job, more particularly in professions involving modern techniques.

QUESTIONS RELATING TO SECURITY AND CO-OPERATION IN THE MEDITERRANEAN

The participating States,

Conscious of the geographical, historical, cultural, economic and political aspects of their relationship with the non-participating Mediterranean States,

Convinced that security in Europe is to be considered in the broader context of world security and is closely linked with security in the Mediterranean area as a whole, and that accordingly the process of improving security should not be confined to Europe but should extend to other parts of the world, and in particular to the Mediterranean area,

Believing that the strengthening of security and the intensification of co-operation in Europe would stimulate positive processes in the Mediterranean region, and expressing their intention to contribute towards peace, security and justice in the region, in which ends the participating States and the non-participating Mediterranean States have a common interest,

Recognizing the importance of their mutual economic relations with the non-participating Mediterranean States, and conscious of their common interest in the further development of co-operation.

Noting with appreciation the interest expressed by the non-participating Mediterranean States in the Conference since its inception, and having duly taken their contributions into account,

Declare their intention:

— to promote the development of good-neighbourly relations with the non-participating Mediterranean States in conformity with the purposes and principles of the Charter of the United Nations, on which their relations are based, and with the United Nations Declaration on Principles of International Law concerning Friendly Relations and Co-operation among States and accordingly, in the context, to conduct their relations with the non-participating Mediterranean States in the spirit of the principles set forth in the Declaration on Principles Guiding Relations between Participating States;

— to seek, by further improving their relations with the non-participating Mediterranean States, to increase mutual confidence, so as to promote security and stability in the Mediterranean area as a whole;

— to encourage with the non-participating Mediterranean States the development of mutually beneficial co-operation in the various fields of economic activity, especially by expanding commercial exchanges, on the basis of a common awareness of the necessity for stability and progress in trade relations, of their mutual economic interests, and of differences in the levels of economic development, thereby promoting their economic advancement and well-being;

— to contribute to a diversified development of the economies of the non-participating Mediterranean countries, whilst taking due account of their national development objectives, and to co-operate with them, especially in the sectors of industry, science and technology, in their efforts to achieve a better utilization of their resources, thus promoting a more harmonious development of economic relations;

— to intensify their efforts and their co-operation on a bilateral and multilateral basis with the non-participating Mediterranean States directed towards the improvement of the environment of the Mediterranean, especially the safeguarding of the biological resources and ecological balance of the sea, by appropriate measures including the prevention and control of pollution; to this end, and in view of the present situation, to co-operate through competent international organizations and in particular within the United Nations Environment Programme (UNEP);

— to promote further contacts and co-operation with the non-participating Mediterranean States in other relevant fields.

In order to advance the objectives set forth above, the participating States also declare their intention of maintaining and amplifying the contacts and dialogue as initiated by the CSCE with the non-participating Mediterranean States to include all the States of the Mediterranean, with the purpose of contributing to peace, reducing armed forces in the region, strengthening security, lessening tensions in the region, and widening the scope of co-operation, ends in which all share a common interest, as well as with the purpose of defining further common objectives.

The participating States would seek, in the framework of their multilateral efforts, to encourage progress and appropriate initiatives and to proceed to an exchange of views on the attainment of the above purposes.

CO-OPERATION IN HUMANITARIAN AND OTHER FIELDS

The participating States,

Desiring to contribute to the strengthening of peace and understanding among peoples and to the spiritual enrichment of the human personality without distinction as to race, sex, language or religion,

Conscious that increased cultural and educational exchanges, broader dissemination of information, contacts between people, and the solution of humanitarian problems will contribute to the attainment of these aims,

Determined therefore to co-operate among themselves, irrespective of their political, economic and social systems, in order to create better conditions in the above fields, to develop and strengthen existing forms of co-operation and to work out new ways and means appropriate to these aims,

Convinced that this co-operation should take place in full respect for the principles guiding relations among participating States as set forth in the relevant document,

Have adopted the following:

1. Human Contacts

The participating States,

Considering the development of contacts to be an important element in the strengthening of friendly relations and trust among peoples,

Affirming, in relation to their present effort to improve conditions in this area, the importance they attach to humanitarian considerations,

Desiring in this spirit to develop, with the continuance of détente, further efforts to achieve continuing progress in this field,

And conscious that the questions relevant hereto must be settled by the States concerned under mutually acceptable conditions,

Make it their aim to facilitate freer movement and contacts, individually and collectively, whether privately or officially, among persons, institutions and organizations of the participating States, and to contribute to the solution of the humanitarian problems that arise in that connexion,

Declare their readiness to these ends to take measures which they consider appropriate and to conclude agreements or arrangements among themselves, as may be needed, and

Express their intention now to proceed to the implementation of the following:

(a)   Contacts and Regular Meetings on the Basis of Family Ties

In order to promote further development of contacts on the basis of family ties the participating States will favourably consider applications for travel with the purpose of allowing persons to enter or leave their territory temporarily, and on a regular basis if desired, in order to visit members of their families.

Applications for temporary visits to meet members of their families will be dealt with without distinction as to the country of origin or destination; existing requirements for travel documents and visas will be applied in this spirit. The preparation and issue of such documents and visas will be effected within reasonable time limits; cases of urgent necessity — such as serious illness or death — will be given priority treatment. They will take such steps as may be necessary to ensure that the fees for official travel documents and visas are acceptable.

They confirm that the presentation of an application concerning contacts on the basis of family ties will not modify the rights and obligations of the applicant or of members of his family.

(b)   Reunification of Families

The participating States will deal in a positive and humanitarian spirit with the applications of persons who wish to be reunited with members of their family, with special attention being given to requests of an urgent character — such as requests submitted by persons who are ill or old.

They will deal with applications in this field as expeditiously as possible.

They will lower where necessary the fees charged in connexion with these applications to ensure that they are at a moderate level.

Applications for the purpose of family reunification which are not granted may be renewed at the appropriate level and will be reconsidered at reasonably short intervals by the authorities of the country of residence or destination, whichever is concerned; under such circumstances fees will be charged only when applications are granted.

Persons whose applications for family reunification are granted may bring with them or ship their household and personal effects; to this end the participating States will use all possibilities provided by existing regulations.

Until members of the same family are reunited meetings and contacts between them may take place in accordance with the modalities for contacts on the basis of family ties.

The participating States will support the efforts of Red Cross and Red Crescent Societies concerned with the problems of family reunification.

They confirm that the presentation of an application concerning family reunification will not modify the rights and obligations of the applicant or of members of his family.

The receiving participating State will take appropriate care with regard to employment for persons from other participating States who take up permanent residence in that State in connexion with family reunification with its citizens and see that they are afforded opportunities equal to those enjoyed by its own citizens for education, medical assistance and social security.

(c)   Marriage between Citizens of Different States

The participating States will examine favourably and on the basis of humanitarian considerations requests for exit or entry permits from persons who have decided to marry a citizen from another participating State.

The processing and issuing of the documents required for the above purposes and for the marriage will be in accordance with the provisions accepted for family reunification.

In dealing with requests from couples from different participating States, once married, to enable them and the minor children of their marriage to transfer their permanent residence to a State in which either one is normally a resident, the participating States will also apply the provisions accepted for family reunification.

(d)   Travel for Personal or Professional Reasons

The participating States intend to facilitate wider travel by their citizens for personal or professional reasons and to this end they intend in particular:

— gradually to simplify and to administer flexibly the procedures for exit and entry;

— to ease regulations concerning movement of citizens from the other participating States in their territory, with due regard to security requirements.

They will endeavour gradually to lower, where necessary, the fees for visas and official travel documents.

They intend to consider, as necessary, means — including, in so far as appropriate, the conclusion of multilateral or bilateral consular conventions or other relevant agreements or understandings — for the improvement of arrangements to provide consular assistance.

They confirm that religious faiths, institutions and organizations, practising within the constitutional framework of the participating States, and their representatives can, in the field of their activities, have contacts and meetings among themselves and exchange information.

(e)   Improvement of Conditions for Tourism on an Individual or Collective Basis

The participating States consider that tourism contributes to a fuller knowledge of the life, culture and history of other countries, to the growth of understanding among peoples, to the improvement of contacts and to the broader use of leisure. They intend to promote the development of tourism, on an individual or collective basis, and, in particular, they intend:

— to promote visits to their respective countries by encouraging the provision of appropriate facilities and the simplification and expediting of necessary formalities relating to such visits;

— to increase, on the basis of appropriate agreements or arrangements where necessary, co-operation in the development of tourism, in particular by considering bilaterally possible ways to increase information relating to travel to other countries and to the reception and service of tourists, and other related questions of mutual interest.

(f)   Meetings among Young People

The participating States intend to further the development of contacts and exchanges among young people by encouraging:

— increased exchanges and contacts on a short or long term basis among young people working, training or undergoing education through bilateral or multilateral agreements or regular programmes in all cases where it is possible;

— study by their youth organizations of the question of possible agreements relating to frameworks of multilateral youth co-operation;

— agreements or regular programmes relating to the organization of exchanges of students, of international youth seminars, of courses of professional training and foreign language study;

— the further development of youth tourism and the provision to this end of appropriate facilities;

— development, where possible, of exchanges, contacts and co-operation on a bilateral or multilateral basis between their organizations which represent wide circles of young people working, training or undergoing education;
— awareness among youth of the importance of developing mutual understanding and of strengthening friendly relations and confidence among peoples.

(g) Sport

In order to expand existing links and co-operation in the field of sport the participating States will encourage contacts and exchanges of this kind, including sports meetings and competitions of all sorts, on the basis of the established international rules, regulations and practice.

(h) Expansion of Contacts

By ways of further developing contacts among governmental institutions and non-governmental organizations and associations, including women's organizations, the participating States will facilitate the convening of meetings as well as travel by delegations, groups and individuals.

2. Information

The participating States,
Conscious of the need for an ever wider knowledge and understanding of the various aspects of life in other participating States,
Acknowledging the contribution of this process to the growth of confidence between peoples,
Desiring, with the development of mutual understanding between the participating States and with the further efforts towards progress in this field,
Recognizing the importance of the dissemination of information from the other participating States and of a better acquaintance with such information,
Emphasizing therefore the essential and influential role of the press, radio, television, cinema and news agencies and of the journalists working in these fields.
Make it their aim to facilitate the freer and wider dissemination of information of all kinds, to encourage co-operation in the field of information and the exchange of information with other countries, and to improve the conditions under which journalists from one participating State exercise their profession in another participating State, and
Express their intention in particular:

(a) Improvement of the Circulation of, Access to, and Exchange of Information

(i) Oral Information
— To facilitate the dissemination of oral information through the encouragement of lectures and lecture tours by personalities and specialists from the other participating States, as well as exchanges of opinions at round table meetings, seminars, symposia, summer schools, congresses and other bilateral and multilateral meetings.

(ii) Printed Information
— To facilitate the improvement of the dissemination, on their territory, of newspapers and printed publications, periodical and non-periodical, from the other participating States. For this purpose:
they will encourage their competent firms and organizations to conclude agreements and contracts designed gradually to increase the quantities and the number of titles of newspapers and publications imported from the other participating States. These agreements and contracts should in particular mention the speediest conditions of delivery and the use of the normal channels existing in each country for the

distribution of its own publications and newspapers, as well as forms and means of payment agreed between the parties making it possible to achieve the objectives aimed at by these agreements and contracts;

where necessary, they will take appropriate measures to achieve the above objectives and to implement the provisions contained in the agreements and contracts.

— To contribute to the improvement of access by the public to periodical and non-periodical printed publications imported on the bases indicated above. In particular:

they will encourage an increase in the number of places where these publications are on sale;

they will facilitate the availability of these periodical publications during congresses, conferences, official visits and other international events and to tourists during the season;

they will develop the possibilities for taking out subscriptions according to the modalities particular to each country;

they will improve the opportunities for reading and borrowing these publications in large public libraries and their reading rooms as well as in university libraries.

They intend to improve the possibilities for acquaintance with bulletins of official information issued by diplomatic missions and distributed by those missions on the basis of arrangements acceptable to the interested parties.

(iii)   Filmed and Broadcast Information
— To promote the improvement of the dissemination of filmed and broadcast information. To this end:

they will encourage the wider showing and broadcasting of a greater variety of recorded and filmed information from the other participating States, illustrating the various aspects of life in their countries and received on the basis of such agreements or arrangements as may be necessary between the organizations and firms directly concerned:

they will facilitate the import by competent organizations and firms of recorded audio-visual material from the other participating States.

The participating States note the expansion in the dissemination of information broadcast by radio, and express the hope for the continuation of this process, so as to meet the interest of mutual understanding among peoples and the aims set forth by this Conference.

(b)   Co-operation in the Field of Information

— To encourage co-operation in the field of information on the basis of short or long term agreements or arrangements. In particular:

they will favour increased co-operation among mass media organizations, including press agencies, as well as among publishing houses and organizations;

they will favour co-operation among public or private, national or international radio and television organizations, in particular through the exchange of both live and recorded radio and television programmes, and through the joint production and the broadcasting and distribution of such programmes;

they will encourage meetings and contacts both between journalists' organizations and between journalists from the participating States;

they will view favourably the possibilities of arrangements between periodical publications as well as between newspapers from the participating States, for the purpose of exchanging and publishing articles;

they will encourage the exchange of technical information as well as the organization of joint research and meetings devoted to the exchange of experience and views between experts in the field of the press, radio and television.

(c)   Improvement of Working Conditions for Journalists

The participating States, desiring to improve the conditions under which journalists from one participating State exercise their profession in another participating State, intend in particular to:

— examine in a favourable spirit and within a suitable and reasonable time scale requests from journalists for visas;

— grant to permanently accredited journalists of the participating States, on the basis of arrangements, multiple entry and exist visas for specified periods;

— facilitate the issue to accredited journalists of the participating States of permits for stay in their country of temporary residence and, if and when these are necessary, of other official papers which it is appropriate for them to have;

— ease, on a basis of reciprocity, procedures for arranging travel by journalists of the participating States in the country where they are exercising their profession, and to provide progressively greater opportunities for such travel, subject to the observance of regulations relating to the existence of areas closed for security reasons;

— ensure that requests by such journalists for such travel receive, in so far as possible, an expeditious response, taking into account the time scale of the request;

— increase the opportunities for journalists of the participating States to communicate personally with their sources, including organizations and official institutions;

— grant to journalists of the participating States the right to import, subject only to its being taken out again, the technical equipment (photographic, cinematographic, tape recorder, radio and television) necessary for the exercise of their profession;*

— enable journalists of the other participating States, whether permanently or temporarily accredited, to transmit completely, normally and rapidly by means recognized by the participating States to the information organs which they represent, the results of their professional activity, including tape recordings and undeveloped film, for the purpose of publication or of broadcasting on the radio or television.

The participating states reaffirm that the legitimate pursuit of their professional activity will neither render journalists liable to expulsion nor otherwise penalize them. If an accredited journalist is expelled, he will be informed of the reasons for this act and may submit an application for reexamination of his case.

3.   Co-operation and Exchanges in the Field of Culture

The participating States

Considering that cultural exchanges and co-operation contribute to a better comprehension among people and among peoples, and thus promote a lasting understanding among States,

Confirming the conclusions already formulated in this field at the multilateral level, particularly at the Intergovernmental Conference on Cultural Policies in Europe, organized by UNESCO in Helsinki in June 1972, where interest was manifested in the active participation of the broadest possible social groups in an increasingly diversified cultural life,

Desiring, with the development of mutual confidence and the further improvement of relations between the participating States, to continue further efforts toward progress in this field,

Disposed in this spirit to increase substantially their cultural exchanges, with regard both to persons and to cultural works, and to develop among them an active co-operation, both at the bilateral and the multilateral level, in all the fields of culture,

---

* While recognizing that appropriate local personnel are employed by foreign journalists in many instances, the participating States note that the above provisions would be applied, subject to the observance of the appropriate rules, to persons from the other participating States, who are regularly and professionally engaged as technicians, photographers or cameramen of the press, radio, television or cinema.

Convinced that such a development of their mutual relations will contribute to the enrichment of the respective cultures, while respecting the originality of each, as well as to the reinforcement among them of a consciousness of common values, while continuing to develop cultural co-operation with other countries of the world,

Declare that they jointly set themselves the following objectives:

(a) to develop the mutual exchange of information with a view to a better knowledge of respective cultural achievements,

(b) to improve the facilities for the exchange and for the dissemination of cultural property,

(c) to promote access by all to respective cultural achievements,

(d) to develop contacts and co-operation among persons active in the field of culture,

(e) to seek new fields and forms of cultural co-operation,

Thus *give expression to* their common will to take progressive, coherent and long-term action in order to achieve the objectives of the present declaration; and

Express their intention now to proceed to the implementation of the following:

Extension of Relations

To expand and improve at the various levels co-operation and links in the field of culture, in particular by:

— concluding, where appropriate, agreements on a bilateral or multilateral basis, providing for the extension of relations among competent State institutions and non-governmental organizations in the field of culture, as well as among people engaged in cultural activities, taking into account the need both for flexibility and the fullest possible use of existing agreements, and bearing in mind that agreements and also other arrangements constitute important means of developing cultural co-operation and exchanges;

— contributing to the development of direct communication and co-operation among relevant State institutions and non-governmental organizations, including, where necessary, such communication and co-operation carried out on the basis of special agreements and arrangements;

— encouraging direct contacts and communications among persons engaged in cultural activities, including, where necessary, such contacts and communications carried out on the basis of special agreements and arrangements.

Mutual Knowledge

Within their competence to adopt, on a bilateral and multilateral level, appropriate measures which would give their peoples a more comprehensive and complete mutual knowledge of their achievements in the various fields of culture, and among them:

— to examine jointly, if necessary with the assistance of appropriate international organizations, the possible creation in Europe and the structure of a bank of cultural data, which would collect information from the participating countries and make it available to its correspondents on their request, and to convene for this purpose a meeting of experts from interested States;

— to consider, if necessary in conjunction with appropriate international organizations, ways of compiling in Europe an inventory of documentary films of a cultural or scientific nature from the participating States;

— to encourage more frequent book exhibitions and to examine the possibility of organizing periodically in Europe a large-scale exhibition of books from the participating States;

— to promote the systematic exchange, between the institutions concerned and publishing houses, of catalogues of available books as well as of pre-publication material which will include, as far as possible, all forthcoming publications; and also

to promote the exchange of material between firms publishing encyclopaedias, with a view of improving the presentation of each country;
— to examine jointly questions of expanding and improving exchanges of information in the various fields of culture, such as theatre, music, library work as well as the conservation and restoration of cultural property.

Exchanges and Dissemination

To contribute to the improvement of facilities for exchanges and the dissemination of cultural property, by appropriate means, in particular by:
— studying the possibilities for harmonizing and reducing the charges relating to international commercial exchanges of books and other cultural materials, and also for new means of insuring works of art in foreign exhibitions and for reducing the risks of damage or loss to which these works are exposed by their movement;
— facilitating the formalities of customs clearance in good time for programmes of artistic events, of the works of art, materials and accessories appearing on lists agreed upon by the organizers of these events;
— encouraging meetings among representatives of competent organizations and relevant firms to examine measures within their field of activity — such as the simplification of orders, time limits for sending supplies and modalities of payment — which might facilitate international commercial exchanges of books;
— promoting the loan and exchange of films among their film institutes and film libraries;
— encouraging the exchange of information among interested parties concerning events of a cultural character foreseen in the participating States, in fields where this is most appropriate, such as music, theatre and the plastic and graphic arts, with a view to contributing to the compilation and publication of a calendar of such events, with the assistance, where necessary, of the appropriate international organizations;
— encouraging a study of the impact which the foreseeable development, and a possible harmonization among interested parties, of the technical means used for the dissemination of culture might have on the development of cultural co-operation and exchanges, while keeping in view the preservation of the diversity and originality of their respective cultures;
— encouraging, in the way they deem appropriate, within their cultural policies, the further development of interest in the cultural heritage of the other participating States, conscious of the merits and the value of each culture;
— endeavouring to ensure the full and effective application of the international agreements and conventions on copyrights and on circulation of cultural property to which they are party or to which they may decide in the future to become party.

Access

To promote fuller mutual access by all to the achievements — works, experiences and performing arts — in the various fields of culture of their countries, and to that end to make the best possible efforts, in accordance with their competence, more particularly:
— to promote wider dissemination of books and artistic works, in particular by such means as:
facilitating, while taking full account of the international copyright conventions to which they are party, international contacts and communications between authors and publishing houses as well as other cultural institutions, with a view to a more complete mutual access to cultural achievements,
recommending that, in determining the size of editions, publishing houses take into account also the demand from the other participating States, and that rights of sale in other participating States be granted, where possible, to several sales organizations of the importing countries, by agreement between interested partners;

encouraging competent organizations and relevant firms to conclude agreements and contracts and contributing, by this means, to a gradual increase in the number and diversity of works by authors from the other participating States available in the original and in translation in their libraries and bookshops;

promoting, where deemed appropriate, an increase in the number of sales outlets where books by authors from the other participating States, imported in the original on the basis of agreements and contracts, and in translation, are for sale;

promoting, on a wider scale, the translation of works in the sphere of literature and other fields of cultural activity, produced in the languages of the other participating States, especially from the less widely-spoken languages, and the publication and dissemination of the translated works by such measures as:

encouraging more regular contracts between interested publishing houses;

developing their efforts in the basic and advanced training of translators;

encouraging, by appropriate means, the publishing houses of their countries to publish translations;

facilitating the exchange between publishers and interested institutions of lists of books which might be translated;

promoting between their countries the professional activity and co-operation of translators;

carrying out joint studies on ways of further promoting translations and their dissemination;

improving and expanding exchanges of books, bibliographies and catalogue cards between libraries;

— to envisage other appropriate measures which would permit, where necessary by mutual agreement among interested parties, the facilitation of access to their respective cultural achievements, in particular in the field of books;

— to contribute by appropriate means to the wider use of the mass media in order to improve mutual acquaintance with the cultural life of each;

— to seek to develop the necessary conditions for migrant workers and their families to preserve their links with their national culture, and also to adapt themselves to their new cultural environment;

— to encourage the competent bodies and enterprises to make a wider choice and effect wider distribution of full-length and documentary films from the other partici-pating States, and to promote more frequent non-commercial showings, such as premieres, film weeks and festivals, giving due consideration to films from countries whose cinematographic works are less well known;

— to promote, by appropriate means, the extension of opportunities for specialists from the other participating States to work with materials of a cultural character from film and audio-visual archives, within the framework of the existing rules for work on such archival materials;

— to encourage a joint study by interested bodies, where appropriate with the assistance of the competent international organizations, of the expediency and the conditions for the establishment of a repertory or their recorded television pro-grammes of a cultural nature, as well as the means of viewing them rapidly in order to facilitate their selection and possible acquisition.

Contacts and Co-operation

To contribute, by appropriate means, to the development of contracts and co-operation in the various fields of culture, especially among creative artists and people engaged in cultural activities, in particular by making efforts to:

— promote for persons active in the field of culture, travel and meetings including, where necessary, those carried out on the basis of agreements, contracts or other special arrangements and which are relevant to their cultural co-operation;

— encourage in this way contracts among creative and performing artists and artistic groups with a view to their working together, making known their works in other participating States or exchanging views on topics relevant to their common activity;

— encourage, where necessary through appropriate arrangements, exchanges of trainees and specialists and the granting of scholarships for basic and advanced training in various fields of culture such as the arts and architecture, museums and libraries, literary studies and translation, and contribute to the creation of favourable conditions of reception in their respective institutions;

— encourage the exchange of experience in the training of organizers of cultural activities as well as of teachers and specialists in fields such as theatre, opera, ballet, music and fine arts.

— continue to encourage the organization of international meetings among creative artists, especially young creative artists, on current questions of artistic and literary creation which are of interest for joint study.

— study other possibilities for developing exchanges and co-operation among persons active in the field of culture, with a view to a better mutual knowledge of the cultural life of the participating States.

Fields and Forms of Co-operation

To encourage the search for new fields and forms of cultural co-operation, to these ends contributing to the conclusion among interested parties, where necessary, of appropriate agreements and arrangements, and in this context to promote:

— joint studies regarding cultural policies, in particular in their social aspects, and as they relate to planning, town-planning, educational and environmental policies, and the cultural aspects of tourism;

— the exchange of knowledge in the realm of cultural diversity, with a view to contributing thus to a better understanding by interested parties of such diversity where it occurs;

— the exchange of information, and as may be appropriate, meetings of experts, the elaboration and the execution of research programmes and projects, as well as their joint evaluation, and the dissemination of the results, on the subjects indicated above;

— such forms of cultural co-operation and the development of such joint projects as:

international events in the fields of the plastic and graphic arts, cinema, theatre, ballet, music, folklore, etc.; book fairs and exhibitions, joint performances of operatic and dramatic works as well as performances given by soloists, instrumental ensembles, orchestras, choirs and other artistic groups, including those composed of amateurs, paying due attention to the organization of international cultural youth events and the exchange of young artists;

the inclusion of works by writers and composers from the other participating States in the repertoires of soloists and artistic ensembles;

the preparation, translation and publication of articles, studies and monographs, as well as of low-cost books and of artistic and literary collections, suited to making better known respective cultural achievements, envisaging for this purpose meetings among experts and representatives of publishing houses;

the co-production and the exchange of films and of radio and television programmes, by promoting, in particular, meetings among producers, technicians and representatives of the public authorities with a view of working out favourable conditions for the execution of specific joint projects and by encouraging, in the field of co-production, the establishment of international filming teams;

the organization of competitions for architects and town-planners, bearing in mind the possible implementation of the best projects and the formation, where possible, of international teams;

the implementation of joint projects for conserving, restoring and showing to advantage works of art, historical and archaeological monuments and sites of cultural interest, with the help, in appropriate cases, of international organizations of a governmental or non-governmental character as well as of private institutions — competent and active in these fields — envisaging for this purpose:

periodic meetings of experts of the interested parties to elaborate the necessary proposals, while bearing in mind the need to consider these questions in a wider social and economic context;

the publication in appropriate periodicals of articles designed to make known and to compare, among the participating States, the most significant achievements and innovations;

a joint study with a view to the improvement and possible harmonization of the different systems used to inventory and catalogue the historical monuments and places of cultural interest in their countries;

the study of the possibilities for organizing international courses for the training of specialists in different disciplines relating to restoration.

National minorities or regional cultures. The participating States, recognizing the contribution that national minorities or regional cultures can make to co-operation among them in various fields of culture, intend, when such minorities or cultures exist within their territory, to facilitate this contribution, taking into account the legitimate interests of their members.

4. Co-operation and Exchanges in the Field of Education

The participating States,

Conscious that the development of relations of an international character in the fields of education and science contributes to a better mutual understanding and is to the advantage of all peoples as well as to the benefit of future generations,

Prepared to facilitate, between organizations, institutions and persons engaged in education and science, the further development of exchanges of knowledge and experience as well as of contacts, on the basis of special arrangements where these are necessary,

Desiring to strengthen the links among educational and scientific establishments and also to encourage their co-operation in sectors of common interest, particularly where the levels of knowledge and resources require efforts to be concerted internationally, and

Convinced that progress in these fields should be accompanied and supported by a wider knowledge of foreign languages.

Express to these ends their intention in particular:

(a) Extension of Relations

To expand and improve at the various levels co-operation and links in the fields of education and science, in particular by:

— concluding, where appropriate, bilateral or multilateral agreements providing for co-operation and exchanges among State institutions, non-governmental bodies and persons engaged in activities in education and science, bearing in mind the need both for flexibility and the fuller use of existing agreements and arrangements;

— promoting the conclusion of direct arrangements between universities and other institutions of higher education and research, in the framework of agreements between governments where appropriate;

— encouraging among persons engaged in education and science direct contacts and communications, including those based on special agreements or arrangements where these are appropriate.

(b) Access and Exchanges

To improve access, under mutually acceptable conditions, for students, teachers and scholars of the participating States to each other's educational, cultural and scientific institutions, and to intensify exchanges among these institutions in all areas of common interest, in particular by:

— increasing the exchange of information on facilities for study and courses open to foreign participants, as well as on the conditions under which they will be admitted and received;

— facilitating travel between the participating States by scholars, teachers and students for purposes of study, teaching and research as well as for improving knowledge of each other's educational, cultural and scientific achievements;

— encouraging the award of scholarships for study, teaching and research in their countries to scholars, teachers and students of other participating States;

— establishing, developing or encouraging programmes providing for the broader exchange of scholars, teachers and students, including the organization of symposia, seminars and collaborative projects, and the exchanges of educational and scholarly information such as university publications and materials from libraries;

— promoting the efficient implementation of such arrangements and programmes by providing scholars, teachers and students in good time with more detailed information about their placing in universities and institutes and the programmes envisaged for them; by granting them the opportunity to use relevant scholarly, scientific and open archival materials; and by facilitating their travel within the receiving State for the purpose of study or research as well as in the form of vacation tours on the basis of the usual procedures;

— promoting a more exact assessment of the problems of comparison and equivalence of academic degrees and diplomas by fostering the exchange of information on the organization, duration and content of studies, the comparison of methods of assessing levels of knowledge and academic qualifications, and, where feasible, arriving at the mutual recognition of academic degrees and diplomas either through governmental agreements, where necessary, or direct arrangements between universities and other institutions of higher learning and research;

— recommending, moreover, to the appropriate international organizations that they should intensify their efforts to reach a generally acceptable solution to the problems of comparison and equivalence between academic degrees and diplomas.

(c) Science

Within their competence to broaden and improve co-operation and exchanges in the field of science, in particular:

To increase, on a bilateral or multilateral basis, the exchange and dissemination of scientific information and documentation by such means as:

— making this information more widely available to scientists and research workers of the other participating States through, for instance, participation in international information-sharing programmes or through other appropriate arrangements;

— broadening and facilitating the exchange of samples and other scientific materials used particularly for fundamental research in the fields of natural sciences and medicine;

— inviting scientific institutions and universities to keep each other more fully and regularly informed about their current and contemplated research work in fields of common interest.

To facilitate the extension of communications and direct contacts between universities, scientific institutions and associations as well as among scientists and research workers, including those based where necessary on special agreements or arrangements, by such means as:

— further developing exchanges of scientists and research workers and encouraging the organization of preparatory meetings or working groups on research topics of common interest;

— encouraging the creation of joint teams of scientists to pursue research projects under arrangements made by the scientific institutions of several countries;

— assisting the organization and successful functioning of international conferences and seminars and participation in them by their scientists and research workers;

— furthermore envisaging, in the near future, a 'Scientific Forum' in the form of a meeting of leading personalities in science from the participating States to discuss interrelated problems of common interest concerning current and future developments in science, and to promote the expansion of contacts, communications and the exchange of information between scientific institutions and among scientists;

— foreseeing, at an early date, a meeting of experts representing the participating States and their national scientific institutions, in order to prepare such a 'Scientific Forum' in consultation with appropriate international organizations, such an UNESCO and the ECE;

— considering in due course what further steps might be taken with respect to the 'Scientific Forum'.

To develop in the field of scientific research, on a bilateral or multilateral basis, the co-ordination of programmes carried out in the participating States and the organization of joint programmes, especially in the areas mentioned below, which may involve the combined efforts of scientists and in certain cases the use of costly or unique equipment. The list of subjects in these areas is illustrative; and specific projects would have to be determined subsequently by the potential partners in the participating States, taking account of the contribution which could be made by appropriate international organizations and scientific institutions:

— *exact and natural sciences,* in particular fundamental research in such fields as mathematics, physics, theoretical physics, geophysics, chemistry, biology, ecology and astronomy;

— *medicine,* in particular basic research into cancer and cardiovascular diseases, studies on the diseases endemic in the developing countries, as well as medico-social research with special emphasis on occupational diseases, the rehabilitation of the handicapped and the care of mothers, children and the elderly;

— *the humanities and social sciences,* such as history, geography, philosophy, psychology, pedagogical research, linguitics, sociology, the legal, political and economic sciences; comparative studies on social, socio-economic and cultural phenomena which are of common interest to the participating States, especially the problems of human environment and urban development; and scientific studies on the methods of conserving and restoring monuments and works of art.

(d)   Foreign Languages and Civilizations

To encourage the study of foreign languages and civilizations as an important means of expanding communication among peoples for their better acquaintance with the culture of each country, as well as for the strengthening of international co-operation; to this end to stimulate, within their competence, the further development and improvement of foreign language teaching and the diversification of choice of languages taught at various levels, paying due attention to less widely-spread or studied languages, and in particular:

— to intensify co-operation aimed at improving the teaching of foreign languages through exchanges of information and experience concerning the development and application of effective modern teaching methods and technical aids, adapted to the needs of different categories of students, including methods of accelerated teaching; and to consider the possibility of conducting, on a bilateral or multilateral basis, studies of new methods of foreign language teaching;

— to encourage co-operation between institutions concerned, on a bilateral or multilateral basis, aimed at exploiting more fully the resources of modern educational technology in language teaching, for example through comparative studies by their specialists and, where agreed, through exchanges or transfers of audio-visual materials, of materials used for preparing textbooks, as well as of information about new types of technical equipment used for teaching languages;

— to promote the exchange of information on the experience acquired in the training of language teachers and intensify exchanges on a bilateral basis of language teachers and students as well as to facilitate their participation in summer courses in languages and civilizations, wherever these are organized;

— to encourage co-operation among experts in the field of lexicography with the aim of defining the necessary terminological equivalents, particularly in the scientific and technical disciplines, in order to facilitate relations among scientific institutions and specialists;

— to promote the wider spread of foreign language study among the different types of secondary education establishments and greater possibilities of choice between an increased number of European languages; and in this context to consider, wherever appropriate, the possibilities for developing the recruitment and training of teachers as well as the organization of the student groups required;

— to favour, in higher education, a wider choice in the languages offered to language students and greater opportunities for other students to study various foreign languages; also to facilitate, where desirable, the organization of courses in languages and civilizations, on the basis of special arrangements as necessary, to be given by foreign lecturers, particularly from European countries having less widely-spread or studied languages;

— to promote, within the framework of adult education, the further development of specialized programmers, adapted to various needs and interests, for teaching foreign languages to their own inhabitants and the languages of host countries to interested adults from other countries; in this context to encourage interested institutions to co-operate, for example, in the elaboration of programmers for teaching by radio and television and by accelerated methods, and also, where desirable, in the definition of study objectives for such programmers, with a view to arriving at comparable levels of language proficiency;

— to encourage the association, where appropriate, of the teaching of foreign languages with the study of the corresponding civilizations and also to make further efforts to stimulate interest in the study of foreign languages, including relevant out-of-class activities.

(e)   Teaching Methods

To promote the exchange of experience, on a bilateral or multilateral basis, in teaching methods at all levels of education, including those used in permanent and adult education, as well as the exchange of teaching materials, in particular by:

— further developing various forms of contacts and co-operation in the different fields of pedagogical science, for example through comparative or joint studies carried out by interested institutions or through exchanges of information on the results of teaching experiments;

— intensifying exchanges of information on teaching methods used in various educational systems and on results of research into the processes by which pupils and students acquire knowledge, taking account of relevant experience in different types of specialized education;

— facilitating exchanges of experience concerning the organization and functioning of education intended for adults and recurrent education, the relationships
between these and other forms and levels of education, as well as concerning the
means of adapting education, including vocational and technical training, to the needs
of economic and social development in their countries;

— encouraging exchanges of experience in the education of youth and adults in
international understanding, with particular reference to those major problems of
mankind whose solution calls for a common approach and wider international
co-operation;

— encouraging exchanges of teaching materials—including school textbooks,
having in mind the possibility of promoting mutual knowledge and facilitating the
presentation of each country in such books—as well as exchanges of information on
technical innovations in the field of education.

National minorities or regional cultures. The participating States, recognizing the
contribution that national minorities or regional cultures can make to co-operation
among them in various fields of education, intend, when such minorities or cultures
exist within their territory, to facilitate this contribution, taking into account the
legitimate interests of their members.

FOLLOW-UP TO THE CONFERENCE

The participating States,

Having considered and evaluated the progress made at the Conference on Security
and Co-operation in Europe,

Considering further that, within the broader context of the world, the Conference is
an important part of the process of improving security and developing co-operation in
Europe and that its results will contribute significantly to this process.

Intending to implement the provisions of the Final Act of the Conference in order
to give full effect to its results and thus to further the process of improving security
and developing co-operation in Europe.

Convinced that, in order to achieve the aims sought by the Conference, they should
make further unilateral, bilateral and multilateral efforts and continue, in the appropriate forms set forth below, the multilateral process initiated by the Conference,

1. *Declare their resolve*, in the period following the Conference, to pay due regard
to and implement the provisions of the Final Act of the Conference:

(a) unilaterally, in all cases which lend themselves to such action;

(b) bilaterally, by negotiations with other participating States;

(c) multilaterally, by meetings of experts of the participating States, and also
within the framework of existing international organizations, such as the United
Nations Economic Commission for Europe and UNESCO, with regard to educational, scientific and cultural co-operation;

2. *Declare furthermore their resolve* to continue the multilateral process initiated by
the Conference:

(a) by proceeding to a thorough exchange of views both on the implementation
of the provisions of the Final Act and of the tasks defined by the Conference, as well
as, in the context of the questions dealt with by the latter, on the deepening of their
mutual relations, the improvement of security and the development of co-operation
in Europe, and the development of the process of détente in the future;

(b) by organizing to these ends meetings among their representatives, beginning
with a meeting at the level of representatives appointed by the Ministers of Foreign Affairs.
This meeting will define the appropriate modalities for the holding of other meetings
which could include further similar meetings and the possibility of a new Conference;

3. The first of the meetings indicated above will be held at Belgrade in 1977. A
preparatory meeting to organize this meeting will be held at Belgrade on 15 June

1977. The preparatory meeting will decide on the date, duration, agenda and other modalities of the meeting of representatives appointed by the Ministers of Foreign Affairs;

4.   The rules of procedure, the working methods and the scale of distribution for the expenses of the Conference will, *mutatis mutandis*, be applied to the meetings envisaged in paragraphs 1 (c), 2 and 3 above. All the above-mentioned meetings will be held in the participating States in rotation. The services of a technical secretariat will be provided by the host country.

The original of this Final Act, drawn up in English, French, German, Italian, Russian and Spanish, will be transmitted to the Government of the Republic of Finland, which will retain it in its archives. Each of the participating States will receive from the Government of the Republic of Finland a true copy of this Final Act.

The text of this Final Act will be published in each participating State, which will disseminate it and make it known as widely as possible.

The Government of the Republic of Finland is requested to transmit to the Secretary-General of the United Nations the text of this Final Act, which is not eligible for registration under Article 102 of the Charter of the United Nations, with a view to its circulation to all the members of the Organization as an official document of the United Nations.

The Government of the Republic of Finland is also requested to transmit the text of this Final Act to the Director-General of UNESCO and to the Executive Secretary of the United Nations Economic Commission for Europe.

Wherefore, the undersigned High Representatives of the participating States, mindful of the high political significance which they attach to the results of the Conference, and declaring their determination to act in accordance with the provisions contained in the above texts, have subscribed their signatures below.

CONCLUDING DOCUMENT OF THE VIENNA MEETING OF REPRESENTATIVES OF THE PARTICIPATING STATES OF THE CONFERENCE ON SECURITY AND CO-OPERATION IN EUROPE, HELD ON THE BASIS OF THE PROVISIONS OF THE FINAL ACT RELATING TO THE FOLLOW-UP TO THE CONFERENCE (1986)

The representatives of the participating States of the Conference on Security and Co-operation in Europe (CSCE), Austria, Belgium, Bulgaria, Canada, Cyprus, Czechoslovakia, Denmark, Finland, France, the German Democratic Republic, the Federal Republic of Germany, Greece, the Holy See, Hungary, Iceland, Ireland, Italy, Liechtenstein, Luxembourg, Malta, Monaco, the Netherlands, Norway, Poland, Portugal, Romania, San Marino, Spain, Sweden, Switzerland, Turkey, the Union of Soviet Socialist Republics, the United Kingdom, the United States of America and Yugoslavia met in Vienna from 4 November 1986 to 19 January 1989 in accordance with the provisions of the Final Act relating to the Follow-Up to the conference, as well as on the basis of the other relevant CSCE documents.

The participants were addressed on 4 November 1986 by the Austrian Federal Chancellor.

Opening statements were made by all Heads of Delegations among whom were Ministers and Deputy Ministers of many participating States. Some Ministers of Foreign Affairs addressed the Meeting also at later stages.

The participants were addressed by a representative of the Secretary-General of the United Nations. Contributions were made by representatives of the United Nations Economic Commission for Europe (ECE) and UNESCO.

Contributions were also made by the following non-participating Mediterranean States: Algeria, Egypt, Israel, Lebanon, Libya, Morocco, Syria and Tunisia.

The representatives of the participating States reaffirmed their commitment to the CSCE process and underlined its essential role in increasing confidence, in opening up new ways for cooperation, in promoting respect for human rights and fundamental freedoms and thus strengthening international security.

The participating States welcomed the favourable developments in the international situation since the conclusion of the Madrid Meeting in 1983 and expressed their satisfaction that the CSCE process has contributed to these developments. Noting the intensification of political dialogue between their countries and the important progress in negotiations on military security and disarmament they agreed that renewed efforts should be undertaken to consolidate these positive trends and to achieve a substantial further improvement of their mutual relations. Accordingly, they reaffirmed their resolve to implement fully, unilaterally, bilaterally and multilaterally, all the provisions of the Final Act and of the other CSCE documents.

As provided for in the Agenda of the Vienna Meeting, the representatives of the participating States held a thorough exchange of views both on the implementation of the provisions of the Final Act, and the Madrid Concluding Document and of the tasks defined by Conference, as well as, in the context of the questions dealt with by the latter, on the deepening of their mutual relations, the improvements of security and the development of cooperation in Europe, and the development of the process of detente in the future.

During this exchange of views the participating States examined thoroughly and in detail the implementation of the Final Act and of the Madrid Concluding Document. Different and at times contradictory opinions were expressed about the extent of the realization of these commitments. While encouraging developments were noted in many areas, the participants criticized the continuing serious deficiencies in the implementation of these documents.

An open and frank discussion was held about the application of and respect for the principles of the Final Act. Concern was expressed about serious violations of a number of these principles. In particular, questions relating to respect for human rights and fundamental freedoms were the focus of intensive and controversial discussion. The participating States agreed that full respect for the principles, in all their aspects, is essential for the improvement of their mutual relations.

The implementation of the provisions of the Final Act concerning confidence-building measures, co-operation in the field of economics, of science and technology and of environment, concerning questions relating to security and cooperation in the Mediterranean as well as cooperation in humanitarian and other fields was discussed. In this context the implementation of the provisions of the Madrid Concluding Document and of other CSCE documents was also discussed. It was considered that the numerous possibilities offered by the Final Act had not been sufficiently utilized.

The participating States also expressed concern about the spread of terrorism and condemned it unreservedly.

The discussion reflected the broader context of the CSCE process and confirmed the importance of taking into account its world dimension in implementing the provisions of the Final Act.

In their deliberations the representatives of the participating States took into account the results of
* the Stockholm Conference on Confidence- and Security-Building Measures and Disarmament in Europe;
* the Athens Meeting of Experts in order to pursue the examination and elaboration of a generally acceptable method for the peaceful settlement of disputes aimed at complementing existing methods;
* the Venice Seminar on Economic, Scientific and Cultural Co-operation in the Mediterranean, the Ottawa Meeting of Experts on Questions concerning Respect, in

their States, for Human Rights and Fundamental Freedoms, in all their Aspects, as embodied in the Final Act;
• the Budapest 'Cultural Forum';
• the Bern Meeting of Experts on Human Contacts.

The participating States noted moreover that the tenth anniversary of the signing of the Final Act had been commemorated at Helsinki on 1 August 1985.

The participating States reaffirmed their commitment to the continuation of the CSCE process as agreed to in the chapter on the Follow-Up to the Conference contained in the Final Act. Recognizing the need for balanced progress in all sections of the Final Act, they expressed their determination also to benefit from new opportunities for their cooperation and reached corresponding decisions concerning joint follow-up activities.

The representatives of the participating States examined all the proposals submitted to the Meeting and agreed on the following:

QUESTIONS RELATING TO SECURITY IN EUROPE

The participating States express their determination
• to build on the current positive developments in their relations in order to make detente a viable, comprehensive and genuine process, universal in scope;
• to assume their responsibility fully to implement the commitments contained in the Final Act and other CSCE documents;
• to intensify their efforts to seek solutions to problems burdening their relations and to strengthen safeguards for international peace and security;
• to promote cooperation and dialogue among them, to ensure the effective exercise of human rights and fundamental freedoms and to facilitate contacts and communication between people;
• to exert new efforts to make further progress to strengthen confidence and security and to promote disarmament.

PRINCIPLES

1. The participating States reaffirm their commitment to all ten principles of the Final Act's Declaration on Principles Guiding Relations between Participating States and their determination to respect them and put them into practice. The participating States reaffirm that all these Principles are of primary significance and, accordingly, will be equally and unreservedly applied, each of them being interpreted taking into account the others.

2. They stress that respect for and full application of these principles as well as strict compliance with all CSCE commitments deriving from them, are of great political importance and essential for building confidence and security as well as for the development of their friendly relations and of their cooperation in all fields.

3. In this context, they confirm that they will respect each other's right freely to choose and develop their political, social, economic and cultural systems as well as their right to determine their laws, regulations, practices and policies. In exercising these rights, they will ensure that their laws, regulations, practices and policies conform with their obligations under international law and are brought into harmony with the provisions of the Declaration on Principles and other CSCE commitments.

4. They also confirm that, by virtue of the principle of equal rights and self-determination of peoples and in conformity with the relevant provisions of the Final Act, all peoples always have the right, in full freedom, to determine, when and as they wish, their internal and external political status, without external interference, and to pursue as they wish their political, economic, social and cultural development.

5. They confirm their commitment strictly and effectively to observe the principle of the territorial integrity of States. They will refrain from any violation of this

principle and thus from any action aimed by direct or indirect means, in contravention of the purposes and principles of the Charter of the United Nations, other obligations under international law or the provisions of the Final Act, at violating the territorial integrity, political independence or the unity of a State. No actions or situations in contravention of this principle will be recognized as legal by the participating States.

6.   The participating States confirm their commitment to the principle of peaceful settlement of disputes, convinced that it is an essential complement to the duty of States to refrain from the threat or use of force, both being essential factors for the maintenance and consolidation of peace and security. They express their determination to pursue continuous efforts to examine and elaborate, on the basis of the relevant provisions of the Final Act and the Madrid Concluding Document, and taking into account the reports of the meetings of experts in Montreux and Athens, a generally acceptable method for the peaceful settlement of disputes aimed at complementing existing methods. In this context they accept, in principle, the mandatory involvement of a third party when a dispute cannot be settled by other peaceful means.

7.   In order to ensure the progressive implementation of this commitment, including, as a first step, the mandatory involvement of a third party in the settlement of certain categories of disputes, they decide to convene a Meeting of Experts in Valletta from 15 January to 8 February 1991 to establish a list of such categories and the related procedures and mechanisms. This list would be subject to subsequent gradual extension. The Meeting will also consider the possibility of establishing mechanisms for arriving at binding third-party decisions. The next CSCE Follow-up meeting will assess the progress achieved at the Meeting of Experts. The agenda, timetable and other organizational modalities are set out in Annex I.

8.   The participating states unreservedly condemn, as criminal, all acts, methods and practices of terrorism, wherever and by whomever committed, including those which jeopardize friendly relations among States and their security, and agree that terrorism cannot be justified under any circumstances.

9.   They express their determination to work for the eradication of terrorism both bilaterally and through multilateral co-operation, particularly in such international fora as the United Nations, the International Civil Aviation Organization and the International Maritime Organization and in accordance with the relevant provisions of the Final Act and the Madrid Concluding Document.

10.   Convinced of the need to combine measures at a national level with reinforced international cooperation, the participating States express their intention

10a •   to pursue a policy of firmness in response to terrorist demands;

10b •   to reinforce and develop bilateral and multilateral co-operation among themselves in order to prevent and combat terrorism as well as to increase efficiency in existing co-operation at the bilateral level or in the framework of groups of States, including, as appropriate, through the exchange of information;

10c •   to prevent on their territories illegal activities of persons, groups or organizations that instigate, organize or engage in the perpetration of acts of terrorism or subversive or other activities directed towards the violent overthrow of the regime of another participating State;

10d •   to take effective measures for the prevention and suppression of acts of terrorism directed at diplomatic or consular representatives and against terrorism involving violations of the Vienna Conventions on Diplomatic and Consular Relations, in particular their provisions relating to diplomatic and consular privileges and immunities;

10e •   to ensure the extradition or prosecution of persons implicated in terrorist acts and to cooperate closely in cases of conflict of jurisdiction where several States are concerned, acting in both respects in accordance with the relevant international agreements;

10f • to consider becoming parties, if they have not yet done so, to the relevant international conventions relating to the suppression of acts of terrorism;

10g • to continue to work in the appropriate international bodies in order to improve and extend measures against terrorism and to ensure that the relevant agreements are accepted and acted upon by as many States as possible.

11. They confirm that they will respect human rights and fundamental freedoms, including the freedom of thought, conscience, religion or belief, for all without distinction as to race, sex, language or religion. They also confirm the universal significance of human rights and fundamental freedoms, respect for which is an essential factor for the peace, justice and security necessary to ensure the development of friendly relations and co-operation among themselves, as among all States.

12. They express their determination to guarantee the effective exercise of human rights and fundamental freedoms, all of which derive from the inherent dignity of the human person and are essential for his free and full development. They recognize that civil, political, economic, social, cultural and other rights and freedoms are all of paramount importance and must be fully realized by all appropriate means.

13. In this context they will

13a • develop their laws, regulations and policies in the field of civil, political, economic, social, cultural and other human rights and fundamental freedoms and put them into practice in order to guarantee the effective exercise of these rights and freedoms;

13b • consider acceding to the International Covenant on Civil and Political Rights, the International Covenant on Economic, Social and Cultural Rights, the Optional Protocol to the Covenant on Civil and Political Rights and other relevant international instruments, if they have not yet done so;

13c • publish and disseminate the text of the Final Act, of the Madrid Concluding Document, and of the present Document as well as those of any relevant international instruments in the field of human rights, in order to ensure the availability of these documents in their entirety, to make them known as widely as possible and to render them accessible to all individuals in their countries, in particular through public library systems;

13d • ensure effectively the right of the individual to know and act upon his rights and duties in this field, and to that end publish and make accessible all laws, regulations and procedures relating to human rights and fundamental freedoms;

13e • respect the right of their citizens to contribute actively, individually or in association with others, to the promotion and protection of human rights and fundamental freedoms;

13f • encourage in schools and other educational institutions consideration of the promotion and protection of human rights and fundamental freedoms;

13g • ensure human rights and fundamental freedoms to everyone within their territory and subject to their jurisdiction, without distinction of any kind such as race, colour, sex, language, religion, political or other opinion, national or social origin, property, birth or other status;

13h • ensure that no individual exercising, expressing the intention to exercise or seeking to exercise these rights and freedoms, or any member of his family, will as a consequence be discriminated against in any manner;

13i • ensure that effective remedies as well as full information about them are available to those who claim that their human rights and fundamental freedoms have been violated; they will, *inter alia*, effectively apply the following remedies:

• the right of the individual to appeal to executive, legislative, judicial or administrative organs;

• the right to a fair and public hearing within a reasonable time before an independent and impartial tribunal, including the right to present legal arguments and to be represented by legal counsel of one's choice;

- the right to be promptly and officially informed of the decision taken on any appeal, including the legal grounds on which this decision was based. This information will be provided as a rule in writing and, in any event, in a way that will enable the individual to make effective use of further available remedies.

14.   The participating States recognize that the promotion of economic, social, cultural rights as well as of civil and political rights is of paramount importance for human dignity and for the attainment of the legitimate aspirations of every individual. They will therefore continue their efforts with a view to achieving progressively the full realization of economic, social and cultural rights by all appropriate means, including in particular by the adoption of legislative measures.

In this context they will pay special attention to problems in the areas of employment, housing, social security, health, education and culture. They will promote constant progress in the realization of all rights and freedoms within their countries, as well as in the development of their relations among themselves and with other States, so that everyone will actually enjoy to the full his economic, social and cultural rights as well as his civil and political rights.

15.   The participating States confirm their determination to ensure equal rights of men and women. Accordingly, they will take all measures necessary, including legislative measures, to promote equally effective participation of men and women in political, economic, social and cultural life. They will consider the possibility of acceding, if they have not yet done so, to the Convention on the Elimination of All Forms of Discrimination Against Women.

16.   In order to ensure the freedom of the individual to profess and practice religion or belief the participating States will, *inter alia*,

16a   • take effective measures to prevent and eliminate discrimination against individuals or communities, on the grounds of religion or belief in the recognition, exercise and enjoyment of human rights and fundamental freedoms in all fields of civil, political, economic, social and cultural life, and ensure the effective equality between believers and non-believers;

16b   • foster a climate of mutual tolerance and respect between believers of different communities as well as between believers and non-believers;

16c   • grant upon their request to communities of believers, practising or prepared to practise their faith within the constitutional framework of their states, recognition of the status provided for them in their respective countries;

16d   • respect the right of religious communities to
  - establish and maintain freely accessible places of worship or assembly,
  - organize themselves according to their own hierarchical and institutional structure,
  - select, appoint and replace their personnel in accordance with their respective requirements and standards as well as with any freely accepted arrangement between them and their State,
  - solicit and receive voluntary financial and other contributions;

16e   • engage in consultations with religious faiths, institutions and organizations in order to achieve a better understanding of the requirements of religious freedom;

16f   • respect the right of everyone to give and receive religious education in the language of his choice, individually or in association with others;

16g   • in this context respect, *inter alia*, the liberty of parents to ensure the religious and moral education of their children in conformity with their own convictions;

16h   • allow the training of religious personnel in appropriate institutions;

16i   • respect the right of individual believers and communities of believers to acquire, possess, and use sacred books, religious publications in the language of their choice and other articles and materials related to the practice of religion or belief;

16j • allow religious faiths, institutions and organizations to produce and import and disseminate religious publications and materials;

16k • favourably consider the interest of religious communities in participating in public dialogue, inter alia, through mass media;

17. The participating States recognize that the exercise of the above-mentioned rights relating to the freedom of religion or belief may be subject only to such limitations as are provided by law and consistent with their obligations under international law and with their international commitments. They will ensure in their laws and regulations and in their application the full and effective implementation of the freedom of thought, conscience, religion or belief;

18. The participating States will exert sustained efforts to implement the provisions of the Final Act and of the Madrid Concluding Document pertaining to national minorities. They will take all the necessary legislative, administrative, judicial and other measures and apply the relevant international instruments by which they may be bound, to ensure the protection of human rights and fundamental freedoms of persons belonging to national minorities within their territory. They will refrain from any discrimination against such persons and contribute to the realization of their legitimate interests and aspirations in the field of human rights and fundamental freedoms.

19. They will protect and create conditions for the promotion of the ethnic, cultural, linguistic and religious identity of national minorities on their territory. They will respect the free exercise of rights by persons belonging to such minorities and ensure their full equality with others.

20. The participating States will respect fully, the right of everyone
    • to freedom of movement and residence within the borders of each State,
and
    • to leave any country, including his own, and to return to his country.

21. The participating States will ensure that the exercise of the above-mentioned rights shall not be subject to any restrictions except to those which are provided by law and consistent with their obligations under international law, in particular the International Covenant on Civil and Political Rights and their international commitments, in particular the Universal Declaration of Human Rights. These restrictions have the character of exceptions. The participating States will ensure that these restrictions are not abused and are not applied in an arbitrary manner, but in such a way that the effective exercise of these rights is ensured.

22. In this context they will allow all refugees who so desire to return in safety to their homes.

23. The participating states will

23a • ensure that no one shall be subjected to arbitrary arrest, detention or exile;

23b • ensure that all individuals in detention or incarceration will be treated with humanity and with respect for the inherent dignity of the human person;

23c • observe the UN Standard Minimum Rules for the Treatment of Prisoners as well as the UN Code of Conduct for Law Enforcement Officials;

23d • prohibit torture and other cruel, inhuman or degrading treatment or punishment and take effective legislative, administrative, judicial and other measures to prevent and punish such practices;

23e • consider acceding to the Convention against Torture and other Cruel, Inhuman or Degrading Treatment or Punishment, if they have not yet done so;

23f • protect individuals from any psychiatric or other medical practices that violate human rights and fundamental freedoms and take effective measures to prevent and punish such practices.

24. With regard to the question of capital punishment, the participating States note that capital punishment has been abolished in a number of them. In participating

States where capital punishment has not been abolished, sentence of death may be imposed only for the most serious crimes in accordance with the law in force at the time of the commission of the crime and not contrary to their international commitments. This question will be kept under consideration. In this context, the participating States will cooperate within relevant international organizations.

25.   The participating States will, with the aim of developing mutual understanding and confidence, promoting friendly and good neighbourly relations, strengthening international peace, security and justice and of improving the implementation of their CSCE commitments, further develop cooperation and promote dialogue between them in all fields and at all levels on the basis of full equality. They agree that full respect for and application of the Principles and the fulfillment of the other CSCE provisions will improve their relations and advance the development of their cooperation. They will refrain from any action inconsistent with the provisions of the Final Act and other CSCE documents and recognize that any such action would impair relations between them and hinder the development of cooperation among them.

26.   They confirm that governments, institutions, organizations and persons have a relevant and positive role to play in contributing to the achievement of the aims of their cooperation and to the full realization of the Final Act. To that end they will respect the right of persons to observe and promote the implementation of CSCE provisions and to associate with others for this purpose. They will facilitate direct contacts and communication among these persons, organizations and institutions within and between participating States and remove, where they exist, legal and administrative impediments inconsistent with the CSCE provisions. They will also take effective measures to facilitate access to information on the implementation of CSCE provisions and the free expression of views on these matters.

27.   The participating States heard accounts of the Meeting of Experts on questions concerning respect, in their states, for Human Rights and Fundamental Freedoms, in all their aspects, as embodied in the Final Act, held in Ottawa from 7 May to 17 June 1985. They welcomed the fact that frank discussions had taken place of matters of key concern. Noting that these discussions had not led to agreed conclusions, they agreed that such thorough exchanges of views themselves constitute a valuable contribution to the CSCE process. In this respect it was noted in particular that proposals made at the meeting had received further consideration at the Vienna Follow-Up Meeting. They also welcomed the decision to allow public access to part of the meeting and noted that this principle was further developed at later meetings.

CONFIDENCE-AND SECURITY-BUILDING MEASURES AND CERTAIN ASPECTS OF SECURITY AND DISARMAMENT IN EUROPE

STOCKHOLM CONFERENCE: ASSESSMENT OF PROGRESS ACHIEVED

The participating States,

In accordance with the relevant provisions of the Madrid Concluding Document, assessed progress achieved during the Conference on Confidence- and Security-building Measures and Disarmament in Europe, which met in Stockholm from 17 January 1984 to 19 September 1986.

They welcomed the adoption at Stockholm of a set of mutually complementary confidence- and security-building measures (CSBMS).

They noted that these measures are in accordance with the criteria of the Madrid mandate and constitute a substantial improvement and extension of the confidence-building measures adopted in the Final Act.

They noted that the adoption of the Stockholm Document was a politically significant achievement and that its measures are an important step in efforts aimed at reducing the risk of military confrontation in Europe. They agreed that the extent to which the measures will in practice contribute to greater confidence and security will depend on the record of implementation. They were encouraged by initial implementation and noted that further experience and detailed review will be required. They reaffirmed their determination to comply strictly with and apply in good faith all the provisions of the Document of the Stockholm Conference.

They reaffirmed their commitment to the provisions of the Madrid Concluding Document relating to the Conference on Confidence- and Security-building Measures and Disarmament in Europe and agreed to resume the work of the Conference with a view to achieving further progress towards it aim.

NEW EFFORTS FOR SECURITY AND DISARMAMENT IN EUROPE

The participating States,

Recalling the relevant provisions of the Final Act and of the Madrid Concluding Document according to which they recognize the interest of all of them in efforts aimed at lessening military confrontation and promoting disarmament,

Reaffirming their determination expressed in the Final Act to strengthen confidence among them and thus to contribute to increasing stability and security in Europe,

Stressing the complementary nature of the efforts within the framework of the CSCE process aimed at building confidence and security and establishing stability and achieving progress in disarmament, in order to lessen military confrontation and to enhance security for all,

Stressing that in undertaking such efforts they will respect the security interests of all CSCE participating States inherent in their sovereign equality,

Having also considered ways and appropriate means to continue their efforts for security and disarmament in Europe,

Have reached the understanding that these efforts should be structured as set forth below:

NEGOTIATIONS ON CONFIDENCE- AND SECURITY-BUILDING MEASURES

The participating States have agreed that Negotiations on Confidence- and Security-building Measures will take place in order to build upon and expand the results already achieved at the Stockholm Conference with the aim of elaborating and adopting a new set of mutually complementary confidence- and security-building measures designed to reduce the risk of military confrontation in Europe. These negotiations will take place in accordance with the Madrid mandate. The decisions of the Preparatory Meeting held in Helsinki from 25 October to 11 November 1983 will be applied *mutatis mutandis* (see Annex II).

These negotiations will take place in Vienna, commencing in the week beginning on 6 March 1989.

The next Follow-up Meeting of the participating States of the CSCE, to be held in Helsinki, commencing on 24 March 1992, will assess the progress achieved in these negotiations.

NEGOTIATION ON CONVENTIONAL ARMED FORCES IN EUROPE

The Negotiation on Conventional Armed Forces in Europe will take place as agreed by those States named in the mandate contained in the Chairman's statement in Annex III of this document, who among themselves have determined the agenda, the rules of procedure and the organizational modalities of these negotiations, and will determine their timetable and results. These negotiations will be conducted within the framework of the CSCE process.

These negotiations will take place in Vienna, commencing in the week beginning on 6 March 1989.

The next Follow-Up Meeting of the participating States of the CSCE, to be held in Helsinki, commencing on 24 March 1992, will exchange views on the progress achieved in these negotiations.

MEETINGS IN ORDER TO EXCHANGE VIEWS AND INFORMATION CONCERNING THE COURSE OF THE NEGOTIATION ON CONVENTIONAL ARMED FORCES IN EUROPE

It has been agreed that the participating States will hold meetings in order to exchange views and information concerning the course of the Negotiation on Conventional Armed Forces in Europe.

These meetings will be held at least twice during each session of the Negotiation on Conventional Armed Forces in Europe.

Provisions on practical modalities relating to these meetings are contained in Annex IV of this document.

At these meetings, substantive information will be provided by the participants in the Negotiation on Conventional Armed Forces in Europe on developments, progress and results in the negotiations with the aim of enabling each participating State to appraise their course.

The participants in these negotiations have undertaken to take into consideration, in the course of their negotiations, the views expressed at such meetings by other participating States concerning their own security.

Information will also be provided on a bilateral basis.

The next Follow-up Meeting of the participating States of the CSCE, to be held in Helsinki, commencing on 24 March 1992, will consider the functioning of these arrangements.

Taking into account the relevant provisions of the Final Act and of the Madrid Concluding Document, and having considered the results achieved in the two negotiations, and also in the light of other relevant negotiations on security and disarmament affecting Europe, a future CSCE follow-up meeting will consider ways and appropriate means for the participating States to continue their efforts for security and disarmament in Europe, including the question of supplementing the Madrid mandate for the next stage of the Conference on Confidence- and Security-building Measures and Disarmament in Europe.

CO-OPERATION IN THE FIELD OF ECONOMICS, OF SCIENCE AND TECHNOLOGY AND OF THE ENVIRONMENT

The participating States reaffirm their willingness to further their co-operation in the field of economics, of science and technology and of the environment, and to promote stable and equitable international economic relations in the interest of all States. They express their readiness to intensify the dialogue in the competent fora with a view to facilitating appropriate solutions for key interrelated economic issues such as money, finance, debt and trade. In this connection, they stress the importance of policies aimed at promoting structural adjustments, stimulating the growth of national economies and creating an international economic environment conducive to development.

The participating States recognize the important role of the United Nations Economic Commission for Europe (ECE) in fostering regional economic co-operation and in contributing to the implementation of the provisions of the Final Act and subsequent CSCE documents. They express their readiness to make further use of the existing framework, resources and experience of the ECE in areas which are of significance for the implementation of recommendations of the CSCE.

TRADE AND INDUSTRIAL COOPERATION

1.   In order to make better use of their economic potential, and to foster the expansion of their commercial exchanges, the participating States will make further efforts to promote favourable conditions for trade and industrial co-operation, taking into account all the relevant provisions of the Final Act and the Madrid Concluding Document.

2.   The participating States recognize the importance of favourable business conditions for the development of trade between them. They will facilitate direct contacts between businesspeople, potential buyers and end-users, including on-site contacts relevant to the business intended or being transacted. They will take measures to improve working conditions for businesspeople regarding, *inter alia*, accreditation, accommodation, communications, recruitment and management of personnel, and to avoid unjustifiable delays in visa procedures and customs clearance. Further, they recognize the opportunities offered by trade fairs and exhibitions for developing commercial contacts and achieving concrete business results.

3.   The participating States will continue their efforts further to reduce or progressively eliminate obstacles of all kinds to trade, thus contributing to the expansion and diversification of their commercial relations. They express their support for the work done in this field in appropriate international fora.

4.   The participating States will encourage forms of trade compatible with the efficient conduct of international business relations and will also encourage business partners to decide independently upon their trading patterns. As to compensation transactions in all their forms, they recommend that such proposals be addressed at the beginning of negotiations and, when agreed upon, dealt with in a flexible way, especially regarding the choice of products. In this connection, the special concerns of small and medium-sized enterprises should be taken into account. The participating States recognize the valuable role of the ECE in dealing with questions related to compensation transactions.

5.   The participating States recognize that, within their respective economies, increased autonomy for enterprises can help achieve a better response to market needs and thus contribute to the development of trade and co-operation among them.

6.   In order to facilitate the identification of market opportunities, the participating States will further promote the publication and availability of comprehensive, comparable and timely economic and commercial information. They will publish up to date macroeconomic information and statistics, and envisage making balance of payments figures available. They will also provide the United Nations trade databank, COM-TRADE, with detailed data in a format relevant to the efficient conduct of foreign trade. They will encourage co-operation between their statistical services and within the framework of the ECE in order, *inter alia*, to facilitate the identification of disparities in foreign trade statistics and to improve the international comparability of such statistics. Furthermore, they consider it useful to increase the publication and exchange of statistics on such topics as demography, public health, agriculture, the environment and energy.

7.   Noting the growing importance of services in their mutual economic relations, the participating States will examine, in appropriate bodies, developments in this area and prospects for improved access to the services' market.

8.   Affirming the importance of industrial co-operation in their long-term economic relations, the participating States will promote measures designed to create favourable conditions for the development of such co-operation. They will therefore examine, within the competent fora, the improvement of the legal, administrative and economic framework for industrial co-operation. Furthermore, they will encourage contacts between potential partners, develop exchanges of appropriate information

and promote the participation of small and medium-sized enterprises in industrial co-operation.

9.   The participating States recognize that productive, competitive and profit-earning joint ventures can play a role in mutually beneficial industrial co-operation. They will improve the legal, administrative and financial conditions for investment in, and operation of, joint ventures. They will also promote the exchange of all information relevant to the establishment of joint ventures, including all necessary technical information, as well as information on management, labour conditions, accounting and taxation, repatriation of profits and the protection of investments, production conditions and access to domestic supplies and markets.

10.   The participating States stress the importance of their standardization policies and practices, and of related activities for the facilitation of international trade, especially regarding products subject to compulsory certification. Accordingly, they will consider mutual recognition of their national testing and certification procedures and practices, and promote co-operation among relevant national bodies and within international organizations including the ECE.

11.   The participating States recognize the growing importance of effective marketing in the development of trade and industrial co-operation, in the production and promotion of new products and in meeting the needs of the consumer. Given the growth of marketing opportunities, they will seek to improve the conditions for firms and organizations engaging in research into domestic or foreign markets and in other marketing activities.

12.   The participating States affirm the usefulness for all enterprises, and especially for small and medium-sized ones, of flexible and mutually agreed arbitration provisions for ensuring the equitable settlement of disputes in international trade and industrial co-operation. Bearing in mind the relevant provisions of the Final Act and the Madrid Concluding Document they attach particular importance to freedom in the choice of arbitrators, including the presiding arbitrator, and of the country of arbitration. They recommend that consideration be given to the adoption of the Model Law on international commercial arbitration of the United Nations Commission on International Trade Law (UNCITRAL). In addition, they recognize the value of agreements on co-operation in the field of commercial arbitration between Chambers of Commerce and other arbitration bodies.

13.   The participating States agree to convene a Conference on Economic Co-operation in Europe. This Conference will take place in Bonn from 19 March to 11 April, 1990. The aim of the conference is to provide new impulses for economic relations between participating States, in particular by improving business conditions for commercial exchanges and industrial co-operation, and by considering new possibilities for, and ways of, economic co-operation. The Conference will be attended by representatives of the participating States and of the business community. The agenda, timetable and other organizational modalities are set out in Annex V. The next Follow-up meeting, to be held in Helsinki, commencing on 24 March 1992, will assess the results achieved at the conference.

SCIENCE AND TECHNOLOGY

14.   The participating States emphasize the important role of science and technology in their overall economic and social development, bearing in mind particularly those sciences and technologies which are of direct relevance to improving the quality of life.

15.   Recognizing the importance of scientific and technological co-operation, the participating States will develop further mutually advantageous co-operation in the fields already set forth in the Final Act, and will examine possibilities for co-operation in new areas of growing importance and common interest. Furthermore, they express

their intention to improve conditions for such co-operation by fostering the exchange of information on, and experience with, scientific and technological achievements, having in mind especially the interests of the countries of the region which are developing from the economic point of view.

16.   The participating States also reaffirm the role of general inter-governmental agreements as well as of bilateral agreements involving universities, scientific and technological institutions and industry, in developing mutually beneficial exchanges. Underlining the importance of freedom of communication and exchange of views for progress in science and technology, they will promote and support direct and individual contacts between scientists, specialists and interested businesspeople. Recalling the conclusions reached at the Hamburg Scientific Forum, they will respect human rights and fundamental freedoms, which represent one of the foundations for a significant improvement in international scientific co-operation at all levels. They will also endeavour to create conditions enabling interested partners to develop appropriate joint research programmes and projects on the basis of reciprocity and mutual advantage and, when appropriate, on a commercial basis.

17.   Given the depletion of natural resources, including non-renewable sources of energy, the participating States will promote co-operation in the rational use of such resources, and in the use of alternative sources of energy, including thermonuclear fusion.

18.   Taking note of the progress made in, and the new opportunities offered by, research and development in biotechnology, the participating States consider it desirable to enhance the exchange of information on laws and regulations relating to the safety aspects of genetic engineering. They will therefore facilitate consultation and exchange of information on safety guidelines. In this context, they emphasize the importance of ethical principles when dealing with genetic engineering and its application.

19.   The participating States will develop their co-operation in medical and related sciences by intensifying research and the exchange of information on drug abuse and on new or increasingly wide-spread diseases. They will co-operate in particular in combating the spread of AIDS, taking into account the global AIDS Strategy of the World Health Organization (WHO). They will also co-operate in research concerning the long-term consequences of radiation.

20.   The participating States recognize the importance of scientific research, of environmentally sound technologies and, in particular, of improved international cooperation in these fields, for the monitoring, prevention and reduction of pollution. They will therefore promote, *inter alia* within the relevant international fora, exchange of information on, and experience with, these technologies. In this respect they will also promote, on a commercial basis, exchanges in the fields of pollution-abatement technologies, technologies and products with less or no emission of ozone-depleting substances, processing and combustion techniques, new methods of waste treatment, including recycling and disposal, and low- and non-waste technologies.

21.   The participating States will exchange appropriate information in specific fields of engineering industries and automation. They will do this on the basis of mutual advantage for potential partners, who will decide independently on the areas of co-operation and with due respect for bilateral and multilateral agreements. To this end they will, *inter alia*, develop statistics in fields of engineering industries of commercial importance.

22.   In the context of their scientific and technological co-operation, the participating States will consider the possibility of encouraging the development and use of alternatives to animal experimentation, including for product testing, on animals.

23.   In the important field of nuclear energy, the participating States recognize that, while individual States should assume full responsibility for the safety of their

own nuclear facilities, nuclear safety requires closer international co-operation, especially within the International Atomic Energy Agency (IAEA). They note that it is essential to maintain the highest possible safety standards in the management and operation of nuclear facilities. They therefore support the work done within the IAEA in developing basic safety principles, and urge all States to use the revised Nuclear Safety Standards—NUSS codes—as a basis for regulating safety practices. They also recall the need further to improve the efficiency of the existing system of nuclear liability.

ENVIRONMENT

24.   Recognizing the need for preventive action, the participating States will strengthen their co-operation and intensify efforts aimed at protecting and improving the environment, bearing in mind the need to maintain and restore the ecological balance in air, water and soil. They will do this by, *inter alia*, developing their internal legislation and international commitments, and by applying the best available means, taking into account levels of development as well as economic and technical constraints. They underline the importance of the Regional Strategy for Environmental Protection and Rational Use of Natural Resources in ECE Member Countries Covering the Period up to the Year 2000 and beyond. They welcome, and will take due account of, the report of the World Commission on Environment and Development and the Environmental Perspective to the year 2000 and beyond, as well as the work already undertaken within the competent international fora, in particular within the framework of the 1979 Convention on Long-Range Transboundary Air Pollution (hereafter called 'the Convention').

25.   The participating States are convinced of the need for timely and effective reductions of sulphur emissions or their transboundary fluxes. They call upon contracting parties and signatories to the Convention to become parties to the Protocol on the reduction of sulphur emissions or their transboundary fluxes by at least 30 per cent. They recommend that further steps to reduce sulphur emissions, in line with the objectives of the Protocol, be taken by those States which are not parties to the Protocol, and that those States where this goal is already accomplished continue to control their emissions. Recalling that the said protocol provides for reductions of sulphur emissions at the latest by 1993, they will work within the framework of the convention for the elaboration at an early date of an arrangement for further reductions of sulphur emissions beyond the level established by the protocol.

26.   The participating States consider that control and reduction of nitrogen oxide emissions, or their transboundary fluxes, deserve high priority in their pollution abatement programmes. They welcome the elaboration and adoption of a protocol on control of nitrogen oxide emissions.

27.   They recognize the need to develop, within the framework of the Convention, arrangements to reduce emissions of other relevant air pollutants such as hydrocarbons and those producing photochemical oxidants. They will strengthen their co-operation accordingly, including by collecting and processing the necessary information.

28.   The participating States agree to strengthen and develop the Cooperative Programme for the Monitoring and Evaluation of the Long-Range Transmission of Air Pollutants in Europe (EMEP), *inter alia* through extending and improving the system of monitoring stations, providing EMEP with the necessary information regarding emissions of pollutants, furthering developing comparable methods of measurement, and expanding coverage to include other relevant air pollutants, in particular nitrogen oxides, hydrocarbons and photochemical oxidants. They also recommend that those countries which have not yet done so should become parties to the Protocol on the Long-Term Financing of EMEP.

29.   The participating States will make every effort to become parties, as soon as possible, to the Vienna Convention for the Protection of the Ozone Layer and to the Montreal Protocol on Substances that Deplete the Ozone Layer. Further, they will foster national action and international co-operation on the control and reduction of the emission of ozone-depleting substances.

30.   The participating States agree that further national and international research efforts should be made regarding the global warming phenomenon, and the role played therein by emissions of carbon dioxide and trace gases in order to provide a scientific basis for mitigative action.

31.   In order to protect and improve freshwater resources and to reduce significantly the pollution of seas and coastal areas, transboundary watercourses and international lakes from all sources of pollution, the participating States will develop and intensify national efforts as well as bilateral and multilateral co-operation. They recommend the elaboration of a framework convention or specific conventions to improve the protection of transboundary watercourses and international lakes. They will reduce significantly discharges of toxic, persistent and potentially hazardous substances. Furthermore, they will devote special attention to the development of appropriate alternatives to sea disposal in order to decrease progressively and substantially the dumping of harmful wastes and the incineration of noxious liquid wastes at sea, with a view to the early termination of such methods.

32.   The participating States recognize the need to improve international co-operation on the transboundary movement of hazardous wastes. Taking into account the valuable work done in other international fora, they will encourage the elaboration of international agreements, including a global convention on the control of transboundary movements of hazardous wastes.

33.   The participating States will seek closer co-operation and greater exchange of information on the problems associated with potentially hazardous chemicals, including assessment of the risks to health and the environment. They will explore possibilities for closer harmonization of their legislation and regulations on the handling of these chemicals.

34.   The participating States will strengthen international co-operation on natural resources and flora and fauna. They will promote early accession to, and effective implementation of, relevant agreements. They will also develop further effective measures to combat soil degradation and to protect flora, fauna and their habitats on the basis of the Declaration on this subject adopted by the ECE. They will intensify their exchanges of views and experience on ways and means of achieving a more rational use of natural resources.

35.   The participating States acknowledge the importance of the contribution of persons and organizations dedicated to the protection and improvement of the environment, and will allow them to express their concerns. They will promote greater public awareness and understanding of environmental issues and will co-operate in the field of environmental education, *inter alia* through exchanges of experience and results of research studies, development of educational programmes and ecological training.

36.   The participating States will co-operate bilaterally and multilaterally with a view to improving and co-ordinating their arrangements for prevention, early warning, exchange of information and mutual assistance in cases of industrial accidents likely to cause transboundary damage to the environment. They will also initiate the examination of key elements related to the transboundary character of industrial accidents, such as clean up, restoration and liability.

37.   The participating States agree to convene a Meeting on the protection of the environment. This Meeting will take place in Sofia from 16 October to 3 November 1989. The aim of the meeting is to elaborate recommendations on principles and

guidelines for further measures and co-operation in new and important areas of environmental protection. The agenda, timetable and other organizational modalities are set out in Annex VII. The next Follow-up meeting, to be held in Helsinki, commencing on 24 March 1992 will assess the results achieved at the meeting.

CO-OPERATION IN OTHER AREAS

38.   The participating States recognize the important role of transport in economic and social development and the overall consequences of increased activity in the transport sector, including problems related to the environment. They will therefore encourage the elaboration of measures for achieving an economically more efficient transport system, taking into account the relative merits of different modes of transport and their potential effects on human health, safety and the environment. In this connection they will, through bilateral and multilateral means, give particular attention to questions concerning multimodal transport networks, combined transport, transit flows and the simplification of transport formalities and, in particular, of transport documents. They also welcome the work done by the ECE in this context.

39.   The participating States underline the economic importance of tourism and its contribution to the mutual understanding of peoples. They therefore favour the development of co-operation in this field and will facilitate normal contacts between tourists and the local population. To this end they will endeavour to improve the infrastructure for tourism, *inter alia*, by diversifying accommodation and by developing facilities for low-budget and youth tourism, including small-scale private accommodation. They will also consider in a positive spirit the progressive phasing out for foreign tourists of minimum exchange requirements where they apply, allow the reconversion of legally acquired local currency, and, furthermore, encourage non-discriminatory pricing for all foreign tourists irrespective of their nationality. They will also reduce arrival and departure procedures to the necessary minimum. The participating States will create conditions conducive to the establishment of joint projects in the field of tourism, including joint ventures and personnel training programmes.

40.   The participating States emphasize the need for effective implementation of the provisions of the Final Act and the Madrid Concluding Document relating to migrant workers and their families in Europe. They invite host countries and countries of origin to make efforts to improve further the economic, social, cultural and other conditions of life for migrant workers and their families legally residing in the host countries. They recommend that host countries and countries of origin should promote their bilateral co-operation in relevant fields with a view to facilitating the reintegration of migrant workers and their families returning to their country of origin.

41.   The participating States will, in accordance with their relevant commitments undertaken in the Helsinki Final Act and the Madrid Concluding Document, consider favourably applications for family reunification as well as family contacts and visits involving migrant workers from other participating States legally residing in the host countries.

42.   The participating States will ensure that migrant workers from other participating States and their families can freely enjoy and maintain their national culture and have access to the culture of the host country.

43.   Aiming at ensuring effective equality of opportunity between the children of migrant workers and the children of their own nationals regarding access to all forms and levels of education, the participating States affirm their readiness to take measures needed for the better use and improvement of educational opportunities. Furthermore, they will encourage or facilitate, where reasonable demand exists, supplementary teaching in their mother tongue for the children of migrant workers.

44.   The participating States recognize that issues of migrant workers have their human dimension.

45. The participating States acknowledge that the impact of economic and technological change is being acutely felt in the work place. They underline their readiness to encourage co-operation in the field of vocational training policy through increased exchange of information and experience, with the aim of enhancing the educational standards, professional knowledge, skills and adaptability of personnel involved in industry and commerce.

46. The participating States recognize the importance of facilitating the integration of young people into professional life. They will therefore continue their efforts to ensure the necessary conditions for the education and vocational training of young people and to promote youth employment opportunities in various sectors of the economy. They will continue their efforts to create conditions for developing the level of scientific and cultural knowledge of their citizens, especially of young people, and for facilitating their access to achievements in the areas of natural and social sciences, as well as culture.

QUESTIONS RELATING TO SECURITY AND COOPERATION IN THE MEDITERRANEAN

The participating States

reaffirm their commitment to, and stress the continuing relevance of, the provisions of the Final Act and the Madrid Concluding Document concerning security and cooperation in the Mediterranean; in this context, they underline the relevance of the Mediterranean paragraph in the Stockholm Document.

They stress the importance of the CSCE process for increasing security and improving cooperation in the Mediterranean area.

They reiterate their conviction that security in Europe is to be considered in the broader context of world security and is closely linked with security in the Mediterranean area as a whole, and that accordingly the process of improving security should not be confined to Europe but should extend to other parts of the world, and in particular to the Mediterranean area.

They express their concern over the continuing tensions in the region and renew their willingness to intensify efforts towards finding just, viable and lasting solutions, through peaceful means, to outstanding crucial problems.

They consider that broader and more active cooperation could contribute to increased mutual understanding and enhanced confidence, thereby promoting stability, security, and peace in the region.

They note the results of existing bilateral and multilateral forms of cooperation and express their readiness to increase efforts in the economic, scientific, and cultural fields, and in the field of environment, taking due account of the interests of the developing countries in the region, and taking into consideration the work underway in these fields.

They note with satisfaction the positive outcome of the Seminar on economic, scientific, and cultural cooperation in the Mediterranean within the framework of the results of the Valetta Meeting of 1979, held in Venice from 16 to 26 October 1984 in accordance with the relevant provisions and objectives of the Madrid Concluding Document. They welcome the concrete contribution of this Seminar to the development of cooperation in the Mediterranean area and they support continued efforts to implement its recommendations as well as those of the Valetta Meeting.

They note the continuing interest of the non-participating Mediterranean States in the CSCE and in efforts with the participating States in strengthening security and promoting cooperation in the Mediterranean. They recognize to this end the need to maintain and amplify their contacts with the non-participating Mediterranean States as initiated by the CSCE and to develop good neighbourly relations with all of them, with due regard to reciprocity and in the spirit of the principles contained in the

Declaration of Principles guiding relations between participating States of the Final Act.

The participating States,

in conformity with the provisions of the Mediterranean chapters of the Final Act and the Madrid Concluding Document, agree to convene a Meeting on the Mediterranean in order to consider ways and means of further enhancing various aspects of cooperation, including the protection and improvement of the Mediterranean ecosystems, with the aim of widening the scope of their cooperation with the non-participating Mediterranean States and contributing to the strengthening of confidence and security in the region.

Representatives of the non-participating Mediterranean States (Algeria, Egypt, Israel, Lebanon, Libya, Morocco, Syria, and Tunisia) and representatives of the competent international organizations (UNESCO, ECE, UNEP, WHO, ITU, IMO) will be invited to this meeting in accordance with the rules and practices adopted for the previous CSCE Mediterranean follow-up events.

The Meeting will be held in Palma de Mallorca from 24 September to 19 October 1990. The agenda, timetable, and other organizational modalities will be as set out in Annex VII.

The next Follow-up Meeting, to be held in Helsinki, commencing on 24 March 1992, will assess the results achieved at this Meeting.

CO-OPERATION IN HUMANITARIAN AND OTHER FIELDS

The participating States,

Considering that co-operation in humanitarian and other fields is an essential factor for the development of their relations,

Agreeing that their co-operation in these fields should take place in full respect for the principles guiding relations between participating States as set forth in the Final Act as well as for the provisions in the Madrid Concluding Document and in the present Document pertaining to those principles,

Confirming that, in implementing the provisions concerning co-operation in humanitarian and other fields in the framework of their laws and regulations, they will ensure that those laws and regulations conform with their obligations under international law and are brought into harmony with their CSCE commitments,

Recognizing that the implementation of the relevant provisions of the Final Act and of the Madrid Concluding Document requires continuous and intensified efforts,

Have adopted and will implement the following:

HUMAN CONTACTS

1.   In implementing the human contacts provisions of the Final Act, the Madrid Concluding Document and the present Document, they will fully respect their obligations under international law as referred to in the subchapter of the present Document devoted to principles, in particular that everyone shall be free to leave any country, including his own, and to return to his country, as well as their international commitments in this field.

2.   They will ensure that their policies concerning entry into their territories are fully consistent with the aims set out in the relevant provisions of the Final Act, the Madrid Concluding Document and the present Document.

3.   They will take the necessary steps to find solutions as expeditiously as possible, but in any case within six months, to all applications based on the human contacts provisions of the Final Act and the Madrid Concluding Document, outstanding at the conclusion of the Vienna Follow-up Meeting.

4.   Thereafter they will conduct regular reviews in order to ensure that all applications based on the human contacts provisions of the Final Act and of the other

afore-mentioned CSCE documents are being dealt with in a manner consistent with those provisions.

5. They will decide upon applications relating to family meetings in accordance with the Final Act and the other afore-mentioned CSCE documents in as short a time as possible and in normal practice within one month.

6. In the same manner they will decide upon applications relating to family reunification or marriage between citizens of different States, in normal practice within three months.

7. In dealing favourably with applications relating to family meetings, they will take due account of the wishes of the applicant, in particular on the timing and sufficiently long duration of such meetings, and on travelling together with other members of his family for joint family meetings.

8. In dealing favourably with applications relating to family meetings, they will also allow visits to and from more distant relatives.

9. In dealing favourably with applications relating to family reunification or marriage between citizens of different States, they will respect the wishes of the applicants on the country of destination ready to accept them.

10. They will pay particular attention to the solution of problems involving the reunification of minor children with their parents. In this context and on the basis of the relevant provisions of the Final Act and of the other afore-mentioned CSCE documents, they will ensure

• that an application in this regard submitted while the child is a minor will be dealt with favourably and expeditiously in order to effect the reunification without delay; and

• that adequate arrangements are made to protect the interests and welfare of the children concerned.

11. They will consider the scope for gradually reducing and eventually eliminating any requirement which might exist for travellers to obtain local currency in excess of actual expenditure, giving priority to persons travelling for the purpose of family meetings. They will accord such persons the opportunity in practice to bring in or to take out with them personal possessions or gifts.

12. They will pay immediate attention to applications for travel of an urgent humanitarian nature and deal with them favourably as follows:

• They will decide within three working days upon applications relating to visits to a seriously ill or dying family member, travel to attend the funeral of a family member or travel by those who have a proven need of urgent medical treatment or who can be shown to be critically or terminally ill.

• They will decide as expeditiously as possible upon applications relating to travel by those who are seriously ill or by the elderly, and other travel of an urgent humanitarian nature.

They will intensify efforts by their local, regional and central authorities concerned with the implementation of the above, and ensure that charges for giving priority treatment to such applications do not exceed costs actually incurred.

13. In dealing with applications for travel for family meetings, family reunification or marriage between citizens of different States, they will ensure that acts or omissions by members of the applicant's family do not adversely affect the rights of the applicant as set forth in the relevant international instruments.

14. They will ensure that all documents necessary for applications based on the human contacts provisions of the Final Act and of the other afore-mentioned CSCE documents are easily accessible to the applicant. The documents will remain valid throughout the application procedure. In the event of a renewed application the documents already submitted by the applicant in connection with previous applications will be taken into consideration.

15.   They will simplify practices and gradually reduce administrative requirements for applications based on the human contacts provisions of the Final Act and of the other afore-mentioned CSCE documents.

16.   They will ensure that, when applications based on the human contacts provisions of the Final Act and of the other afore-mentioned CSCE documents are refused for reasons specified in the relevant international instruments, the applicant is promptly provided in writing with an official notification of the grounds on which the decision was based. As a rule and in all cases where the applicant so requests, he will be given the necessary information about the procedure for making use of any effective administrative or judicial remedies against the decision available to him as envisaged in the abovementioned international instruments. In cases where exit for permanent settlement abroad is involved, this information will be provided as part of the official notification foreseen above.

17.   If in this context an individual's application for travel abroad has been refused for reasons of national security, they will ensure that, within strictly warranted time limits, any restriction on that individual's travel is as short as possible and is not applied in an arbitrary manner. They will also ensure that the applicant can have the refusal reviewed within six months and, should the need arise, at regular intervals thereafter so that any changes in the circumstances surrounding the refusal, such as the time elapsed since the applicant was last engaged in work or duties involving national security, are taken into account. Before individuals take up work or duties involving national security, they will be formally notified if and how this could affect applications they might submit for such travel.

18.   Within one year of the conclusion of the Vienna Follow-up Meeting they will publish and make easily accessible, where this has not already been done, all their laws and statutory regulations concerning movement by individuals within their territory and travel between States.

19.   In dealing favourably with applications based on the human contacts provisions of the Final Act and of the other afore-mentioned CSCE documents, they will ensure that these are dealt with in good time in order, inter alia, to take due account of important family, personal or professional considerations significant for the applicant.

20.   They will deal favourably with applications for travel abroad without distinction of any kind, such as race, colour, sex, language, religion, political or other opinion, national or social origin, property, birth, age or other status. They will ensure that any refusal does not affect applications submitted by other persons.

21.   They will further facilitate travel on an individual or collective basis for personal or professional reasons and for tourism, such as travel by delegations, groups and individuals. To this end they will reduce the time for the consideration of applications for such travel to a minimum.

22.   They will give serious consideration to proposals for concluding agreements on the issuing of multiple entry visas and the reciprocal easing of visa processing formalities, and consider possibilities for the reciprocal abolition of entry visas on the basis of agreements between them.

23.   They will consider adhering to the relevant multilateral instruments as well as concluding complementary or other bilateral agreements, if necessary, in order to improve arrangements for ensuring effective consular, legal and medical assistance for citizens of other participating States temporarily on their territory.

24.   They will take any necessary measures to ensure that citizens of other participating States temporarily on their territory for personal or professional reasons, inter alia for the purpose of participating in cultural, scientific and educational activities, are afforded appropriate personal safety, where this is not already the case.

25.   They will facilitate and encourage the establishment and maintenance of direct personal contacts between their citizens as well as between representatives of their

institutions and organizations through travel between States and other means of communication.

26. They will facilitate such contacts and co-operation among their peoples through such measures as direct sports exchanges on a local and regional level, the unimpeded establishment and implementation of town-twinning arrangements, as well as student and teacher exchanges.

27. They will encourage the further development of direct contacts between young people, as well as between governmental and non-governmental youth and student organizations and institutions; the conclusion between such organizations and institutions of bilateral and multilateral arrangements and programmes; and the holding on a bilateral and multilateral basis of educational, cultural and other events and activities by and for young people.

28. They will make further efforts to facilitate travel and tourism by young people, *inter alia*, by recommending to those of their railway authorities which are members of the International Union of Railways (UIC) that they expand the Inter-Rail system to cover all their European networks and by recommending to those of their railway authorities which are not members of the UIC that they consider establishing similar facilities.

29. In accordance with the Universal Postal Convention and the International Telecommunication Convention, they will
   • guarantee the freedom of transit of postal communication;
   • ensure the rapid and unhindered delivery of correspondence,
including personal mail and parcels;
   • respect the privacy and integrity of postal and telephone communications; and
   • ensure the conditions necessary for rapid and uninterrupted telephone calls, including the use of international direct dialling systems, where they exist, and their development.

30. They will encourage direct personal contacts between the citizens of their States, *inter alia* by facilitating individual travel within their countries and by allowing foreigners to meet their citizens as well as, when invited to do so, to stay in private homes.

31. They will ensure that the status of persons belonging to national minorities or regional cultures on their territories is equal to that of other citizens with regard to human contacts under the Final Act and the other afore-mentioned CSCE documents and that these persons can establish and maintain such contacts through travel and other means of communication, including contacts with citizens of other States with whom they share a common national origin or cultural heritage.

32. They will allow believers, religious faiths and their representatives, in groups or on an individual basis, to establish and maintain direct personal contacts and communication with each other, in their own and other countries, *inter alia* through travel, pilgrimages and participation in assemblies and other religious events. In this context and commensurate with such contacts and events, those concerned will be allowed to acquire, receive and carry with them religious publications and objects related to the practice of their religion or belief.

33. They heard accounts of the Meeting of Experts on Human Contacts held in Bern from 15 April to 26 May 1986. Noting that no conclusions had been agreed upon at the Meeting, they regarded both the frankness of the discussion and the greater degree of openness in the exchanges as welcome developments. In this respect they noted the particular importance of the fact that proposals made at the Meeting had received further consideration at the Vienna Follow-up Meeting.

INFORMATION

34. They will continue efforts to contribute to an ever wider knowledge and understanding of life in their States, thus promoting confidence between peoples.

They will make further efforts to facilitate the freer and wider dissemination of information of all kinds, to encourage co-operation in the field of information and to improve the working conditions for journalists.

In this connection and in accordance with the International Covenant on Civil and Political Rights, the Universal Declaration of Human Rights and their relevant international commitments concerning seeking, receiving and imparting information of all kinds, they will ensure that individuals can freely choose their sources of information. In this context they will

• ensure that radio services operating in accordance with the ITU Radio Regulations can be directly and normally received in their states; and

• allow individuals, institutions and organizations, while respecting intellectual property rights, including copyright, to obtain, possess, reproduce and distribute information material of all kinds.

To these ends they will remove any restrictions inconsistent with the above-mentioned obligations and commitments.

35.   They will take every opportunity offered by modern means of communication, including cable and satellites, to increase the freer and wider dissemination of information of all kinds. They will also encourage co-operation and exchanges between their relevant institutions, organizations and technical experts, and work towards the harmonization of technical standards and norms. They will bear in mind the effects of these modern means of communication on their mass media.

36.   They will ensure in practice that official information bulletins can be freely distributed on their territory by the diplomatic and other official missions and consular posts of the other participating States.

37.   They will encourage radio and television organizations, on the basis of arrangements between them, to broadcast live, especially in the organizing countries, programmes and discussions with participants from different States and to broadcast statements of and interviews with political and other personalities from the participating States.

38.   They will encourage radio and television organizations to report on different aspects of life in other participating States and to increase the number of telebridges between their countries.

39.   Recalling that the legitimate pursuit of journalists' professional activity will neither render them liable to expulsion nor otherwise penalize them, they will refrain from taking restrictive measures such as withdrawing a journalist's accreditation or expelling him because of the content of the reporting of the journalist or of his information media.

40.   They will ensure that, in pursuing this activity, journalists, including those representing media from other participating States, are free to seek access to and maintain contacts with public and private sources of information and that their need for professional confidentiality is respected.

41.   They will respect the copyright of journalists.

42.   On the basis of arrangements between them, where necessary, and for the purpose of regular reporting, they will grant accreditation, where it is required, and multiple entry visas to journalists from other participating States, regardless of their domicile. On this basis they will reduce to a maximum of two months the period for issuing both accreditation and multiple entry visas to journalists.

43.   They will facilitate the work of foreign journalists by providing relevant information, on request, on matters of practical concern, such as import regulations, taxation and accommodation.

44.   They will ensure that official press conferences and, as appropriate, other similar official press events are also open to foreign journalists, upon accreditation, where this is required.

45.   They will ensure in practice that persons belonging to national minorities or regional cultures on their territories can disseminate, have access to, and exchange information in their mother tongue.

46.   They agree to convene an Information Forum to discuss improvement of the circulation of, access to and exchange of information; co-operation in the field of information; and the improvement of working conditions for journalists. The Forum will be held in London from 18 April to 12 May 1989. It will be attended by personalities from the participating States in the field of information. The agenda, time-table and other organizational modalities are set out in Annex VIII.

CO-OPERATION AND EXCHANGES IN THE FIELD OF CULTURE

47.   They will promote and give full effect to their cultural co-operation, *inter alia* through the implementation of any relevant bilateral and multilateral agreements concluded among them in the various fields of culture.

48.   They will encourage non-governmental organizations interested in the field of culture, to participate, together with state institutions, in the elaboration and implementation of these agreements and specific projects, as well as in the elaboration of practical measures concerning cultural exchange and co-operation.

49.   They will favour the establishment, by mutual agreement, of cultural institutes or centres of other participating States on their territory. Unhindered access by the public to such institutes or centres as well as their normal functioning will be assured.

50.   They will assure unhindered access by the public to cultural events organized on their territory by persons or institutions from other participating States and ensure that the organizers can use all means available in the host country to publicize such events.

51.   They will facilitate and encourage direct personal contacts in the field of culture, on both an individual and a collective basis, as well as contacts between cultural institutions, associations of creative and performing artists and other organizations in order to increase the opportunities for their citizens to acquaint themselves directly with the creative work in and from other participating States.

52.   They will ensure the unimpeded circulation of works of art and other cultural objects, subject only to those restrictions aimed at preserving their cultural heritage which are based on respect for intellectual and artistic property rights or derive from their international commitments on the circulation of cultural property.

53.   They will encourage co-operation between and joint artistic endeavours of persons from different participating states who are engaged in cultural activities; as appropriate, facilitate specific initiatives to this end by such persons, institutions and organizations and encourage the participation of young people in such initiatives. In this context they will encourage meetings and symposia, exhibitions, festivals and tours by ensembles or companies, and research and training programmes in which persons from the other participating States may also freely take part and make their contribution.

54.   The replacement of persons or groups invited to participate in a cultural activity will be exceptional and subject to prior agreement by the inviting party.

55.   They will encourage the holding of film weeks including, as appropriate, meetings of artists and experts as well as lectures on cinematographic art; facilitate and encourage direct contacts between film directors and producers with a view to co-producing films; and encourage co-operation in the protection of film material and the exchange of technical information and publications about the cinema.

56.   They will explore the scope for computerizing bibliographies and catalogues of cultural works and productions in a standard form and disseminating them.

57.   They will encourage museums and art galleries to develop direct contacts, *inter alia* with a view to organizing exhibitions, including loans of works of art, and exchanging catalogues.

58.   They will renew their efforts to give effect to the provisions of the Final Act and the Madrid Concluding Document relating to less widely spoken languages. They will also encourage initiatives aimed at increasing the number of translations of literature from and into these languages and improving their quality, in particular by the holding of workshops involving translators, authors and publishers, by the publication of dictionaries and, where appropriate, by the exchange of translators through scholarships.

59.   They will ensure that persons belonging to national minorities or regional cultures on their territories can maintain and develop their own culture in all its aspects, including language, literature and religion; and that they can preserve their cultural and historical monuments and objects.

60.   They heard accounts of the work done and the ideas advanced during the Cultural Forum held in Budapest from 15 October to 25 November 1985. Noting that no conclusions had been agreed upon at the Forum, they welcomed the fact that many of the useful ideas and proposals put forward there had received renewed consideration at the Vienna Follow-up Meeting and that institutions and organizations in the participating States have based many activities on these ideas. They expressed their appreciation of the significant contributions made to the event by leading personalities in the field of culture, and noted, in the light of the experience gained, the importance of securing, both inside and outside future meetings of this nature, arrangements which would permit a freer and more spontaneous discussion.

61.   Taking duly into account the originality and diversity of their respective cultures, they will encourage efforts to explore common features and to foster greater awareness of their cultural heritage. Accordingly they will encourage initiatives which may contribute to a better knowledge of the cultural heritage of the other participating States in all its forms, including regional aspects and folk art.

62.   They agree to convene a Symposium on the Cultural Heritage of the CSCE participating States. The symposium will take place in Cracow from 28 May to 7 June 1991. It will be attended by scholars and other personalities from the participating States who are engaged in cultural activities. The agenda, timetable and other organizational modalities are set out in Annex IX.

CO-OPERATION AND EXCHANGES IN THE FIELD OF EDUCATION

63.   They will ensure access by all to the various types and levels of education without discrimination as to race, colour, sex, language, religion, political or other opinion, national or social origin, property, birth or other status.

64.   In order to encourage wider co-operation in science and education, they will facilitate unimpeded communication between universities and other institutions of higher education and research. They will also facilitate direct personal contacts, including contacts through travel, between scholars, scientists and other persons active in these fields.

65.   In this context they will also ensure unimpeded access by scholars, teachers and students from the other participating States to open information material available in public archives, libraries, research institutes and similar bodies.

66.   They will facilitate exchanges of schoolchildren between their countries on the basis of bilateral arrangements, where necessary, including meeting and staying with families of the host country in their homes, with the aim of acquainting schoolchildren with life, traditions and education in other participating States.

67.   They will encourage their relevant government agencies or educational institutions to include, as appropriate, the Final Act as a whole in the curricula of schools and universities.

68.   They will ensure that persons belonging to national minorities or regional cultures on their territories can give and receive instruction on their own culture,

including instruction through parental transmission of language, religion and cultural identity to their children.

69.   They will encourage their radio and television organizations to inform each other of the educational programmes they produce and to consider exchanging such programmes.

70.   They will encourage direct contacts and co-operation between relevant governmental institutions or organizations in the field of education and science.

71.   They will encourage further co-operation and contacts between specialized institutions and experts in the field of education and rehabilitation of handicapped children.

HUMAN DIMENSION OF THE CSCE

The participating States,

Recalling the undertakings entered into in the Final Act and in other CSCE documents concerning respect for all human rights and fundamental freedoms, human contacts and other issues of a related humanitarian character,

Recognizing the need to improve the implementation of their CSCE commitments and their co-operation in these areas which are hereafter referred to as the human dimension of the CSCE,

Have, on the basis of the principles and provisions of the Final Act and of other relevant CSCE documents, decided:

1.   to exchange information and respond to requests for information and to representations made to them by other participating States on questions relating to the human dimension of the CSCE. Such communications may be forwarded through diplomatic channels or be addressed to any agency designated for these purposes;

2.   to hold bilateral meetings with other participating States that so request, in order to examine questions relating to the human dimension of the CSCE, including situations and specific cases with a view to resolving them. The date and place of such meetings will be arranged by mutual agreement through diplomatic channels;

3.   that any participating State which deems it necessary may bring situations and cases in the human dimensions of the CSCE, including those which have been raised at the bilateral meetings described in paragraph 2, to the attention of other participating States though diplomatic channels;

4.   that any participating State which deems it necessary may provide information on the exchange of information and the responses to its requests for information and to representations (paragraph 1) and on the results of the bilateral meetings (paragraph 2), including information concerning situations and specific cases, at the meetings of the Conference of the Human Dimension as well as at the main CSCE Follow-up Meetings.

The participating States decide further to convene a Conference on the Human Dimension of the CSCE in order to achieve further progress concerning respect for all human rights and fundamental freedoms, human contacts and other issues of a related humanitarian character. The Conference will hold three meetings before the next CSCE Follow-up meeting.

The Conference will:

• review developments in the human dimension of the CSCE including the implementation of the relevant CSCE commitments;

• evaluate the functioning of the procedure described in paragraphs 1 to 4 and discuss the information provided according to paragraph 4;

• consider practical proposals for new measures aimed at improving the implementation of the commitments relating to the human dimension of the CSCE and enhancing the effectiveness of the procedures described in paragraphs 1 to 4.

On the basis of these proposals, the Conference will consider adopting new measures.

The first Meeting of the Conference will be held in Paris from 30 May to 23 June 1989.

The second Meeting of the Conference will be held in Copenhagen from 5 June to 29 June 1990.

The third Meeting of the Conferece will be held in Moscow from 10 September to 4 October 1991.

The agenda, timetable and other organizational modalities are set out in Annex X.

The next main CSCE Follow-up Meeting, to be held in Helsinki, commencing on 24 March 1992, will assess the functioning of the procedures set out in paragraphs 1 to 4 above and the progress made at the Meetings of the Conference on the Human Dimension of the CSCE. It will consider ways of further strengthening and improving these procedures and will take appropriate decisions.

FOLLOW-UP TO THE CONFERENCE

In conformity with the relevant provisions of the Final Act and with their resolve and commitment to continue the multilateral process initiated by the CSCE, the participating States will hold further meetings regularly among their representatives.

The fourth main Follow-up meeting will be held in Helsinki, commencing on 24 March 1992.

The agenda, work programme and modalities of the main Vienna Meeting will be applied *mutatis mutandis* to the main Helsinki Meeting, unless other decisions on these questions are taken by the preparatory meeting mentioned below.

For the purpose of making the adjustments to the agenda, work programme and modalities applied at the main Vienna Meeting, a preparatory meeting will be held in Helsinki, commencing on 10 March 1992. It is understood that in this context adjustments concern those items requiring change as a result of the change in date and place, the drawing of lots, and the mention of the other meetings held in conformity with the decisions of the Vienna Meeting 1986. The duration of the preparatory meeting shall not exceed two weeks.

The agenda, work programme and modalities for CSCE follow-up meetings mentioned in this document have been prepared by the main Vienna Meeting. The results of these meetings will be taken into account, as appropriate, at the main Helsinki Meeting.

All the meetings referred to in this chapter will be held in conformity with paragraph 4 of the chapter on 'Follow-up to the Conference' of the Final Act.

The participating States examined the scope for rationalising the modalities for future CSCE follow-up meetings, for enhancing their effectiveness and for ensuring the best possible use of resources. In the light of their examination and in connection with the steps taken at the main Vienna Meeting, including the drawing up of mandates annexed to this document, they decided:

- to dispense with preparatory meetings unless otherwise agreed;
- bearing in mind the purpose of the meeting, to limit the number of subsidiary working bodies meeting simultaneously to the lowest possible;
- to limit the duration of meetings, unless otherwise agreed, to a period not exceeding four weeks;
- in the case of meetings to which non-governmental participants are invited to contribute, to make maximum use of the possibility of having informal meetings in order to allow for a more spontaneous discussion;
- to observe to the same extent as the host country its national day.

The main Helsinki Meeting will review these arrangements and other modalities in the light of experience, with a view to making any improvements which may be necessary.

The Government of Austria is requested to transmit the present document to the Secretary-General of the United Nations, to the Director-General of UNESCO and to the Executive Secretary of the United Nations Economic Commission for Europe and to other international organizations mentioned in this document. The Government of Austria is also requested to transmit the present document to the Governments of the non-participating Mediterranean States.

The text of this document will be published in each participating State, which will disseminate it and make it known as widely as possible.

The representatives of the participating States express their profound gratitude to the people and Government of Austria for the excellent organization of the Vienna Meeting and warm hospitality extended to the delegations which participated in the Meeting.

Vienna, 15 January 1989

DOCUMENT OF THE COPENHAGEN MEETING OF THE CONFERENCE ON THE HUMAN DIMENSION OF THE CSCE (1990)

The representatives of the participating States of the Conference on Security and Co-operation in Europe (CSCE), Austria, Belgium, Bulgaria, Canada, Cyprus, Czechoslovakia, Denmark, Finland, France, the German Democratic Republic, the Federal Republic of Germany, Greece, the Holy See, Hungary, Iceland, Ireland, Italy, Liechtenstein, Luxembourg, Malta, Monaco, the Netherlands, Norway, Poland, Portugal, Romania, San Marino, Spain, Sweden, Switzerland, Turkey, the Union of Soviet Socialist Republics, the United Kingdom, the United States of America and Yugoslavia, met in Copenhagen from 5 to 29 June 1990, in accordance with the provisions relating to the Conference on the Human Dimension of the CSCE contained in the Concluding Document of the Vienna Follow-up Meeting of the CSCE.

The representative of Albania attended the Copenhagen Meeting as observer.

The first Meeting of the Conference was held in Paris from 30 May to 23 June 1989.

The Copenhagen Meeting was opened and closed by the Minister for Foreign Affairs of Denmark.

The formal opening of the Copenhagen Meeting was attended by Her Majesty the Queen of Denmark and His Royal Highness the Prince Consort.

Opening statements were made by Ministers and Deputy Ministers of the participating States.

At a special meeting of the Ministers for Foreign Affairs of the participating States of the CSCE on 5 June 1990, convened on the invitation of the Minister for Foreign Affairs of Denmark, it was agreed to convene a Preparatory Committee in Vienna on 10 July 1990 to prepare a Summit Meeting in Paris of their Heads of State or Government.

The participating States welcome with great satisfaction the fundamental political changes that have occurred in Europe since the first Meeting of the Conference on the Human Dimension of the CSCE in Paris in 1989. They note that the CSCE process has contributed significantly to bringing about these changes and that these developments in turn have greatly advanced the implementation of the provisions of the Final Act and of the other CSCE documents.

They recognize that pluralistic democracy and the rule of law are essential for ensuring respect for all human rights and fundamental freedoms, the development of human contacts and the resolution of other issues of a related humanitarian character. They therefore welcome the commitment expressed by all participating States to the ideals of democracy and political pluralism as well as their common determination to build democratic societies based on free elections and the rule of law.

At the Copenhagen Meeting the participating States held a review of the implementation of their commitments in the field of the human dimension. They considered that the degree of compliance with the commitments contained in the relevant provisions of the CSCE documents had shown a fundamental improvement since the Paris Meeting. They also expressed the view, however, that further steps are required for the full realization of their commitments relating to the human dimension.

The participating States express their conviction that full respect for human rights and fundamental freedoms and the development of societies based on pluralistic democracy and the rule of law are prerequisites for progress in setting up the lasting order of peace, security, justice and co-operation that they seek to establish in Europe. They therefore reaffirm their commitment to implement fully all provisions of the Final Act and of the other CSCE documents relating to the human dimension and undertake to build on the progress they have made.

They recognize that co-operation among themselves, as well as the active involvement of persons, groups, organizations and institutions, will be essential to ensure continuing progress towards their shared objectives.

In order to strengthen respect for, and enjoyment of, human rights and fundamental freedoms, to develop human contacts and to resolve issues of a related humanitarian character, the participating States agree on the following:

I

(1) The participating States express their conviction that the protection and promotion of human rights and fundamental freedoms is one of the basic purposes of government, and reaffirm that the recognition of these rights and freedoms constitutes the foundation of freedom, justice and peace.

(2) They are determined to support and advance those principles of justice which form the basis of the rule of law. They consider that the rule of law does not mean merely a formal legality which assures regularity and consistency in the achievement and enforcement of democratic order, but justice based on the recognition and full acceptance of the supreme value of the human personality and guaranteed by institutions providing a framework for its fullest expression.

(3) They reaffirm that democracy is an inherent element of the rule of law. They recognize the importance of pluralism with regard to political organizations.

(4) They confirm that they will respect each other's right freely to choose and develop, in accordance with international human rights standards, their political, social, economic and cultural systems. In exercising this right, they will ensure that their laws, regulations, practices and policies conform with their obligations under international law and are brought into harmony with the provisions of the Declaration on Principles and other CSCE commitments.

(5) They solemnly declare that among those elements of justice which are essential to the full expression of the inherent dignity and of the equal and inalienable rights of all human beings are the following:

(5.1) — free elections that will be held at reasonable intervals by secret ballot or by equivalent free voting procedure, under conditions which ensure in practice the free expression of the opinion of the electors in the choice of their representatives;

(5.2) — a form of government that is representative in character, in which the executive is accountable to the elected legislature or the electorate;

(5.3) — the duty of the government and public authorities to comply with the constitution and to act in a manner consistent with law;

(5.4) — a clear separation between the State and political parties; in particular, political parties will not be merged with the State;

(5.5) — the activity of the government and the administration as well as that of the judiciary will be exercised in accordance with the system established by law. Respect for that system must be ensured;

(5.6) — military forces and the police will be under the control of, and accountable to, the civil authorities;

(5.7) — human rights and fundamental freedoms will be guaranteed by law and in accordance with their obligations under international law;

(5.8) — legislation, adopted at the end of a public procedure, and regulations will be published, that being the condition for their applicability. Those texts will be accessible to everyone;

(5.9) — all persons are equal before the law and are entitled without any discrimination to the equal protection of the law. In this respect, the law will prohibit any discrimination and guarantee to all persons equal and effective protection against discrimination on any ground;

(5.10) — everyone will have an effective means of redress against administrative decisions, so as to guarantee respect for fundamental rights and ensure legal integrity;

(5.11) — administrative decisions against a person must be fully justifiable and must as a rule indicate the usual remedies available;

(5.12) — the independence of judges and the impartial operation of the public judicial service will be ensured;

(5.13) — the independence of legal practitioners will be recognized and protected, in particular as regards conditions for recruitment and practice;

(5.14) — the rules relating to criminal procedure will contain a clear definition of powers in relation to prosecution and the measures preceding and accompanying prosecution;

(5.15) — any person arrested or detained on a criminal charge will have the right, so that the lawfulness of his arrest or detention can be decided, to be brought promptly before a judge or other officer authorized by law to exercise this function;

(5.16) — in the determination of any criminal charge against him, or of his rights and obligations in a suit at law, everyone will be entitled to a fair and public hearing by a competent, independent and impartial tribunal established by law;

(5.17) —— any person prosecuted will have the right to defend himself in person or through prompt legal assistance of his own choosing or, if he does not have sufficient means to pay for legal assistance, to be given it free when the interests of justice so require;

(5.18) — no one will be charged with, tried for or convicted of any criminal offence unless the offence is provided for by a law which defines the elements of the offence with clarity and precision;

(5.19) — everyone will be presumed innocent until proved guilty according to law;

(5.20) — considering the important contribution of international instruments in the field of human rights to the rule of law at a national level, the participating States reaffirm that they will consider acceding to the International Covenant on Civil and Political Rights, the International Covenant on Economic, Social and Cultural Rights and other relevant international instruments, if they have not yet done so;

(5.21) — in order to supplement domestic remedies and better to ensure that the participating States respect the international obligations they have undertaken, the participating States will consider acceding to a regional or global international convention concerning the protection of human rights, such as the European Convention on Human Rights or the Optional Protocol to the International Covenant on Civil and Political Rights, which provide for procedures of individual recourse to international bodies.

(6) The participating States declare that the will of the people, freely and fairly expressed through periodic and genuine elections, is the basis of the authority and legitimacy of all government. The participating States will accordingly respect the

right of their citizens to take part in the governing of their country, either directly or through representatives freely chosen by them through fair electoral processes. They recognize their responsibility to defend and protect, in accordance with their laws, their international human rights obligations and their international commitments, the democratic order freely established through the will of the people against the activities of persons, groups or organizations that engage in or refuse to renounce terrorism or violence aimed at the overthrow of that order or of that of another participating State.

(7)   To ensure that the will of the people serves as the basis of the authority of government, the participating States will

(7.1)   —   hold free elections at reasonable intervals, as established by law;

(7.2)   —   permit all seats in at least one chamber of the national legislature to be freely contested in a popular vote;

(7.3)   —   guarantee universal and equal suffrage to adult citizens;

(7.4)   —   ensure that votes are cast by secret ballot or by equivalent free voting procedure, and that they are counted and reported honestly with the official results made public;

(7.5)   —   respect the right of citizens to seek political or public office, individually or as representatives of political parties or organizations, without discrimination;

(7.6)   —   respect the right of individuals and groups to establish, in full freedom, their own political parties or other political organizations and provide such political parties and organizations with the necessary legal guarantees to enable them to compete with each other on a basis of equal treatment before the law and by the authorities;

(7.7)   —   ensure that law and public work to permit political campaigning to be conducted in a fair and free atmosphere in which neither administrative action, violence nor intimidation bars the parties and the candidates from freely presenting their views and qualifications, or prevents the voters from learning and discussing them or from casting their vote free of fear of retribution;

(7.8)   —   provide that no legal or administrative obstacle stands in the way of unimpeded access to the media on a non-discriminatory basis for all political groupings and individuals wishing to participate in the electoral process;

(7.9)   —   ensure that candidates who obtain the necessary number of votes required by law are duly installed in office and are permitted to remain in office until their term expires or is otherwise brought to an end in a manner that is regulated by law in conformity with democratic parliamentary and constitutional procedures.

(8)   The participating States consider that the presence of observers, both foreign and domestic, can enhance the electoral process for States in which elections are taking place. They therefore invite observers from any other CSCE participating States and any appropriate private institutions and organizations who may wish to do so to observe the course of their national election proceedings, to the extent permitted by law. They will also endeavour to facilitate similar access for election proceedings held below the national level. Such observers will undertake not to interfere in the electoral proceedings.

II

(9)   The participating States reaffirm that

(9.1)   —   everyone will have the right to freedom of expression including the right to communication. This right will include freedom to hold opinions and to receive and impart information and ideas without interference by public authority and regardless of frontiers. The exercise of this right may be subject only to such restrictions as are prescribed by law and are consistent with international standards. In particular, no limitation will be imposed on access to, and use of, means of reproducing documents of any kind, while respecting, however, rights relating to intellectual property, including copyright;

(9.2) — everyone will have the right of peaceful assembly and demonstration. Any restrictions which may be placed on the exercise of these rights will be prescribed by law and consistent with international standards;

(9.3) — the right of association will be guaranteed. The right to form and — subject to the general right of a trade union to determine its own membership — freely to join a trade union will be guaranteed. These rights will exclude any prior control. Freedom of association for workers, including the freedom to strike, will be guaranteed, subject to limitations prescribed by law and consistent with international standards;

(9.4) — everyone will have the right to freedom of thought, conscience and religion. This right includes freedom to change one's religion or belief and freedom to manifest one's religion or belief, either alone or in community with others, in public or in private, through worship, teaching, practice and observance. The exercise of these rights may be subject only to such restrictions as are prescribed by law and are consistent with international standards;

(9.5) — they will respect the right of everyone to leave any country, including his own, and to return to his country, consistent with a State's international obligations and CSCE commitments. Restrictions on this right will have the character of very rare exceptions, will be considered necessary only if they respond to a specific public need, pursue a legitimate aim and are proportionate to that aim, and will not be abused or applied in an arbitrary manner;

(9.6) — everyone has the right peacefully to enjoy his property either on his own or in common with others. No one may be deprived of his property except in the public interest and subject to the conditions provided for by law and consistent with international commitments and obligations.

(10) In reaffirming their commitment to ensure effectively the rights of the individual to know and act upon human rights and fundamental freedoms, and to contribute actively, individually or in association with others, to their promotion and protection, the participating States express their commitment to

(10.1) — respect the right of everyone, individually or in association with others, to seek, receive and impart freely views and information on human rights and fundamental freedoms, including the rights to disseminate and publish such views and information;

(10.2) — respect the rights of everyone, individually or in association with others, to study and discuss the observance of human rights and fundamental freedoms and to develop and discuss ideas for improved protection of human rights and better means for ensuring compliance with international human rights standards;

(10.3) — ensure that individuals are permitted to exercise the right to association, including the right to form, join and participate effectively in non-governmental organizations which seek the promotion and protection of human rights and fundamental freedoms, including trade unions and human rights monitoring groups;

(10.4) — allow members of such groups and organizations to have unhindered access to and communication with similar bodies within and outside their countries and with international organizations, to engage in exchanges, contacts and cooperation with such groups and organizations and to solicit, receive and utilize for the purpose of promoting and protecting human rights and fundamental freedoms voluntary financial contributions from national and international sources as provided for by law.

(11) The participating States further affirm that, where violations of human rights and fundamental freedoms are alleged to have occurred, the effective remedies available include

(11.1) — the right of the individual to seek and receive adequate legal assistance;

(11.2) — the right of the individual to seek and receive assistance from others in defending human rights and fundamental freedoms, and to assist others in defending human rights and fundamental freedoms;

(11.3) — the right of individuals or groups acting on their behalf to communicate with international bodies with competence to receive and consider information concerning allegations of human rights abuses.

(12) The participating States, wishing to ensure greater transparency in the implementation of the commitments undertaken in the Vienna Concluding Document under the heading of the human dimension of the CSCE, decide to accept as a confidence-building measure the presence of observers sent by participating States and representatives of non-governmental organizations and other interested persons at proceedings before courts as provided for in national legislation and international law; it is understood that proceedings may only be held *in camera* in the circumstances prescribed by law and consistent with obligations under international law and international commitments.

(13) The participating States decide to accord particular attention to the recognition of the rights of the child, his civil rights and his individual freedoms, his economic, social and cultural rights, and his right to special protection against all forms of violence and exploitation. They will consider acceding to the Convention on the Rights of the Child, if they have not yet done so, which was opened for signature by States on 26 January 1990. They will recognize in their domestic legislation the rights of the child as affirmed in the international agreements to which they are Parties.

(14) The participating States agree to encourage the creation, within their countries, of conditions for the training of students and trainees from other participating States, including persons taking vocational and technical courses. They also agree to promote travel by young people from their countries for the purpose of obtaining education in other participating States and to that end to encourage the conclusion, where appropriate, of bilateral and multilateral agreements between their relevant governmental institutions, organizations and educational establishments.

(15) The participating States will act in such a way as to facilitate the transfer of sentenced persons and encourage those participating States which are not Parties to the Convention on the Transfer of Sentenced Persons, signed at Strasbourg on 21 November 1983, to consider acceding to the Convention.

(16) The participating States

(16.1) — reaffirm their commitment to prohibit torture and other cruel, inhuman or degrading treatment or punishment, to take effective legislative, administrative, judicial and other measures to prevent and punish such practices, to protect individuals from any psychiatric or other medical practices that violate human rights and fundamental freedoms and to take effective measures to prevent and punish such practices;

(16.2) — intend, as a matter of urgency, to consider acceding to the Convention against Torture and Other Cruel, Inhuman or Degrading Treatment or Punishment, if they have not yet done so, and recognizing the competences of the Committee against Torture under articles 21 and 22 of the Convention and withdrawing reservations regarding the competence of the Committee under article 20;

(16.3) — stress that no exceptional circumstances whatsoever, whether a state of war or a threat of war, internal political instability or any other public emergency, may be invoked as a justification of torture;

(16.4) — will ensure that education and information regarding the prohibition against torture are fully included in the training of law enforcement personnel, civil or military, medical personnel, public officials and other persons who may be involved in the custody, interrogation or treatment of any individual subjected to any form of arrest, detention or imprisonment;

(16.5)   —   will keep under systematic review interrogation rules, instructions, methods and practices as well as arrangements for the custody and treatment of persons subjected to any form of arrest, detention or imprisonment in any territory under their jurisdiction, with a view to preventing any cases of torture;

(16.6)   —   will take up with priority for consideration and for appropriate action, in accordance with the agreed measures and procedures for the effective implementation of the commitments relating to the human dimension of the CSCE, any cases of torture and other inhuman or degrading treatment or punishment made known to them through official channels or coming from any other reliable source of information;

(16.7)   —   will act upon the understanding that preserving and guaranteeing the life and security of any individual subjected to any form of torture and other inhuman or degrading treatment or punishment will be the sole criterion in determining the urgency and priorities to be accorded in taking appropriate remedial action; and, therefore, the consideration of any cases of torture and other inhuman or degrading treatment or punishment within the framework of any other international body or mechanism may not be invoked as a reason for refraining from consideration and appropriate action in accordance with the agreed measures and procedures for the effective implementation of the commitments relating to the human dimension of the CSCE.

(17)   The participating States

(17.1)   —   recall the commitment undertaken in the Vienna Concluding Document to keep the question of capital punishment under consideration and to co-operate within relevant international organizations;

(17.2)   —   recall, in this context, the adoption by the General Assembly of the United Nations, on 15 December 1989, of the Second Optional Protocol to the International Covenant on Civil and Political Rights, aiming at the abolition of the death penalty;

(17.3)   —   note the restrictions and safeguards regarding the use of the death penalty which have been adopted by the international community, in particular article 6 of the International Covenant on Civil and Political Rights;

(17.4)   —   note the provisions of the Sixth Protocol to the European Convention for the Protection of Human Rights and Fundamental Freedoms, concerning the abolition of the death penalty;

(17.5)   —   note recent measures taken by a number of participating States towards the abolition of capital punishment;

(17.6)   —   note the activities of several non-governmental organizations on the question of the death penalty;

(17.7)   —   will exchange information within the framework of the Conference on the Human Dimension on the question of the abolition of the death penalty and keep that question under consideration;

(17.8)   —   will make available to the public information regarding the use of the death penalty.

(18)   The participating States

(18.1)   —   note that the United Nations Commission on Human Rights has recognized the right of everyone to have conscientious objections to military service;

(18.2)   —   note recent measures taken by a number of participating States to permit exemption from compulsory military service on the basis of conscientious objections;

(18.3)   —   note the activities of several non-governmental organizations on the question of conscientious objections to compulsory military service;

(18.4)   —   agree to consider introducing, where this has not yet been done, various forms of alternative service, which are compatible with the reasons for conscientious objection, such forms of alternative service being in principle of a non-combatant or civilian nature, in the public interest and of a non-punitive nature;

(18.5) — will make available to the public information on this issue;

(18.6) — will keep under consideration, within the framework of the Conference on the Human Dimension, the relevant questions related to the exemption from compulsory military service, where it exists, of individuals on the basis of conscientious objections to armed service, and will exchange information on these questions.

(19) The participating States affirm that freer movement and contacts among their citizens are important in the context of the protection and promotion of human rights and fundamental freedoms. They will ensure that their policies concerning entry into their territories are fully consistent with the aims set out in the relevant provisions of the Final Act, the Madrid Concluding Document and the Vienna Concluding Document. While reaffirming their determination not to recede from the commitments contained in CSCE documents, they undertake to implement fully and improve present commitments in the field of human contacts, including on a bilateral and multilateral basis. In this context they will

(19.1) — strive to implement the procedures for entry into their territories, including the issuing of visas and passport and customs control, in good faith and without unjustified delay. Where necessary, they will shorten the waiting time for visa decisions, as well as simplify practices and reduce administrative requirements for visa applications;

(19.2) — ensure, in dealing with visa applications, that these are processed as expeditiously as possible in order, *inter alia*, to take due account of important family, personal or professional considerations, especially in cases of an urgent, humanitarian nature;

(19.3) — endeavour, where necessary, to reduce fees charged in connection with visa applications to the lowest possible level.

(20) The participating States concerned will consult and, where appropriate, co-operate in dealing with problems that might emerge as a result of the increased movement of persons.

(21) The participating States recommend the consideration, at the next CSCE Follow-up Meeting in Helsinki, of the advisability of holding a meeting of experts on consular matters.

(22) The participating States reaffirm that the protection and promotion of the rights of migrant workers have their human dimension. In this context, they

(22.1) — agree that the protection and promotion of the rights of migrant workers are the concern of all participating States and that as such they should be addressed within the CSCE process;

(22.2) — reaffirm their commitment to implement fully in their domestic legislation the rights of migrant workers provided for in international agreements to which they are parties;

(22.3) — consider that, in future international instruments concerning the rights of migrant workers, they should take into account the fact that this issue is of importance for all of them;

(22.4) — express their readiness to examine, at future CSCE meetings, the relevant aspects of the further promotion of the rights of migrant workers and their families.

(23) The participating States reaffirm their conviction expressed in the Vienna Concluding Document that the promotion of economic, social and cultural rights as well as of civil and political rights is of paramount importance for human dignity and for the attainment of the legitimate aspirations of every individual. They also reaffirm their commitment taken in the Document of the Bonn Conference on Economic Co-operation in Europe to the promotion of social justice and the improvement of living

and working conditions. In the context of continuing their efforts with a view to achieving progressively the full realization of economic, social and cultural rights by all appropriate means, they will pay special attention to problems in the areas of employment, housing, social security, health, education and culture.

(24)   The participating States will ensure that the exercise of all the human rights and fundamental freedoms set out above will not be subject to any restrictions except those which are provided by law and are consistent with their obligations under international law, in particular the International Covenant on Civil and Political Rights, and with their international commitments, in particular the Universal Declaration of Human Rights. These restrictions have the character of exceptions. The participating States will ensure that these restrictions are not abused and are not applied in an arbitrary manner, but in such a way that the effective exercise of these rights is ensured.

Any restriction on rights and freedoms must, in a democratic society, relate to one of the objectives of the applicable law and be strictly proportionate to the aim of that law.

(25)   The participating States confirm that any derogations from obligations relating to human rights and fundamental freedoms during a state of public emergency must remain strictly within the limits provided for by international law, in particular the relevant international instruments by which they are bound, especially with respect to rights from which there can be no derogation. They also reaffirm that

(25.1)   —   measures derogating from such obligations must be taken in strict conformity with the procedural requirements laid down in those instruments;

(25.2)   —   the imposition of a state of public emergency must be proclaimed officially, publicly, and in accordance with the provisions laid down by law;

(25.3)   —   measures derogating from obligations will be limited to the extent strictly required by the exigencies of the situation;

(25.4)   such measures will not discriminate solely on the grounds of race, colour, sex, language, religion, social origin or of belonging to a minority.

III

(26)   The participating States recognize that vigorous democracy depends on the existence as an integral part of national life of democratic values and practices as well as an extensive range of democratic institutions. They will therefore encourage, facilitate and, where appropriate, support practical co-operative endeavours and the sharing of information, ideas and expertise among themselves and by direct contacts and co-operation between individuals, groups and organizations in areas including the following:

—   constitutional law, reform and development,
—   electoral legislation, administration and observation,
—   establishment and management of courts and legal systems,
—   the development of an impartial and effective public service where recruitment and advancement are based on a merit system,
—   law enforcement,
—   local government and decentralization,
—   access to information and protection of privacy,
—   developing political parties and their role in pluralistic societies,
—   free and independent trade unions,
—   co-operative movements,
—   developing other forms of free associations and public interest groups,
—   journalism, independent media, and intellectual and cultural life,
—   the teaching of democratic values, institutions and practices in educational institutions and the fostering of an atmosphere of free enquiry.

Such endeavours may cover the range of co-operation encompassed in the human dimension of the CSCE, including training, exchange of information, books and instructional materials, co-operative programmes and projects, academic and professional exchanges and conferences, scholarships, research grants, provision of expertise and advice, business and scientific contacts and programmes.

(27) The participating States will also facilitate the establishment and strengthening of independent national institutions in the area of human rights and the rule of law, which may also serve as focal points for co-ordination and collaboration between such institutions in the participating States. They propose that co-operation be encouraged between parliamentarians from participating States, including through existing inter-parliamentary associations and, *inter alia*, through joint commissions, television debates involving parliamentarians, meetings and round-table discussions. They will also encourage existing institutions, such as organizations within the United Nations system and the Council of Europe, to continue and expand the work they have begun in this area.

(28) The participating States recognize the important expertise of the Council of Europe in the field of human rights and fundamental freedoms and agree to consider further ways and means to enable the Council of Europe to make a contribution to the human dimension of the CSCE. They agree that the nature of this contribution could be examined further in a future CSCE forum.

(29) The participating States will consider the idea of convening a meeting or seminar of experts to review and discuss co-operative measures designed to promote and sustain viable democratic institutions in participating States, including comparative studies of legislation in participating States in the area of human rights and fundamental freedoms, *inter alia* drawing upon the experience acquired in this area by the Council of Europe and the activities of the Commission 'Democracy through Law'.

IV

(30) The participating States recognize that the questions relating to national minorities can only be satisfactorily resolved in a democratic political framework based on the rule of law, with a functioning independent judiciary. This framework guarantees full respect for human rights and fundamental freedoms, equal rights and status for all citizens, the free expression of all their legitimate interests and aspirations, political pluralism, social tolerance and the implementation of legal rules that place effective restraints on the abuse of governmental power.

They also recognize the important role of non-governmental organizations, including political parties, trade unions, human rights organizations and religious groups, in the promotion of tolerance, cultural diversity and the resolution of questions relating to national minorities.

They further reaffirm that respect for the rights of persons belonging to national minorities as part of universally recognized human rights is an essential factor for peace, justice, stability and democracy in the participating States.

(31) Persons belonging to national minorities have the right to exercise fully and effectively their human rights and fundamental freedoms without any discrimination and in full equality before the law.

The participating States will adopt, where necessary, special measures for the purpose of ensuring to persons belonging to national minorities full equality with the other citizens in the exercise and enjoyment of human rights and fundamental freedoms.

(32) To belong to a national minority is a matter of a person's individual choice and no disadvantage may arise from the exercise of such choice.

Persons belonging to national minorities have the right freely to express, preserve and develop their ethnic, cultural, linguistic or religious identity and to maintain and develop their culture in all its aspects, free of any attempts at assimilation against their will. In particular, they have the right

(32.1) — to use freely their mother tongue in private as well as in public;

(32.2) — to establish and maintain their own educational, cultural and religious institutions, organizations or associations, which can seek voluntary financial and other contributions as well as public assistance, in conformity with national legislation;

(32.3) — to profess and practise their religion, including the acquisition, possession and use of religious materials, and to conduct religious educational activities in their mother tongue;

(32.4) — to establish and maintain unimpeded contacts among themselves within their country as well as contacts across frontiers with citizens of other States with whom they share a common ethnic or national origin, cultural heritage or religious beliefs;

(32.5) — to disseminate, have access to and exchange information in their mother tongue;

(32.6) — to establish and maintain organizations or associations within their country and to participate in international non-governmental organizations.

Persons belonging to national minorities can exercise and enjoy their rights individually as well as in community with other members of their group. No disadvantage may arise for a person belonging to a national minority on account of the exercise or non-exercise of any such rights.

(33) The participating States will protect the ethnic, cultural, linguistic and religious identity of national minorities on their territory and create conditions for the promotion of that identity. They will take the necessary measures to that effect after due consultations, including contacts with organizations or associations of such minorities, in accordance with the decision-making procedures of each State.

Any such measures will be in conformity with the principles of equality and non-discrimination with respect to the other citizens of the participating State concerned.

(34) The participating States will endeavour to ensure that persons belonging to national minorities, notwithstanding the need to learn the official language or languages of the State concerned, have adequate opportunities for instruction of their mother tongue or in their mother tongue, as well as, wherever possible and necessary, for its use before public authorities, in conformity with applicable national legislation.

In the context of the teaching of history and culture in educational establishments, they will also take account of the history and culture of national minorities.

(35) The participating States will respect the right of persons belonging to national minorities to effective participation in public affairs, including participation in the affairs relating to the protection and promotion of the identity of such minorities.

The participating States note the efforts undertaken to protect and create conditions for the promotion of the ethnic, cultural, linguistic and religious identity of certain national minorities by establishing, as one of the possible means to achieve these aims, appropriate local or autonomous administrations corresponding to the specific historical and territorial circumstances of such minorities and in accordance with the policies of the State concerned.

(36) The participating States recognize the particular importance of increasing constructive co-operation among themselves on questions relating to national minorities. Such co-operation seeks to promote mutual understanding and confidence, friendly and good-neighbourly relations, international peace, security and justice.

Every participating State will promote a climate of mutual respect, understanding, co-operation and solidarity among all persons living on its territory, without distinction as to ethnic or national origin or religion, and will encourage the solution of problems through dialogue based on the principles of the rule of law.

(37)   None of these commitments may be interpreted as implying any right to engage in any activity or perform any action in contravention of the purposes and principles of the Charter of the United Nations, other obligations under international law or the provisions of the Final Act, including the principle of territorial integrity of States.

(38)   The participating States, in their efforts to protect and promote the rights of persons belonging to national minorities, will fully respect their undertakings under existing human rights conventions and other relevant international instruments and consider adhering to the relevant conventions, if they have not yet done so, including those providing for a right of complaint by individuals.

(39)   The participating States will co-operate closely in the competent inter-national organizations to which they belong, including the United Nations and, as appropriate, the Council of Europe, bearing in mind their on-going work with respect to questions relating to national minorities.

They will consider convening a meeting of experts for a thorough discussion of the issue of national minorities.

(40)   The participating States clearly and unequivocally condemn totalitarianism, racial and ethnic hatred, anti-semitism, xenophobia and discrimination against anyone as well as persecution on religious and ideological grounds. In this context, they also recognize the particular problems of Roma (gypsies).

They declare their firm intention to intensify the efforts to combat these phenomena in all their forms and therefore will

(40.1)   —   take effective measures, including the adoption, in conformity with their constitutional systems and their international obligations, of such laws as may be necessary, to provide protection against any acts that constitute incitement to violence against persons or groups based on national, racial, ethnic or religious discrimination, hostility or hatred, including anti-semitism;

(40.2)   —   commit themselves to take appropriate and proportionate measures to protect persons or groups who may be subject to threats or acts of discrimination, hostility or violence as a result of their racial, ethnic, cultural, linguistic or religious identity, and to protect their property;

(40.3)   —   take effective measures, in conformity with their constitutional systems, at the national, regional and local levels to promote understanding and tolerance, particularly in the fields of education, culture and information;

(40.4)   —   endeavour to ensure that the objectives of education include special attention to the problem of racial prejudice and hatred and to the development of respect for different civilizations and cultures;

(40.5)   —   recognize the right of the individual to effective remedies and endeavour to recognize, in conformity with national legislation, the right of interested persons and groups to initiate and support complaints against acts of discrimination, including racist and xenophobic acts;

(40.6)   —   consider adhering, if they have not yet done so, to the international instruments which address the problem of discrimination and ensure full compliance with the obligations therein, including those relating to the submission of periodic reports;

(40.7)   —   consider, also, accepting those international mechanisms which allow States and individuals to bring communications relating to discrimination before international bodies.

V

(41)   The participating States reaffirm their commitment to the human dimension of the CSCE and emphasize its importance as an integral part of a balanced approach to security and co-operation in Europe. They agree that the Conference on the

Human Dimension of the CSCE and the human dimension mechanism described in the section on the human dimension of the CSCE of the Vienna Concluding Document have demonstrated their value as methods of furthering their dialogue and co-operation and assisting in the resolution of relevant specific questions. They express their conviction that these should be continued and developed as part of an expanding CSCE process.

(42)   The participating States recognize the need to enhance further the effectiveness of the procedures described in paragraphs 1 to 4 of the section on the human dimension of the CSCE of the Vienna Concluding Document and with this aim decide

(42.1)   —   to provide in as short a time as possible, but no later than four weeks, a written response to requests for information and to representations made to them in writing by other participating States under paragraph 1;

(42.2)   —   that the bilateral meetings, as contained in paragraph 2, will take place as soon as possible, as a rule within three weeks of the date of the request;

(42.3)   —   to refrain, in the course of a bilateral meeting held under paragraph 2, from raising situations and cases not connected with the subject of the meeting, unless both sides have agreed to do so.

(43)   The participating States examined practical proposals for new measures aimed at improving the implementation of the commitments relating to the human dimension of the CSCE. In this regard, they considered proposals related to the sending of observers to examine situations and specific cases, the appointment of rapporteurs to investigate and suggest appropriate solutions, the setting up of a Committee on the Human Dimension of the CSCE, greater involvement of persons, organizations and institutions in the human dimension mechanism and further bilateral and multilateral efforts to promote the resolution of relevant issues.

They decide to continue to discuss thoroughly in subsequent relevant CSCE fora these and other proposals designed to strengthen the human dimension mechanism, and to consider adopting, in the context of the further development of the CSCE process, appropriate new measures. They agree that these measures should contribute to achieving further effective progress, enhance conflict prevention and confidence in the field of the human dimension of the CSCE.

(44)   The representatives of the participating States express their profound gratitude to the people and Government of Denmark for the excellent organization of the Copenhagen Meeting and the warm hospitality extended to the delegations which participated in the Meeting.

(45)   In accordance with the provisions relating to the Conference on the Human Dimension of the CSCE contained in the Concluding Document of the Vienna Follow-up Meeting of the CSCE, the third Meeting of the Conference will take place in Moscow from 10 September to 4 October 1991.

Copenhagen, 29 June 1990

CHARTER OF PARIS FOR A NEW EUROPE (1990)

Meeting of the Heads of State or Government of the participating States of the Conference on Security and Co-operation in Europe (CSCE): Austria, Belgium, Bulgaria, Canada, Cyprus, Czech and Slovak Federal Republic, Denmark, Finland, France, Germany, Greece, Holy See, Hungary, Iceland, Ireland, Italy-European Community, Liechtenstein, Luxembourg, Malta, Monaco, Netherlands, Norway, Poland, Portugal, Romania, San Marino, Spain, Sweden, Switzerland, Turkey, Union of Soviet Socialist Republics, United Kingdom, United States of America and Yugoslavia

Paris, 19–21 November 1990

A NEW ERA OF DEMOCRACY, PEACE AND UNITY

We, the Heads of State or Government of the States participating in the Conference on Security and Co-operation in Europe, have assembled in Paris at a time of profound change and historic expectations. The era of confrontation and division of Europe has ended. We declare that henceforth our relations will be founded on respect and co-operation.

Europe is liberating itself from the legacy of the past. The courage of men and women, the strength of the will of the peoples and the power of the ideas of the Helsinki Final Act have opened a new era of democracy, peace and unity in Europe.

Ours is a time for fulfilling the hopes and expectations our peoples have cherished for decades: steadfast commitment to democracy based on human rights and fundamental freedoms; prosperity through economic liberty and social justice; and equal security for all our countries.

The Ten Principles of the Final Act will guide us towards this ambitious future, just as they have lighted our way towards better relations for the past fifteen years. Full implementation of all CSCE commitments must form the basis for the initiatives we are now taking to enable our nations to live in accordance with their aspirations.

Human Rights, Democracy and Rule of Law

We undertake to build, consolidate and strengthen democracy as the only system of government of our nations. In this endeavour, we will abide by the following:

Human rights and fundamental freedoms are the birthright of all human beings, are inalienable and are guaranteed by law. Their protection and promotion is the first responsibility of government. Respect for them is an essential safeguard against an over-mighty State. Their observance and full exercise are the foundation of freedom, justice and peace.

Democratic government is based on the will of the people, expressed regularly through free and fair elections. Democracy has as its foundation respect for the human person and the rule of law. Democracy is the best safeguard of freedom of expression, tolerance of all groups of society, and equality of opportunity for each person.

Democracy, with its representative and pluralist character, entails accountability to the electorate, the obligation of public authorities to comply with the law and justice administered impartially. No one will be above the law.

We affirm that, without discrimination,

every individual has the right to:

freedom of thought, conscience and religion or belief,

freedom of expression,

freedom of association and peaceful assembly,

freedom of movement;

no one will be:

subject to arbitrary arrest or detention,

subject to torture or other cruel, inhuman or degrading treatment or punishment;

everyone also has the right:

to know and act upon his rights,

to participate in free and fair elections,

to fair and public trial if charged with an offence,

to own property alone or in association and to exercise individual enterprise,

to enjoy his economic, social and cultural rights.

We affirm that the ethnic, cultural, linguistic and religious identity of national minorities will be protected and that persons belonging to national minorities have the right freely to express, preserve and develop that identity without any discrimination and in full equality before the law.

We will ensure that everyone will enjoy recourse to effective remedies, national or international, against any violation of his rights.

Full respect for these precepts is the bedrock on which we will seek to construct the new Europe.

Our States will co-operate and support each other with the aim of making democratic gains irreversible.

Economic Liberty and Responsibility

Economic liberty, social justice and environmental responsibility are indispensable for prosperity.

The free will of the individual, exercised in democracy and protected by the rule of law, forms the necessary basis for successful economic and social development. We will promote economic activity which respects and upholds human dignity.

Freedom and political pluralism are necessary elements in our common objective of developing market economies towards sustainable economic growth, prosperity, social justice, expanding employment and efficient use of economic resources. The success of the transition to market economy by countries making efforts to this effect is important and in the interest of us all. It will enable us to share a higher level of prosperity which is our common objective. We will co-operate to this end.

Preservation of the environment is a shared responsibility of all our nations. While supporting national and regional efforts in this field, we must also look to the pressing need for joint action on a wider scale.

Friendly Relations among Participating States

Now that a new era is dawning in Europe, we are determined to expand and strengthen friendly relations and co-operation among the States of Europe, the United States of America and Canada, and to promote friendship among our peoples.

To uphold and promote democracy, peace and unity in Europe, we solemnly pledge our full commitment to the Ten Principles of the Helsinki Final Act. We affirm the continuing validity of the Ten Principles and our determination to put them into practice. All the Principles apply equally and unreservedly, each of them being interpreted taking into account the others. They form the basis for our relations.

In accordance with our obligations under the Charter of the United Nations and commitments under the Helsinki Final Act, we renew our pledge to refrain from the threat or use of force against the territorial integrity or political independence of any State, or from acting in any other manner inconsistent with the principles or purposes of those documents. We recall that non-compliance with obligations under the Charter of the United Nations constitutes a violation of international law.

We reaffirm our commitment to settle disputes by peaceful means. We decide to develop mechanisms for the prevention and resolution of conflicts among the participating States.

With the ending of the division of Europe, we will strive for a new quality in our security relations while fully respecting each other's freedom of choice in that respect. Security is indivisible and the security of every participating State is inseparably linked to that of all the others. We therefore pledge to co-operate in strengthening confidence and security among us and in promoting arms control and disarmament.

We welcome the Joint Declaration of Twenty-Two States on the improvement of their relations.

Our relations will rest on our common adherence to democratic values and to human rights and fundamental freedoms. We are convinced that in order to strengthen peace and security among our States, the advancement of democracy, and respect for and effective exercise of human rights, are indispensable. We reaffirm the equal rights of peoples and their right to self-determination in conformity with the Charter of the United Nations and with the relevant norms of international law, including those relating to territorial integrity of States.

We are determined to enhance political consultation and to widen co-operation to solve economic, social, environmental, cultural and humanitarian problems. This common resolve and our growing interdependence will help to overcome the mistrust of decades, to increase stability and to build a united Europe.

We want Europe to be a source of peace, open to dialogue and to co-operation with other countries, welcoming exchanges and involved in the search for common responses to the challenges of the future.

Security

Friendly relations among us will benefit from the consolidation of democracy and improved security.

We welcome the signature of the Treaty on Conventional Armed Forces in Europe by twenty-two participating States, which will lead to lower levels of armed forces. We endorse the adoption of a substantial new set of Confidence- and Security-building Measures which will lead to increased transparency and confidence among all participating States. These are important steps towards enhanced stability and security in Europe.

The unprecedented reduction in armed forces resulting from the Treaty on Conventional Armed Forces in Europe, together with new approaches to security and co-operation within the CSCE process, will lead to a new perception of security in Europe and a new dimension in our relations. In this context we fully recognize the freedom of States to choose their own security arrangements.

Unity

Europe whole and free is calling for a new beginning. We invite our peoples to join in this great endeavour.

We note with great satisfaction the Treaty on the Final Settlement with respect to Germany signed in Moscow on 12 September 1990 and sincerely welcome the fact that the German people have united to become one State in accordance with the principles of the Final Act of the Conference on Security and Co-operation in Europe and in full accord with their neighbours. The establishment of the national unity of Germany is an important contribution to a just and lasting order of peace for a united, democratic Europe aware of its responsibility for stability, peace and co-operation.

The participation of both North American and European States is a fundamental characteristic of the CSCE; it underlies its past achievements and is essential to the future of the CSCE process. An abiding adherence to shared values and our common heritage are the ties which bind us together. With all the rich diversity of our nations, we are united in our commitment to expand our co-operation in all fields. The challenges confronting us can only be met by common action, co-operation and solidarity.

The CSCE and the World

The destiny of our nations is linked to that of all other nations. We support fully the United Nations and the enhancement of its role in promoting international peace, security and justice. We reaffirm our commitment to the principles and purposes of the United Nations as enshrined in the Charter and condemn all violations of these principles. We recognize with satisfaction the growing role of the United Nations in world affairs and its increasing effectiveness, fostered by the improvement in relations among our States.

Aware of the dire needs of a great part of the world, we commit ourselves to solidarity with all other countries. Therefore, we issue a call from Paris today to all the nations of the world. We stand ready to join with any and all States in common efforts to protect and advance the community of fundamental human values.

GUIDELINES FOR THE FUTURE

Proceeding from our firm commitment to the full implementation of all CSCE principles and provisions, we now resolve to give a new impetus to a balanced and comprehensive development of our co-operation in order to address the needs and aspirations of our peoples.

Human Dimension
We declare our respect for human rights and fundamental freedoms to be irrevocable. We will fully implement and build upon the provisions relating to the human dimension of the CSCE.

Proceeding from the Document of the Copenhagen Meeting of the Conference on the Human Dimension, we will co-operate to strengthen democratic institutions and to promote the application of the rule of law. To that end, we decide to convene a seminar of experts in Oslo from 4 to 15 November 1991.

Determined to foster the rich contribution of national minorities to the life of our societies, we undertake further to improve their situation. We reaffirm our deep conviction that friendly relations among our peoples, as well as peace, justice, stability and democracy, require that the ethnic, cultural, linguistic and religious identity of national minorities be protected and conditions for the promotion of that identity be created. We declare that questions related to national minorities can only be satisfactorily resolved in a democratic political framework. We further acknowledge that the rights of persons belonging to national minorities must be fully respected as part of universal human rights. Being aware of the urgent need for increased co-operation on, as well as better protection of, national minorities, we decide to convene a meeting of experts on national minorities to be held in Geneva from 1 to 19 July 1991.

We express our determination to combat all forms of racial and ethnic hatred, anti-semitism, xenophobia and discrimination against anyone as well as persecution on religious and ideological grounds.

In accordance with our CSCE commitments, we stress that free movement and contacts among our citizens as well as the free flow of information and ideas are crucial for the maintenance and development of free societies and flourishing cultures. We welcome increased tourism and visits among our countries.

The human dimension mechanism has proved its usefulness, and we are consequently determined to expand it to include new procedures involving, *inter alia*, the services of experts or a roster of eminent persons experienced in human rights issues which could be raised under the mechanism. We shall provide, in the context of the mechanism, for individuals to be involved in the protection of their rights. Therefore, we undertake to develop further our commitments in this respect, in particular at the Moscow Meeting of the Conference on the Human Dimension, without prejudice to obligations under existing international instruments to which our States may be parties.

We recognize the important contribution of the Council of Europe to the promotion of human rights and the principles of democracy and the rule of law as well as to the development of cultural co-operation. We welcome moves by several participating States to join the Council of Europe and adhere to its European Convention on Human Rights. We welcome as well the readiness of the Council of Europe to make its experience available to the CSCE.

Security
The changing political and military environment in Europe opens new possibilities for common efforts in the field of military security. We will build on the important achievements attained in the Treaty on Conventional Armed Forces in Europe and in the Negotiations on Confidence- and Security-building Measures. We undertake to continue the CSBM negotiations under the same mandate, and to seek to conclude them no later than the Follow-up Meeting of the CSCE to be held in Helsinki in 1992. We also welcome the decision of the participating States concerned to continue the CFE negotiation under the same mandate and to seek to conclude it no later than

the Helsinki Follow-up Meeting. Following a period for national preparations, we look forward to a more structured co-operation among all participating States on security matters, and to discussions and consultations among the thirty-four participating States aimed at establishing by 1992, from the conclusion of the Helsinki Follow-up Meeting, new negotiations on disarmament and confidence and security building open to all participating States.

We call for the earliest possible conclusion of the Convention on an effectively verifiable, global and comprehensive ban on chemical weapons, and we intend to be original signatories to it.

We reaffirm the importance of the Open Skies initiative and call for the successful conclusion of the negotiations as soon as possible.

Although the threat of conflict in Europe has diminished, other dangers threaten the stability of our societies. We are determined to co-operate in defending democratic institutions against activities which violate the independence, sovereign equality or territorial integrity of the participating States. These include illegal activities involving outside pressure, coercion and subversion.

We unreservedly condemn, as criminal, all acts, methods and practices of terrorism and express our determination to work for its eradication both bilaterally and through multilateral co-operation. We will also join together in combating illicit trafficking in drugs.

Being aware that an essential complement to the duty of States to refrain from the threat or use of force is the peaceful settlement of disputes, both being essential factors for the maintenance and consolidation of international peace and security, we will not only seek effective ways of preventing, through political means, conflicts which may yet emerge, but also define, in conformity with international law, appropriate mechanisms for the peaceful resolution of any disputes which may arise. Accordingly, we undertake to seek new forms of co-operation in this area, in particular a range of methods for the peaceful settlement of disputes, including mandatory third-party involvement. We stress that full use should be made in this context of the opportunity of the Meeting on the Peaceful Settlement of Disputes which will be convened in Valletta at the beginning of 1991. The Council of Ministers for Foreign Affairs will take into account the Report of the Valletta Meeting.

Economic Co-operation
We stress that economic co-operation based on market economy constitutes an essential element of our relations and will be instrumental in the construction of a prosperous and united Europe. Democratic institutions and economic liberty foster economic and social progress, as recognized in the Document of the Bonn Conference on Economic Co-operation, the results of which we strongly support.

We underline that co-operation in the economic field, science and technology is now an important pillar of the CSCE. The participating States should periodically review progress and give new impulses in these fields.

We are convinced that our overall economic co-operation should be expanded, free enterprise encouraged and trade increased and diversified according to GATT rules. We will promote social justice and progress and further the welfare of our peoples. We recognize in this context the importance of effective policies to address the problem of unemployment.

We reaffirm the need to continue to support democratic countries in transition towards the establishment of market economy and the creation of the basis for self-sustained economic and social growth, as already undertaken by the Group of twenty-four countries. We further underline the necessity of their increased integration, involving the acceptance of disciplines as well as benefits, into the international economic and financial system.

We consider that increased emphasis on economic co-operation within the CSCE process should take into account the interests of developing participating States.

We recall the link between respect for and promotion of human rights and fundamental freedoms and scientific progress. Co-operation in the field of science and technology will play an essential role in economic and social development. Therefore, it must evolve towards a greater sharing of appropriate scientific and technological information and knowledge with a view to overcoming the technological gap which exists among the participating States. We further encourage the participating States to work together in order to develop human potential and the spirit of free enterprise.

We are determined to give the necessary impetus to co-operation among our States in the fields of energy, transport and tourism for economic and social development. We welcome, in particular, practical steps to create optimal conditions for the economic and rational development of energy resources, with due regard for environmental considerations.

We recognize the important role of the European Community in the political and economic development of Europe. International economic organizations such as the United Nations Economic Commission for Europe (ECE), the Bretton Woods Institutions, the Organisation for Economic Co-operation and Development (OECD), the European Free Trade Association (EFTA) and the International Chamber of Commerce (ICC) also have a significant task in promoting economic co-operation, which will be further enhanced by the establishment of the European Bank for Reconstruction and Development (EBRD). In order to pursue our objectives, we stress the necessity for effective co-ordination of the activities of these organizations and emphasize the need to find methods for all our States to take part in these activities.

Environment
We recognize the urgent need to tackle the problems of the environment and the importance of individual and co-operative efforts in this area. We pledge to intensify our endeavours to protect and improve our environment in order to restore and maintain a sound ecological balance in air, water and soil. Therefore, we are determined to make full use of the CSCE as a framework for the formulation of common environmental commitments and objectives, and thus to pursue the work reflected in the Report of the Sofia Meeting on the Protection of the Environment.

We emphasize the significant role of a well-informed society in enabling the public and individuals to take initiatives to improve the environment. To this end, we commit ourselves to promoting public awareness and education on the environment as well as the public reporting of the environmental impact of policies, projects and programmes.

We attach priority to the introduction of clean and low-waste technology, being aware of the need to support countries which do not yet have their own means for appropriate measures.

We underline that environmental policies should be supported by appropriate legislative measures and administrative structures to ensure their effective implementation.

We stress the need for new measures providing for the systematic evaluation of compliance with the existing commitments and, moreover, for the development of more ambitious commitments with regard to notification and exchange of information about the state of the environment and potential environmental hazards. We also welcome the creation of the European Environment Agency (EEA).

We welcome the operational activities, problem-oriented studies and policy reviews in various existing international organizations engaged in the protection of the environment, such as the United Nations Environment Programme (UNEP), the United Nations Economic Commission for Europe (ECE) and the Organisation for

Economic Co-operation and Development (OECD). We emphasize the need for strengthening their co-operation and for their efficient co-ordination.

Culture
We recognize the essential contribution of our common European culture and our shared values in overcoming the division of the continent. Therefore, we underline our attachment to creative freedom and to the protection and promotion of our cultural and spiritual heritage, in all its richness and diversity.

In view of the recent changes in Europe, we stress the increased importance of the Cracow Symposium and we look forward to its consideration of guidelines for intensified co-operation in the field of culture. We invite the Council of Europe to contribute to this Symposium.

In order to promote greater familiarity amongst our peoples, we favour the establishment of cultural centres in cities of other participating States as well as increased co-operation in the audio-visual field and wider exchange in music, theatre, literature and the arts.

We resolve to make special efforts in our national policies to promote better understanding, in particular among young people, through cultural exchanges, co-operation in all fields of education and, more specifically, through teaching and training in the languages of other participating States. We intend to consider first results of this action at the Helsinki Follow-up Meeting in 1992.

Migrant Workers
We recognize that the issues of migrant workers and their families legally residing in host countries have economic, cultural and social aspects as well as their human dimension. We reaffirm that the protection and promotion of their rights, as well as the implementation of relevant international obligations, is our common concern.

Mediterranean
We consider that the fundamental political changes that have occurred in Europe have a positive relevance to the Mediterranean region. Thus, we will continue efforts to strengthen security and co-operation in the Mediterranean as an important factor for stability in Europe. We welcome the Report of the Palma de Mallorca Meeting on the Mediterranean, the results of which we all support.

We are concerned with the continuing tensions in the region, and renew our determination to intensify efforts towards finding just, viable and lasting solutions, through peaceful means, to outstanding crucial problems, based on respect for the principles of the Final Act.

We wish to promote favourable conditions for a harmonious development and diversification of relations with the non-participating Mediterranean States. Enhanced co-operation with these States will be pursued with the aim of promoting economic and social development and thereby enhancing stability in the region. To this end, we will strive together with these countries towards a substantial narrowing of the prosperity gap between Europe and its Mediterranean neighbours.

Non-governmental Organizations
We recall the major role that non-governmental organizations, religious and other groups and individuals have played in the achievement of the objectives of the CSCE and will further facilitate their activities for the implementation of the CSCE commitments by the participating States. These organizations, groups and individuals must be involved in an appropriate way in the activities and new structures of the CSCE in order to fulfil their important tasks.

NEW STRUCTURES AND INSTITUTIONS OF THE CSCE PROCESS

Our common efforts to consolidate respect for human rights, democracy and the rule of law, to strengthen peace and to promote unity in Europe require a new quality of political dialogue and co-operation and thus development of the structures of the CSCE.

The intensification of our consultations at all levels is of prime importance in shaping our future relations. To this end, we decide on the following:

We, the Heads of State or Government, shall meet next time in Helsinki on the occasion of the CSCE Follow-up Meeting 1992. Thereafter, we will meet on the occasion of subsequent follow-up meetings.

Our Ministers for Foreign Affairs will meet, as a Council, regularly and at least once a year. These meetings will provide the central forum for political consultations within the CSCE process. The Council will consider issues relevant to the Conference on Security and Co-operation in Europe and take appropriate decisions.

The first meeting of the Council will take place in Berlin.

A Committee of Senior Officials will prepare the meetings of the Council and carry out its decisions. The Committee will review current issues and may take appropriate decisions, including in the form of recommendations to the Council. Additional meetings of the representatives of the participating States may be agreed upon to discuss questions of urgent concern.

The Council will examine the development of provisions for convening meetings of the Committee of Senior Officials in emergency situations.

Meetings of other Ministers may also be agreed by the participating States.

In order to provide administrative support for these consultations we establish a Secretariat in Prague.

Follow-up meetings of the participating States will be held, as a rule, every two years to allow the participating States to take stock of developments, review the implementation of their commitments and consider further steps in the CSCE process.

We decide to create a Conflict Prevention Centre in Vienna to assist the Council in reducing the risk of conflict.

We decide to establish an Office for Free Elections in Warsaw to facilitate contacts and the exchange of information on elections within participating States.

Recognizing the important role parliamentarians can play in the CSCE process, we call for greater parliamentary involvement in the CSCE, in particular through the creation of a CSCE parliamentary assembly, involving members of parliaments from all participating States. To this end, we urge that contacts be pursued at parliamentary level to discuss the field of activities, working methods and rules of procedure of such a CSCE parliamentary structure, drawing on existing experience and work already undertaken in this field.

We ask our Ministers for Foreign Affairs to review this matter on the occasion of their first meeting as a Council.

Procedural and organizational modalities relating to certain provisions contained in the Charter of Paris for a New Europe are set out in the Supplementary Document which is adopted together with the Charter of Paris.

We entrust to the Council the further steps which may be required to ensure the implementation of decisions contained in the present document, as well as in the Supplementary Document, and to consider further efforts for the strengthening of security and co-operation in Europe. The Council may adopt any amendment to the supplementary document which it may deem appropriate.

The original of the Charter of Paris for a New Europe, drawn up in English, French, German, Italian, Russian and Spanish, will be transmitted to the Government of the French Republic, which will retain it in its archives. Each of the participating States will receive from the Government of the French Republic a true copy of the Charter of Paris.

The text of the Charter of Paris will be published in each participating State, which will disseminate it and make it known as widely as possible.

The Government of the French Republic is requested to transmit to the Secretary-General of the United Nations the text of the Charter of Paris for a New Europe which is not eligible for registration under Article 102 of the Charter of the United Nations, with a view to its circulation to all the members of the Organization as an official document of the United Nations.

The Government of the French Republic is also requested to transmit the text of the Charter of Paris to all the other international organizations mentioned in the text.

Wherefore, we, the undersigned High Representatives of the participating States, mindful of the high political significance we attach to the results of the Summit Meeting, and declaring our determination to act in accordance with the provisions we have adopted, have subscribed our signatures below.

DOCUMENT OF THE MOSCOW MEETING OF THE CONFERENCE ON THE HUMAN DIMENSION OF THE CSCE (1991)

The representatives of the participating States of the Conference on Security and Co-operation in Europe (CSCE), Albania, Austria, Belgium, Bulgaria, Canada, Cyprus, the Czech and Slovak Federal Republic, Denmark, Estonia, Finland, France, Germany, Greece, the Holy See, Hungary, Iceland, Ireland, Italy, Latvia, Liechtenstein, Lithuania, Luxembourg, Malta, Monaco, the Netherlands-European Community, Norway, Poland, Portugal, Romania, San Marino, Spain, Sweden, Switzerland, Turkey, the USSR, the United Kingdom, the United States of America and Yugoslavia, met in Moscow from 10 September to 4 October 1991, in accordance with the provisions relating to the Conference on the Human Dimension of the CSCE contained in the Concluding Document of the Vienna Follow-up Meeting of the CSCE.

They welcomed the admission as participating States of Estonia, Latvia and Lithuania decided at an additional Meeting at ministerial level of the representatives of the participating States in Moscow on 10 September 1991, convened by the Federal Minister for Foreign Affairs of the Federal Republic of Germany, Chairman-in-Office of the CSCE Council, prior to the opening of the Moscow Meeting.

The first Meeting of the Conference was held in Paris from 30 May to 23 June 1989. The second Meeting of the Conference was held in Copenhagen from 5 to 29 June 1990.

The Moscow Meeting was opened by the Minister for Foreign Affairs of the USSR. An opening address was delivered by the President of the USSR on behalf of the host country.

Opening statements were made by delegates of the participating States, among them Ministers, Deputy Ministers and the Vice-President of the Commission of the European Communities. A contribution to the Meeting was made by the Secretary General of the Council of Europe.

The participating States renew their commitment to implement fully all the principles and provisions of the Final Act of the Conference on Security and Co-operation in Europe, of the Charter of Paris for a New Europe and of the other CSCE documents relating to the human dimension, including, in particular, the Document of the Copenhagen Meeting of the Conference on the Human Dimension of the CSCE, and are determined to achieve still further progress in the implementation of these provisions, as full respect for human rights and fundamental freedoms and the development of societies based on pluralistic democracy and the rule of law are prerequisites for a lasting order of peace, security, justice and co-operation in Europe.

In this context, the participating States underlined that, in accordance with the Final Act of the Conference on Security and Co-operation in Europe and the Charter of Paris for a New Europe, the equal rights of peoples and their right to self-determination are to be respected in conformity with the Charter of the United Nations and the relevant norms of international law, including those relating to territorial integrity of States.

At the Moscow Meeting views were expressed by the participating States on the implementation of their commitments in the field of the human dimension. They considered that the degree of compliance with the commitments contained in the relevant provisions of the CSCE documents had shown further substantial improvement since the Copenhagen Meeting. They also considered that, in spite of the significant progress made, serious threats to and violations of CSCE principles and provisions continue to exist and have a sobering effect on the assessment of the over all situation in Europe. In particular, they deplored acts of discrimination, hostility and violence against persons or groups on national, ethnic or religious grounds. The participating States therefore expressed the view that, for the full realization of their commitments relating to the human dimension, continued efforts are still required which should benefit substantially from the profound political changes that have occurred.

The participating States emphasize that issues relating to human rights, fundamental freedoms, democracy and the rule of law are of international concern, as respect for these rights and freedoms constitutes one of the foundations of the international order. They categorically and irrevocably declare that the commitments undertaken in the field of the human dimension of the CSCE are matters of direct and legitimate concern to all participating States and do not belong exclusively to the internal affairs of the State concerned. They express their determination to fulfil all of their human dimension commitments and to resolve by peaceful means any related issue, individually and collectively, on the basis of mutual respect and co-operation. In this context they recognize that the active involvement of persons, groups, organizations and institutions is essential to ensure continuing progress in this direction.

The participating States express their collective determination to further safeguard human rights and fundamental freedoms and to consolidate democratic advances in their territories. They also recognize a compelling need to increase the CSCE's effectiveness in addressing human rights concerns that arise in their territories at this time of profound change in Europe.

In order to strengthen and expand the human dimension mechanism described in the section on the human dimension of the CSCE in the Concluding Document of the Vienna Meeting and to build upon and deepen the commitments set forth in the Document of the Copenhagen Meeting of the Conference on the Human Dimension of the CSCE, the participating States adopt the following:

I

(1)   The participating States emphasize that the human dimension mechanism described in paragraphs 1 to 4 of the section on the human dimension of the CSCE in the Vienna Concluding Document constitutes an essential achievement of the CSCE process, having demonstrated its value as a method of furthering respect for human rights, fundamental freedoms, democracy and the rule of law through dialogue and co-operation and assisting in the resolution of specific relevant questions. In order to improve further the implementation of the CSCE commitments in the human dimension, they decide to enhance the effectiveness of this mechanism and to strengthen and expand it as outlined in the following paragraphs.

(2)   The participating States amend paragraphs 42.1 and 42.2 of the Document of the Copenhagen Meeting to the effect that they will provide in the shortest possible

time, but no later than ten days, a written response to requests for information and to representations made to them in writing by other participating States under paragraph 1 of the human dimension mechanism. Bilateral meetings, as referred to in paragraph 2 of the human dimension mechanism, will take place as soon as possible, and as a rule within one week of the date of the request.

(3)   A resource list comprising up to three experts appointed by each participating State will be established without delay at the CSCE institution*. The experts will be eminent persons, preferably experienced in the field of the human dimension, from whom an impartial performance of their functions may be expected.

The experts will be appointed for a period of three to six years at the discretion of the appointing State, no expert serving more than two consecutive terms. Within four weeks after notification by the CSCE Institution of the appointment, any participating State may make reservations regarding no more than two experts to be appointed by another participating State. In such case, the appointing State may, within four weeks of being notified of such reservations, reconsider its decision and appoint another expert or experts; if it confirms the appointment originally intended, the expert concerned cannot take part in any procedure with respect to the State having made the reservation without the latter's express consent.

The resource list will become operational as soon as 45 experts have been appointed.

(4)   A participating State may invite the assistance of a CSCE mission, consisting of up to three experts, to address or contribute to the resolution of questions in its territory relating to the human dimension of the CSCE. In such case, the State will select the person or persons concerned from the resource list. The mission of experts will not include the participating State's own nationals or residents or any of the persons it appointed to the resource list or more than one national or resident of any particular State.

The inviting State will inform without delay the CSCE Institution when a mission of experts is established, which in turn will notify all participating States. The CSCE institutions will also, whenever necessary, provide appropriate support to such a mission.

(5)   The purpose of a mission of experts is to facilitate resolution of a paticular question or problem relating to the human dimension of the CSCE. Such mission may gather the information necessary for carrying out its tasks and, as appropriate, use its good offices and mediation services to promote dialogue and co-operation among interested parties. The State concerned will agree with the mission on the precise terms of reference and may thus assign any further functions to the mission of experts, *inter alia* fact-finding and advisory services, in order to suggest ways and means of facilitating the observance of CSCE commitments.

(6)   The inviting State will co-operate fully with the mission of experts and facilitate its work. It will grant the mission all the facilities necessary for the independent exercise of its functions. It will, *inter alia*, allow the mission, for the purpose of carrying out its tasks, to enter its territory without delay, to hold discussions and to travel freely therein, to meet freely with officials, non-governmental organizations and any group or person from whom it wishes to receive information. The mission may also receive information in confidence from any individual, group or organization on questions it is addressing. The members of such missions will respect the confidential nature of their task.

The participating States will refrain from any action against persons, organizations or institutions on account of their contact with the mission of experts or of any publicly available information transmitted to it. The inviting State will comply with

---

* The Council will take the decision on the institution.

any request from a mission of experts to be accompanied by officials of that State if the mission considers this to be necessary to facilitate its work or guarantee its safety.

(7)   The mission of experts will submit its observations to the inviting State as soon as possible, preferably within three weeks after the mission has been established. The inviting State will transmit the observations of the mission, together with a description of any action it has taken or intends to take upon it, to the other participating States via the CSCE Institution no later than three weeks after the submission of the observations.

These observations and any comments by the inviting State may be discussed by the Committee of Senior Officials, which may consider any possible follow-up action. The observations and comments will remain confidential until brought to the attention of the Senior Officials. Before the circulation of the observations and any comments, no other mission of experts may be appointed for the same issue.

(8)   Furthermore, one or more participating States, having put into effect paragraphs 1 or 2 of the human dimension mechanism, may request that the CSCE Institution inquire of another participating State whether it would agree to invite a mission of experts to address a particular, clearly defined question on its territory relating to the human dimension of the CSCE. If the other participating State agrees to invite a mission of experts for the purpose indicated, the procedure set forth in paragraphs 4 to 7 will apply.

(9)   If a participating State (a) has directed an enquiry under paragraph 8 to another participating State and that State has not established a mission of experts within a period of ten days after the enquiry has been made, or (b) judges that the issue in question has not been resolved as a result of a mission of experts, it may, with the support of at least five other participating States, initiate the establishment of a mission of up to three CSCE rapporteurs. Such a decision will be addressed to the CSCE Institution, which will notify without delay the State concerned as well as all the other participating States.

(10)   The requesting State or States may appoint one person from the resource list to serve as a CSCE rapporteur. The requested State may, if it so chooses, appoint a further rapporteur from the resource list within six days after notification by the CSCE Institution of the appointment of the rapporteur. In such case the two designated rapporteurs, who will not be nationals or residents of, or persons appointed to the resource list by any of the States concerned, will by common agreement and without delay appoint a third rapporteur from the resource list. In case they fail to reach agreement within eight days, a third rapporteur who will not be a national or resident of, or a person appointed to the resource list by any of the States concerned, will be appointed from the resource list by the ranking official of the CSCE body designated by the Council. The provisions of the second part of paragraph 4 and the whole of paragraph 6 also apply to a mission of rapporteurs.

(11)   The CSCE rapporteur(s) will establish the facts, report on them and may give advice on possible solutions to the question raised. The report of the rapporteur(s), containing observations of facts, proposals or advice, will be submitted to the participating State or States concerned and, unless all the States concerned agree otherwise, to the CSCE Institution no later than three weeks after the last rapporteur has been appointed. The requested State will submit any observations on the report to the CSCE Institution, unless all the States concerned agree otherwise, no later than three weeks after the submission of the report.

The CSCE Institution will transmit the report, as well as any observations by the requested State or any other participating State, to all participating States without delay. The report may be placed on the agenda of the next regular meeting of the Committee of Senior Officials, which may decide on any possible follow-up action. The report will remain confidential until after that meeting of the Committee. Before the circulation of the report no other rapporteur may be appointed for the same issue.

(12)   If a participating State considers that a particularly serious threat to the fulfilment of the provisions of the CSCE human dimension has arisen in another participating State, it may, with the support of at least nine other participating States, engage the procedure set forth in paragraph 10. The provisions of paragraph 11 will apply.

(13)   Upon the request of any participating State the Committee of Senior Officials may decide to establish a mission of experts or of CSCE rapporteurs. In such case the Committee will also determine whether to apply the appropriate provisions of the preceding paragraphs.

(14)   The participating State or States that have requested the establishment of a mission of experts or rapporteurs will cover the expenses of that mission. In case of the appointment of experts or rapporteurs pursuant to a decision of the Committee of Senior Officials, the expenses will be covered by the participating States in accordance with the usual scale of distribution of expenses. These procedures will be reviewed by the Helsinki Follow-up Meeting of the CSCE.

(15)   Nothing in the foregoing will in any way affect the right of participating States to raise within the CSCE process any issue relating to the implementation of any CSCE commitment, including any commitment relating to the human dimension of the CSCE.

(16)   In considering whether to invoke the procedures in paragraphs 9 and 10 or 12 regarding the case of an individual, participating States should pay due regard to whether that individual's case is already *sub judice* in an international judicial procedure.

II

(17)   The participating States

(17.1)   — condemn unreservedly forces which seek to take power from a representative government of a participating State against the will of the people as expressed in free and fair elections and contrary to the justly established constitutional order;

(17.2)   — will support vigorously, in accordance with the Charter of the United Nations, in case of overthrow or attempted overthrow of a legitimately elected government of a participating State by undemocratic means, the legitimate organs of that State upholding human rights, democracy and the rule of law, recognizing their common commitment to countering any attempt to curb these basic values;

(17.3)   — recognize the need to make further peaceful efforts concerning human rights, democracy and the rule of law within the context of security and co-operation in Europe, individually and collectively, to make democratic advances irreversible and prevent any falling below the standards laid down in the principles and provisions of the Final Act, the Vienna Concluding Document, the Document of the Copenhagen Meeting, the Charter of Paris for a New Europe and the present document.

(18)   The participating States recall their commitment to the rule of law in the Document of the Copenhagen Meeting and affirm their dedication to supporting and advancing those principles of justice which form the basis of the rule of law. In particular, they again reaffirm that democracy is an inherent element in the rule of law and that pluralism is important in regard to political organizations.

(18.1)   Legislation will be formulated and adopted as the result of an open process reflecting the will of the people, either directly or through their elected representatives.

(18.2)   Everyone will have an effective means of redress against administrative decisions, so as to guarantee respect for fundamental rights and ensure legal integrity.

Any reference to the Committee of Senior Officials in this document is subject to the decision of that Committee and the Council.

(18.3) To the same end, there will be effective means of redress against administrative regulations for individuals affected thereby.

(18.4) The participating States will endeavour to provide for judicial review of such regulations and decisions.

(19) The participating States

(19.1) — will respect the internationally recognized standards that relate to the independence of judges and legal practitioners and the impartial operation of the public judicial service including, *inter alia*, the Universal Declaration of Human Rights and the International Covenant on Civil and Political Rights;

(19.2) — will, in implementing the relevant standards and commitments, ensure that the independence of the judiciary is guaranteed and enshrined in the constitution or the law of the country and is respected in practice, paying particular attention to the Basic Principles on the Independence of the Judiciary, which, *inter alia*, provide for

(i) prohibiting improper influence on judges;

(ii) preventing revision of judicial decisions by administrative authorities, except for the rights of the competent authorities to mitigate or commute sentences imposed by judges, in conformity with the law;

(iii) protecting the judiciary's freedom of expression and association, subject only to such restrictions as are consistent with its functions;

(iv) ensuring that judges are properly qualified, trained and selected on a non-discriminatory basis;

(v) guaranteeing tenure and appropriate conditions of service, including on the matter of promotion of judges, where applicable;

(vi) respecting conditions of immunity;

(vii) ensuring that the disciplining, suspension and removal of judges are determined according to law.

(20) For the promotion of the independence of the judiciary, the participating States will

(20.1) — recognize the important function national and international associations of judges and lawyers can perform in strengthening respect for the independence of their members and in providing education and training on the role of the judiciary and the legal profession in society;

(20.2) — promote and facilitate dialogue, exchanges and co-operation among national associations and other groups interested in ensuring respect for the independence of the judiciary and the protection of lawyers;

(20.3) — co-operate among themselves through, *inter alia*, dialogue, contacts and exchanges in order to identify where problem areas exist concerning the protection of the independence of judges and legal practitioners and to develop ways and means to address and resolve such problems;

(20.4) — co-operate on an ongoing basis in such areas as the education and training of judges and legal practitioners, as well as the preparation and enactment of legislation intended to strengthen respect for their independence and the impartial operation of the public judicial service.

(21) The participating States will

(21.1) — take all necessary measures to ensure that law enforcement personnel, when enforcing public order, will act in the public interest, respond to a specific need and pursue a legitimate aim, as well as use ways and means commensurate with the circumstances, which will not exceed the needs of enforcement;

(21.2) — ensure that law enforcement acts are subject to judicial control, that law enforcement personnel are held accountable for such acts, and that due compensation may be sought, according to domestic law, by the victims of acts found to be in violation of the above commitments.

(22)   The participating States will take appropriate measures to ensure that education and information regarding the prohibition of excess force by law enforcement personnel as well as relevant international and domestic codes of conduct are included in the training of such personnel.

(23)   The participating States will treat all persons deprived of their liberty with humanity and with respect for the inherent dignity of the human person and will respect the internationally recognized standards that relate to the administration of justice and the human rights of detainees.

(23.1)   The participating States will ensure that

(i)   no one will be deprived of his liberty except on such grounds and in accordance with such procedures as are established by law;

(ii)   anyone who is arrested will be informed promptly in a language which he understands of the reason for his arrest, and will be informed of any charges against him;

(iii)   any person who has been deprived of his liberty will be promptly informed about his rights according to domestic law;

(iv)   any person arrested or detained will have the right to be brought promptly before a judge or other officer authorized by law to determine the lawfulness of his arrest or detention, and will be released without delay if it is unlawful;

(v)   anyone charged with a criminal offence will have the right to defend himself in person or through legal assistance of his own choosing or, if he has not sufficient means to pay for legal assistance, to be given it free when the interests of justice so require;

(vi)   any person arrested or detained will have the right, without undue delay, to notify or to require the competent authority to notify appropriate persons of his choice of his arrest, detention, imprisonment and whereabouts; any restriction in the exercise of this right will be prescribed by law and in accordance with international standards;

(vii)   effective measures will be adopted, if this has not already been done, to provide that law enforcement bodies do not take undue advantage of the situation of a detained or imprisoned person for the purpose of compelling him to confess, or otherwise to incriminate himself, or to force him to testify against any other person;

(viii)   the duration of any interrogation and the intervals between them will be recorded and certified, consistent with domestic law;

(ix)   a detained person or his counsel will have the right to make a request or complaint regarding his treatment, in particular when torture or other cruel, inhuman or degrading treatment has been applied, to the authorities responsible for the administration of the place of detention and to higher authorities, and when necessary, to appropriate authorities vested with reviewing or remedial power;

(x)   such request or complaint will be promptly dealt with and replied to without undue delay; if the request or complaint is rejected or in case of inordinate delay, the complainant will be entitled to bring it before a judicial or other authority; neither the detained or imprisoned person nor any complainant will suffer prejudice for making a request or complaint;

(xi)   anyone who has been the victim of an unlawful arrest or detention will have a legally enforceable right to seek compensation.

(23.2)   The participating States will

(i)   endeavour to take measures, as necessary, to improve the conditions of individuals in detention or imprisonment;

(ii)   pay particular attention to the question of alternatives to imprisonment.

(24)   The participating States reconfirm the right to the protection of private and family life, domicile, correspondence and electronic communications. In order to avoid any improper or arbitrary intrusion by the State in the realm of the individual,

which would be harmful to any democratic society, the exercise of this right will be subject only to such restrictions as are prescribed by law and are consistent with internationally recognized human rights standards. In particular, the participating States will ensure that searches and seizures of persons and private premises and property will take place only in accordance with standards that are judicially enforceable.

(25)   The participating States will

(25.1)   —   ensure that their military and paramilitary forces, internal security and intelligence services, and the police are subject to the effective direction and control of the appropriate civil authorities;

(25.2)   —   maintain and, where necessary, strengthen executive control over the use of military and paramilitary forces as well as the activities of the internal security and intelligence services and the police;

(25.3)   —   take appropriate steps to create, wherever they do not already exist, and maintain effective arrangements for legislative supervision of all such forces, services and activities.

(26)   The participating States reaffirm the right to freedom of expression, including the right to communication and the right of the media to collect, report and disseminate information, news and opinions. Any restriction in the exercise of this right will be prescribed by law and in accordance with international standards. They further recognize that independent media are essential to a free and open society and accountable systems of government and are of particular importance in safeguarding human rights and fundamental freedoms.

(26.1)   They consider that the print and broadcast media in their territory should enjoy unrestricted access to foreign news and information services. The public will enjoy similar freedom to receive and impart information and ideas without interference by public authority regardless of frontiers, including through foreign publications and foreign broadcasts. Any restriction in the exercise of this right will be prescribed by law and in accordance with international standards.

(26.2)   The participating States will not discriminate against independent media with respect to affording access to information, material and facilities.

(27)   The participating States

(27.1)   —   express their intention to co-operate in the field of constitutional, administrative, commercial, civil and social welfare laws and other relevant areas, in order to develop, particularly in States where they do not yet exist, legal systems based on respect for human rights, the rule of law and democracy;

(27.2)   —   to this end, envisage the continuation and enhancement of bilateral and multilateral legal and administrative co-operation, *inter alia* in the following fields:

—   development of an efficient administrative system;
—   assistance in formulating law and regulations;
—   training of administrative and legal staff;
—   exchange of legal works and periodicals.

(28)   The participating States consider it important to protect human rights and fundamental freedoms during a state of public emergency, to take into account the relevant provisions of the Document of the Copenhagen Meeting, and to observe the international conventions to which they are parties.

(28.1)   The participating States reaffirm that a state of public emergency is justified only by the most exceptional and grave circumstances, consistent with the State's international obligations and CSCE commitments. A state of public emergency may not be used to subvert the democratic constitutional order, nor aim at the destruction of internationally recognized human rights and fundamental freedoms. If recourse to force cannot be avoided, its use must be reasonable and limited as far as possible.

(28.2)   A state of public emergency may be proclaimed only by a constitutionally lawful body, duly empowered to do so. In cases where the decision to impose a state of public emergency may be lawfully taken by the executive authorities, that decision should be subject to approval in the shortest possible time or to control by the legislature.

(28.3)   The decision to impose a state of public emergency will be proclaimed officially, publicly, and in accordance with provisions laid down by law. The decision will, where possible, lay down territorial limits of a state of public emergency. The State concerned will make available to its citizens information, without delay, about which measures have been taken. The state of public emergency will be lifted as soon as possible and will not remain in force longer than strictly required by the exigencies of the situation.

(28.4)   A *de facto* imposition or continuation of a state of public emergency not in accordance with provisions laid down by law is not permissible.

(28.5)   The participating States will endeavour to ensure that the normal functioning of the legislative bodies will be guaranteed to the highest possible extent during a state of public emergency.

(28.6)   The participating States confirm that any derogation from obligations relating to human rights and fundamental freedoms during a state of public emergency must remain strictly within the limits provided for by international law, in particular the relevant international instruments by which they are bound, especially with respect to rights from which there can be no derogation.

(28.7)   The participating States will endeavour to refrain from making derogations from those obligations from which, according to international conventions to which they are parties, derogation is possible under a state of public emergency. Measures derogating from such obligations must be taken in strict conformity with the procedural requirements laid down in those instruments. Such measures will neither go further nor remain in force longer than strictly required by the exigencies of the situation; they are by nature exceptional and should be interpreted and applied with restraint. Such measures will not discriminate solely on the grounds of race, colour, sex, language, religion, social origin or of belonging to a minority.

(28.8)   The participating States will endeavour to ensure that the legal guarantees necessary to uphold the rule of law will remain in force during a state of public emergency. They will endeavour to provide in their law for control over the regulations related to the state of public emergency, as well as the implementation of such regulations.

The participating States will endeavour to maintain freedom of expression and freedom of information, consistent with their international obligations and commitments, with a view to enabling public discussion on the observance of human rights and fundamental freedoms as well as on the lifting of the state of public emergency. They will, in conformity with international standards regarding the freedom of expression, take no measures aimed at barring journalists from the legitimate exercise of their profession other than those strictly required by the exigencies of the situation.

(28.10)   When a state of public emergency is declared or lifted in a participating State, the State concerned will immediately inform the CSCE Institution* of this decision, as well as of any derogation made from the State's international human rights obligations. The Institution will inform the other participating States without delay.

(29)   The participating States, recognizing their common interest in promoting contacts and the exchange of information amongst Ombudsmen and other institutions entrusted with similar functions of investigating individual complaints of citizens

---

* The Council will take the decision on the institution.

against public authorities, note with appreciation an offer by Spain to host a meeting of Ombudsmen.

(30)   The participating States suggest that the appropriate CSCE fora consider expanding the functions of the Office for Free Elections to enable it to assist in strengthening democratic institutions within the participating States.

(31)   The participating States acknowledge the extensive experience and expertise of the Council of Europe in the field of human rights. They welcome its contribution to strengthening democracy in Europe including its readiness to make its experience available to the CSCE.

III

(32)   The participating States reaffirm their enduring commitment to the principles and provisions of the Final Act, the Vienna Concluding Document, and other relevant CSCE documents in which they undertook, *inter alia*, to respect human rights and fundamental freedoms and to ensure that they are guaranteed for all without distinction of any kind.

(33)   The participating States will remove all legal and other restrictions with respect to travel within their territories for their own nationals and foreigners, and with respect to residence for those entitled to permanent residence, except those restrictions which may be necessary and officially declared for military, safety, ecological or other legitimate government interests, in accordance with their national laws, consistent with CSCE commitments and international human rights obligations. The participating States undertake to keep such restrictions to a minimum.

(34)   The participating States will adopt, where appropriate, all feasible measures to protect journalists engaged in dangerous professional missions, particularly in cases of armed conflict, and will co-operate to that effect. These measures will include tracing missing journalists, ascertaining their fate, providing appropriate assistance and facilitating their return to their families.

(35)   The participating States reaffirm that guaranteeing the freedom of artistic creation and preserving the cultural heritage form part of the human dimension of the CSCE. They consider that independent intellectual and cultural life is crucial for the maintenance of free societies and democratic institutions. They will implement their commitments in the cultural field, as laid down in the Document of the Cracow Symposium on the Cultural Heritage, and express the view that cultural issues, including cultural freedom, creativity and co-operation, should be further considered in the CSCE.

(36)   The participating States recall their commitment in the Vienna Concluding Document to keep the question of capital punishment under consideration and reaffirm their undertakings in the Document of the Copenhagen Meeting to exchange information on the question of the abolition of the death penalty and to make available to the public information regarding the use of the death penalty.

(36.1)   They note

(i)   that the Second Optional Protocol to the International Covenant on Civil and Political Rights aiming at the abolition of the death penalty entered into force on 11 July 1991;

(ii)   that a number of participating States have recently taken steps towards the abolition of capital punishment;

(iii)   the activities of several non-governmental organizations concerning the question of the death penalty.

(37)   The participating States confirm the provisions and commitments of all CSCE documents, in particular the Document of the Copenhagen Meeting of the Conference on the Human Dimension of the CSCE, concerning questions relating to national minorities and the rights of persons belonging to them, and the Report of the Geneva CSCE Meeting of Experts on National Minorities, and call for their full and

early implementation. They believe that, in particular, the use of the new and expanded CSCE mechanisms and procedures will contribute to further protection and promotion of the rights of persons belonging to national minorities.

(38) The participating States recognize the need to ensure that the rights of migrant workers and their families lawfully residing in the participating States are respected and underline their right to express freely their ethnic, cultural, religious and linguistic characteristics. The exercise of such rights may be subject to such restrictions as are prescribed by law and are consistent with international standards.

(38.1) They condemn all acts of discrimination on the ground of race, colour and ethnic origin, intolerance and xenophobia against migrant workers. They will, in conformity with domestic law and international obligations, take effective measures to promote tolerance, understanding, equality of opportunity and respect for the fundamental human rights of migrant workers and adopt, if they have not already done so, measures that would prohibit acts that constitute incitement to violence based on national, racial, ethnic or religious discrimination, hostility or hatred.

(38.2) They will adopt appropriate measures that would enable migrant workers to participate in the life of the society of the participating States.

(38.3) They note that issues which concern the human dimension of migrant workers residing on their territory could, as any other issue of the human dimension, be raised under the human dimension mechanism.

(38.4) They recommend that the CSCE in its future work on the human dimension consider appropriate means to hold focused discussions on all issues regarding migrant workers, including *inter alia*, familiarization with the language and social life of the country concerned.

(39) The participating States will

(39.1) — increase their preparedness and co-operate fully to enable humanitarian relief operations to be undertaken speedily and effectively;

(39.2) — take all necessary steps to facilitate speedy and unhindered access to the affected areas for such relief operations;

(39.3) — make the necessary arrangements for those relief operations to be carried out.

(40) The participating States recognize that full and true equality between men and women is a fundamental aspect of a just and democratic society based on the rule of law. They recognize that the full development of society and the welfare of all its members require equal opportunity for full and equal participation of men and women. In this context they will

(40.1) — ensure that all CSCE commitments relating to the protection and promotion of human rights and fundamental freedoms are applied fully and without discrimination with regard to sex;

(40.2) — comply with the Convention on the Elimination of All Forms of Discrimination against Women (CEDAW), if they are parties, and, if they have not already done so, consider ratifying or acceding to this Convention; States that have ratified or acceded to this Convention with reservations will consider withdrawing them;

(40.3) — effectively implement the obligations in international instruments to which they are parties and take appropriate measures to implement the United Nations Nairobi Forward-looking Strategies for the Advancement of Women (FLS);

(40.4) — affirm that it is their goal to achieve not only *de jure* but *de facto* equality of opportunity between men and women and to promote effective measures to that end;

(40.5) — establish or strengthen national machinery, as appropriate, for the advancement of women in order to ensure that programmes and policies are assessed for their impact on women;

(40.6) — encourage measures effectively to ensure full economic opportunity for women, including non-discriminatory employment policies and practices, equal access to education and training, and measures to facilitate combining employment with family responsibilities for female and male workers; and will seek to ensure that any structural adjustment policies or programmes do not have an adversely discriminatory effect on women;

(40.7) — seek to eliminate all forms of violence against women, and all forms of traffic in women and exploitation of prostitution of women including by ensuring adequate legal prohibitions against such acts and other appropriate measures;

(40.8) — encourage and promote equal opportunity for full participation by women in all aspects of political and public life, in decision-making processes and in international co-operation in general;

(40.9) — recognize the vital role women and women's organizations play in national and international efforts to promote and enhance women's rights by providing, inter alia, direct services and support to women and encouraging a meaningful partnership between governments and these organizations for the purpose of advancing equality for women;

(40.10) — recognize the rich contribution of women to all aspects of political, cultural, social and economic life and promote a broad understanding of these contributions, including those made in the informal and unpaid sectors;

(40.11) — take measures to encourage that information regarding women and women's rights under international and domestic law is easily accessible.

(40.12) — develop educational policies, consistent with their constitutional systems, to support the participation of women in all areas of study and work, including non-traditional areas, and encourage and promote a greater understanding of issues relating to equality between men and women;

(40.13) — ensure the collection and analysis of data to assess adequately, monitor and improve the situation of women; these data should not contain any personal information.

(41) The participating States decide

(41.1) — to ensure protection of the human rights of persons with disabilities;

(41.2) — to take steps to ensure the equal opportunity of such persons to participate fully in the life of their society;

(41.3) — to promote the appropriate participation of such persons in decision-making in fields concerning them;

(41.4) — to encourage services and training of social workers for the vocational and social rehabilitation of persons with disabilities;

(41.5) — to encourage favourable conditions for the access of persons with disabilities to public buildings and services, housing, transport, and cultural and recreational activities.

(42) The participating States

(42.1) — affirm that human rights education is fundamental and that it is therefore essential that their citizens are educated on human rights and fundamental freedoms and the commitment to respect such rights and freedoms in domestic legislation and international instruments to which they may be parties;

(42.2) — recognize that effective human rights education contributes to combating intolerance, religious, racial and ethnic prejudice and hatred, including against Roma, xenophobia and anti-semitism;

(42.3) — will encourage their competent authorities responsible for education programmes to design effective human rights related curricula and courses for students at all levels, particularly students of law, administration and social sciences as well as those attending military, police and public service schools;

(42.4) — will make information on all CSCE human dimension provisions available to their educators;

(42.5) — will encourage organizations and educational establishments to co-operate in drawing up and exchanging human rights programmes at the national as well as the international level;

(42.6) — will seek to ensure that activities undertaken with a view to promoting human rights education in the broader sense take into account experience, programmes and forms of co-operation within existing international governmental and non-governmental bodies, such as the United Nations and the Council of Europe.

(43) The participating States will recognize as NGOs those which declare themselves as such, according to existing national procedures, and will facilitate the ability of such organizations to conduct their activities freely on their territories; to that effect they will

(43.1) — endeavour to seek ways of further strengthening modalities for contacts and exchanges of views between NGOs and relevant national authorities and governmental institutions;

(43.2) — endeavour to facilitate visits to their countries by NGOs from within any of the participating States in order to observe human dimension conditions;

(43.3) — welcome NGO activities, including, *inter alia*, observing compliance with CSCE commitments in the field of the human dimension;

(43.4) — allow NGOs, in view of their important function within the human dimension of the CSCE, to convey their views to their own governments and the governments of all the other participating States during the future work of the CSCE on the human dimension.

(43.5) During the future work of the CSCE on the human dimension, NGOs will have the opportunity to distribute written contributions on specific issues of the human dimension of the CSCE to all delegations.

(43.6) The CSCE Secretariat will, within the framework of the resources at its disposal, respond favourably to requests by NGOs for non-restricted documents of the CSCE.

(43.7) Guidelines for the participation of NGOs in the future work of the CSCE on the human dimension might, *inter alia*, include the following:

(i) NGOs should be allotted common space at such meeting sites or in their immediate vicinity for their use as well as reasonable access, at their own expense, to technical facilities, including photocopying machines, telephones and fax machines,

(ii) NGOs should be informed and briefed on openness and access procedures in a timely manner,

(iii) delegations to CSCE meetings should be further encouraged to include or invite NGO members.

The participating States recommend that the Helsinki Follow-up Meeting consider establishing such guidelines.

(44) The representatives of the participating States express their profound gratitude to the people and Government of the USSR for the excellent organization of the Moscow Meeting and the warm hospitality extended to the delegations which participated in the Meeting.

Moscow, 3 October 1991

PRAGUE DOCUMENT ON FURTHER DEVELOPMENT OF CSCE INSTITUTIONS AND STRUCTURES (1992)

1. The Ministers reaffirmed their commitment to pursue actively all the objectives set out in the Charter of Paris for a New Europe, and their determination to further strengthen CSCE institutions and structures for this purpose. To this end they took

the following decisions and established certain guidelines for the discussions at the Helsinki Follow-up Meeting.

I

Overview and co-ordination

2.   Between meetings of the CSCE Council, the Committee of Senior Officials will be responsible for overview, management and co-ordination and will act as the Council's agent in taking appropriate decisions.

3.   In order to increase its effectiveness, the Committee of Senior Officials will meet more regularly, at least every three months. In conformity with the Charter of Paris and building on established practice, the Committee of Senior Officials may delegate tasks to other CSCE institutions or to open-ended *ad hoc* groups of participating States with a precise mandate.

II

Political consultations

4.   In order to further strengthen the political consultation process, the Committee of Senior Officials may set aside certain meetings, or parts thereof, for addressing previously agreed specific issues. Other relevant policy-level officials could attend such meetings.

5.   The facilities of the CSCE communications network will be made available to the Chairman-in-Office of the Committee of Senior Officials for transmission of urgent messages related to the work of the Committee.

III

Human dimension

6.   The Ministers agreed that monitoring and promoting progress in the human dimension remains a key function of the CSCE.

7.   Issues related to the human dimension will therefore be considered by the Council or the Committee of Senior Officials whenever necessary.

8.   In addition, meetings of a short duration may also be decided upon by the Committee of Senior Officials to address clearly defined issues. Results of such meetings will be submitted to the Council through the Committee of Senior Officials for consideration or decisions as required.

9.   In order to extend practical co-operation among participating States in the human dimension, the Ministers decided to give additional functions to the Office for Free Elections which will henceforth be called the Office for Democratic Institutions and Human Rights.

10.   Under the general guidance of the CSO, the Office should, *inter alia*:

—   organize a short CSCE meeting at the seat of the Office for Democratic Institutions and Human Rights to address implementation of CSCE human dimension commitments every year in which a follow-up meeting does not take place. The Helsinki Follow-up Meeting will work out the organizational modalities for such meetings;

—   serve as an institutional framework for sharing and exchanging information on available technical assistance, expertise, and national and international programmes aimed at assisting the new democracies in their institution-building;

—   facilitate contacts between those offering such resources and those wishing to make use of them;

—   develop co-operation with the Council of Europe in order to make use of its database of such resources and services;

— establish contacts with non-governmental organizations active in the field of democratic institution-building, with a view to enabling interested participating States to make use of their extensive resources and expertise;

— facilitate co-operation in training and education in disciplines relevant to democratic institutions;

— organize meetings and seminars among all participating States on subjects related to the building and revitalization of democratic institutions, such as a short seminar on free media and, at an appropriate time, one on migration. These meetings and seminars will be held in Warsaw unless otherwise decided.

11.   In order to avoid duplication of work specially in the fields enumerated above, the Ministers directed the Office to work closely with other institutions active in the field of democratic institution-building and human rights, particularly the Council of Europe and the European Commission for Democracy through Law.

12.   The CSO will on an annual basis examine the need for meetings and seminars on the human dimension and democratic institutions and will establish a work programme.

13.   The Ministers requested the Helsinki Follow-up Meeting to further specify the task of the Warsaw Office and to decide how the human dimension activities of the CSCE may be further carried forward.

14.   The Office for Democratic Institutions and Human Rights is designated as the CSCE institution charged with the tasks in connection with expert and rapporteur missions according to the Document of the Moscow Meeting of the Conference on the Human Dimension of the CSCE.

15.   The Office for Democratic Institutions and Human Rights will be connected to the CSCE communications network.

IV

Safeguarding human rights, democracy and the rule of law

16.   The Council decided, in order to develop further the CSCE's capability to safeguard human rights, democracy and the rule of law through peaceful means, that appropriate action may be taken by the Council or the Committee of Senior Officials, if necessary in the absence of the consent of the State concerned, in cases of clear, gross and uncorrected violations of relevant CSCE commitments. Such actions would consist of political declarations or other political steps to apply outside the territory of the State concerned. This decision is without prejudice to existing CSCE mechanisms.

17.   The Council requested the Helsinki Follow-up Meeting to consider further modalities in applying this decision.

V

Economic Co-operation

18.   The Ministers agreed on the need to continue their efforts to strengthen the focus of CSCE on the transition to and development of free-market economies as an essential contribution to the building of democracy.

19.   To this end, they agreed to establish an Economic Forum within the framework of the CSO. The CSO would convene as the economic forum to give political stimulus to the dialogue on these topics, to suggest practical efforts for the development of free-market systems and economic co-operation, and to encourage activities already underway within organizations such as the Organisation for Economic Co-operation and Development (OECD), the European Investment Bank (EIB), the European Bank for Reconstruction and Development (EBRD) and the United Nations Economic Commission for Europe (ECE). The Forum will meet periodically

in Prague and can invite contributions to its meetings by those European and transatlantic organizations relevant to the subject under discussion. It was agreed that the first meeting of the Economic Forum would be in early 1993.

20.   The Ministers agreed that the Helsinki Follow-up Meeting will consider appropriate further measures to promote discussions in the framework of the CSCE on economic co-operation and related topics.

VI

Crisis management and conflict prevention instruments

21.   The Council agreed that the capabilities of the CSCE to engage in crisis management and conflict prevention and resolution should be improved.

22.   To this end, the Council requested the Helsinki Follow-up Meeting to study possibilities for improving the following instruments:
— fact finding and rapporteur missions;
— monitor missions;
— good offices;
— counselling and conciliation;
— dispute settlement.

23.   In this context the Helsinki Follow-up Meeting should also give careful consideration to possibilities for CSCE peacekeeping or a CSCE role in peacekeeping.

24.   Provision should be made for the further operational implementation within the CSCE of decisions by the Council or the Committee of Senior Officials.

25.   Tasks may be delegated to the Chairman-in-Office of the Committee of Senior Officials, to the Consultative Committee of the Conflict Prevention Centre or to open-ended groups of participating States of an *ad hoc* character. In each case a precise mandate and arrangements for reporting back should be established.

Conflict Prevention Centre

26.   In addition to the tasks already given to the Conflict Prevention Centre in the Supplementary Document of the Paris Charter and in the Summary of Conclusions of the Berlin Meeting of the CSCE Council, the functions and working methods of the CPC are enhanced as follows:

27.   The Consultative Committee will serve as a forum in the security field wherein the CSCE participating States will conduct comprehensive and regular consultations on security issues with politico-military implications. In this context, any participating State may, in order to reduce the risk of conflict, promptly raise an issue which in its view has such implications. This is without prejudice to later decisions on the structure of a new security/arms control forum and the relationship it may have to the CPC.

28.   The Consultative Committee will serve as a forum for consultation and co-operation in conflict prevention and for co-operation in the implementation of decisions on crisis management taken by the Council or by the CSO acting as its agent.

29.   The Consultative Committee has the authority to initiate and, with the assistance of the CPC Secretariat, execute fact-finding and monitor missions in connection with paragraph 17 of the Vienna Document 1990 (Mechanism for Consultation and Co-operation as regards Unusual Military Activities).

30.   The Consultative Committee, with the assistance of the CPC Secretariat, will execute any additional tasks assigned to it by the Council, or by the Committee of Senior Officials acting as its agent. This will include full responsibility in the implementation of such tasks. The Consultative Committee will report in an appropriate manner on the implementation of these tasks to the Committee of Senior Officials.

31.   The Consultative Committee will develop general guidelines for the imple-mentation of its operational tasks including, in due time, those that may be assigned to it by the Helsinki Follow-up Meeting and in the future.

32.   In addition to the existing support to the implementation of CSBMs, the CPC will fulfil other functions as regards the implementation and verification of agreements in the field of disarmament and arms control, if so requested by the parties to those agreements and agreed upon by the Consultative Committee.

33.   The Consultative Committee may at any time draw the attention of the Committee of Senior Officials to a situation which it considers requires the consider-ation of the Committee of Senior Officials.

34.   The Consultative Committee will meet regularly, as a rule at least once a month. Working schedules should be flexible and additional meetings may be held, in the light of circumstances and future requirements.

35.   The Consultative Committee may establish subsidiary working bodies, includ-ing open-ended ad hoc groups entrusted with specific tasks.

36.   The regular meetings of the Consultative Committee will be chaired in alphabetical rotation. The Chairmanship will rotate immediately after the last regular meeting in every month.

37.   The Chairman of the Consultative Committee and the Chairman of the Committee of Senior Officials will maintain contact with each other.

38.   The Chairman of the Consultative Committee or his representative will attend meetings of the Committee of Senior Officials which are relevant to the tasks of the CPC.

39.   In accordance with the paragraph on 'CSCE Relationship with International Organizations', European, Transatlantic and other international organizations, such as the North Atlantic Treaty Organization (NATO), the Western European Union (WEU) and relevant United Nations bodies, will be invited to make appropriate contributions to future seminars organized by the CPC.

40.   The Helsinki Follow-up Meeting should also examine further how the CSCE could co-operate with other international organizations in these fields.

VII

Parliamentary Assembly

41.   In the interest of encouraging an active dialogue with the CSCE Parliamentary Assembly, the Chairman-in-Office of the Council will be in contact with the Chairman of the Committee of Heads of Delegation of the Assembly in order to explore possible interest in the presence of the Chairman of the Council at the Budapest Meeting of the Assembly in July 1992. The Chairman of the Council will be prepared to make himself available to report on the work of the CSCE; to answer parliamentarians' questions in this regard; and to take note of parliamentarians' views for subsequent transmission to the Council.

VIII

Non-Governmental Organizations

42.   The Council requests the Helsinki Follow-up Meeting to strengthen relations between the CSCE and non-governmental organizations, in order to increase the role of non-governmental organizations in implementing CSCE goals and commitments. In particular, the Follow-up Meeting will develop opportunities and procedures for meaningful non-governmental organization involvement in the CSCE and possibilities for non-governmental organizations to communicate with CSCE structures and institutions, recalling *inter alia* the texts on non-governmental organizations agreed by the Sofia and Moscow Meetings and by the Oslo Seminar.

IX

CSCE relationship with international organizations

43.   The Council of Europe, ECE, NATO, the Western European Union, OECD, EBRD, EIB and other European and transatlantic organizations which may be agreed will be invited to make contributions on the basis of CSCE precedent and practice to specialized CSCE Meetings where they have relevant expertise.

44.   To ensure full co-ordination, the Ministers would welcome it if the above organizations would inform the CSCE Secretariat annually of their current work programme and of the facilities available for work relevant to the CSCE.

X

Relations with non-participating States

45.   The Council requests the Helsinki Follow-up Meeting to recommend practical ways to establish a flexible dialogue between the CSCE and interested non-participating States or groups of States, for example through contacts between the said States and the Chairman-in-Office of the Council or of the Committee of Senior Officials.

XI

Financial arrangements of the CSCE and cost-effectiveness

46.   The Council requested the Helsinki Follow-up Meeting to develop procedures which would ensure greater predictability and transparency of the costs of CSCE meetings and other activities. Measures to provide for increased cost-effectiveness should also be examined.

47.   States proposing to host future CSCE meetings will present draft budgets along with their proposals. Detailed provisions in this respect will be developed at the Helsinki Follow-up Meeting.

CSCE HELSINKI DOCUMENT (1992)

HELSINKI SUMMIT DECLARATION

Promises and problems of change

1.   We, the Heads of State or Government of the States participating in the Conference on Security and Co-operation in Europe, have returned to the birthplace of the Helsinki process, to give new impetus to our common endeavour.

2.   The Charter of Paris for a New Europe, signed at the last Summit, defined a common democratic foundation, established institutions for co-operation and set forth guidelines for realization of a community of free and democratic States from Vancouver to Vladivostok.

3.   We have witnessed the end of the cold war, the fall of totalitarian regimes and the demise of the ideology on which they were based. All our countries now take democracy as the basis for their political, social and economic life. The CSCE has played a key role in these positive changes. Still, the legacy of the past remains strong. We are faced with challenges and opportunities, but also with serious difficulties and disappointments.

4.   We have met here to review recent developments, to consolidate the achievements of the CSCE and to set its future direction. To meet new challenges we are approving here today a programme to enhance our capabilities for concerted action and to intensify our co-operation for democracy, prosperity and equal rights of security.

5. The aspirations of peoples freely to determine their internal and external political status have led to the spread of democracy and have recently found expression in the emergence of a number of sovereign States. Their full participation brings a new dimension to the CSCE.

6. We welcome the commitment of all participating States to our shared values. Respect for human rights and fundamental freedoms, including the rights of persons belonging to national minorities, democracy, the rule of law, economic liberty, social justice and environmental responsibility are our common aims. They are immutable. Adherence to our commitments provides the basis for participation and co-operation in the CSCE and a cornerstone for further development of our societies.

7. We reaffirm the validity of the guiding principles and common values of the Helsinki Final Act and the Charter of Paris, embodying responsibilities of States towards each other and of governments towards their people. These are the collective conscience of our community. We recognize our accountability to each other for complying with them. We underline the democratic rights of citizens to demand from their governments respect for these values and standards.

8. We emphasize that the commitments undertaken in the field of the human dimension of the CSCE are matters of direct and legitimate concern to all participating States and do not belong exclusively to the internal affairs of the State concerned. The protection and promotion of human rights and fundamental freedoms and the strengthening of democratic institutions continue to be a vital basis for our comprehensive security.

9. The transition to and development of democracy and market economy by the new democracies is being carried forward with determination amidst difficulties and varying conditions. We offer our support and solidarity to participating States undergoing transformation to democracy and market economy. We welcome their efforts to become fully integrated into the wider community of States. Making this transition irreversible will ensure the security and prosperity of us all.

10. Encouragement of this sense of wider community remains one of our fundamental goals. We welcome in this connection the rapid adaptation of European and transatlantic institutions and organizations which are increasingly working together to face up to the challenges before us and to provide a solid foundation for peace and prosperity.

The European Community (EC), fulfilling its important role in the political and economic development of Europe, is moving towards a union and has decided to broaden its membership. It is closely involved in CSCE activities.

The North Atlantic Treaty Organization (NATO), one of the essential transatlantic links, has adopted a new strategic concept and strengthened its role as an integral aspect for security in Europe. Through establishment of the North Atlantic Co-operation Council (NACC) it has established patterns of co-operation with new partners in harmony with the goals of the CSCE. It has also offered practical support for the work of the CSCE.

The Western European Union (WEU) is an integral part of the development of the European Union; it is also the means to strengthen the European pillar of the Atlantic Alliance; it is developing an operational capacity; it is opening itself to additional co-operation with new partners and has offered to provide resources in support of the CSCE.

The Council of Europe is elaborating its own programmes for new democracies, opening up to new members and is co-operating with the CSCE in the human dimension.

The Group of Seven and the Group of Twenty-Four are deeply engaged in assistance to countries in transition.

The Organisation for Economic Co-operation and Development (OECD), United Nations Economic Commission for Europe (ECE) and the European Bank for

Reconstruction and Development (EBRD) have a key role to play in the construction of a new Europe.

The Commonwealth of Independent States (CIS) has stated its readiness to assist the CSCE in pursuit of its objectives.

These and the other forms of regional and sub-regional co-operation which continue to develop, such as the Council of the Baltic Sea States, the Visegrad Triangle, the Black Sea Economic Co-operation and the Central European Initiative, multiply the links uniting CSCE participating States.

11.   We welcome the adoption of the Vienna 1992 Document on Confidence- and Security-building Measures and the signature of the Treaty on Open Skies, with the adoption of the Declaration on the Treaty on Open Skies. We also welcome the imminent entry into force of the Treaty on Conventional Armed Forces in Europe (CFE) and the Concluding Act of the Negotiation on Personnel Strength of Conventional Armed Forces in Europe. These agreements provide a solid foundation for our further security co-operation. We welcome the recent United States-Russian joint understanding on Strategic Offensive Arms. We reaffirm our commitment to become original signatories to the forthcoming convention on the prohibition of the development, production, stockpiling and use of chemical weapons and on their destruction, and urge other States to do so.

12.   This is a time of promise but also a time of instability and insecurity. Economic decline, social tension, aggressive nationalism, intolerance, xenophobia and ethnic conflicts threaten stability in the CSCE area. Gross violations of CSCE commitments in the field of human rights and fundamental freedoms, including those related to national minorities, pose a special threat to the peaceful development of society, in particular in new democracies.

There is still much work to be done in building democratic and pluralistic societies, where diversity is fully protected and respected in practice. Consequently, we reject racial, ethnic and religious discrimination in any form. Freedom and tolerance must be taught and practised.

13.   For the first time in decades we are facing warfare in the CSCE region. New armed conflicts and massive use of force to achieve hegemony and territorial expansion continue to occur. The loss of life, human misery, involving huge numbers of refugees have been the worst since the Second World War. Damage to our cultural heritage and the destruction of property have been appalling.

Our community is deeply concerned by these developments. Individually and jointly within the CSCE and the United Nations and other international organizations, we have sought to alleviate suffering and seek long term solutions to the crises which have arisen.

With the Helsinki decisions, we have put in place a comprehensive programme of co-ordinated action which will provide additional tools for the CSCE to address tensions before violence erupts and to manage crises which may regrettably develop. The Council and the Committee of Senior Officials have already established for the CSCE an important role in dealing with crises which have developed within our area.

No international effort can be successful if those engaged in conflicts do not reaffirm their will to seek peaceful solutions to their differences. We stress our determination to hold parties to conflicts accountable for their actions.

14.   In times of conflict the fulfilment of basic human needs is most at risk. We will exert every effort to ensure that they are met and that humanitarian commitments are respected. We will strive to relieve suffering by humanitarian cease-fires and to facilitate the delivery of assistance under international supervision, including its safe passage. We recognize that the refugee problems resulting from these conflicts require the co-operation of all of us. We express our support for and solidarity with those countries which bear the brunt of the refugee problems resulting from these conflicts. In this context we recognize the need for co-operation and concerted action.

15.   Even where violence has been contained, the sovereignty and independence of some States still needs to be upheld. We express support for efforts by CSCE participating States to remove, in a peaceful manner and through negotiations, the problems that remain from the past, like the stationing of foreign armed forces on the territories of the Baltic States without the required consent of those countries.

Therefore, in line with basic principles of international law and in order to prevent any possible conflict, we call on the participating States concerned to conclude, without delay, appropriate bilateral agreements, including timetables, for the early, orderly and complete withdrawal of such foreign troops from the territories of the Baltic States.

16.   The degradation of the environment over many years threatens us all. The danger of nuclear accidents is a pressing concern. So are, in several parts of the CSCE area, defence-related hazards for the environment.

17.   The present proliferation of weapons increases the danger of conflict and is an urgent challenge. Effective export controls on nuclear materials, conventional weapons and other sensitive goods and technologies are a pressing need.

The CSCE and the management of change

18.   The CSCE has been instrumental in promoting changes; now it must adapt to the task of managing them. Our decisions in Helsinki are making the CSCE more operational and effective. We are determined to fully use consultations and concerted action to enable a common response to the challenges facing us.

19.   In approaching these tasks, we emphasize the central role of the CSCE in fostering and managing change in our region. In this era of transition, the CSCE is crucial to our efforts to forestall aggression and violence by addressing the root causes of problems and to prevent, manage and settle conflicts peacefully by appropriate means.

20.   To this end, we have further developed structures to ensure political management of crises and created new instruments of conflict prevention and crisis management. We have strengthened the Council and the Committee of Senior Officials (CSO) and devised means to assist them. The CSCE capacities in the field of early warning will be strengthened in particular by the activities of the newly established High Commissioner on National Minorities.

We have provided for CSCE peacekeeping according to agreed modalities. CSCE peacekeeping activities may be undertaken in cases of conflict within or among participating States to help maintain peace and stability in support of an ongoing effort at a political solution. In this respect, we are also prepared to seek, on a case-by-case basis, the support of international institutions and organizations, such as the EC, NATO and WEU, as well as other institutions and mechanisms, including the peacekeeping mechanism of the CIS. We welcome their readiness to support CSCE peacekeeping activities, including by making available their resources.

We are further developing our possibilities for peaceful settlement of disputes.

21.   Our approach is based on our comprehensive concept of security as initiated in the Final Act. This concept relates the maintenance of peace to the respect for human rights and fundamental freedoms. It links economic and environmental solidarity and co-operation with peaceful inter-State relations. This is equally valid in managing change as it was necessary in mitigating confrontation.

22.   The CSCE is a forum for dialogue, negotiation and co-operation, providing direction and giving impulse to the shaping of the new Europe. We are determined to use it to give new impetus to the process of arms control, disarmament and confidence- and security-building, to the enhancement of consultation and co-operation on security matters and to furthering the process of reducing the risk of conflict. In this context, we will also consider new steps to further strengthen norms

of behaviour on politico-military aspects of security. We will ensure that our efforts in these fields are coherent, interrelated and complementary.

23. We remain convinced that security is indivisible. No State in our CSCE community will strengthen its security at the expense of the security of other States. This is our resolute message to States which resort to the threat or use of force to achieve their objectives in flagrant violation of CSCE commitments.

24. Essential to the success of our efforts to foster democratic change within the CSCE framework will be increased co-operation with other European and transatlantic organizations and institutions. Therefore, we are convinced that a lasting and peaceful order for our community of States will be built on mutually reinforcing institutions, each with its own area of action and responsibility.

25. Reaffirming the commitments to the Charter of the United Nations as subscribed to by our States, we declare our understanding that the CSCE is a regional arrangement in the sense of Chapter VIII of the Charter of the United Nations. As such, it provides an important link between European and global security. The rights and responsibilities of the Security Council remain unaffected in their entirety. The CSCE will work together closely with the United Nations especially in preventing and settling conflicts.

26. We restate our unreserved condemnation of all acts, methods and practices of terrorism. We are determined to enhance our co-operation to eliminate this threat to security, democracy and human rights. To this end, we will take measures to prevent in our territories criminal activities that support acts of terrorism in other States. We will encourage exchange of information concerning terrorist activities. We will seek further effective avenues for co-operation as appropriate. We will also take the necessary steps at a national level to fulfil our international obligations in this field.

27. Illicit trafficking in drugs represents a danger to the stability of our societies and democratic institutions. We will act together to strengthen all forms of bilateral and multilateral co-operation in the fight against illicit trafficking in drugs and other forms of international organized crime.

28. We will work to reinforce the close link which exists between political pluralism and the operation of a market economy. Enhanced co-operation in the field of economy, science and technology has a crucial role to play in strengthening security and stability in the CSCE region.

29. Economic co-operation remains an essential element of the CSCE. We will continue to support the transformations under way to introduce market economies as the means to enhance economic performance and increased integration into the international economic and financial systems.

30. We will also facilitate expanded economic co-operation which must take account of the prevailing political and economic conditions. We welcome the contribution of economic, financial and technical assistance programmes of the Group of Seven and the Group of Twenty-Four to the transition process.

In the framework of our co-operation we fully support the further development of the European Energy Charter which is of particular importance in the period of transition.

31. We will work together to help facilitate means of transportation and communication in order to deepen co-operation among us.

32. We renew our commitment to co-operate in protecting and improving the environment for present and future generations. We stress in particular the importance of co-operation to effectively ensure the safety of nuclear installations and to bring defence-related hazards for the environment under control.

We emphasize the need for greater public awareness and understanding of environmental issues and for public involvement in the planning and decision-making process.

We welcome the important outcome of the United Nations Conference on Environment and Development (UNCED) held in Rio de Janeiro in June 1992. We emphasize the need for effective and sustained implementation of UNCED decisions.
33.   Further steps must be taken to stop the proliferation of weapons. It remains vital to ensure non-proliferation of nuclear weapons and the relevant technology and expertise. We urge all States which have not acceded to the Treaty on Non-proliferation of Nuclear Weapons to do so as non-nuclear weapons States and to conclude safeguards agreements with the International Atomic Energy Agency (IAEA). We commit ourselves to intensify our co-operation in the field of effective export controls applicable to nuclear materials, conventional weapons and other sensitive goods and technologies.
34.   We welcome the development of regional co-operation among CSCE participating States as a valuable means of promoting pluralistic structures of stability. Based on the CSCE principles and commitments, regional co-operative activities serve the purpose of uniting us and promoting comprehensive security.
35.   We encourage wide-ranging transfrontier co-operation, including human contacts, involving local and regional communities and authorities. This co-operation contributes to overcoming economic and social inequalities and enhancing ethnic understanding, fostering good-neighbourly relations among States and peoples.
36.   In order to ensure full participation and co-operation by recently admitted participating States we are initiating a programme of co-ordinated support.
37.   We reaffirm our conviction that strengthening security and co-operation in the Mediterranean is important for stability in the CSCE region. We recognize that the changes which have taken place in Europe are relevant to the Mediterranean region and that, conversely, economic, social, political and security developments in that region have a direct bearing on Europe.
38.   We will therefore widen our co-operation and enlarge our dialogue with the non-participating Mediterranean States as a means to promote social and economic development, thereby enhancing stability in the region, in order to narrow the prosperity gap between Europe and its Mediterranean neighbours and protect the Mediterranean ecosystems. We stress the importance of intra-Mediterranean relations and the need for increased co-operation within the region.
39.   We welcome and encourage the continuation of initiatives and negotiations aimed at finding just, lasting and viable solutions, through peaceful means, to the outstanding crucial problems of the Mediterranean region.
40.   We have expanded dialogue with non-participating States, inviting them to take part in our activities on a selective basis when they can make a contribution.
41.   We welcome the establishment of the CSCE Parliamentary Assembly which held its first meeting in Budapest on 3 to 5 July and look forward to the active participation of parliamentarians in the CSCE process.
42.   We attach particular importance to the active involvement of our publics in the CSCE. We will expand the opportunities for contributions by and co-operation with individuals and non-governmental organizations in our work.
43.   In order to foster our partnership, and to better manage change, we have today in Helsinki adopted an agenda for a strengthened and effective CSCE through the Helsinki Decisions. These decisions will be implemented fully and in good faith.
44.   We entrust the Council with the further steps which may be required to implement them. The Council may adopt any amendment to the decisions which it may deem appropriate.
45.   The full text of the Helsinki Document will be published in each participating State, which will make it known as widely as possible.
46.   The Government of Finland is requested to transmit to the Secretary-General of the United Nations the text of the Helsinki Document, which is not eligible for

registration under Article 102 of the Charter of the United Nations, with a view to its circulation to all the members of the Organization as an official document of the United Nations.

47. The next review conference will be held in Budapest in 1994 on the basis of modalities of the Helsinki Follow-up Meeting, *mutatis mutandis*, to be further specified by the CSO which may decide to organize a special preparatory meeting.

Helsinki, 10 July 1992

HELSINKI DECISIONS

I

STRENGTHENING CSCE INSTITUTIONS AND STRUCTURES

(1) In order to enhance the coherence of their consultations and the efficiency of their concerted action based on their joint political will, as well as to further develop the practical aspects of co-operation among them, the participating States have decided to reaffirm and develop the decisions on CSCE structures and institutions set forth in the Charter of Paris and the Prague Document on Further Development of CSCE Institutions and Structures.

To this end, they have agreed as follows:

Meetings of Heads of State or Government

(2) Meetings of Heads of State or Government, as laid down in the Charter of Paris, will take place, as a rule, every two years on the occasion of review conferences.

(3) They will set priorities and provide orientation at the highest political level.

Review conferences

(4) Review conferences will precede the meetings of Heads of State or Government. They will be operational and of short duration. They will:

— review the entire range of activities within the CSCE, including a thorough implementation debate, and consider further steps to strengthen the CSCE process;

— prepare a decision-oriented document to be adopted at the meeting.

(5) Preparation of review conferences, including the agenda and modalities, will be carried out by the Committee of Senior Officials (CSO), which may decide to organize a special preparatory meeting.

CSCE Council

(6) The Council constitutes the central decision-making and governing body of the CSCE.

(7) The Council will ensure that the various CSCE activities relate closely to the central political goals of the CSCE.

(8) The participating States have agreed to enhance the working methods of the Council and promote effective consultations at its meetings.

Committee of senior officials

(9) Further to the decisions contained in the Charter of Paris and as set forth in the Prague document, the CSO, between the meetings of the CSCE Council, will be responsible for overview, management and co-ordination and will act as the Council's agent in taking appropriate decisions. Additional responsibilities are described in Chapter III of this document.

(10) Greater use will be made of the points of contact and communications network order to manage the flow of information more efficiently.

(11) The functions of the CSO convening as the Economic Forum are set out in Chapter VII of this document.

Chairman-in-Office

(12)   The Chairman-in-Office will be responsible on behalf of the Council/CSO for the co-ordination of and consultation on current CSCE business.

(13)   The Chairman-in-Office will be requested to communicate Council and CSO decisions to the CSCE institutions and to give them such advice regarding those decisions as may be required.

(14)   In carrying out entrusted tasks, the Chairman-in-Office may be assisted, *inter alia*, by:

— the preceding and succeeding Chairmen, operating together as a Troika;
— *ad hoc* steering groups;
— personal representatives, if necessary.

Assistance to the Chairman-in-Office

Troika

(15)   The Chairman-in-Office may be assisted by the preceding and succeeding Chairmen, operating together as a Troika, in carrying out entrusted tasks. The Chairman-in-Office will retain the responsibility for such tasks and for reporting on Troika activities to the Council/CSO.

Ad hoc steering groups

(16)   *Ad hoc* steering groups may be established on a case-by-case basis in order to further assist the Chairman-in-Office, in particular in the field of conflict prevention, crisis management and dispute resolution.

(17)   The decision of the Council/CSO to establish an *ad hoc* steering group will, in principle, be taken upon recommendation of the Chairman-in-Office and will include a description of its composition and mandate which will set out the specific tasks and objectives and specify the duration.

(18)   If the matter is urgent, the Chairman-in-Office may consult the participating States to propose the establishment of an *ad hoc* steering group under a silence procedure. If objections to the proposal are voiced within five days and if further consultations by the Chairman-in-Office have not led to consensus, the CSO must address the question.

(19)   In order to ensure efficiency, an *ad hoc* steering group will be composed of a restricted number of participating States which will include the Troika. Its composition and size will be decided taking into account the need for impartiality and efficiency.

(20)   The Council/CSO may decide to terminate or extend for a specific period of time the term of the activities of an *ad hoc* steering group as well as to amend the mandate, composition and instructions given to a steering group.

(21)   The Chairman-in-Office will report comprehensively and on a regular basis to the CSO on the activities of the *ad hoc* steering group and on related developments.

Personal representatives

(22)   When dealing with a crisis or a conflict, the Chairman-in-Office may, on his/her own responsibility, designate a personal representative with a clear and precise mandate in order to provide support. The Chairman-in-Office will inform the CSO of the intention to appoint a personal representative and of the mandate. In reports to the Council/CSO, the Chairman-in-Office will include information on the activities of the personal representative as well as any observations or advice submitted by the latter.

High Commissioner on national minorities

(23)   The Council will appoint a High Commissioner on National Minorities. The High Commissioner provides 'early warning' and, as appropriate, 'early action' at the

earliest possible stage in regard to tensions involving national minority issues that have the potential to develop into a conflict within the CSCE area, affecting peace, stability, or relations between participating States. The High Commissioner will draw upon the facilities of the Office for Democratic Institutions and Human Rights (ODIHR) in Warsaw.

Other institutions and structures

(24)   Further to the Charter of Paris and the Prague Document, additional functions of the other CSCE institutions and structures are described in Chapters II, III, IV, V and VI of this document.

(25)   The participating States mandate the CSO to study ways and means which would enable the three CSCE institutional arrangements to better accomplish their functions. In this regard they will consider the relevance of an agreement granting an internationally recognized status to the CSCE Secretariat, the Conflict Prevention Centre (CPC) and the ODIHR.

Implementation reviews

(26)   Thorough review of the implementation of CSCE commitments will continue to play a prominent role in CSCE activities, thus enhancing co-operation among participating States.

(27)   Reviews of implementation will be held regularly at review conferences as well as at special meetings convened for this purpose at the ODIHR and the CPC, and when the CSO convenes as the Economic Forum as provided for in the relevant CSCE documents.

(28)   These reviews of implementation will be of a co-operative nature, comprehensive in scope and at the same time able to address specific issues.

(29)   The participating States will be invited to offer contributions on their implementation experience, with particular reference to difficulties encountered, and to provide their views of implementation throughout the CSCE area. Participating States are encouraged to circulate descriptions of contributions in advance of the meeting.

(30)   Reviews should offer the opportunity to identify action which may be required to address problems. Meetings at which reviews of implementation take place may draw to the attention of the CSO any suggestions for measures to improve implementation which they deem advisable.

Communications

(31)   The CSCE communications network is an important instrument for the implementation of the Vienna Document 1992 and other documents and agreements. As the CSCE's capacity to deal with emergency situations is being developed, the network is assuming a new and vital role in providing the participating States with up-to-date means for urgent communications. In this respect, it is essential that all participating States be connected to the system. The Consultative Committee of the CPC will monitor progress and, if necessary, recommend solutions for technical problems.

II
CSCE HIGH COMMISSIONER ON NATIONAL MINORITIES

(1)   The participating States decide to establish a High Commissioner on National Minorities.

Mandate

(2)   The High Commissioner will act under the aegis of the CSO and will thus be an instrument of conflict prevention at the earliest possible stage.

(3)   The High Commissioner will provide 'early warning' and, as appropriate, 'early action' at the earliest possible stage in regard to tensions involving national minority issues which have not yet developed beyond an early warning stage, but, in the judgement of the High Commissioner, have the potential to develop into a conflict within the CSCE area, affecting peace, stability or relations between participating States, requiring the attention of and action by the Council or the CSO.

(4)   Within the mandate, based on CSCE principles and commitments, the High Commissioner will work in confidence and will act independently of all parties directly involved in the tensions.

(5a)   The High Commissioner will consider national minority issues occurring in the State of which the High Commissioner is a national or a resident, or involving a national minority to which the High Commissioner belongs, only if all parties directly involved agree, including the State concerned.

(5b)   The High Commissioner will not consider national minority issues in situations involving organized acts of terrorism.

(5c)   Nor will the High Commissioner consider violations of CSCE commitments with regard to an individual person belonging to a national minority.

(6)   In considering a situation, the High Commissioner will take fully into account the availability of democratic means and international instruments to respond to it, and their utilization by the parties involved.

(7)   When a particular national minority issue has been brought to the attention of the CSO, the involvement of the High Commissioner will require a request and a specific mandate from the CSO.

Profile, appointment, support

(8)   The High Commissioner will be an eminent international personality with long-standing relevant experience from whom an impartial performance of the function may be expected.

(9)   The High Commissioner will be appointed by the Council by consensus upon the recommendation of the CSO for a period of three years, which may be extended for one further term of three years only.

(10)   The High Commissioner will draw upon the facilities of the ODIHR in Warsaw, and in particular upon the information relevant to all aspects of national minority questions available at the ODIHR.

Early warning

(11)   The High Commissioner will:

(11a)   collect and receive information regarding national minority issues from sources described below (see Supplement paragraphs (23)–(25));

(11b)   assess at the earliest possible stage the role of the parties directly concerned, the nature of the tensions and recent developments therein and, where possible, the potential consequences for peace and stability within the CSCE area;

(11c)   to this end, be able to pay a visit, in accordance with paragraph (17) and Supplement paragraphs (27)–(30), to any participating State and communicate in person, subject to the provisions of paragraph (25), with parties directly concerned to obtain first-hand information about the situation of national minorities.

(12)   The High Commissioner may during a visit to a participating State, while obtaining first-hand information from all parties directly involved, discuss the questions with the parties, and where appropriate promote dialogue, confidence and co-operation between them.

Provision of early warning

(13)   If, on the basis of exchanges of communications and contacts with relevant parties, the High Commissioner concludes that there is a *prima facie* risk of potential conflict (as set out in paragraph (3)) he/she may issue an early warning, which will be communicated promptly by the Chairman-in-Office to the CSO.

(14)   The Chairman-in-Office will include this early warning in the agenda for the next meeting of the CSO. If a State believes that such an early warning merits prompt consultation, it may initiate the procedure set out in Annex 2 of the Summary of Conclusions of the Berlin Meeting of the Council ('Emergency Mechanism').

(15)   The High Commissioner will explain to the CSO the reasons for issuing the early warning.

Early action

(16)   The High Commissioner may recommend that he/she be authorized to enter into further contact and closer consultations with the parties concerned with a view to possible solutions, according to a mandate to be decided by the CSO. The CSO may decide accordingly.

Accountability

(17)   The High Commissioner will consult the Chairman-in-Office prior to a departure for a participating State to address a tension involving national minorities. The Chairman-in-Office will consult, in confidence, the participating State(s) concerned and may consult more widely.

(18)   After a visit to a participating State, the High Commissioner will provide strictly confidential reports to the Chairman-in-Office on the findings and progress of the High Commissioner's involvement in a particular question.

(19)   After termination of the involvement of the High Commissioner in a particular issue, the High Commissioner will report to the Chairman-in-Office on the findings, results and conclusions. Within a period of one month, the Chairman-in-Office will consult, in confidence, on the findings, results and conclusions the participating State(s) concerned and may consult more widely. Thereafter the report, together with possible comments, will be transmitted to the CSO.

(20)   Should the High Commissioner conclude that the situation is escalating into a conflict, or if the High Commissioner deems that the scope for action by the High Commissioner is exhausted, the High Commissioner shall, through the Chairman-in-Office, so inform the CSO.

(21)   Should the CSO become involved in a particular issue, the High Commissioner will provide information and, on request, advice to the CSO, or to any other institution or organization which the CSO may invite, in accordance with the provisions of Chapter III of this document, to take action with regard to the tensions or conflict.

(22)   The High Commissioner, if so requested by the CSO and with due regard to the requirement of confidentiality in his/her mandate, will provide information about his/her activities at CSCE implementation meetings on Human Dimension issues.

Sources of information about national minority issues

(23)   The High Commissioner may:

(23a)   collect and receive information regarding the situation of national minorities and the role of parties involved therein from any source, including the media and non-governmental organizations with the exception referred to in paragraph (25);

(23b)   receive specific reports from parties directly involved regarding developments concerning national minority issues. These may include reports on violations of CSCE commitments with respect to national minorities as well as other violations in the context of national minority issues.

(24)   Such specific reports to the High Commissioner should meet the following requirements:

— they should be in writing, addressed to the High Commissioner as such and signed with full names and addresses;

— they should contain a factual account of the developments which are relevant to the situation of persons belonging to national minorities and the role of the parties involved therein, and which have taken place recently, in principle not more than 12 months previously. The reports should contain information which can be sufficiently substantiated.

(25)   The High Commissioner will not communicate with and will not acknowledge communications from any person or organization which practises or publicly condones terrorism or violence.

Parties directly concerned

(26)   Parties directly concerned in tensions who can provide specific reports to the High Commissioner and with whom the High Commissioner will seek to communicate in person during a visit to a participating State are the following:

(26a)   governments of participating States, including, if appropriate, regional and local authorities in areas in which national minorities reside;

(26b)   representatives of associations, non-governmental organizations, religious and other groups of national minorities directly concerned and in the area of tension, which are authorized by the persons belonging to those national minorities to represent them.

Conditions for travel by the High Commissioner

(27)   Prior to an intended visit, the High Commissioner will submit to the participating State concerned specific information regarding the intended purpose of that visit. Within two weeks the State(s) concerned will consult with the High Commissioner on the objectives of the visit, which may include the promotion of dialogue, confidence and co-operation between the parties. After entry the State concerned will facilitate free travel and communication of the High Commissioner subject to the provisions of paragraph (25) above.

(28)   If the State concerned does not allow the High Commissioner to enter the country and to travel and communicate freely, the High Commissioner will so inform the CSO.

(29)   In the course of such a visit, subject to the provision of paragraph (25) the High Commissioner may consult the parties involved, and may receive information in confidence from any individual, group or organization directly concerned on questions the High Commissioner is addressing. The High Commissioner will respect the confidential nature of the information.

(30)   The participating States will refrain from taking any action against persons, organizations or institutions on account of their contact with the High Commissioner.

High Commissioner and involvement of experts

(31)   The High Commissioner may decide to request assistance from not more than three experts with relevant expertise in specific matters on which brief, specialized investigation and advice are required.

(32)   If the High Commissioner decides to call on experts, the High Commissioner will set a clearly defined mandate and time-frame for the activities of the experts.

(33)   Experts will only visit a participating State at the same time as the High Commissioner. Their mandate will be an integral part of the mandate of the High Commissioner and the same conditions for travel will apply.

(34)   The advice and recommendations requested from the experts will be submitted in confidence to the High Commissioner, who will be responsible for the activities and for the reports of the experts and who will decide whether and in what form the advice and recommendations will be communicated to the parties concerned. They will be non-binding. If the High Commissioner decides to make the advice and recommendations available, the State(s) concerned will be given the opportunity to comment.

(35)   The experts will be selected by the High Commissioner with the assistance of the ODIHR from the resource list established at the ODIHR as laid down in the Document of the Moscow Meeting.

(36)   The experts will not include nationals or residents of the participating State concerned, or any person appointed by the State concerned, or any expert against whom the participating State has previously entered reservations. The experts will not include the participating State's own nationals or residents or any of the persons it appointed to the resource list, or more than one national or resident of any particular State.

Budget

(37)   A separate budget will be determined at the ODIHR, which will provide, as appropriate, logistical support for travel and communication. The budget will be funded by the participating States according to the established CSCE scale of distribution. Details will be worked out by the Financial Committee and approved by the CSO.

III
EARLY WARNING, CONFLICT PREVENTION AND CRISIS MANAGEMENT (INCLUDING FACT-FINDING AND RAPPORTEUR MISSIONS AND CSCE PEACEKEEPING), PEACEFUL SETTLEMENT OF DISPUTES
Early warning, conflict prevention and crisis management (including fact-finding and rapporteur missions and CSCE peacekeeping)

(1)   The participating States have decided to strengthen the structure of their political consultations and increase their frequency, and to provide for more flexible and active dialogue and better early warning and dispute settlement, resulting in a more effective role in conflict prevention and resolution, complemented, when necessary, by peacekeeping operations.

(2)   The participating States have decided to enhance their capability to identify the root causes of tensions through a more rigorous review of implementation to be conducted both through the ODIHR and the CPC. They have also decided to improve their capability to gather information and to monitor developments, as well as their ability to implement decisions about further steps. They have recommitted themselves to co-operating constructively in using the full range of possibilities within the CSCE to prevent and resolve conflicts.

Early warning and preventive action

(3)   In order to have early warning of situations within the CSCE area which have the potential to develop into crises, including armed conflicts, the participating States will make intensive use of regular, in-depth political consultations, within the structures and institutions of the CSCE, including implementation review meetings.

(4)   The CSO, acting as the Council's agent, will have primary responsibility in this regard.

(5)   Without prejudice to the right of any State to raise any issue, the attention of the CSO may be drawn to such situations through the Chairman-in-Office, *inter alia*, by:

— any State directly involved in a dispute;
— a group of 11 States not directly involved in the dispute;
— the High Commissioner on National Minorities in situations he/she deems escalating into a conflict or exceeding the scope of his/her action;
— the Consultative Committee of the CPC in accordance with paragraph 33 of the Prague Document;
— the Consultative Committee of the CPC following the use of the mechanism for consultations and co-operation as regards unusual military activities;
— the use of the Human Dimension Mechanism or the Valletta Principles for Dispute Settlement and Provisions for a CSCE Procedure for Peaceful Settlement of Disputes.

Political management of crisis

(6) The CSO will promote steps by the State or States concerned to avoid any action which could aggravate the situation and, if appropriate, recommend other procedures and mechanisms to resolve the dispute peacefully.

(7) In order to facilitate its consideration of the situation, it may seek independent advice and counsel from relevant experts, institutions and international organizations.

(8) If the CSO concludes that concerted CSCE action is required, it will determine the procedure to be employed in the light of the nature of the situation. It will have, acting on behalf of the Council, overall CSCE responsibility for managing the crisis with a view to its resolution. It may, *inter alia*, decide to set up a framework for a negotiated settlement, or to dispatch a rapporteur or fact-finding mission. The CSO may also initiate or promote the exercise of good offices, mediation or conciliation.

(9) In this context the CSO may delegate tasks to:
— the Chairman-in-Office, who may designate a personal representative to carry out certain tasks, as defined in paragraph (22) of Chapter I of this document;
— the Chairman-in-Office, assisted by the preceding and succeeding Chairmen-in-Office operating together as a Troika, as defined in paragraph (15) of Chapter I of this document;
— an *ad hoc* steering group of participating States, as defined in paragraphs (16) to (21) of Chapter I of this document;
— the Consultative Committee of the CPC, or other CSCE institutions.

(10) Once the CSO has determined the procedure to be applied, it will establish a precise mandate for action, including provisions for reporting back within an agreed period. Within the limits of that mandate, those to whom the CSO has delegated tasks under the preceding paragraph will retain the freedom to determine how to proceed, with whom to consult, and the nature of any recommendations to be made.

(11) All participating States concerned in the situation will fully co-operate with the CSO and the agents it has designated.

Instruments of conflict prevention and crisis management

Fact-finding and rapporteur missions

(12) Fact-finding and rapporteur missions can be used as an instrument of conflict prevention and crisis management.

(13) Without prejudice to the provisions of paragraph 13 of the Moscow Document in respect of Human Dimension issues, and paragraph 29 of the Prague Document in respect of Unusual Military Activities, the CSO or the Consultative Committee of the CPC may decide, by consensus, to establish such missions. Such decisions will in every case contain a clear mandate.

(14) The participating State(s) will co-operate fully with the mission on its territory in pursuance of the mandate and facilitate its work.

(15) Reports of fact-finding and rapporteur missions will be submitted for discussion to the CSO or the Consultative Committee of the CPC as applicable. Such reports and any observations submitted by the State(s) visited will remain confidential until they are discussed. The reports will normally be made public. If, however, the mission or the participating State(s) visited request that they should be kept confidential, they will not be made public, unless otherwise decided by the participating States.

(16) Except where provided on a voluntary basis, the expenses of fact-finding and rapporteur missions will be borne by all participating States in accordance with the scale of distribution.

CSCE peacekeeping

(17) Peacekeeping constitutes an important operational element of the overall capability of the CSCE for conflict prevention and crisis management intended to complement the political process of dispute resolution. CSCE peacekeeping activities may be undertaken in cases of conflict within or among participating States to help maintain peace and stability in support of an ongoing effort at a political solution.

(18) A CSCE peacekeeping operation, according to its mandate, will involve civilian and/or military personnel, may range from small-scale to large-scale, and may assume a variety of forms including observer and monitor missions and larger deployments of forces. Peacekeeping activities could be used, inter alia, to supervise and help maintain cease-fires, to monitor troop withdrawals, to support the maintenance of law and order, to provide humanitarian and medical aid and to assist refugees.

(19) CSCE peacekeeping will be undertaken with due regard to the responsibilities of the United Nations in this field and will at all times be carried out in conformity with the Purposes and Principles of the Charter of the United Nations. CSCE peacekeeping will take place in particular within the framework of Chapter VIII of the Charter of the United Nations. The CSCE, in planning and carrying out peacekeeping operations, may draw upon the experience and expertise of the United Nations.

(20) The Chairman-in-Office will keep the United Nations Security Council fully informed of CSCE peacekeeping activities.

(21) The Council, or the CSO acting as its agent, may conclude because of the specific character of an operation and its envisaged size that the matter should be referred by the participating States to the United Nations Security Council.

(22) CSCE peacekeeping operations will not entail enforcement action.

(23) Peacekeeping operations require the consent of the parties directly concerned.

(24) Peacekeeping operations will be conducted impartially.

(25) Peacekeeping operations cannot be considered a substitute for a negotiated settlement and therefore must be understood to be limited in time.

(26) Requests to initiate peacekeeping operations by the CSCE may be addressed by one or more participating States to the CSO through the Chairman-in-Office.

(27) The CSO may request the Consultative Committee of the CPC to consider which peacekeeping activities might be most appropriate to the situation and to submit its recommendations to the CSO for decision.

(28) The CSO will exercise overall political control and guidance of a peacekeeping operation.

(29) Decisions to initiate and dispatch peacekeeping operations will be taken by consensus by the Council or the CSO acting as its agent.

(30) The Council/CSO will only take such decisions when all parties concerned have demonstrated their commitment to creating favourable conditions for the execution of the operation, inter alia, through a process of peaceful settlement and their willingness to co-operate. Before the decision to dispatch a mission is taken, the following conditions must be fulfilled:

— establishment of an effective and durable cease-fire;

— agreement on the necessary Memoranda of Understanding with the parties concerned, and

— provision of guarantees for the safety at all times of personnel involved.

(31) Missions will be dispatched as soon as possible following such a decision.

(32) Decisions by the CSO to establish a peacekeeping operation will include the adoption of a clear and precise mandate.

(33) When establishing a mission, the CSO will take into account the financial implications involved.

(34) The terms of reference of a peacekeeping operation will define practical modalities and determine requirements for personnel and other resources. Preparation of the terms of reference will be carried out, as appropriate, by the Consultative Committee of the CPC. They will be adopted by the CSO unless it has agreed otherwise.

(35) All participating States are eligible to take part in CSCE peacekeeping operations. Appropriate consultations by the Chairman-in-Office will take place. Participating States will be invited by the Chairman-in-Office of the CSO to contribute, on an individual basis, to an operation case by case.

(36) Personnel will be provided by individual participating States.

(37) Parties concerned will be consulted about which participating States will contribute personnel to the operation.

(38) The Council/CSO will regularly review an operation and make any necessary decision related to its conduct, taking into account political developments and developments in the field.

Chain of command

(39) The Council/CSO will assign overall operational guidance of an operation to the Chairman-in-Office assisted by an *ad hoc* group established at the CPC. The Chairman-in-Office will chair the *ad hoc* group and, in this capacity, be accountable to it, and will receive, on behalf of the *ad hoc* group, the reports of the Head of Mission. The *ad hoc* group will, as a rule, consist of representatives of the preceding and succeeding Chairmen-in-Office, of the participating States providing personnel for the mission and of participating States making other significant practical contributions to the operation.

(40) The *ad hoc* group will provide overall operational support for the mission and will monitor it. It will act as a 24-hour point of contact for the Head of Mission and assist the Head of Mission as required.

(41) Continuous liaison between the operation and all participating States will be ensured by the Consultative Committee of the CPC through the regular provision of information to it by the *ad hoc* group.

(42) In all cases where the CSO assigns tasks related to peacekeeping to the CPC, the Consultative Committee of the CPC will be responsible to the CSO for the execution of those tasks.

Head of Mission

(43) The Chairman-in-Office, after appropriate consultations, will nominate a Head of Mission for endorsement by the CSO.

(44) The Head of Mission will be responsible to the Chairman-in-Office. The Head of Mission will consult and be guided by the *ad hoc* group.

(45) The Head of Mission will have operational command in the mission area.

Financial arrangements

(46) Peacekeeping operations require a sound financial basis and must be planned with maximum efficiency and cost-effectiveness on the basis of clear cost projections.

(47)   Costs of CSCE peacekeeping activities will be borne by all CSCE participating States. At the beginning of each calendar year, the CSO will establish a reasonable ceiling for the cost of peacekeeping operations to which the CSCE scale of distribution will be applied. Beyond that limit, other special arrangements will be negotiated and agreed to by consensus. Full and timely payments will be required.

(48)   Additional contributions could be provided by participating States on a voluntary basis.

(49)   Financial accountability will be ensured by the Chairman-in-Office through regular reports to the participating States.

(50)   A start-up fund will, if appropriate, be established to cover the initial costs of an operation. Contributions by a participating State to the start-up fund will be deducted from that State's regular assessed share of the costs relating to the operation.

(51)   The Consultative Committee of the CPC is charged to submit to the CSO by the end of 1992 a recommendation with regard to financial modalities of CSCE peacekeeping operations, specifying, *inter alia*, the costs to be shared among participating States in accordance with the preceding paragraphs.

Co-operation with regional and transatlantic organizations

(52)   The CSCE may benefit from resources and possible experience and expertise of existing organizations such as the EC, NATO and the WEU, and could therefore request them to make their resources available in order to support it in carrying out peacekeeping activities. Other institutions and mechanisms, including the peacekeeping mechanism of the Commonwealth of Independent States (CIS), may also be asked by the CSCE to support peacekeeping in the CSCE region.

(53)   Decisions by the CSCE to seek the support of any such organization will be made on a case-by-case basis, having allowed for prior consultations with the participating States which belong to the organization concerned. The CSCE participating States will also take into account the consultations by the Chairman-in-Office regarding prospective participation in the mission, in light of the envisaged size of the operation and the specific character of the conflict.

(54)   Contributions by such organizations will not affect the procedures for the establishment, conduct and command of CSCE peacekeeping operations as set out in paragraphs (17) to (51) above, nor does the involvement of any such organization affect the principle that all participating States are eligible to take part in CSCE peacekeeping operations as set out in paragraph (35) above.

(55)   Organizations contributing to CSCE peacekeeping would carry out defined and mutually agreed tasks in connection with the practical implementation of a CSCE mandate.

(56)   The *ad hoc* group will establish and maintain effective communication with any organization whose resources may be drawn upon in connection with CSCE peacekeeping activities.

Peaceful settlement of disputes

(57)   The participating States consider their commitment to settle disputes among themselves by peaceful means to form a cornerstone of the CSCE process. In their view, the peaceful settlement of disputes is an essential component of the CSCE's overall ability to manage change effectively and to contribute to the maintenance of international peace and security.

(58)   The participating States welcome the work done to this end by the Helsinki Follow-up Meeting. In particular they were encouraged by significant progress made on issues relating to creating a conciliation and arbitration court within the CSCE, enhancing the Valletta mechanism and establishing a CSCE procedure for conciliation including directed conciliation, for which proposals were submitted.

(59)   In the light of the important subject matter and of the discussions held here in Helsinki, they have decided to continue to develop a comprehensive set of measures to expand the options available within the CSCE to assist States to resolve their disputes peacefully.

(60)   In this respect, the Council of Ministers and the CSO could play an important role, in particular by encouraging wider use of conciliation.

(61)   Accordingly, intending to reach early results, they have decided to convene a CSCE meeting in Geneva, with a first round from 12 to 23 October 1992, to negotiate a comprehensive and coherent set of measures as mentioned above. They will take into account the ideas expressed regarding procedures for a compulsory element in conciliation, setting up of a court of conciliation and arbitration within the CSCE, and other means.

(62)   The results of the meeting will be submitted to the Council of Ministers at the Stockholm Meeting on 14 and 15 December 1992 for approval and, as appropriate, opening for signature.

IV
RELATIONS WITH INTERNATIONAL ORGANIZATIONS, RELATIONS WITH NON-PARTICIPATING STATES, ROLE OF NON-GOVERNMENTAL ORGANIZATIONS (NGOs)

(1)   The new tasks before the CSCE require clearer relations and closer contacts with international organizations, in particular with the United Nations, and non-participating States. The CSCE remains at the same time a process whose activities go far beyond formal relations among governments to involve citizens and societies of the participating States. Successful efforts to build a lasting peaceful and democratic order and to manage the process of change require more structured and substantive input from groups, individuals, States and organizations outside the CSCE process. To this end, the participating States have decided as follows:

Relations with international organizations

(2)   The participating States, reaffirming their commitments to the Charter of the United Nations as subscribed to by them, declare their understanding that the CSCE is a regional arrangement in the sense of Chapter VIII of the Charter of the United Nations and as such provides an important link between European and global security. The rights and responsibilities of the United Nations Security Council remain unaffected in their entirety.

(3)   Recalling the relevant decisions of the Prague Document, the participating States will improve contact and practical co-operation with appropriate international organizations.

(4)   They may accordingly agree to invite presentations by those international organizations and institutions mentioned in the Prague Document and others, as appropriate.

(5)   Those organizations, institutions and others as agreed may be invited to attend CSCE meetings and seminars as guests of honour with appropriate name-plates.

(6)   They will make full use of the information exchange under paragraph 44 of the Prague Document.

Relations with non-participating Mediterranean States

(7)   Recalling the provisions of the Final Act and other CSCE relevant documents and consistent with established practice, the non-participating Mediterranean States will continue to be invited to contribute to CSCE activities.

(8)   Measures to widen the scope of co-operation with non-participating Mediterranean States are set forth in Chapter X.

Relations with non-participating States

(9)   In accordance with paragraph 45 of the Prague Document, the participating States intend to deepen their co-operation and develop a substantial relationship with non-participating States, such as Japan, which display an interest in the CSCE, share its principles and objectives, and are actively engaged in European co-operation through relevant organizations.

(10)   To this end, Japan will be invited to attend CSCE meetings, including those of Heads of State and Government, the CSCE Council, the Committee of Senior Officials and other appropriate CSCE bodies which consider specific topics of expanded consultation and co-operation.

(11)   Representatives of Japan may contribute to such meetings, without participating in the preparation and adoption of decisions, on subjects in which Japan has a direct interest and/or wishes to co-operate actively with the CSCE.

Increasing openness of CSCE activities, promoting understanding of the CSCE,
expanding the role of NGOs

(12)   The participating States will increase the openness of the CSCE institutions and structures and ensure wide dissemination of information on the CSCE.

(13)   To this end:

— the Chairman-in-Office assisted by the CSCE Secretariat will arrange briefings on the political consultation process;

— the CSCE institutions will, within existing budgets, provide information to the public and organize public briefings on their activities;

— the Secretariat will facilitate the flow of information to and contacts with the media, bearing in mind that CSCE policy issues remain the responsibility of participating States.

(14)   The participating States will provide opportunities for the increased involvement of non-governmental organizations in CSCE activities.

(15)   They will, accordingly:

— apply to all CSCE meetings the guidelines previously agreed for NGO access to certain CSCE meetings;

— make open to NGOs all plenary meetings of review conferences, ODIHR seminars, workshops and meetings, the CSO when meeting as the Economic Forum, and human rights implementation meetings, as well as other expert meetings. In addition each meeting may decide to open some other sessions to attendance by NGOs;

— instruct Directors of CSCE institutions and Executive Secretaries of CSCE meetings to designate an 'NGO liaison person' from among their staff;

— designate, as appropriate, one member of their Foreign Ministries and a member of their delegations to CSCE meetings to be responsible for NGO liaison;

— promote contacts and exchanges of views between NGOs and relevant national authorities and governmental institutions between CSCE meetings;

— facilitate during CSCE meetings informal discussion meetings between representatives of participating States and of NGOs;

— encourage written presentations by NGOs to CSCE institutions and meetings, titles of which may be kept and provided to the participating States upon request;

— provide encouragement to NGOs organizing seminars on CSCE-related issues;

— notify NGOs through the CSCE institutions of the dates of future CSCE meetings, together with an indication, when possible, of the subjects to be addressed, as well as, upon request, the activations of CSCE mechanisms which have been made known to all participating States.

(16)	The above provisions will not be applied to persons or organizations which resort to the use of violence or publicly condone terrorism or the use of violence.
(17)	The participating States will use all appropriate means to disseminate as widely as possible within their societies knowledge of the CSCE, its principles, commitments and activities.
(18)	The concept of a CSCE Prize will be considered.

V
CSCE FORUM FOR SECURITY CO-OPERATION

The participating States of the Conference on Security and Co-operation in Europe,
(1)	Reaffirming their commitments undertaken in the Charter of Paris for a New Europe and, in particular, their determination to establish new negotiations on disarmament and confidence- and security-building open to all participating States,
(2)	Encouraged by the opportunities for new co-operative approaches to strengthening security offered by the historic changes and by the process of consolidation of democracy in the CSCE community of States,
(3)	Welcoming the adoption of the Vienna Document 1992 on Confidence- and Security-building Measures, the conclusion of the Treaty on Open Skies and the adoption of the CSCE Declaration on the Treaty on Open Skies and the Concluding Act of the Negotiation on Personnel Strength of Conventional Armed Forces in Europe as well as the imminent entry into force of the Treaty on Conventional Armed Forces in Europe (CFE),
(4)	Determined to build upon those important achievements and to give a new impetus to arms control, disarmament and confidence- and security-building, security co-operation and conflict prevention in order to better contribute to the strengthening of security and stability and the establishment of a just and lasting peace within the CSCE community of States,
(5)	Underlining the equality of rights and the equal respect for the security interests of all CSCE participating States,
(6)	Reaffirming their right to choose their own security arrangements,
(7)	Recognizing that security is indivisible and that the security of every participating State is inseparably linked to that of all others,
(8)	Have decided
—	to start a new negotiation on arms control, disarmament and confidence- and security-building,
—	to enhance regular consultation and to intensify co-operation among them on matters related to security, and
—	to further the process of reducing the risk of conflict.
(9)	To carry out these tasks the participating States have decided to establish a new CSCE Forum for Security Co-operation, with a strengthened Conflict Prevention Centre, as an integral part of the CSCE.
(10)	The participating States will ensure that their efforts in the Forum towards arms control, disarmament and confidence- and security-building, security co-operation and conflict prevention are coherent, interrelated and complementary.

Objectives

(11)	The participating States will strengthen security and stability through the negotiation of concrete measures aimed at keeping or achieving the levels of armed forces to a minimum commensurate with common or individual legitimate security needs within Europe and beyond. These new measures may entail reductions of and limitations on conventional armed forces and may, as appropriate, include measures of a regional character.

(12)   They will address the question of the harmonization of obligations agreed among participating States under the various existing instruments concerning arms control, disarmament and confidence- and security-building.

(13)   They will develop the Vienna Document 1992 on the basis of a review of its implementation.

(14)   They will negotiate new stabilizing measures in respect of military forces and new confidence- and security-building measures designed to ensure greater transparency in the military field. Such measures may be of a regional character and/or may apply in relation to certain border areas.

(15)   The participating States will aim at establishing among themselves new security relations based upon co-operative and common approaches to security. To this end, they will develop consultation, goal-oriented continuing dialogue and co-operation in the field of security.

(16)   They will promote increased predictability about their military plans, programmes and capabilities, including the introduction of major new weapons systems.

(17)   They will support and enhance regimes on non-proliferation and arms transfers.

(18)   They will enhance contacts, liaison, exchanges and co-operation between their armed forces.

(19)   They will promote consultation and co-operation in respect of challenges to their security from outside their territories.

(20)   They will also consider other measures to foster security among the participating States in order to contribute to a just and lasting peace among them, including the possibility of further strengthening the norms of behaviour among them through the elaboration of additional security instruments.

(21)   They will make every effort to prevent conflict and give full effect to relevant provisions.

(22)   They will further enhance the capability of the CPC to reduce the risks of such conflicts through relevant conflict prevention techniques.

(23)   They will foster their co-operation in the field of the implementation and verification of existing and future arms control, disarmament and confidence- and security-building agreements.

(24)   The negotiations on new measures of arms control, disarmament and confidence- and security-building will proceed in distinct phases, taking into account progress made in the implementation of existing arms control agreements. They will also take into consideration ongoing reduction, restructuring and redeployment processes regarding armed forces as well as further relevant political and military developments. Such new measures will build upon the achievements of existing agreements and will be effective, concrete and militarily significant.

(25)   All measures negotiated in the Forum will be developed in a way which precludes circumvention.

Programme for immediate action

(26)   A Programme for Immediate Action is set out in the Annex. It can be amended, supplemented or extended by consensus. It will be reviewed, together with the progress and results obtained, at the review conference preceding the next meeting of CSCE Heads of State or Government.

(27)   Additional proposals can be tabled and discussed at any time.

Area of application

(28)   Each measure to be negotiated in the Forum will have an area of application according to its nature. The areas of application for negotiations under the Programme for Immediate Action are set out therein in relation to its relevant elements.

This is without prejudice to subsequent negotiations on arms control, disarmament and confidence- and security-building or security co-operation in the Forum. Consideration of decisions concerning the area of application will take into account existing agreements and the need for greater transparency.

Constitution and organization of the Forum

(29)   The arrangements for the Forum will be as follows:

(30)   *The Special Committee* meeting either:

(a)   for negotiations on arms control, disarmament and confidence- and security-building, or

(b)   for consideration of, goal-oriented dialogue on and, as appropriate, elaboration or negotiation of proposals for security enhancement and co-operation.

(31)   *The Consultative Committee* in respect of the existing and future tasks of the CPC.

(32)   In order to ensure coherence the representation of the participating States on the Special Committee and the Consultative Committee will in principle be assured by the same delegation. Appropriate meetings will be held as necessary for organizational purposes.

Procedures

(33)   The Forum will, unless otherwise agreed below, work according to the CSCE procedures.

1. The Special Committee

(34)   The Special Committee may establish under its authority subsidiary working bodies open to all participating States. They will work on an *ad referendum* basis and report regularly to the Special Committee. Any question under consideration by such subsidiary working bodies may at any time be raised before the Special Committee.

(35)   Consideration and negotiation of regional measures undertaken within the CSCE framework will form an integral part of the activity of the Forum.

(36)   They will be dealt with in open-ended working groups established by the Special Committee.

(37)   Alternatively, the Special Committee may decide, on the initiative of a limited number of participating States, and on the basis of information provided by them on the nature and the scope of the measures envisaged, that these States form a working group in order to consider, negotiate or develop among themselves certain regional measures. Such working groups will on a regular basis provide appropriate information on their activities to the Special Committee and will submit to it the results.

(38)   Any question under consideration by such working groups may at any time be raised before the Special Committee.

(39)   This is without prejudice to the right of States to consider, negotiate or develop measures among themselves outside the framework of the CSCE. In such cases they are invited to inform the Forum about progress and results of their work.

2. The Consultative Committee

(40)   The procedures of the Consultative Committee will be based on the relevant decisions of the CSCE Council.

Form of commitments

(41)   The results of the negotiations of the Forum will be expressed in international commitments. The nature of obligations will be determined by the character of the measures agreed. They will enter into force in the forms and according to the procedures to be agreed by the negotiators.

Verification

(42)   Measures will, if appropriate, be provided with suitable forms of verification according to their nature.

Conference services

(43)   Common conference services for the Special Committee and the Consultative Committee as well as for all their subsidiary bodies (including seminars) will be provided by an Executive Secretary to be nominated by the host country. The Executive Secretary may also, if so decided by those concerned, provide conference services for meetings of the CFE Joint Consultative Group and the Open Skies Consultative Commission. The Executive Secretary will assume full responsibility for the organization of all the relevant meetings as well as for all related administrative and budgeting arrangements, for which he will be accountable to the participating States according to procedures to be agreed.

(44)   The Special Committee and the Consultative Committee will use the same premises.

(45)   The new CSCE Forum for Security Co-operation shall commence in Vienna on 22 September 1992.

Programme for immediate action

(46)   The participating States have decided to give early attention to the following:

A.   ARMS CONTROL, DISARMAMENT AND CONFIDENCE- AND
SECURITY-BUILDING

Measures to be negotiated under paragraphs 1–3 will apply to the territory of the participating States in Europe or in Asia as defined below in relation to the area of application of each measure. Measures to be negotiated under paragraphs 4 and 5 will apply to the conventional armed forces and facilities of the participating States both on the territory of all the participating States and beyond. Measures to be negotiated under paragraph 6 will apply to the territory or part thereof of the participating States involved in the measures. Exceptions to these rules on the area of application may be agreed by consensus.

1.   Harmonization of obligations concerning arms control, disarmanent and confidence- and security-building
An appropriate harmonization of the obligations of participating States under existing international instruments applicable to conventional armed forces in Europe, in particular of those concerning the exchange of information, verification and force levels. The harmonization of obligations concerning arms control, disarmament and confidence- and security-building will apply to the areas of application in respect of which the obligations have been undertaken.

2.   Development of the Vienna Document 1992
Improvement and further development of confidence- and security-building measures contained in this document. The area of application will be as set out in the Vienna Document 1992.

3.   The further enhancement of stability and confidence
The negotiation of new stabilizing measures and confidence-building measures related to conventional armed forces, including, with due regard to the specific characteristics of the armed forces of individual participating States, measures to address force generation capabilities of active and non-active forces. These measures may be of a constraining kind. They will apply within the area of application set out in the Vienna Document 1992. This is without prejudice to the possibility that participating States

may, if they so choose, decide to offer certain assurances in respect of their conventional armed forces in parts of their territory adjacent to this area of application if they consider such forces relevant to the security of other CSCE participating States.

4. Global exchange of military information
The negotiation of further transparency by means of a global annual appropriately aggregated or disaggregated exchange of information encompassing armaments and equipment, including information on armaments and equipment categories limited by the CFE Treaty, and personnel in the conventional armed forces of the participating States. The regime will also include information on the production of military equipment. The regime will be separate from other information exchange regimes and, because of its special nature, will not involve limitations, constraints or verification.

5. Co-operation in respect of non-proliferation
Co-operation in respect of the strengthening of multilateral non-proliferation regimes, including the transfer of sensitive expertise, and the establishment of a responsible approach to international armaments transfers.

6. Regional measures
The negotiation by the participating States of suitable measures, including, where appropriate, reductions or limitations in accordance with the objectives set out above, for example in relation to certain regions or border areas. The area of application will be the territory or part thereof of the participating States' territories involved in a regional measure.

B. SECURITY ENHANCEMENT AND CO-OPERATION

Proposals for and dialogue on measures and activities under paragraphs 7–12 will apply to all participating States, unless otherwise agreed or specified below.

7. Force planning
The elaboration of provisions to provide transparency about each CSCE participating State's intentions in the medium to long term as regards the size, structure, training and equipment of its armed forces, as well as defence policy, doctrines and budgets related thereto. Such a system should be based on each participating State's national practice, and should provide the background for a dialogue among the participating States.

8. Co-operation in defence conversion
The development of a programme of exchanges, co-operation and the sharing of expertise in the field of defence conversion throughout all the territory of the participating States.

9. Co-operation in respect of non-proliferation
Co-operation in respect of the strengthening of multilateral non-proliferation regimes, including the transfer of sensitive expertise, and the establishment of a responsible approach to international armaments transfers.

10. Development of provisions on military co-operation and contacts
The development of a programme of military contacts, liaison arrangements, co-operation and exchanges, particularly in the fields of the training and organization of armed forces. Participation in this programme will be open to all CSCE participating States in respect of all their armed forces and territory.

11. Regional security issues
Discussion and clarification of regional security issues or specific security problems for example in relation to border areas.

12. Security enhancement consultations

Goal-oriented dialogue and consultations aimed at enhancing security co-operation, including through the further encouragement of responsible and co-operative norms of behaviour on politico-military aspects of security. The participating States will undertake consultations with a view to strengthening the role of the CSCE, by establishing a code of conduct governing their mutual relations in the field of security.

Conflict prevention

Consistent with and further to the decisions taken in Paris, Prague and Helsinki about the tasks of the CPC, the following parts of this work programme will be undertaken in the CPC:

13. Relevant techniques

Without prejudice to other tasks of the CPC or to the competence of the Committee of Senior Officials in the field of conflict prevention and crisis management, the Consultative Committee will, particularly in the light of experience gained in the execution of its own tasks, maintain under consideration the need for improvements in relevant techniques.

14. Co-operation in the field of verification

The encouragement of practical co-operation, through training, exchanges and participation in evaluation and inspection teams, in the implementation of the verification provisions of arms control, disarmament and confidence- and security-building agreements among CSCE participants who are parties to such agreements. The area of application will correspond to that of the relevant agreements.

VI
THE HUMAN DIMENSION

(1) The participating States conducted a useful review of implementation of CSCE commitments in the Human Dimension. They based their discussion on the new community of values established among them, as set forth by the Charter of Paris for a New Europe and developed by the new standards created within the CSCE in recent years. They noted major progress in complying with Human Dimension commitments, but recognized developments of serious concern and thus the need for further improvement.

(2) The participating States express their strong determination to ensure full respect for human rights and fundamental freedoms, to abide by the rule of law, to promote the principles of democracy and, in this regard, to build, strengthen and protect democratic institutions, as well as to promote tolerance throughout society. To these ends, they will broaden the operational framework of the CSCE, including by further enhancing the ODIHR, so that information, ideas, and concerns can be exchanged in a more concrete and meaningful way, including as an early warning of tension and potential conflict. In doing so, they will focus their attention on topics in the Human Dimension of particular importance. They will therefore keep the strengthening of the Human Dimension under constant consideration, especially in a time of change.

(3) In this regard, the participating States adopt the following:

Framework for monitoring compliance with CSCE commitments and for promoting co-operation in the Human Dimension

(4) In order to strengthen and monitor compliance with CSCE commitments as well as to promote progress in the Human Dimension, the participating States agree to enhance the framework of their co-operation and to this end decide the following:

Enhanced role of the ODIHR
(5)   Under the general guidance of the CSO and in addition to its existing tasks as set out in the Charter of Paris for a New Europe and in the Prague Document on Further Development of CSCE Institutions and Structures, the ODIHR will, as the main institution of the Human Dimension:
(5a)   assist the monitoring of implementation of commitments in the Human Dimension by:
—   serving as a venue for bilateral meetings under paragraph 2 and as a channel for information under paragraph 3 of the Human Dimension Mechanism as set out in the Vienna Concluding Document;
—   receiving any comments from States visited by CSCE missions of relevance to the Human Dimension other than those under the Human Dimension Mechanism; it will transmit the report of those missions as well as eventual comments to all participating States with a view to discussion at the next implementation meeting or review conference;
—   participating in or undertaking missions when instructed by the Council or the CSO;
(5b)   act as a clearing-house for information on:
—   a state of public emergency according to paragraph 28.10 of the Document of the Moscow Meeting of the Conference on the Human Dimension;
—   resource lists, and assistance, e.g. in the field of censuses or on democracy at a local and regional level, and the holding of national seminars on such issues;
(5c)   assist other activities in the field of the Human Dimension, including the building of democratic institutions by:
—   fulfilling the tasks as defined in the 'Programme of co-ordinated support to recently admitted participating States';
—   arranging 'Seminars on the democratic process' at the request of participating States. The same procedural provisions as set out in the 'Programme of co-ordinated support for recently admitted participating States' will also apply to these seminars;
—   contributing, within the resources at its disposal, to the preparation of seminars at the request of one or more participating States;
—   providing, as appropriate, facilities to the High Commissioner on National Minorities;
—   communicating, as appropriate, with relevant international and non-governmental organizations;
—   consulting and co-operating with relevant bodies of the Council of Europe and those associated with it, and examining how they can contribute, as appropriate, to the ODIHR's activities. The ODIHR will also, at the request of participating States, supply them with information about programmes within the framework of the Council of Europe which are open to all participating States.
(6)   The activities on Human Dimension issues undertaken by the ODIHR may, *inter alia*, contribute to early warning in the prevention of conflicts.

Human Dimension Mechanism
(7)   In order to align the Human Dimension Mechanism with present CSCE structures and institutions the participating States decide that:
Any participating State which deems it necessary may provide information on situations and cases which have been the subject of requests under paragraphs 1 or 2 of the chapter entitled the 'Human Dimension of the CSCE' of the Vienna Concluding Document or on the results of those procedures, to the participating States through the ODIHR—which can equally serve as a venue for bilateral meetings under paragraph 2 — or diplomatic channels. Such information may be

discussed at meetings of the CSO, at implementation meetings on Human Dimension issues and review conferences.

(8)   Procedures concerning the covering of expenses of expert and rapporteur missions of the Human Dimension Mechanism may be considered by the next review conference in the light of experience gained.

Implementation

Implementation meetings on Human Dimension issues
(9)   Every year in which a review conference does not take place, the ODIHR will organize a three-weeks meeting at expert-level of all participating States at its seat to review implementation of CSCE Human Dimension commitments. The meeting will perform the following tasks:

(9a)   a thorough exchange of views on the implementation of Human Dimension commitments, including discussion on the information provided in accordance with paragraph 4 of the Human Dimension Mechanism and on the Human Dimension aspects of the reports of CSCE missions, as well as the consideration of ways and means of improving implementation;

(9b)   an evaluation of the procedures for monitoring compliance with commitments.

(10)   The implementation meeting may draw to the attention of the CSO measures to improve implementation which it deems necessary.

(11)   The implementation meeting will not produce a negotiated document.

(12)   Written contributions and information material will be of a non-restricted or restricted character as indicated by the submitting State.

(13)   Implementation meetings will be organized to meet in formal and informal sessions. All formal sessions will be open. In addition, the participating States may decide, on a case-by-case basis, to open informal sessions.

(14)   The Council of Europe, the European Commission for Democracy through Law and the European Bank for Reconstruction and Development (EBRD), as well as other relevant international organizations and institutions, will be encouraged by the implementation meeting to attend and make contributions.

(15)   Non-governmental organizations having relevant experience in the field of the Human Dimension are invited to make written presentations to the implementation meeting, e.g. through the ODIHR, and may be invited by the implementation meeting, on the basis of their written presentations, to address specific questions orally as appropriate.

(16)   During two half days in the course of the implementation meeting no formal session will be scheduled in order to provide better opportunities for possible contacts with NGOs. To this purpose, a hall at the meeting site will be placed at the disposal of NGOs.

CSCE Human Dimension seminars
(17)   Under the general guidance of the CSO, the ODIHR will organize CSCE Human Dimension seminars which will address specific questions of particular relevance to the Human Dimension and of current political concern. The CSO will establish an annual work programme including the titles and dates of such seminars. The agenda and modalities of each seminar will be approved by the CSO at the latest three months before the seminar. In doing so, the CSO will take into account views expressed by the ODIHR. Unless otherwise decided, seminars will be held at the seat of the ODIHR and will not exceed one week. The work programme will take into account work by relevant international organizations and institutions.

(18)   These seminars will be organized in an open and flexible manner. Relevant international organizations and institutions may be invited to attend and to make

contributions. So may NGOs with relevant experience. Independent experts attending the seminar as members of national delegations will also be free to speak in their own capacity.

(19) CSCE seminars will be organized to meet in formal and informal sessions. All formal sessions will be open. In addition, the participating States may decide, on a case-by-case basis, to open informal sessions.

(20) CSCE seminars will not produce a negotiated document or follow-up programmes.

(21) Contributions by independent experts will be of a non-restricted character.

(22) In order to launch the new CSCE Human Dimension Seminars without delay, the participating States decide now at the Helsinki Follow-up Meeting that the ODIHR will organize the following four seminars:

— Migration
— Case Studies on National Minorities Issues: Positive Results
— Tolerance
— Free Media

These seminars will be held before 31 December 1993. The agenda and modalities of the seminars will be decided by the CSO. Seminars on migrant workers and on local democracy will be included in the first annual work programme of seminars. The financial implications of the seminar programme will be kept under consideration by the CSO.

Enhanced commitments and co-operation in the Human Dimension

National minorities
The participating States:

(23) Reaffirm in the strongest terms their determination to implement in a prompt and faithful manner all their CSCE commitments, including those contained in the Vienna Concluding Document, the Copenhagen Document and the Geneva Report, regarding questions relating to national minorities and rights of persons belonging to them;

(24) Will intensify in this context their efforts to ensure the free exercise by persons belonging to national minorities, individually or in community with others, of their human rights and fundamental freedoms, including the right to participate fully, in accordance with the democratic decision-making procedures of each State, in the political, economic, social and cultural life of their countries including through democratic participation in decision-making and consultative bodies at the national, regional and local level, *inter alia*, through political parties and associations;

(25) Will continue through unilateral, bilateral and multilateral efforts to explore further avenues for more effective implementation of their relevant CSCE commitments, including those related to the protection and the creation of conditions for the promotion of the ethnic, cultural, linguistic and religious identity of national minorities;

(26) Will address national minority issues in a constructive manner, by peaceful means and through dialogue among all parties concerned on the basis of CSCE principles and commitments;

(27) Will refrain from resettling and condemn all attempts, by the threat or use of force, to resettle persons with the aim of changing the ethnic composition of areas within their territories;

(28) Direct the ODIHR to organize, in spring 1993, a CSCE Human Dimension Seminar on Case Studies on National Minorities Issues: Positive Results.

Indigenous populations
The participating States:

(29)   Noting that persons belonging to indigenous populations may have special problems in exercising their rights, agree that their CSCE commitments regarding human rights and fundamental freedoms apply fully and without discrimination to such persons.

Tolerance and non-discrimination
The participating States:
(30)   Express their concern over recent and flagrant manifestations of intolerance, discrimination, aggressive nationalism, xenophobia, anti-semitism and racism and stress the vital role of tolerance, understanding and co-operation in the achievement and preservation of stable democratic societies;

(31)   Direct the ODIHR to organize, in autumn 1992, a CSCE Human Dimension Seminar on Tolerance;

(32)   Will consider adhering to the International Convention on the Elimination of All Forms of Racial Discrimination, if they have not already done so;

(33)   Will consider taking appropriate measures within their constitutional framework and in conformity with their international obligations to assure to everyone on their territory protection against discrimination on racial, ethnic and religious grounds, as well as to protect all individuals, including foreigners, against acts of violence, including on any of these grounds. Moreover, they will make full use of their domestic legal processes, including enforcement of existing laws in this regard;

(34)   Will consider developing programmes to create the conditions for promoting non-discrimination and cross-cultural understanding which will focus on human rights education, grass-roots action, cross-cultural training and research;

(35)   Reaffirm, in this context, the need to develop appropriate programmes addressing problems of their respective nationals belonging to Roma and other groups traditionally identified as Gypsies and to create conditions for them to have equal opportunities to participate fully in the life of society, and will consider how to co-operate to this end.

Migrant workers
The participating States:
(36)   Restate that human rights and fundamental freedoms are universal, that they are also enjoyed by migrant workers wherever they live and stress the importance of implementing all CSCE commitments on migrant workers and their families lawfully residing in the participating States;

(37)   Will encourage the creation of conditions to foster greater harmony in relations between migrant workers and the rest of the society of the participating State in which they lawfully reside. To this end, they will seek to offer, *inter alia*, measures to facilitate the familiarization of migrant workers and their families with the languages and social life of the respective participating State in which they lawfully reside so as to enable them to participate in the life of the society of the host country;

(38)   Will, in accordance with their domestic policies, laws and international obligations, seek, as appropriate, to create the conditions for promoting equality of opportunity in respect of working conditions, education, social security and health services, housing, access to trade unions as well as cultural rights for lawfully residing and working migrant workers.

Refugees and displaced persons
The participating States:
(39)   Express their concern over the problem of refugees and displaced persons;

(40)   Emphasize the importance of preventing situations that may result in mass flows of refugees and displaced persons and stress the need to identify and address the root causes of displacement and involuntary migration;

(41)   Recognize the need for international co-operation in dealing with mass flows of refugees and displaced persons;

(42)   Recognize that displacement is often a result of violations of CSCE commitments, including those relating to the Human Dimension;

(43)   Reaffirm the importance of existing international standards and instruments related to the protection of and assistance to refugees and will consider acceding to the Convention relating to the Status of Refugees and the Protocol, if they have not already done so;

(44)   Recognize the importance of the United Nations High Commissioner for Refugees and the International Committee of the Red Cross, as well as of non-governmental organizations involved in relief work, for the protection of and assistance to refugees and displaced persons;

(45)   Welcome and support unilateral, bilateral and multilateral efforts to ensure protection of and assistance to refugees and displaced persons with the aim of finding durable solutions;

(46)   Direct the ODIHR to organize, in early 1993, a CSCE Human Dimension Seminar on Migration, Including Refugees and Displaced Persons.

International humanitarian law
The participating States:

(47)   Recall that international humanitarian law is based upon the inherent dignity of the human person;

(48)   Will in all circumstances respect and ensure respect for international humanitarian law including the protection of the civilian population;

(49)   Recall that those who violate international humanitarian law are held personally accountable;

(50)   Acknowledge the essential role of the International Committee of the Red Cross in promoting the implementation and development of international humanitarian law, including the Geneva Conventions and their relevant Protocols;

(51)   Reaffirm their commitment to extend full support to the International Committee of the Red Cross, as well as to the Red Cross and Red Crescent Societies, and to the United Nations organizations, particularly in times of armed conflict, respect their protective emblems, prevent the misuse of these emblems and, as appropriate, exert all efforts to ensure access to the areas concerned;

(52)   Commit themselves to fulfilling their obligation to teach and disseminate information about their obligations under international humanitarian law.

Democracy at a local and regional level
The participating States:

(53)   Will endeavour, in order to strengthen democratic participation and institution building and in developing co-operation among them, to share their respective experience on the functioning of democracy at a local and regional level, and welcome against this background the Council of Europe information and education network in this field;

(54)   Will facilitate contacts and encourage various forms of co-operation between bodies at a local and regional level.

Nationality
The participating States:

(55)   Recognize that everyone has the right to a nationality and that no one should be deprived of his/her nationality arbitrarily;

(56)   Underline that all aspects of nationality will be governed by the process of law. They will, as appropriate, take measures, consistent with their constitutional framework, not to increase statelessness;

(57)   Will continue within the CSCE the discussion on these issues.

Capital punishment
The participating States:
(58) Confirm their commitments in the Copenhagen and Moscow Documents concerning the question of capital punishment.

Free media
The participating States:
(59) Direct the ODIHR to organize a CSCE Human Dimension Seminar on Free Media, to be held in 1993. The goal of the Seminar will be to encourage the discussion, demonstration, establishment of contacts and exchange of information between governmental representatives and media practitioners.

Education
The participating States:
(60) Would welcome, in view of the importance of education as to the dissemination of the ideas of democracy, human rights and democratic institutions, especially in a period of change, the organization to this end of a seminar entitled 'Education: Structures, Policies and Strategies' by the Council of Europe, open to all participating States.

Compilation of Human Dimension commitments
The participating States:
(61) Welcome the drawing up of compilations of existing CSCE Human Dimension commitments in order to promote greater understanding for the implementation of these commitments.

Domestic implementation guidelines
The participating States:
(62) Will promote, where appropriate, the drawing up of guidelines to assist the effective implementation of domestic legislation on human rights issues related to CSCE commitments.

VII
ECONOMIC CO-OPERATION

(1) The participating States will intensify co-operation among them in order to achieve sustainable economic development. They will continue to co-operate in supporting those participating States which are engaged in the transition process to market economies.

(2) The participating States welcome the fact that, in response to the Document of the Bonn Conference on Economic Co-operation and the Charter of Paris for a New Europe, the United Nations Economic Commission for Europe (ECE) has identified priority areas for its activities and considers the promotion of the process of reform in economies in transition important in the preparation of its work programme. They also welcome the establishment within OECD of the Centre for Co-operation with European Economies in Transition (CCEET), through which countries in transition have access to the expertise of that organization. They express their satisfaction that the EBRD is now in a position to provide substantial support for the restructuring and modernization of the economies in transition.

(3) The participating States invite these and other international economic and financial organizations to pursue their work, so as to facilitate the integration of the economies in transition into the international economic and financial system and to promote economic co-operation in the CSCE area. They call for increased co-ordination among them in order to ensure greater coherence and effectiveness of action and to avoid duplication.

(4) The participating States will work to ensure the further implementation of their existing commitments. They agree to give renewed impetus in particular in the

areas of human resources, industrial co-operation, trade, statistics, infrastructure, energy, defence conversion, agriculture, tourism and science and technology.

(5)   The participating States emphasize the need for continuing co-operation and investment in human resources development in order to cope with problems of transition to market economies, rapid technological changes and the evolution of society. Recognizing the importance of education and training, including management and vocational training at all levels, they will intensify their dialogue on education and training systems and promote further co-operation in this area.

(6)   The participating States will enhance opportunities for industrial co-operation by providing an appropriate legal and economic environment for business, particularly with the aim of strengthening the private sector and developing small and medium-sized enterprises. They will create favourable conditions for business by progressively reducing obstacles to trade, to freedom of establishment and to contacts among business communities. They will, if appropriate, improve legislation in particular with regard to customs, standardization, competition, property and intellectual property rights, banking, accounting and company law, capital movement and investment protection.

(7)   The participating States recognize that the maintenance of an open multilateral trading system based on General Agreement on Tariffs and Trade (GATT) rules is an essential element in stimulating economic development. They will intensify their efforts to help economies in transition through increased market access.

(8)   The participating States stress the importance of comprehensive, transparent and reliable statistics and commercial and administrative information as a basis for policy making and, in particular, for economic decision making, as well as for the efficient operation of a market economy. They will further improve the quality, timeliness and availability of this information. They recognize the valuable role of the ECE in this field, as well as the contribution by OECD of related fundamental analysis and information.

(9)   The participating States emphasize the importance of the development of infrastructure, especially in the transport and telecommunication sectors, for a successful transition period and a greater share in international trade.

(10)   In view of the impact of increasing transport activities on transport capacity, the environment and safety, they will co-operate in order to improve the efficiency and quality of transport by land, water and air. They will also co-operate in developing an efficient transport system within the CSCE area based on the principles of the market economy, safety and transparent and fully competitive conditions among operators and different modes of transport, with due consideration for the environment and social aspects. They stress the importance of further development and early completion of joint road and rail infrastructure projects, including those being undertaken by the ECE and United Nations Development Programme (UNDP).

(11)   Taking into account the impact on the environment, they will pay particular attention to the development of low-emission transport systems, notably rail, inland waterways and combined transport operations.

(12)   They will co-operate in creating an integrated telecommunications market, paying particular attention to the development of modern telecommunications infrastructure and related service capabilities, the establishment and expansion of telecommunications networks throughout the CSCE region, technical co-operation and the facilitation of the free flow of information.

(13)   The participating States fully support the further development of the European Energy Charter and stress the importance of completing work on and implementing the Basic Agreement and the protocols. They consider these documents of particular importance for the period of transition and, recognizing their mutual interests in this field, they will co-operate to take advantage of the available opportunities.

(14) They emphasize the need for further energy sector co-operation with the objective of improving the security of energy supply, maximizing the efficiency of the production, conversion, transport, distribution and use of energy, enhancing safety and minimizing environmental problems, on an acceptable economic basis. In this context they also recognize the importance of existing international programmes, such as Energy Efficiency 2000 under the auspices of the ECE. The participating States underline the need for close co-operation in related areas such as commercial development of and research into renewable energy sources, as well as the free movement of energy products.

(15) The participating States stress the social and economic importance of the conversion of military production to civilian purposes. They support co-operation in the conversion of military production with interested participating States on a bilateral level, as well as within the framework of international organizations.

(16) The participating States stress the importance of agricultural reforms carried out in certain economies in transition. They will expand co-operation in sharing agricultural production expertise, including issues of privatization, co-operation and training in the agricultural and food industries.

(17) In order to take advantage of the enhanced opportunities for tourism since the opening of borders, the participating States will co-operate in improving, *inter alia*, infrastructure, services and harmonization of definitions and indicators, while giving due consideration to the impact of tourism on the environment. They will enhance their co-operation in the field of training and education in this sector and encourage the exchange of know-how and relevant information and the setting up of joint operations.

(18) Reaffirming the essential role of science and technology in the process of sustainable economic and social development, the participating States will enhance their co-operation in this field giving priority to areas which are of direct concern to their populations and to their production systems. This will include areas such as environmental research, biomedicine and health research, nuclear safety, energy and raw material saving techniques, agro- and food-processing technologies as well as measurement and testing techniques in order to facilitate the progressive introduction of international standards and codes of good practice to support the development of trade.

(19) They will take steps towards a greater sharing, where appropriate, of scientific and technological information and knowledge to overcome the technological gap, and recognize that the transfer of technology and exchange of up-to-date know-how should be consistent with non-proliferation obligations and the protection of intellectual property rights.

(20) Recognizing the need to develop human resources in the field of science and technology, they welcome the opportunity for further collaboration within appropriate international organizations and in research programmes such as COST and EUREKA, as well as the recent establishment of the International Centre for Science and Technology with centres in the Russian Federation and Ukraine. They will work towards the development of scientific networks and joint research projects.

Economic Forum

Mandate

(21) The CSCE Ministers agreed at the Prague Council, Meeting (30 January 1992) to establish an Economic Forum within the framework of the CSO.

(22) The CSO will convene as the Economic Forum to give political stimulus to the dialogue on the transition to and development of free-market economies as an essential contribution to the building of democracy, to suggest practical efforts for the development of free-market systems and economic co-operation, and to encourage

activities already under way within organizations such as the Organisation for Economic Co-operation and Development (OECD), the European Investment Bank (EIB), the EBRD and the ECE.

Organization
(23)   The CSO will convene as the Economic Forum. The Economic Forum will thus be governed by the same arrangements as those applying to all regular CSO meetings.
(24)   The Forum can invite contributions to its work by those European and transatlantic organizations relevant to the subject under discussion.
(25)   The work of the Forum should be so structured as to avoid duplication of the work of international organizations and overcommitment of scarce resources.
(26)   The Economic Forum will meet on an annual basis as a rule. The meeting will last for two to three days, and the discussion will focus on two to three specific subjects.
(27)   The Economic Forum will consider topics and subjects that may require further study by experts. This will take the form of open-ended seminars on specific subjects during the course of the year. These meetings of experts may, with the agreement of the Forum, be organized and financed by one or more CSCE States and/or by international organizations, possibly in co-operation with private organizations.
(28)   These meetings of experts can bring together economic policy makers, parliamentary leaders and representatives of non-governmental organizations and the private sector in a positive dialogue on co-operation and the transition to market economies.
(29)   The Forum will welcome reports of meetings of expert groups and encourages their distribution to all CSCE States. However, these groups of experts will not produce documents with commitments binding on CSCE States.

Functions
(30)   The Economic Forum will permit the exchange of views and experiences concerning key issues of the transition process, as well as on the work of relevant international organizations.
(31)   The Economic Forum should serve as an important mechanism for reviewing the implementation of CSCE commitments in the areas of economics, the environment and science and technology. The Forum should disseminate information, help to identify structural problems and suggest practical efforts for the development of economic co-operation in these areas during the period of transition.
(32)   The political impulses which the Economic Forum is mandated to give to the discussion on the economic, environmental and science and technology aspects of the transition process will complement and support work in the international economic and environmental organizations that are addressing these problems at an operational level.

INDICATIVE AGENDA FOR THE FIRST MEETING OF THE
ECONOMIC FORUM
Prague 16–18 March 1993

1. Opening

2. Discussion items
Exchange of views and experiences concerning key issues of the transition process, and in this respect an implementation review, with particular focus on the following three areas, with an eye to the possibility for further co-operation:

— key elements of a favourable business climate in the light of the provisions of the Document of the Bonn Conference, including the protection of all types of property and with particular emphasis of the place and role of public policy;
— the human factors of the economic transition process, with emphasis on the development of human capital, including vocational and professional training and technical training, the development of managerial skills, fostering an entrepreneurial spirit, and working conditions;
— integrating economic and environmental factors during the transition to market economies.

3. **Consideration of proposals for topics for seminars in 1993**

4. **Dates and agenda for the next meeting of the economic forum**

VIII

ENVIRONMENT

(1)   The participating States will intensify the existing and growing co-operation between them in order to restore and maintain a sound ecological balance in air, water and soil and they recognize their individual and common commitment towards achieving these goals.

(2)   The participating States stress the need to develop, in the appropriate fora, efficient systems for monitoring and evaluating compliance with existing environmental commitments. They are looking forward to the results of environmental policy performance reviews being carried out in co-operation between OECD and the ECE. They encourage the ECE and other international organizations to consider ways of enabling all CSCE participating States to adhere to relevant conventions.

(3)   The participating States underline that the integration of environmental protection in other policies and in the economic decision-making process is an essential condition both for the creation of sustainable economic development and for a prudent use of natural resources. In this respect, the use of economic and fiscal instruments in addition to regulatory instruments is important in order to implement, at national level, the 'polluter-pays' principle, as well as the precautionary approach.

(4)   They emphasize that environmental protection should be a major consideration in international co-operation among them. They encourage work towards elaborating an Action Programme for Central and Eastern Europe, as well as elements for an Environmental Programme for the whole of Europe, in the follow-up to the 1991 ministerial conference 'Environment for Europe'.

(5)   The participating States will support intensified work within the relevant international organizations to make liberalized international trade and the protection of the environment mutually supportive.

(6)   The participating States stress the need to ensure effectively the safety of all nuclear installations, in order to protect the population and the environment. They will co-operate in the appropriate international fora on defining and establishing nuclear safety objectives.

(7)   They recommend the widest possible adherence to the IAEA Conventions on Early Notification of a Nuclear Accident and on Assistance in the Case of a Nuclear Accident or Radiological Emergency and express their support for active work on the early elaboration of an international convention on nuclear safety in the framework of IAEA. The participating States welcome the International Nuclear Events Scale (INES) and Incident Reporting System.

(8)   They will work to support the technical co-operation programmes of IAEA aimed at enhancing nuclear safety. They will support other international efforts in this direction aimed at, *inter alia*, upgrading the safety of nuclear installations where technically feasible, and where not feasible by developing and implementing plans, as

soon as practically possible, to substitute them with facilities using environmentally sound energy production processes and through the improvement of energy efficiency.

(9)   The participating States should ascertain that their military establishments conform to their nationally applicable environmental norms in the treatment and disposal of hazardous wastes.

(10)   The participating States express their concern about the illegal international transport and disposal of toxic and hazardous wastes. They will co-operate to prevent the illegal movement and disposal of such wastes and to prohibit their export to and import by countries that do not have the technical means to process and dispose of them in an environmentally sound manner, in the context of the Basel Convention on the Control of Transboundary Movements of Hazardous Wastes and Their Disposal. With regard to international transport of radioactive waste they will take into account the IAEA Code of Practice on International Transboundary Movement of Radioactive Waste.

(11)   The participating States will work towards the development of policies aimed at increasing environmental awareness and educating citizens to reduce the risks of natural and technological disasters, as well as preparing appropriate actions when such disasters occur. To this end, the participating States recognize the important work under way through the United Nations Environment Programme (UNEP) Awareness and Preparedness for Emergencies at the Local Level (APELL) programme. The participating States will take appropriate steps to enhance public participation in environmental planning and decision making.

(12)   The participating States urge the implementation of principles regarding the exchange of information on the state of the environment, consultation, early warning and assistance in environmental emergencies contained in the OECD Guiding Principles for Chemical Accident Prevention, Preparedness and Response, and in the ECE Convention on the Transboundary Effects of Industrial Accidents.

(13)   They encourage the designation of national environmental arrangements, such as task forces, which could co-ordinate the dissemination of relevant information on expertise and equipment to countries facing emergencies, to the United Nations Centre for Urgent Environmental Assistance, and to other relevant international organizations. These arrangements will take into account the ECE Conventions on the Transboundary Effects of Industrial Accidents and on Environmental Impact Assessment in a Transboundary Context, as well as other relevant agreements.

(14)   They would welcome the designation by the United Nations Centre for Urgent Environmental Assistance of one of its staff as liaison officer for the CSCE region, and recommend that the Centre be connected to the CSCE communications network, which could serve as a supplementary information system in emergency situations, taking into account the fact that the Centre will be subject to evaluation by the UNEP Governing Council in June 1993.

(15)   The participating States will encourage in the appropriate fora the development of a network of protection areas in the CSCE region to conserve and safeguard the large-scale natural and near-natural biotopes and ecosystems still in existence, as part of their natural heritage, as well as further development of the protection and conservation of animals.

(16)   Encouraging early implementation of the forest principles adopted at UNCED and recognizing the importance of sustaining the forest ecosystems of the CSCE region, the participating States decide to give impetus to this issue through practical discussions. In this regard, a Seminar of CSCE Experts on the subject of 'Sustainable Development of Boreal and Temperate Forests', will be convened in Montreal from 27 September to 6 October 1993. A proposal outlining the budget, agenda and modalities of this seminar will be presented by Canada for approval by the CSO before the end of 1992.

IX
THE CSCE AND REGIONAL AND TRANSFRONTIER CO-OPERATION

(1)   The participating States welcome the various regional co-operation activities among the CSCE participating States as well as transfrontier co-operation and consider them an effective form of promoting CSCE principles and objectives as well as implementing and developing CSCE commitments.

(2)   The participating States will encourage appropriate links among the various forms of regional co-operation as well as steps to provide the CSCE with relevant information on their activities in the framework of regional co-operation, including future work plans.

(3)   The participating States will encourage and promote, both bilaterally and, as appropriate, multilaterally, including through initiatives in European and other international organizations, transfrontier co-operation between territorial communities or authorities, involving border areas of two or more participating States with the aim of promoting friendly relations between States.

(4)   The development of transfrontier co-operation should involve governments, regional and local authorities and communities.

(5)   Transfrontier co-operation should be as comprehensive as possible, promoting increased contacts at all levels, including contacts among persons sharing a common origin, cultural heritage and religious belief.

(6)   Special attention should be paid, *inter alia*, to co-operative infrastructural development, joint economic activity, ecology, tourism and administrative co-operation.

X
MEDITERRANEAN

(1)   The participating States recognize that the changes which have taken place in Europe are relevant to the Mediterranean region and that, conversely, economic, social, political and security developments in that region can have a bearing on Europe. In this context, the CSO will seek to relate issues regarding co-operation in the Mediterranean to the goals of the CSCE process and will examine, as appropriate, practical modalities for possible contributions to the CSCE by non-participating Mediterranean States.

(2)   The Chairman-in-Office of the CSO is encouraged to foster contacts with non-participating Mediterranean States in order to establish an effective information exchange.

(3)   Non-participating Mediterranean States will be invited to future review conferences to make contributions concerning security and co-operation in the Mediterranean.

(4)   A CSCE Mediterranean Seminar will be convened under the auspices of the CSO in the course of the year following this Follow-up Meeting. It will meet for a duration of no more than five working days. The date, location and agenda will be decided upon by the CSO.

(5)   The Seminar can be attended by non-participating Mediterranean States, to which invitations will be extended.

(6)   The agenda of the Seminar may comprise topics such as the environment, demographic trends or economic development and other areas of bilateral and multilateral co-operation between CSCE participating States and non-participating Mediterranean States reflecting the general framework of principles of co-operation in the Mediterranean region as provided for in the Final Act and other CSCE documents. The Seminar will not produce a document with commitments binding on CSCE participating States.

XI
PROGRAMME OF CO-ORDINATED SUPPORT FOR RECENTLY ADMITTED PARTICIPATING STATES

Further to paragraph 19 of the Summary of Conclusions of the Prague Meeting of the Council, the participating States decide to establish a programme of co-ordinated support for those participating States which have been admitted to the CSCE since 1991. Through the programme, *inter alia*, diplomatic, academic, legal and administrative expertise and advice on CSCE matters will be made available as follows.

(1)   The programme will be co-ordinated by the ODIHR under the overall guidance of the CSO. The ODIHR will act as a centre of information for relevant activities of the CSCE and the participating States as well as international organizations, including the Council of Europe, as provided for in the mandate of the ODIHR. The ODIHR will make the information received available on request by the participating States.

(2)   Subject to the approval of the CSO, the ODIHR will arrange meetings and seminars on CSCE matters, specially designed for recently admitted participating States. Such meetings and seminars will, where possible, be held in the recently admitted participating States. They will be focused on enhancing knowledge on matters dealt with in the CSCE among, *inter alia*, civil servants, the media and the public at large.

(3)   Within its field of competence the CPC will arrange meetings and seminars on CSCE matters, specially designed for the recently admitted participating States. Such meetings and seminars will, where possible, be held in those States.

(4)   The CSCE Secretariat will devote special attention to distributing CSCE documents to the recently admitted participating States.

(5)   The officers of the CSCE Secretariat, the CPC Secretariat and the ODIHR will, when on missions to recently admitted participating States, make themselves available, to the extent possible to share their expertise in a relevant manner.

(6)   Participating States may make available to the ODIHR any national inventories of CSCE expertise available within the diplomatic, academic, legal, administrative and other relevant fields. Persons, institutions and organizations thus listed could, through national initiatives and following requests from the recently admitted participating States, be invited for, *inter alia*, lectures, seminars, courses and advisory services on CSCE matters in the recently admitted participating States. Such persons, institutions and organizations may also be invited to the seminars arranged by the ODIHR on CSCE matters for recently admitted States, in order to provide expertise in various areas of the democratic process.

(7)   The participating States are encouraged to include representatives of the recently admitted participating States in government-sponsored internships, study and training programmes.

(8)   Costs ensuing from national initiatives will be borne by the participating States providing the support in question. Costs of the CSCE institutions will be covered within their regular budgets. The provision of accommodation and full board, as well as of interpreters and meeting facilities, by those recently admitted participating States where activities take place will be welcomed as contributions to the costs of the programme of co-ordinated support. The participating States will be invited to contribute financially on a voluntary basis to the seminars and meetings envisaged.

(9)   The next review conference will assess the results of this programme.

ABBREVIATIONS

APELL   Awareness and Preparedness for Emergencies at the Local Level
CCEET   Centre for Co-operation with European Economies in Transition

CFE	Conventional Armed Forces in Europe
CIS	Commonwealth of Independent States
COST	European Co-operation in the field of Scientific and Technical Research
CPC	Conflict Prevention Centre
CSCE	Conference on Security and Co-operation in Europe
CSO	Committee of Senior Officials
EBRD	European Bank for Reconstruction and Development
EC	European Community
ECE	United Nations Economic Commission for Europe
EIB	European Investment Bank
GATT	General Agreement on Tariffs and Trade
IAEA	International Atomic Energy Agency
INES	International Nuclear Events Scale
NACC	North Atlantic Co-operation Council
NATO	North Atlantic Treaty Organization
NGO	Non-governmental organization
ODIHR	Office for Democratic Institutions and Human Rights
OECD	Organisation for Economic Co-operation and Development
UNCED	United Nations Conference on Environment and Development
UNDP	United Nations Development Programme
UNEP	United Nations Environment Programme
WEU	Western European Union

UNITED NATIONS WORLD CONFERENCES ON HUMAN RIGHTS INSTRUMENTS

THE PROCLAMATION OF TEHERAN (1968)

The International Conference on Human Rights,
Having met at Teheran from April 22 to May 13, 1968 to review the progress made in the twenty years since the adoption of the Universal Declaration of Human Rights and to formulate a programme for the future,
Having considered the problems relating to the activities of the United Nations for the promotion and encouragement of respect for human rights and fundamental freedoms,
Bearing in mind the resolutions adopted by the Conference,
Noting that the observance of the International Year for Human Rights takes place at a time when the world is undergoing a process of unprecedented change,
Having regard to the new opportunities made available by the rapid progress of science and technology,
Believing that, in an age when conflict and violence prevail in many parts of the world, the fact of human interdependence and the need for human solidarity are more evident than ever before,
Recognizing that peace is the universal aspiration of mankind and that peace and justice are indispensable to the full realization of human rights and fundamental freedoms,
Solemnly proclaims that:
  1. It is imperative that the members of the international community fulfil their solemn obligations to promote and encourage respect for human rights and fundamental freedoms for all without distinctions of any kind such as race, colour, sex, language, religion, political or other opinions;
  2. The Universal Declaration of Human Rights states a common understanding of the peoples of the world concerning the inalienable and inviolable rights of all members of the human family and constitutes an obligation for the members of the international community;
  3. The International Covenant on Civil and Political Rights, the International Covenant on Economic, Social and Cultural Rights, the Declaration on the Granting of Independence to Colonial Countries and Peoples, the International Convention on the Elimination of All Forms of Racial Discrimination as well as other conventions and declarations in the field of human rights adopted under the auspices of the United Nations, the specialized agencies and the regional intergovernmental organizations, have created new standards and obligations to which States should conform;
  4. Since the adoption of the Universal Declaration of Human Rights the United Nations has made substantial progress in defining standards for the enjoyment and protection of human rights and fundamental freedoms. During this period many important international instruments were adopted but much remains to be done in regard to the implementation of those rights and freedoms;
  5. The primary aim of the United Nations in the sphere of human rights is the achievement by each individual of the maximum freedom and dignity. For the realization of this objective, the laws of every country should grant each individual, irrespective of race, language, religion or political belief, freedom of expression, of information, of conscience and of religion, as well as the right to participate in the political, economic, cultural and social life of his country;
  6. States should reaffirm their determination effectively to enforce the principles enshrined in the Charter of the United Nations and in other international instruments that concern human rights and fundamental freedoms;

7. Gross denials of human rights under the repugnant policy of *apartheid* is a matter of the gravest concern to the international community. This policy of *apartheid*, condemned as a crime against humanity, continues seriously to disturb international peace and security. It is therefore imperative for the international community to use every possible means to eradicate this evil. The struggle against *apartheid* is recognized as legitimate;

8. The peoples of the world must be made fully aware of the evils of racial discrimination and must join in combating them. The implementation of this principle of non-discrimination, embodied in the Charter of the United Nations, the Universal Declaration of Human Rights, and other international instruments in the field of human rights, constitutes a most urgent task of mankind at the international as well as at the national level. All ideologies based on racial superiority and intolerance must be condemned and resisted;

9. Eight years after the General Assembly's Declaration on the Granting of Independence to Colonial Countries and Peoples the problems of colonialism continue to preoccupy the international community. It is a matter of urgency that all Member States should co-operate with the appropriate organs of the United Nations so that effective measures can be taken to ensure that the Declaration is fully implemented;

10. Massive denials of human rights, arising out of aggression or any armed conflict with their tragic consequences, and resulting in untold human misery, engender reactions which could engulf the world in ever growing hostilities. It is the obligation of the international community to co-operate in eradicating such scourges;

11. Gross denials of human rights arising from discrimination on grounds of race, religion, belief or expressions of opinion outrage the conscience of mankind and endanger the foundations of freedom, justice and peace in the world;

12. The widening gap between the economically developed and developing countries impedes the realization of human rights in the international community. The failure of the Development Decade to reach its modest objectives makes it all the more imperative for every nation, according to its capacities, to make the maximum possible effort to close this gap;

13. Since human rights and fundamental freedoms are indivisible, the full realization of civil and political rights without the enjoyment of economic, social and cultural rights is impossible. The achievement of lasting progress in the implementation of human rights is dependent upon sound and effective national and international policies of economic and social development;

14. The existence of over seven hundred million illiterates throughout the world is an enormous obstacle to all efforts at realizing the aims and purposes of the Charter of the United Nations and the provisions of the Universal Declaration of Human Rights. International action aimed at eradicating illiteracy from the face of the earth and promoting education at all levels requires urgent attention;

15. The discrimination of which women are still victims in various regions of the world must be eliminated. An inferior status for women is contrary to the Charter of the United Nations as well as the provisions of the Universal Declaration of Human Rights. The full implementation of the Declaration on the Elimination of Discrimination against Women is a necessity for the progress of mankind;

16. The protection of the family and of the child remains the concern of the international community. Parents have a basic human right to determine freely and responsibly the number and the spacing of their children;

17. The aspirations of the younger generation for a better world, in which human rights and fundamental freedoms are fully implemented, must be given the highest encouragement. It is imperative that youth participate in shaping the future of mankind;

18. While recent scientific discoveries and technological advances have opened vast prospects for economic, social and cultural progress, such developments may nevertheless endanger the rights and freedoms of individuals and will require continuing attention;

19. Disarmament would release immense human and material resources now devoted to military purposes. These resources should be used for the promotion of human rights and fundamental freedoms. General and complete disarmament is one of the highest aspirations of all peoples;

Therefore,

The International Conference on Human Rights

1. *Affirming* its faith in the principles of the Universal Declaration of Human Rights and other international instruments in this field,

2. *Urges* all peoples and governments to dedicate themselves to the principles enshrined in the Universal Declaration of Human Rights and to redouble their efforts to provide for all human beings a life consonant with freedom and dignity and conductive to physical, mental, social and spiritual welfare.

WORLD CONFERENCE ON HUMAN RIGHTS — THE VIENNA DECLARATION AND PROGRAMME OF ACTION (1993)

The World Conference on Human Rights,

Considering that the promotion and protection of human rights is a matter of priority for the international community, and that the Conference affords a unique opportunity to carry out a comprehensive analysis of the international human rights system and of the machinery for the protection of human rights, in order to enhance and thus promote a fuller observance of those rights, in a just and balanced manner,

Recognizing and affirming that all human rights derive from the dignity and worth inherent in the human person, and that the human person is the central subject of human rights and fundamental freedoms, and consequently should be the principal beneficiary and should participate actively in the realization of these rights and freedoms,

Reaffirming their commitment to the purposes and principles contained in the Charter of the United Nations and the Universal Declaration of Human Rights,

Reaffirming the commitment contained in Article 56 of the Charter of the United Nations to take joint and separate action, placing proper emphasis on developing effective international cooperation for the realization of the purposes set out in Article 55, including universal respect for, and observance of, human rights and fundamental freedoms for all,

Emphasizing the responsibilities of all States, in conformity with the Charter of the United Nations, to develop and encourage respect for human rights and fundamental freedoms for all, without distinction as to race, sex, language or religion,

Recalling the Preamble to the Charter of the United Nations, in particular the determination to reaffirm faith in fundamental human rights, in the dignity and worth of the human person, and in the equal rights of men and women and of nations large and small,

Recalling also the determination expressed in the Preamble of the Charter of the United Nations to save succeeding generations from the scourge of war, to establish conditions under which justice and respect for obligations arising from treaties and other sources of international law can be maintained, to promote social progress and better standards of life in larger freedom, to practice tolerance and good neighbourliness, and to employ international machinery for the promotion of the economic and social advancement of all peoples,

Emphasizing that the Universal Declaration of Human Rights, which constitutes a common standard of achievement for all peoples and all nations, is the source of inspiration and has been the basis for the United Nations in making advances in standard setting as contained in the existing international human rights instruments, in particular the International Covenant on Civil and Political Rights and the International Covenant on Economic, Social and Cultural Rights.

Considering the major changes taking place on the international scene and the aspirations of all the peoples for an international order based on the principles enshrined in the Charter of the United Nations, including promoting and encouraging respect for human rights and fundamental freedoms for all and respect for the principle of equal rights and self-determination of peoples, peace, democracy, justice, equality, rule of law, pluralism, development, better standards of living and solidarity,

Deeply concerned by various forms of discrimination and violence, to which women continue to be exposed all over the world,

Recognizing that the activities of the United Nations in the field of human rights should be rationalized and enhanced in order to strengthen the United Nations machinery in this field and to further the objectives of universal respect for observance of international human rights standards,

Having taken into account the Declarations adopted by the three regional meetings at Tunis, San José and Bangkok and the contributions made by Governments, and bearing in mind the suggestions made by intergovernmental and non-governmental organizations, as well as the studies prepared by independent experts during the preparatory process leading to the World Conference on Human Rights,

Welcoming the International Year of the World's Indigenous People 1993 as a reaffirmation of the commitment of the international community to ensure their enjoyment of all human rights and fundamental freedoms and to respect the value and diversity of their cultures and identities,

Recognizing also that the international community should devise ways and means to remove the current obstacles and meet challenges to the full realization of all human rights and to prevent the continuation of human rights violations resulting thereof throughout the world,

Invoking the spirit of our age and the realities of our time which call upon the peoples of the world and all States Members of the United Nations to rededicate themselves to the global task of promoting and protecting all human rights and fundamental freedoms so as to secure full and universal enjoyment of these rights,

Determined to take new steps forward in the commitment of the international community with a view to achieving substantial progress in human rights endeavours by an increased and sustained effort of international cooperation and solidarity,

Solemnly adopts the Vienna Declaration and Programme of Action.

I

1.   The World Conference on Human Rights reaffirms the solemn commitment of all States to fulfil their obligations to promote universal respect for, and observance and protection of, all human rights and fundamental freedoms for all in accordance with the Charter of the United Nations, other instruments relating to human rights, and international law. The universal nature of these rights and freedoms is beyond question.

In this framework, enhancement of international cooperation in the field of human rights is essential for the full achievement of the purposes of the United Nations.

Human rights and fundamental freedoms are the birthright of all human beings; their protection and promotion is the first responsibility of Governments.

2.   All peoples have the right of self-determination. By virtue of that right they freely determine their political status, and freely pursue their economic, social and cultural development.

Taking into account the particular situation of peoples under colonial or other forms of alien domination or foreign occupation, the World Conference on Human Rights recognizes the right of peoples to take any legitimate action, in accordance with the Charter of the United Nations, to realize their inalienable right of self-determination. The World Conference on Human Rights considers the denial of the right of self-determination as a violation of human rights and underlines the importance of the effective realization of this right.

In accordance with the Declaration on Principles of International Law concerning Friendly Relations and Cooperation Among States in accordance with the Charter of the United Nations, this shall not be construed as authorizing or encouraging any action which would dismember or impair, totally or in part, the territorial integrity or political unity of sovereign and independent States conducting themselves in compliance with the principle of equal rights and self-determination of peoples and thus possessed of a Government representing the whole people belonging to the territory without distinction of any kind.

3.   Effective international measures to guarantee and monitor the implementation of human rights standards should be taken in respect of people under foreign occupation, and effective legal protection against the violation of their human rights should be provided, in accordance with human rights norms and international law, particularly the Geneva Convention relative to the Protection of Civilian Persons in Time of War, of 14 August 1949, and other applicable norms of humanitarian law.

4.   The promotion and protection of all human rights and fundamental freedoms must be considered as a priority objective of the United Nations in accordance with its purposes and principles, in particular the purpose of international cooperation. In the framework of these purposes and principles, the promotion and protection of all human rights is a legitimate concern of the international community. The organs and specialized agencies related to human rights should therefore further enhance the coordination of their activities based on the consistent and objective application of international human rights instruments.

5.   All human rights are universal, indivisible and interdependent and interrelated. The international community must treat human rights globally in a fair and equal manner, on the same footing, and with the same emphasis. While the significance of national and regional particularities and various historical, cultural and religious backgrounds must be borne in mind, it is the duty of States, regardless of their political, economic and cultural systems, to promote and protect all human rights and fundamental freedoms.

6.   The efforts of the United Nations system towards the universal respect for, and observance of, human rights and fundamental freedoms for all, contribute to the stability and well-being necessary for peaceful and friendly relations among nations, and to improved conditions for peace and security as well as social and economic development, in conformity with the Charter of the United Nations.

7.   The processes of promoting and protecting human rights should be conducted in conformity with the purposes and principles of the Charter of the United Nations, and international law.

8.   Democracy, development and respect for human rights and fundamental freedoms are interdependent and mutually reinforcing. Democracy is based on the freely expressed will of the people to determine their own political, economic, social and cultural systems and their full participation in all aspects of their lives. In the context of the above, the promotion and protection of human rights and fundamental freedoms at the national and international levels should be universal and conducted without conditions attached. The international community should support the strengthening and promoting of democracy, development and respect for human rights and fundamental freedoms in the entire world.

9. The World Conference on Human Rights reaffirms that least developed countries committed to the process of democratization and economic reforms, many of which are in Africa, should be supported by the international community in order to succeed in their transition to democracy and economic development.

10. The World Conference on Human Rights reaffirms the right to development, as established in the Declaration on the Right to Development, as a universal and inalienable right and an integral part of fundamental human rights.

As stated in the Declaration on the Right to Development, the human person is the central subject of development.

While development facilitates the enjoyment of all human rights, the lack of development may not be invoked to justify the abridgement of internationally recognized human rights.

States should cooperate with each other in ensuring development and eliminating obstacles to development. The international community should promote an effective international cooperation for the realization of the right to development and the elimination of obstacles to development.

Lasting progress towards the implementation of the right to development requires effective development policies at the national level, as well as equitable economic relations and a favourable economic environment at the international level.

11. The right to development should be fulfilled so as to meet equitably the developmental and environmental needs of present and future generations. The World Conference on Human Rights recognizes that illicit dumping of toxic and dangerous substances and waste potentially constitutes a serious threat to the human rights to life and health of everyone.

Consequently, the World Conference on Human Rights calls on all States to adopt and vigorously implement existing conventions relating to the dumping of toxic and dangerous products and waste and to cooperate in the prevention of illicit dumping.

Everyone has the right to enjoy the benefits of scientific progress and its applications. The World Conference on Human Rights notes that certain advances, notably in the biomedical and life sciences as well as in information technology, may have potentially adverse consequences for the integrity, dignity and human rights of the individual, and calls for international cooperation to ensure that human rights and dignity are fully respected in this area of universal concern.

12. The World Conference on Human Rights calls upon the international community to make all efforts to help alleviate the external debt burden of developing countries, in order to supplement the efforts of the Governments of such countries to attain the full realization of the economic, social and cultural rights of their people.

13. There is a need for States and international organizations, in cooperation with non-governmental organizations, to create favourable conditions at the national, regional and international levels to ensure the full and effective enjoyment of human rights. States should eliminate all violations of human rights and their causes, as well as obstacles to the enjoyment of these rights.

14. The existence of widespread extreme poverty inhibits the full and effective enjoyment of human rights; its immediate alleviation and eventual elimination must remain a high priority for the international community.

15. Respect for human rights and for fundamental freedoms without distinction of any kind is a fundamental rule of international human rights law. The speedy and comprehensive elimination of all forms of racism and racial discrimination, xenophobia and related intolerance is a priority task for the international community. Governments should take effective measures to prevent and combat them. Groups, institutions, intergovernmental and non-governmental organizations and individuals are urged to intensify their efforts in cooperating and coordinating their activities against these evils.

16. The World Conference on Human Rights welcomes the progress made in dismantling apartheid and calls upon the international community and the United Nations system to assist in this process.

The World Conference on Human Rights also deplores the continuing acts of violence aimed at undermining the quest for a peaceful dismantling of apartheid.

17. The acts, methods and practices of terrorism in all its forms and manifestations as well as linkage in some countries to drug trafficking are activities aimed at the destruction of human rights, fundamental freedoms and democracy, threatening territorial integrity, security of States and destabilizing legitimately constituted Governments. The international community should take the necessary steps to enhance cooperation to prevent and combat terrorism.

18. The human rights of women and of the girl-child are an inalienable, integral and indivisible part of universal human rights. The full and equal participation of women in political, civil, economic, social and cultural life, at the national, regional and international levels, and the eradication of all forms of discrimination on grounds of sex are priority objectives of the international community.

Gender-based violence and all forms of sexual harassment and exploitation, including those resulting from cultural prejudice and international trafficking, are incompatible with the dignity and worth of the human person, and must be eliminated. This can be achieved by legal measures and through national action and international cooperation in such fields as economic and social development, education, safe maternity and health care, and social support.

The human rights of women should form an integral part of the United Nations human rights activities, including the promotion of all human rights instruments relating to women.

The World Conference on Human Rights urges Governments, institutions, inter-governmental and non-governmental organizations to intensify their efforts for the protection and promotion of human rights of women and the girl-child.

19. Considering the importance of the promotion and protection of the rights of persons belonging to minorities and the contribution of such promotion and protection to the political and social stability of the States in which such persons live,

The World Conference on Human Rights reaffirms the obligation of States to ensure that persons belonging to minorities may exercise fully and effectively all human rights and fundamental freedoms without any discrimination and in full equality before the law in accordance with the Declaration on the Rights of Persons Belonging to National or Ethnic, Religious and Linguistic Minorities.

The persons belonging to minorities have the right to enjoy their own culture, to profess and practise their own religion and to use their own language in private and in public, freely and without interference or any form of discrimination.

20. The World Conference on Human Rights recognizes the inherent dignity and the unique contribution of indigenous people to the development and plurality of society and strongly reaffirms the commitment of the international community to their economic, social and cultural well-being and their enjoyment of the fruits of sustainable development. States should ensure the full and free participation of indigenous people in all aspects of society, in particular in matters of concern to them. Considering the importance of the promotion and protection of the rights of indigenous people, and the contribution of such promotion and protection to the political and social stability of the States in which such people live, States should, in accordance with international law, take concerted positive steps to ensure respect for all human rights and fundamental freedoms of indigenous people, on the basis of equality and non-discrimination, and recognize the value and diversity of their distinct identities, cultures and social organization.

21. The World Conference on Human Rights, welcoming the early ratification of the Convention on the Rights of the Child by a large number of States and noting the

recognition of the human rights of children in the World Declaration on the Survival, Protection and Development of Children and Plan of Action adopted by the World Summit for Children, urges universal ratification of the Convention by 1995 and its effective implementation by States parties through the adoption of all the necessary legislative, administrative and other measures and the allocation to the maximum extent of the available resources. In all actions concerning children, non-discrimination and the best interest of the child should be primary considerations and the views of the child given due weight. National and international mechanisms and programmes should be strengthened for the defence and protection of children, in particular, the girl-child, abandoned children, street children, economically and sexually exploited children, including through child pornography, child prostitution or sale of organs, children victims of diseases including acquired immunodeficiency syndrome, refugee and displaced children, children in detention, children in armed conflict, as well as children victims of famine and drought and other emergencies. International cooperation and solidarity should be promoted to support the implementation of the Convention and the rights of the child should be a priority in the United Nations system-wide action on human rights.

The World Conference on Human Rights also stresses that the child for the full and harmonious development of his or her personality should grow up in a family environment which accordingly merits broader protection.

22.   Special attention needs to be paid to ensuring non-discrimination, and the equal enjoyment of all human rights and fundamental freedoms by disabled persons, including their active participation in all aspects of society.

23.   The World Conference on Human Rights reaffirms that everyone, without distinction of any kind, is entitled to the right to seek and to enjoy in other countries asylum from persecution, as well as the right to return to one's own country. In this respect it stresses the importance of the Universal Declaration of Human Rights, the 1951 Convention relating to the Status of Refugees, its 1967 Protocol and regional instruments. It expresses its appreciation to States that continue to admit and host large numbers of refugees in their territories, and to the Office of the United Nations High Commissioner for Refugees for its dedication to its task. It also expresses its appreciation to the United Nations Relief and Works Agency for Palestine Refugees in the Near East.

The World Conference on Human Rights recognizes that gross violations of human rights, including in armed conflicts, are among the multiple and complex factors leading to displacement of people.

The World Conference on Human Rights recognizes that, in view of the complexities of the global refugee crisis and in accordance with the Charter of the United Nations, relevant international instruments and international solidarity and in the spirit of burden-sharing, a comprehensive approach by the international community is needed in coordination and cooperation with the countries concerned and relevant organizations, bearing in mind the mandate of the United Nations High Commissioner for Refugees. This should include the development of strategies to address the root causes and effects of movements of refugees and other displaced persons, the strengthening of emergency preparedness and response mechanisms, the provision of effective protection and assistance, bearing in mind the special needs of women and children, as well as the achievement of durable solutions, primarily through the preferred solution of dignified and safe voluntary repatriation, including solutions such as those adopted by the international refugee conferences. The World Conference on Human Rights underlines the responsibilities of States, particularly as they relate to the countries of origin.

In the light of the comprehensive approach, the World Conference on Human Rights emphasizes the importance of giving special attention including through intergovernmental and humanitarian organizations and finding lasting solutions to questions related to internally displaced persons including their voluntary and safe return and rehabilitation.

In accordance with the Charter of the United Nations and the principles of humanitarian law, the World Conference on Human Rights further emphasizes the importance of and the need for humanitarian assistance to victims of all natural and man-made disasters.

24. Great importance must be given to the promotion and protection of the human rights of persons belonging to groups which have been rendered vulnerable, including migrant workers, the elimination of all forms of discrimination against them, and the strengthening and more effective implementation of existing human rights instruments. States have an obligation to create and maintain adequate measures at the national level, in particular in the fields of education, health and social support, for the promotion and protection of the rights of persons in vulnerable sectors of their populations and to ensure the participation of those among them who are interested in finding a solution to their own problems.

25. The World Conference on Human Rights affirms that extreme poverty and social exclusion constitute a violation of human dignity and that urgent steps are necessary to achieve better knowledge of extreme poverty and its causes, including those related to the problem of development, in order to promote the human rights of the poorest, and to put an end to extreme poverty and social exclusion and to promote the enjoyment of the fruits of social progress. It is essential for States to foster participation by the poorest people in the decision-making process by the community in which they live, the promotion of human rights and efforts to combat extreme poverty.

26. The World Conference on Human Rights welcomes the progress made in the codification of human rights instruments, which is a dynamic and evolving process, and urges the universal ratification of human rights treaties. All States are encouraged to accede to these international instruments; all States are encouraged to avoid, as far as possible, the resort to reservations.

27. Every State should provide an effective framework of remedies to redress human rights grievances or violations. The administration of justice, including law enforcement and prosecutorial agencies and, especially, an independent judiciary and legal profession in full conformity with applicable standards contained in international human rights instruments, are essential to the full and non-discriminatory realization of human rights and indispensable to the processes of democracy and sustainable development. In this context, institutions concerned with the administration of justice should be properly funded, and an increased level of both technical and financial assistance should be provided by the international community. It is incumbent upon the United Nations to make use of special programmes of advisory services on a priority basis for the achievement of a strong and independent administration of justice.

28. The World Conference on Human Rights expresses its dismay at massive violations of human rights especially in the form of genocide, 'ethnic cleansing' and systematic rape of women in war situations, creating mass exodus of refugees and displaced persons. While strongly condemning such abhorrent practices it reiterates the call that perpetrators of such crimes be punished and such practices immediately stopped.

29. The World Conference on Human Rights expresses grave concern about continuing human rights violations in all parts of the world in disregard of standards as contained in international human rights instruments and international humanitarian law and about the lack of sufficient and effective remedies for the victims.

The World Conference on Human Rights is deeply concerned about violations of human rights during armed conflicts, affecting the civilian population, especially women, children, the elderly and the disabled. The Conference therefore calls upon States and all parties to armed conflicts strictly to observe international humanitarian law, as set forth in the Geneva Conventions of 1949 and other rules and principles of international law, as well as minimum standards for protection of human rights, as laid down in international conventions.

The World Conference on Human Rights reaffirms the right of the victims to be assisted by humanitarian organizations, as set forth in the Geneva Conventions of 1949 and other relevant instruments of international humanitarian law, and calls for the safe and timely access for such assistance.

30.   The World Conference on Human Rights also expresses its dismay and condemnation that gross and systematic violations and situations that constitute serious obstacles to the full enjoyment of all human rights continue to occur in different parts of the world. Such violations and obstacles include, as well as torture and cruel, inhuman and degrading treatment or punishment, summary and arbitrary executions, disappearances, arbitrary detentions, all forms of racism, racial discrimination and apartheid, foreign occupation and alien domination, xenophobia, poverty, hunger and other denials of economic, social and cultural rights, religious intolerance, terrorism, discrimination against women and lack of the rule of law.

31.   The World Conference on Human Rights calls upon States to refrain from any unilateral measure not in accordance with international law and the Charter of the United Nations that creates obstacles to trade relations among States and impedes the full realization of the human rights set forth in the Universal Declaration of Human Rights and international human rights instruments, in particular the rights of everyone to a standard of living adequate for their health and well-being, including food and medical care, housing and the necessary social services. The World Conference on Human Rights affirms that food should not be used as a tool for political pressure.

32.   The World Conference on Human Rights reaffirms the importance of ensuring the universality, objectivity and non-selectivity of the consideration of human rights issues.

33.   The World Conference on Human Rights reaffirms that States are duty-bound, as stipulated in the Universal Declaration of Human Rights and the International Covenant on Economic, Social and Cultural Rights and in other international human rights instruments, to ensure that education is aimed at strengthening the respect of human rights and fundamental freedoms. The World Conference on Human Rights emphasizes the importance of incorporating the subject of human rights education programmes and calls upon States to do so. Education should promote understanding, tolerance, peace and friendly relations between the nations and all racial or religious groups and encourage the development of United Nations activities in pursuance of these objectives. Therefore, education on human rights and the dissemination of proper information, both theoretical and practical, play an important role in the promotion and respect of human rights with regard to all individuals without distinction of any kind such as race, sex, language or religion, and this should be integrated in the education policies at the national as well as international levels. The World Conference on Human Rights notes that resource constraints and institutional inadequacies may impede the immediate realization of these objectives.

34.   Increased efforts should be made to assist countries which so request to create the conditions whereby each individual can enjoy universal human rights and fundamental freedoms. Governments and the United Nations system as well as other multilateral organizations are urged to increase considerably the resources allocated to programmes aiming at the establishment and strengthening of national legislation, national institutions and related infrastructures which uphold the rule of law and

democracy, electoral assistance, human rights awareness through training, teaching and education, popular participation and civil society.

The programmes of advisory services and technical cooperation under the Centre for Human Rights should be strengthened as well as made more efficient and transparent and thus become a major contribution to improving respect for human rights. States are called upon to increase their contributions to these programmes, both through promoting a larger allocation from the United Nations regular budget and through voluntary contributions.

35. The full and effective implementation of United Nations activities to promote and protect human rights must reflect the high importance accorded to human rights by the Charter of the United Nations and the demands of the United Nations human rights activities, as mandated by Member States. To this end, United Nations human rights activities should be provided with increased resources.

36. The World Conference on Human Rights reaffirms the important and constructive role played by national institutions for the promotion and protection of human rights, in particular in their advisory capacity to the competent authorities, their role in remedying human rights violations, in the dissemination of human rights information, and education in human rights.

The World Conference on Human Rights encourages the establishment and strengthening of national institutions, having regard to the 'Principles relating to the status of national institutions' and recognizing that it is the right of each State to choose the framework which is best suited to its particular needs at the national level.

37. Regional arrangements play a fundamental role in promoting and protecting human rights. They should reinforce universal human rights standards, as contained in international human rights instruments, and their protection. The World Conference on Human Rights endorses efforts under way to strengthen these arrangements and to increase their effectiveness, while at the same time stressing the importance of cooperation with the United Nations human rights activities.

The World Conference on Human Rights reiterates the need to consider the possibility of establishing regional and sub-regional arrangements for the promotion and protection of human rights where they do not already exist.

38. The World Conference on Human Rights recognizes the important role of non-governmental organizations in the promotion of all human rights and in humanitarian activities at national, regional and international levels. The World Conference on Human Rights appreciates their contribution to increasing public awareness of human rights issues, to the conduct of education, training and research in this field, and to the promotion and protection of all human rights and fundamental freedoms. While recognizing that the primary responsibility for standard-setting lies with States, the Conference also appreciates the contribution of non-governmental organizations to this process. In this respect, the World Conference on Human Rights emphasizes the importance of continued dialogue and cooperation between Governments and non-governmental organizations. Non-governmental organizations and their members genuinely involved in the field of human rights should enjoy the rights and freedoms recognized in the Universal Declaration of Human Rights, and the protection of the national law. These rights and freedoms may not be exercised contrary to the purposes and principles of the United Nations. Non-governmental organizations should be free to carry out their human rights activities, without interference, within the framework of national law and the Universal Declaration of Human Rights.

39. Underlining the importance of objective, responsible and impartial information about human rights and humanitarian issues, the World Conference on Human Rights encourages the increased involvement of the media, for whom freedom and protection should be guaranteed within the framework of national law.

II
A. INCREASED COORDINATION ON HUMAN RIGHTS WITHIN
THE UNITED NATIONS SYSTEM

1. The World Conference on Human Rights recommends increased coordination in support of human rights and fundamental freedoms within the United Nations system. To this end, the World Conference on Human Rights urges all United Nations organs, bodies and the specialized agencies whose activities deal with human rights to cooperate in order to strengthen, rationalize and streamline their activities, taking into account the need to avoid unnecessary duplication. The World Conference on Human Rights also recommends to the Secretary-General that high-level officials of relevant United Nations bodies and specialized agencies at their annual meeting, besides coordinating their activities, also assess the impact of their strategies and policies on the enjoyment of all human rights.

2. Furthermore, the World Conference on Human Rights calls on regional organizations and prominent international and regional finance and development institutions to assess also the impact of their policies and programmes on the enjoyment of human rights.

3. The World Conference on Human Rights recognizes that relevant specialized agencies and bodies and institutions of the United Nations system as well as other relevant intergovernmental organizations whose activities deal with human rights play a vital role in the formulation, promotion and implementation of human rights standards, within their respective mandates, and should take into account the outcome of the World Conference on Human Rights within their fields of competence.

4. The World Conference on Human Rights strongly recommends that a concerted effort be made to encourage and facilitate the ratification of and accession or succession to international human rights treaties and protocols adopted within the framework of the United Nations system with the aim of universal acceptance. The Secretary-General, in consultation with treaty bodies, should consider opening a dialogue with States not having acceded to these human rights treaties, in order to identify obstacles and to seek ways of overcoming them.

5. The World Conference on Human Rights encourages States to consider limiting the extent of any reservations they lodge to international human rights instruments, formulate any reservations as precisely and narrowly as possible, ensure that none is incompatible with the object and purpose of the relevant treaty and regularly review any reservations with a view to withdrawing them.

6. The World Conference on Human Rights, recognizing the need to maintain consistency with the high quality of existing international standards and to avoid proliferation of human rights instruments, reaffirms the guidelines relating to the elaboration of new international instruments contained in General Assembly resolution 41/120 of 4 December 1986 and calls on the United Nations human rights bodies, when considering the elaboration of new international standards, to keep those guidelines in mind, to consult with human rights treaty bodies on the necessity for drafting new standards and to request the Secretariat to carry out technical reviews of proposed new instruments.

7. The World Conference on Human Rights recommends that human rights officers be assigned if and when necessary to regional offices of the United Nations Organization with the purpose of disseminating information and offering training and other technical assistance in the field of human rights upon the request of concerned Member States. Human rights training for international civil servants who are assigned to work relating to human rights should be organized.

8. The World Conference on Human Rights welcomes the convening of emergency sessions of the Commission on Human Rights as a positive initiative and that

other ways of responding to acute violations of human rights be considered by the relevant organs of the United Nations system.

Resources

9. The World Conference on Human Rights, concerned by the growing disparity between the activities of the Centre for Human Rights and the human, financial and other resources available to carry them out, and bearing in mind the resources needed for other important United Nations programmes, requests the Secretary-General and the General Assembly to take immediate steps to increase substantially the resources for the human rights programme from within the existing and future regular budgets of the United Nations, and to take urgent steps to seek increased extrabudgetary resources.

10. Within this framework, an increased proportion of the regular budget should be allocated directly to the Centre for Human Rights to cover its costs and all other costs borne by the Centre for Human Rights, including those related to the United Nations human rights bodies. Voluntary funding of the Centre's technical cooperation activities should reinforce this enhanced budget; the World Conference on Human Rights calls for generous contributions to the existing trust funds.

11. The World Conference on Human Rights requests the Secretary-General and the General Assembly to provide sufficient human, financial and other resources to the Centre for Human Rights to enable it effectively, efficiently and expeditiously to carry out its activities.

12. The World Conference on Human Rights, noting the need to ensure that human and financial resources are available to carry out the human rights activities, as mandated by intergovernmental bodies, urges the Secretary-General, in accordance with Article 101 of the Charter of the United Nations, and Member States to adopt a coherent approach aimed at securing that resources commensurate to the increased mandates are allocated to the Secretariat. The World Conference on Human Rights invites the Secretary-General to consider whether adjustments to procedures in the programme budget cycle would be necessary or helpful to ensure the timely and effective implementation of human rights activities as mandated by Member States.

Centre for Human Rights

13. The World Conference on Human Rights stresses the importance of strengthening the United Nations Centre for Human Rights.

14. The Centre for Human Rights should play an important role in coordinating system-wide attention for human rights. The focal role of the Centre can best be realized if it is enabled to cooperate fully with other United Nations bodies and organs. The coordinating role of the Centre for Human Rights also implies that the office of the Centre for Human Rights in New York is strengthened.

15. The Centre for Human Rights should be assured adequate means for the system of thematic and country rapporteurs, experts, working groups and treaty bodies. Follow-up on recommendations should become a priority matter for consideration by the Commission on Human Rights.

16. The Centre for Human Rights should assume a larger role in the promotion of human rights. This role could be given shape through cooperation with Member States and by an enhanced programme of advisory services and technical assistance. The existing voluntary funds will have to be expanded substantially for these purposes and should be managed in a more efficient and coordinated way. All activities should follow strict and transparent project management rules and regular programme and project evaluations should be held periodically. To this end, the results of such evaluation exercises and other relevant information should be made available regularly. The Centre should, in particular, organize at least once a year information meetings open to all Member States and organizations directly involved in these projects and programmes.

Adaptation and strengthening of the United Nations machinery for human rights, including the question of the establishment of a United Nations High Commissioner for Human Rights

17. The World Conference on Human Rights recognizes the necessity for a continuing adaptation of the United Nations human rights machinery to the current and future needs in the promotion and protection of human rights, as reflected in the present Declaration and within the framework of a balanced and sustainable development for all people. In particular, the United Nations human rights organs should improve their coordination, efficiency and effectiveness.

18. The World Conference on Human Rights recommends to the General Assembly that, when examining the report of the Conference at its forty-eighth session, it begin, as a matter of priority, consideration of the question of the establishment of a High Commissioner for Human Rights for the promotion and protection of all human rights.

B. EQUALITY, DIGNITY AND TOLERANCE

1. Racism, racial discrimination, xenophobia and other forms of intolerance

19. The World Conference on Human Rights considers the elimination of racism and racial discrimination, in particular in their institutionalized forms such as apartheid or resulting from doctrines of racial superiority or exclusivity or contemporary forms and manifestations of racism, as a primary objective for the international community and a world-wide promotion programme in the field of human rights. United Nations organs and agencies should strengthen their efforts to implement such a programme of action related to the third decade to combat racism and racial discrimination as well as subsequent mandates to the same end. The World Conference on Human Rights strongly appeals to the international community to contribute generously to the Trust Fund for the Programme for the Decade for Action to Combat Racism and Racial Discrimination.

20. The World Conference on Human Rights urges all Governments to take immediate measures and to develop strong policies to prevent and combat all forms and manifestations of racism, xenophobia or related intolerance, where necessary by enactment of appropriate legislation, including penal measures, and by the establishment of national institutions to combat such phenomena.

21. The World Conference on Human Rights welcomes the decision of the Commission on Human Rights to appoint a Special Rapporteur on contemporary forms of racism, racial discrimination, xenophobia and related intolerance. The World Conference on Human Rights also appeals to all States parties to the International Convention on the Elimination of All Forms of Racial Discrimination to consider making the declaration under article 14 of the Convention.

22. The World Conference on Human Rights calls upon all Governments to take all appropriate measures in compliance with their international obligations and with due regard to their respective legal systems to counter intolerance and related violence based on religion or belief, including practices of discrimination against women and including the desecration of religious sites, recognizing that every individual has the right to freedom of thought, conscience, expression and religion. The Conference also invites all States to put into practice the provisions of the Declaration on the Elimination of All Forms of Intolerance and of Discrimination Based on Religion or Belief.

23. The World Conference on Human Rights stresses that all persons who perpetrate or authorize criminal acts associated with ethnic cleansing are individually responsible and accountable for such human rights violations, and that the international community should exert every effort to bring those legally responsible for such violations to justice.

24.   The World Conference on Human Rights calls on all States to take immediate measures, individually and collectively, to combat the practice of ethnic cleansing to bring it quickly to an end. Victims of the abhorrent practice of ethnic cleansing are entitled to appropriate and effective remedies.

2.   *Persons belonging to national or ethnic, religious and linguistic minorities*

25.   The World Conference on Human Rights calls on the Commission on Human Rights to examine ways and means to promote and protect effectively the rights of persons belonging to minorities as set out in the Declaration on the Rights of Persons belonging to National or Ethnic, Religious and Linguistic Minorities. In this context, the World Conference on Human Rights calls upon the Centre for Human Rights to provide, at the request of Governments concerned and as part of its programme of advisory services and technical assistance, qualified expertise on minority issues and human rights, as well as on the prevention and resolution of disputes, to assist in existing or potential situations involving minorities.

26.   The World Conference on Human Rights urges States and the international community to promote and protect the rights of persons belonging to national or ethnic, religious and linguistic minorities in accordance with the Declaration on the Rights of Persons belonging to National or Ethnic, Religious and Linguistic Minorities.

27.   Measures to be taken, where appropriate, should include facilitation of their full participation in all aspects of the political, economic, social, religious and cultural life of society and in the economic progress and development in their country.

Indigenous people

28.   The World Conference on Human Rights calls on the Working Group on Indigenous Populations of the Sub-commission on Prevention of Discrimination and Protection of Minorities to complete the drafting of a declaration on the rights of indigenous people at its eleventh session.

29.   The World Conference on Human Rights recommends that the Commission on Human Rights consider the renewal and updating of the mandate of the Working Group on Indigenous Populations upon completion of the drafting of a declaration on the rights of indigenous people.

30.   The World Conference on Human Rights also recommends that advisory services and technical assistance programmes within the United Nations system respond positively to requests by States for assistance which would be of direct benefit to indigenous people. The World Conference on Human Rights further recommends that adequate human and financial resources be made available to the Centre for Human Rights within the overall framework of strengthening the Centre's activities as envisaged by this document.

31.   The World Conference on Human Rights urges States to ensure the full and free participation of indigenous people in all aspects of society, in particular in matters of concern to them.

32.   The World Conference on Human Rights recommends that the General Assembly proclaim an international decade of the world's indigenous people, to begin from January 1994, including action-orientated programmes, to be decided upon in partnership with indigenous people. An appropriate voluntary trust fund should be set up for this purpose. In the framework of such a decade, the establishment of a permanent forum for indigenous people in the United Nations system should be considered.

Migrant workers

33.   The World Conference on Human Rights urges all States to guarantee the protection of the human rights of all migrant workers and their families.

34.   The World Conference on Human Rights considers that the creation of
conditions to foster greater harmony and tolerance between migrant workers and the
rest of the society of the State in which they reside is of particular importance.
35.   The World Conference on Human Rights invites States to consider the
possibility of signing and ratifying, at the earliest possible time, the International
Convention on the Rights of All Migrant Workers and Members of Their Families.

3.   The equal status and human rights of women

36.   The World Conference on Human Rights urges the full and equal enjoyment
by women of all human rights and that this be a priority for Governments and for the
United Nations. The World Conference on Human Rights also underlines the
importance of the integration and full participation of women as both agents and
beneficiaries in the development process, and reiterates the objectives established on
global action for women towards sustainable and equitable development set forth in
the Rio Declaration on Environment and Development and chapter 24 of Agenda 21,
adopted by the United Nations Conference on Environment and Development (Rio
de Janeiro, Brazil, 3–14 June 1992).
37.   The equal status of women and the human rights of women should be
integrated into the mainstream of United Nations system-wide activity. These issues
should be regularly and systematically addressed throughout relevant United Nations
bodies and mechanisms. In particular, steps should be taken to increase cooperation
and promote further integration of objectives and goals between the Commission on
the Status of Women, the Commission on Human Rights, the Committee for the
Elimination of Discrimination against Women, the United Nations Development
Fund for Women, the United Nations Development Programme and other United
Nations agencies. In this context, cooperation and coordination should be
strengthened between the Centre for Human Rights and the Division for the
Advancement of Women.
38.   In particular, the World Conference on Human Rights stresses the importance
of working towards the elimination of violence against women in public and private
life, the elimination of all forms of sexual harassment, exploitation and trafficking in
women, the elimination of gender bias in the administration of justice and the
eradication of any conflicts which may arise between the rights of women and the
harmful effects of certain traditional or customary practices, cultural prejudices and
religious extremism. The World Conference on Human Rights calls upon the General
Assembly to adopt the draft declaration on violence against women and urges States
to combat violence against women in accordance with its provisions. Violations of the
human rights of women in situations of armed conflict are violations of the fundamental principles of international human rights and humanitarian law. All violations of this
kind, including in particular murder, systematic rape, sexual slavery, and forced
pregnancy, require a particularly effective response.
39.   The World Conference on Human Rights urges the eradication of all forms of
discrimination against women, both hidden and overt. The United Nations should
encourage the goal of universal ratification by all States of the Convention on the
Elimination of All Forms of Discrimination against Women by the year 2000. Ways
and means of addressing the particularly large number of reservations to the Convention should be encouraged. *Inter alia*, the Committee on the Elimination of Discrimination against Women should continue its review of reservations to the Convention.
States are urged to withdraw reservations that are contrary to the object and purpose
of the Convention or which are otherwise incompatible with international treaty law.
40.   Treaty monitoring bodies should disseminate necessary information to enable
women to make more effective use of existing implementation procedures in their
pursuits of full and equal enjoyment of human rights and non-discrimination. New

procedures should also be adopted to strengthen implementation of the commitment to women's equality and the human rights of women. The Commission on the Status of Women and the Committee on the Elimination of Discrimination against Women should quickly examine the possibility of introducing the right of petition through the preparation of an optional protocol to the Convention on the Elimination of All Forms of Discrimination against Women. The World Conference on Human Rights welcomes the decision of the Commission on Human Rights to consider the appointment of a special rapporteur on violence against women at its fiftieth session.

41.   The World Conference on Human Rights recognizes the importance of the enjoyment by women of the highest standard of physical and mental health throughout their life-span. In the context of the World Conference on Women and the Convention on the Elimination of All Forms of Discrimination against Women, as well as the Proclamation of Tehran of 1968, the World Conference on Human Rights reaffirms, on the basis of equality between women and men, a woman's right to accessible and adequate health care and the widest range of family planning services, as well as equal access to education at all levels.

42.   Treaty monitoring bodies should include the status of women and the human rights of women in their deliberations and findings, making use of gender-specific data. States should be encouraged to supply information on the situation of women *de jure* and de facto in their reports to treaty monitoring bodies. The World Conference on Human Rights notes with satisfaction that the Commission on Human Rights adopted at its forty-ninth session resolution 1993/46 of 8 March 1993 stating that rapporteurs and working groups in the field of human rights should also be encouraged to do so. Steps should also be taken by the Division for the Advancement of Women in cooperation with other United Nations bodies, specifically the Centre for Human Rights, to ensure that the human rights activities of the United Nations regularly address violations of women's human rights, including gender-specific abuses. Training for United Nations human rights and humanitarian relief personnel to assist them to recognize and deal with human rights abuses particular to women and to carry out their work without gender bias should be encouraged.

43.   The World Conference on Human Rights urges Governments and regional and international organizations to facilitate the access of women to decision-making posts and their greater participation in the decision-making process. It encourages further steps within the United Nations Secretariat to appoint and promote women staff members in accordance with the Charter of the United Nations, and encourages other principal and subsidiary organs of the United Nations to guarantee the participation of women under conditions of equality.

44.   The World Conference on Human Rights welcomes the World Conference on Women to be held in Beijing in 1995 and urges that human rights of women should play an important role in its deliberations, in accordance with the priority themes of the World Conference on Women of equality, development and peace.

4.   The rights of the child

45.   The World Conference on Human Rights reiterates the principle of 'First Call for Children' and, in this respect, underlines the importance of major national and international efforts, especially those of the United Nations Children's Fund, for promoting respect for the rights of the child to survival, protection, development and participation.

46.   Measures should be taken to achieve universal ratification of the Convention on the Rights of the Child by 1995 and the universal signing of the World Declaration on the Survival, Protection and Development of Children and Plan of Action adopted by the World Summit for Children, as well as their effective implementation. The World Conference on Human Rights urges States to withdraw reservations to the

Convention on the Rights of the Child contrary to the object and purpose of the Convention or otherwise contrary to international treaty law.

47. The World Conference on Human Rights urges all nations to undertake measures to the maximum extent of their available resources, with the support of international cooperation, to achieve the goals in the World Summit Plan of Action. The Conference calls on States to integrate the Convention on the Rights of the Child into their national action plans. By means of these national action plans and through international efforts, particular priority should be placed on reducing infant and maternal mortality rates, reducing malnutrition and illiteracy rates and providing access to safe drinking-water and to basic education. When ever so called for, national plans of action should be devised to combat devastating emergencies resulting from natural disasters and armed conflicts and the equally grave problem of children in extreme poverty.

48. The World Conference on Human Rights urges all States, with the support of international cooperation, to address the acute problem of children under especially difficult circumstances. Exploitation and abuse of children should be actively combated, including by addressing their root causes. Effective measures are required against female infanticide, harmful child labour, sale of children and organs, child prostitution, child pornography, as well as other forms of sexual abuse.

49. The World Conference on Human Rights supports all measures by the United Nations and its specialized agencies to ensure the effective protection and promotion of human rights of the girl child. The World Conference on Human Rights urges States to repeal existing laws and regulations and remove customs and practices which discriminate against and cause harm to the girl child.

50. The World Conference on Human Rights strongly supports the proposal that the Secretary-General initiate a study into means of improving the protection of children in armed conflicts. Humanitarian norms should be implemented and measures taken in order to protect and facilitate assistance to children in war zones. Measures should include protection for children against indiscriminate use of all weapons of war, especially antipersonnel mines. The need for after-care and rehabilitation of children traumatized by war must be addressed urgently. The Conference calls on the Committee on the Rights of the Child to study the question of raising the minimum age of recruitment into armed forces.

51. The World Conference on Human Rights recommends that matters relating to human rights and the situation of children be regularly reviewed and monitored by all relevant organs and mechanisms of the United Nations system and by the supervisory bodies of the specialized agencies in accordance with their mandates.

52. The World Conference on Human Rights recognizes the important role played by non-governmental organizations in the effective implementation of all human rights instruments and, in particular, the Convention on the Rights of the Child.

53. The World Conference on Human Rights recommends that the Committee on the Rights of the Child, with the assistance of the Centre for Human Rights, be enabled expeditiously and effectively to meet its mandate, especially in view of the unprecedented extent of ratification and subsequent submission of country reports.

5. Freedom from torture

54. The World Conference on Human Rights welcomes the ratification by many Member States of the Convention against Torture and Other Cruel, Inhuman or Degrading Treatment or Punishment and encourages its speedy ratification by all other Member States.

55. The World Conference on Human Rights emphasizes that one of the most atrocious violations against human dignity is the act of torture, the result of which destroys the dignity and impairs the capability of victims to continue their lives and their activities.

56. The World Conference on Human Rights reaffirms that under human rights law and international humanitarian law, freedom from torture is a right which must be protected under all circumstances, including in times of internal or international disturbance or armed conflicts.

57. The World Conference on Human Rights therefore urges all States to put an immediate end to the practice of torture and eradicate this evil for ever through full implementation of the Universal Declaration of Human Rights as well as the relevant conventions and, where necessary, strengthening of existing mechanisms. The World Conference on Human Rights calls on all States to cooperate fully with the Special Rapporteur on the question of torture in the fulfilment of his mandate.

58. Special attention should be given to ensure universal respect for, and effective implementation of, the Principles of Medical Ethics relevant to the Role of Health Personnel, particularly Physicians, in the Protection of Prisoners and Detainees against Torture and other Cruel, Inhuman or Degrading Treatment or Punishment adopted by the General Assembly of the United Nations.

59. The World Conference on Human Rights stresses the importance of further concrete action within the framework of the United Nations with the view to providing assistance to victims of torture and ensuring more effective remedies for their physical, psychological and social rehabilitation. Providing the necessary resources for this purpose should be given high priority, *inter alia*, by additional contributions to the United Nations Voluntary Fund for the Victims of Torture.

60. States should abrogate legislation leading to impunity for those responsible for grave violations of human rights such as torture and prosecute such violations, thereby providing a firm basis for the rule of law.

61. The World Conference on Human Rights reaffirms that efforts to eradicate torture should, first and foremost, be concentrated on prevention and, therefore, calls for the early adoption of an optional protocol to the Convention against Torture and Other Cruel, Inhuman and Degrading Treatment or Punishment, which is intended to establish a preventive system of regular visits to places of detention.

Enforced disappearances

62. The World Conference on Human Rights, welcoming the adoption by the General Assembly of the Declaration on the Protection of All Persons from Enforced Disappearance, calls upon all States to take effective legislative, administrative, judicial or other measures to prevent, terminate and punish acts of enforced disappearances. The World Conference on Human Rights reaffirms that it is the duty of all States, under any circumstances, to make investigations whenever there is reason to believe that an enforced disappearance has taken place on a territory under their jurisdiction and, if allegations are confirmed, to prosecute its perpetrators.

6. The rights of the disabled person

63. The World Conference on Human Rights reaffirms that all human rights and fundamental freedoms are universal and thus unreservedly include persons with disabilities. Every person is born equal and has the same rights to life and welfare, education and work, living independently and active participation in all aspects of society. Any direct discrimination or other negative discriminatory treatment of a disabled person is therefore a violation of his or her rights. The World Conference on Human Rights calls on Governments, where necessary, to adopt or adjust legislation to assure access to these and other rights for disabled persons.

64. The place of disabled persons is everywhere. Persons with disabilities should be guaranteed equal opportunity through the elimination of all socially determined barriers, be they physical, financial, social or psychological, which exclude or restrict full participation in society.

65. Recalling the World Programme of Action concerning Disabled Persons, adopted by the General Assembly at its thirty-seventh session, the World Conference on Human Rights calls upon the General Assembly and the Economic and Social Council to adopt the draft standard rules on the equalization of opportunities for persons with disabilities, at their meetings in 1993.

C. CO-OPERATION, DEVELOPMENT AND STRENGTHENING OF HUMAN RIGHTS

66. The World Conference on Human Rights recommends that priority be given to national and international action to promote democracy, development and human rights.

67. Special emphasis should be given to measures to assist in the strengthening and building of institutions relating to human rights, strengthening of a pluralistic civil society and the protection of groups which have been rendered vulnerable. In this context, assistance provided upon the request of Governments for the conduct of free and fair elections, including assistance in the human rights aspects of elections and public information about elections, is of particular importance. Equally important is the assistance to be given to the strengthening of the rule of law, the promotion of freedom of expression and the administration of justice, and to the real and effective participation of the people in the decision-making processes.

68. The World Conference on Human Rights stresses the need for the implementation of strengthened advisory services and technical assistance activities by the Centre for Human Rights. The Centre should make available to States upon request assistance on specific human rights issues, including the preparation of reports under human rights treaties as well as for the implementation of coherent and comprehensive plans of action for the promotion and protection of human rights. Strengthening the institutions of human rights and democracy, the legal protection of human rights, training of officials and others, broad-based education and public information aimed at promoting respect for human rights should all be available as components of these programmes.

69. The World Conference on Human Rights strongly recommends that a comprehensive programme be established within the United Nations in order to help States in the task of building and strengthening adequate national structures which have a direct impact on the overall observance of human rights and the maintenance of the rule of law. Such a programme, to be coordinated by the Centre for Human Rights, should be able to provide, upon the request of the interested Government, technical and financial assistance to national projects in reforming penal and correctional establishments, education and training of lawyers, judges and security forces in human rights, and any other sphere of activity relevant to the good functioning of the rule of law. That programme should make available to States assistance for the implementation of plans of action for the promotion and protection of human rights.

70. The World Conference on Human Rights requests the Secretary-General of the United Nations to submit proposals to the United Nations General Assembly, containing alternatives for the establishment, structure, operational modalities and funding of the proposed programme.

71. The World Conference on Human Rights recommends that each State consider the desirability of drawing up a national action plan identifying steps whereby that State would improve the promotion and protection of human rights.

72. The World Conference on Human Rights reaffirms that the universal and inalienable right to development, as established in the Declaration on the Right to Development, must be implemented and realized. In this context, the World Conference on Human Rights welcomes the appointment by the Commission on Human Rights of a thematic working group on the right to development and urges that the Working Group, in consultation and co-operation with other organs and agencies of

the United Nations system, promptly formulate, for early consideration by the United Nations General Assembly, comprehensive and effective measures to eliminate obstacles to the implementation and realization of the Declaration on the Right to Development and recommending ways and means towards the realization of the right to development by all States.

73.   The World Conference on Human Rights recommends that non-governmental and other grass-roots organizations active in development and/or human rights should be enabled to play a major role on the national and international levels in the debate, activities and implementation relating to the right to development and, in co-operation with Governments, in all relevant aspects of development co-operation.

74.   The World Conference on Human Rights appeals to Governments, competent agencies and institutions to increase considerably the resources devoted to building well-functioning legal systems able to protect human rights, and to national institutions working in this area. Actors in the field of development co-operation should bear in mind the mutually reinforcing inter-relationship between development, democracy and human rights. Co-operation should be based on dialogue and transparency. The World Conference on Human Rights also calls for the establishment of comprehensive programmes, including resource banks of information and personnel with expertise relating to the strengthening of the rule of law and of democratic institutions.

75.   The World Conference on Human Rights encourages the Commission on Human Rights, in co-operation with the Committee on Economic, Social and Cultural Rights, to continue the examination of optional protocols to the International Covenant on Economic, Social and Cultural Rights.

76.   The World Conference on Human Rights recommends that more resources be made available for the strengthening or the establishment of regional arrangements for the promotion and protection of human rights under the programmes of advisory services and technical assistance of the Centre for Human Rights. States are encouraged to request assistance for such purposes as regional and subregional workshops, seminars and information exchanges designed to strengthen regional arrangement for the promotion and protection of human rights in accord with universal human rights standards as contained in international human rights instruments.

77.   The World Conference on Human Rights supports all measures by the United Nations and its relevant specialized agencies to ensure the effective promotion and protection of trade union rights, as stipulated in the International Covenant on Economic, Social and Cultural Rights and other relevant international instruments. It calls on all States to abide fully by their obligations in this regard contained in international instruments.

D.   HUMAN RIGHTS EDUCATION

78.   The World Conference on Human Rights considers human rights education, training and public information essential for the promotion and achievement of stable and harmonious relations among communities and for fostering mutual understanding, tolerance and peace.

79.   States should strive to eradicate illiteracy and should direct education towards the full development of the human personality and to the strengthening of respect for human rights and fundamental freedoms. The World Conference on Human Rights calls on all States and institutions to include human rights, humanitarian law, democracy and rule of law as subjects in the curricula of all learning institutions in formal and non-formal settings.

80.   Human rights education should include peace, democracy, development and social justice, as set forth in international and regional human rights instruments, in order to achieve common understanding and awareness with a view to strengthening universal commitment to human rights.

81.   Taking into account the World Plan of Action on Education for Human Rights and Democracy, adopted in March 1993 by the International Congress on Education for Human Rights and Democracy of the United Nations Educational, Scientific and Cultural Organization, and other human rights instruments, the World Conference on Human Rights recommends that States develop specific programmes and strategies for ensuring the widest human rights education and the dissemination of public information, taking particular account of the human rights needs of women.

82.   Governments, with the assistance of intergovernmental organizations, national institutions and non-governmental organizations, should promote an increased awareness of human rights and mutual tolerance. The World Conference on Human Rights underlines the importance of strengthening the World Public Information Campaign for Human Rights carried out by the United Nations. They should initiate and support education in human rights and undertake effective dissemination of public information in this field. The advisory services and technical assistance programmes of the United Nations system should be able to respond immediately to requests from States for educational and training activities in the field of human rights as well as for special education concerning standards as contained in international human rights instruments and in humanitarian law and their application to special groups such as military forces, law enforcement personnel, police and the health profession. The proclamation of a United Nations decade for human rights education in order to promote, encourage and focus these educational activities should be considered.

E.   IMPLEMENTATION AND MONITORING METHODS

83.   The World Conference on Human Rights urges Governments to incorporate standards as contained in international human rights instruments in domestic legislation and to strengthen national structures, institutions and organs of society which play a role in promoting and safeguarding human rights.

84.   The World Conference on Human Rights recommends the strengthening of United Nations activities and programmes to meet requests for assistance by States which want to establish or strengthen their own national institutions for the promotion and protection of human rights.

85.   The World Conference on Human Rights also encourages the strengthening of co-operation between national institutions for the promotion and protection of human rights, particularly through exchanges of information and experience, as well as co-operation with regional organizations and the United Nations.

86.   The World Conference on Human Rights strongly recommends in this regard that representatives of national institutions for the promotion and protection of human rights convene periodic meetings under the auspices of the Centre for Human Rights to examine ways and means of improving their mechanisms and sharing experiences.

87.   The World Conference on Human Rights recommends to the human rights treaty bodies, to the meetings of chairpersons of the treaty bodies and to the meetings of States parties that they continue to take steps aimed at coordinating the multiple reporting requirements and guidelines for preparing State reports under the respective human rights conventions and study the suggestion that the submission of one overall report on treaty obligations undertaken by each State would make these procedures more effective and increase their impact.

88.   The World Conference on Human Rights recommends that the States parties to international human rights instruments, the General Assembly and the Economic and Social Council should consider studying the existing human rights treaty bodies and the various thematic mechanisms and procedures with a view to promoting greater efficiency and effectiveness through better coordination of the various bodies, mechanisms and procedures, taking into account the need to avoid unnecessary duplication and overlapping of their mandates and tasks.

89. The World Conference on Human Rights recommends continued work on the improvement of the functioning, including the monitoring tasks, of the treaty bodies, taking into account multiple proposals made in this respect, in particular those made by the treaty bodies themselves and by the meetings of the chairpersons of the treaty bodies. The comprehensive national approach taken by the Committee on the Rights of the Child should also be encouraged.

90. The World Conference on Human Rights recommends that States parties to human rights treaties consider accepting all the available optional communication procedures.

91. The World Conference on Human Rights views with concern the issue of impunity of perpetrators of human rights violations, and supports the efforts of the Commission on Human Rights and the Subcommission on Prevention of Discrimination and Protection of Minorities to examine all aspects of the issue.

92. The World Conference on Human Rights recommends that the Commission on Human Rights examine the possibility for better implementation of existing human rights instruments at the international and regional levels and encourages the International Law Commission to continue its work on an international criminal court.

93. The World Conference on Human Rights appeals to States which have not yet done so to accede to the Geneva Conventions of 12 August 1949 and the Protocols thereto, and to take all appropriate national measures, including legislative ones, for their full implementation.

94. The World Conference on Human Rights recommends the speedy completion and adoption of the draft declaration on the right and responsibility of individuals, groups and organs of society to promote and protect universally recognized human rights and fundamental freedoms.

95. The World Conference on Human Rights underlines the importance of preserving and strengthening the system of special procedures, rapporteurs, representatives, experts and working groups of the Commission on Human Rights and the Subcommission on the Prevention of Discrimination and Protection of Minorities, in order to enable them to carry out their mandates in all countries throughout the world, providing them with the necessary human and financial resources. The procedures and mechanisms should be enabled to harmonize and rationalize their work through periodic meetings. All States are asked to co-operate fully with these procedures and mechanisms.

96. The World Conference on Human Rights recommends that the United Nations assume a more active role in the promotion and protection of human rights in ensuring full respect for international humanitarian law in all situations of armed conflict, in accordance with the purposes and principles of the Charter of the United Nations.

97. The World Conference on Human Rights, recognizing the important role of human rights components in specific arrangements concerning some peace-keeping operations by the United Nations, recommends that the Secretary-General take into account the reporting, experience and capabilities of the Centre for Human Rights and human rights mechanisms, in conformity with the Charter of the United Nations.

98. To strengthen the enjoyment of economic, social and cultural rights, additional approaches should be examined, such as a system of indicators to measure progress in the realization of the rights set forth in the International Covenant on Economic, Social and Cultural Rights. There must be a concerted effort to ensure recognition of economic, social and cultural rights at the national, regional and international levels.

F. FOLLOW-UP TO THE WORLD CONFERENCE ON HUMAN RIGHTS

99. The World Conference on Human Rights recommends that the General Assembly, the Commission on Human Rights and other organs and agencies of the

United Nations system related to human rights consider ways and means for the full implementation, without delay, of the recommendations contained in the present Declaration, including the possibility of proclaiming a United Nations decade for human rights. The World Conference on Human Rights further recommends that the Commission on Human Rights annually review the progress towards this end.

100.   The World Conference on Human Rights requests the Secretary-General of the United Nations to invite on the occasion of the fiftieth anniversary of the Universal Declaration of Human Rights all States, all organs and agencies of the United Nations system related to human rights, to report to him on the progress made in the implementation of the present Declaration and to submit a report to the General Assembly at its fifty-third session, through the Commission on Human Rights and the Economic and Social Council. Likewise, regional and, as appropriate, national human rights institutions, as well as non-governmental organizations, may present their views to the Secretary-General on the progress made in the implementation of the present Declaration. Special attention should be paid to assessing the progress towards the goal of universal ratification of international human rights treaties and protocols adopted within the frame-work of the United Nations system.

INDEX

BLACKSTONE'S STATUTES

TITLES IN THE SERIES